T0147050

PRAISE FOR THE AUTHOR

"Thanks to Paul Krassner for continuing to be the lobster claw in the tuna casserole of modern America."   —Tom Robbins

"Krassner is one of the best minds of his generation to be destroyed by madness, starving, hysterical, naked—but mainly hysterical. His true wacky, wackily true autobiography is the definitive book on the sixties."

—Art Spiegelman

"Paul's own writing, in particular, seemed daring and adventurous to me; it took big chances and made important arguments in relentlessly funny ways. I felt, down deep, that maybe I had some of that in me, too; that maybe I could be using my skills to better express my beliefs. *The Realist* was the inspiration that kept pushing me to the next level; there was no way I could continue reading it and remain the same."   —George Carlin

"Krassner loves ironies, especially stinging ironies that nettle public figures. He would rather savor a piquant irony about a public figure than eat a bowl of fresh strawberries and ice cream."   —Ken Kesey

"I told Krassner one time that his writings made me hopeful. He found this an odd compliment to offer a satirist. I explained that he made supposedly serious matters seem ridiculous, and that this inspired many of his readers to decide for themselves what was ridiculous and what was not. Knowing that there were people doing that, better late than never, made me optimistic."

—Kurt Vonnegut

"Father of the underground press."   —*People*

"This is one funniest book. Flip on, boot up any page and you'll be instantly sassed-out, Krassed-out by this excruciatingly honest, accurately demented, twisted underground history of our times."   —Timothy Leary

"Enjoy this transcendent experience of compassionate acerbity served on dark wry."   —Ram Dass

"As counterculture revives and breathes again, Paul Krassner's personal histories and inside-dope anecdotes chronicle the national nuttiness of America's last decades before a new millennium."   —Allen Ginsberg

"The real story of our times is seldom told in the horse-puckey-filled memoirs of dopey, self-serving presidents or generals, but in the outrageous, demented lives of guys like Lenny Bruce, Giordano Bruno, Scott Fitzgerald . . . and Paul Krassner. The burrs under society's saddle. The pains in the ass."

—Harlan Ellison

"Krassner says he lost his sanity when he lost his sense of humor; his *Confessions* prove he's got them back."   —*Newsweek*

"He is an expert at ferreting out hypocrisy and absurdism from the more solemn crannies of American culture." —*The New York Times*

"Krassner has the uncanny ability to alter your perceptions permanently." —*Los Angeles Times*

"Wickedly funny . . . Chillingly funny . . . A convincing look at a man who knows how to wield absurdity." —*San Francisco Chronicle*

"Uproarious and mostly delightful . . . There is so much soulful humor and precious daffiness in this book." —*The Village Voice*

"Sheds wild light on what could be called America's psychotic episode." —*Spin*

"The dean of countercultural journalism." —*High Times*

"Ranks with Tom Wolfe's *Electric Kool-Aid Acid Test* as one of the most informative and entertaining studies of a time and place that now seem, like it or not, long ago and far away." —*The Baltimore Sun*

"I have been a fan of his since I was a snot-nosed kid, and his words have been a driving force and influence on my life . . . If you have read his work before, you know the joys that you are in for. If you haven't, start reading, and consider this your lucky day. For Paul Krassner is an activist, a philosopher, a lunatic, and a saint, but most of all he is funny." —Lewis Black

"I predict in time Paul Krassner will wind up as the only live Lenny Bruce." —Groucho Marx

"Paul taught me that extreme stylistic accuracy could make even the most bizarre comedic concept credible . . . He is a unique character on the American landscape. A self-described 'investigative satirist,' he straddles the lines between politics, culture, pornography, and drugs—in other words, the land where all of us, were we really honest with ourselves, would choose to dwell." —Harry Shearer

"Paul Krassner—confidant of Lenny Bruce, cofounder of the Yippies, defiler of Disney characters, publisher of *The Realist*, investigative satirist extraordinaire —as soon as we decided to create *The Huffington Post*, I knew I wanted Paul involved. His irreverence was just what the blog doctor ordered." —Arianna Huffington

"Krassner lives in a world where Truth and Satire are swingers, changing partners so often you never know who belongs with whom." —*Playboy*

CONFESSIONS
OF A RAVING,
UNCONFINED NUT

MISADVENTURES IN THE COUNTERCULTURE

UPDATED AND EXPANDED EDITION

PAUL KRASSNER

Soft Skull Press

Library of Congress Cataloging-in-Publication Data is available.

ISBN: 978-1-59376-503-3

Interior design by Neuwirth & Associates
Cover design by Kalynn Campbell

Soft Skull Press
New York, NY
www.softskull.com

Printed in the United States of America

OTHER BOOKS BY PAUL KRASSNER

How a Satirical Editor Became a Yippie Conspirator in Ten Easy Years

Tales of Tongue Fu

Best of The Realist [Editor]

The Winner of the Slow Bicycle Race:
The Satirical Writings of Paul Krassner

Impolite Interviews

Pot Stories for the Soul [Editor]

Sex, Drugs, and the Twinkie Murders:
40 Years of Countercultural Journalism

Psychedelic Trips for the Mind [Editor]

Murder at the Conspiracy Convention and Other American Absurdities

Magic Mushrooms and Other Highs:
From Toad Slime to Ecstasy [Editor]

One Hand Jerking: Reports from an Investigative Satirist

In Praise of Indecency: Dispatches from the Valley of Porn

Who's to Say What's Obscene?: Politics,
Culture and Comedy in America Today

To the Unknown Reporter—
who brought romance to a press conference once
by asking the widow of a slain voter registration worker
whose mutilated body had just been found in a Mississippi swamp:
"Did you love your husband?"

"It is quite true that I have invented for myself a good many experiences which I never really had. But they were all experiences which belonged to me by right of temperament and character. I should have had them, if I had but had my rights. I was despoiled of them by the rough tyranny of Circumstance. On the other hand, I have suppressed a number of incidents which actually happened, because I did not, upon mature reflection, find them in consonance with my nature as I like to think it is—they were lies that were told about me by the slinking facts of life. Evangelists of various descriptions assure us that we can make the future what we will, if we can but attain a sufficient degree of spirituality. It has been my endeavor to attain such a degree of spirituality that I may be able to influence the past as well as the future."

—Don Marquis

AUTHOR'S NOTE

Confessions of a Raving, Unconfined Nut was originally published by Simon & Schuster in 1993. All rights have since been reverted back to me, providing an opportunity to correct, clarify, expand, and update this new and improved edition. Also, I've added a couple of new chapters. So, enjoy your ass off.

TABLE OF CONTENTS

CHAPTER 1

HOW DO YOU ESCAPE FROM CARNEGIE HALL?

I FIRST WOKE UP AT THE AGE OF SIX.

It began with an itch in my leg. My left leg. But somehow I knew I wasn't supposed to scratch it. Although my eyes were closed, I was standing up. In fact, I was standing on a huge stage. And I was playing the violin. I was in the middle of playing the "Vivaldi Concerto in A Minor." I was wearing a *Little Lord Fauntleroy* suit—ruffled white silk shirt with puffy sleeves, black velvet short pants with ivory buttons and matching vest—white socks and black patent-leather shoes. My hair was platinum blond and wavy. On this particular Saturday evening—January 14, 1939—I was in the process of becoming the youngest concert artist in any field ever to perform at Carnegie Hall. But all I knew was that I was being taunted by an itch. An itch that had become my adversary.

I was tempted to stop playing the violin, just for a second, and scratch my leg with the bow, yet I was vaguely aware that this would not be appropriate. I had been well trained. I was a true professional. But that itch kept getting fiercer and fiercer. Then, suddenly, an impulse surfaced from my hidden laboratory of alternative possibilities, and I surrendered to it. Balancing on my left foot, I scratched my left leg with my right foot, without missing a note of the "Vivaldi Concerto."

Between the impulse and the surrender, there was a choice—I had *decided* to balance on one foot—and it was that simple act of choosing which triggered the precise moment of my awakening to the mystery of consciousness. *This is me!* The relief of scratching my leg was overshadowed by a surge of energy throughout my body. I was being engulfed by some kind of spiritual orgasm. By a wave of born-again ecstasy with no ideological context. No doctrine to explain the shock of my own existence. No dogma to function as a metaphor for the mystery. Instead, I woke up to the sound of laughter.

I had heard that sound before, sweet and comforting, but never like this. Now I could hear a whole *symphony* of delight and reassurance, like clarinets and guitars harmonizing with saxophones and drums. It was the audience laughing. I opened my eyes. There were rows upon rows of people sitting out there in the dark, and they were all laughing together.

They had understood my plight. It was easier for them to identify with the urge to scratch than with a little freak playing the violin. And I could identify with *them* identifying with me. I knew that laughter felt good, and I was pleased that it made the audience feel good—but I hadn't *intended* to make them laugh. I was merely trying to solve a personal dilemma. So the lesson I woke up to—this totally nonverbal, internal *buzz*—would serve as my lifetime filter for perceiving reality and its rules. If you could somehow translate that buzz into words, it would spell out: *One person's logic is another person's humor.*

I finished playing "Vivaldi" by rote. Then I bowed to the audience and walked off stage. The applause continued, and I was pushed back on stage by my violin teacher, Mischa Goodman, to play an encore, "Orientale." I had previously asked him—while rehearsing the encore—why it wasn't listed on the program since we already knew that I would play it at the concert. But instead of answering my question, he poked me in the chest, verbalizing each poke: "Violin *up!* Violin *up!*" Now, while playing "Orientale," I heard the echo of his voice, and I automatically raised my violin higher.

Then I popped my ears and the music sounded clearer. I wondered if it sounded clearer to the audience too. They had no idea that their laughter had woken me up. I was overwhelmed by the notion that everybody in the audience had their own individual *this-is-me*, but maybe some of *them* were still asleep and didn't know it. How could you tell who was awake and who was asleep? After all, I hadn't known that *I* was asleep, and look what I accomplished *before* I woke up. If it hadn't been for that itch, I might *still* be asleep.

There was, of course, an objective, scientific explanation for what happened on the stage of Carnegie Hall. According to a textbook, *Physiological Psychology*, "It is now rather well accepted that 'itch' is a variant of the pain experience and employs the same sensory mechanisms." But for me, something beyond an ordinary itch had occurred that night.

It was as though I had been zapped by the god of Absurdity. I didn't even know there was such a concept as absurdity. I simply experienced an overpowering awareness of *something* when the audience applauded me for doing what I had learned while I was asleep. But it was only when they laughed that we had really connected, and I imprinted on that sound. I wanted to hear it again. I was hooked. And the first laugh was free.

*　*　*

My mother, Ida, was born in Russia. Her family came to the United States when she was one year old. Her first and only job was legal secretary for the district attorney of Queens County in New York. My father, Michael, was born in America, his family having come from Hungary. He was a printer. When my mother told him she liked his mustache, he shaved it off, put the hair in an envelope, and presented it to her as a gift.

On April 9, 1932, my mother having been knocked out for the occasion, I emerged from her womb in a terrible drug stupor. There are those who claim that an individual soul chooses the specific parents of the fetus it will occupy. I had no such recollection. But even if I decided to be born, I was circumcised against my will.

It was an act of anti-Semitism by a kosher butcher—a *moyl* who not only practiced surgery without a license but also was slightly drunk that afternoon. He accidentally left an extra flap of foreskin clinging to the underside of my pippy. (That was our family name for penis.) As a child, because the rumpled foreskin on my pippy stuck uncomfortably to the loose skin of my scrotum, I would occasionally be observed trying to separate them through my clothing. Grown-ups became extremely concerned that I was playing with myself, and they offered various diversions. Among these was the violin. However, the program notes for that Carnegie Hall recital implied a certain basic sibling rivalry as my *own* motivation:

> Paul Krassner, six years old, was born in New York City. While his older brother, George, took violin lessons from Mischa Goodman, Paul's interest impressed Mr. Goodman, who then decided to start the youngster seriously. Paul was barely three years old. The compositions he now plays are far removed from the student's repertoire.

But it all seemed extremely hazy to me. There's a classic joke: Somebody stops a man on the street and says, "Excuse me, can you tell me how to get to Carnegie Hall?" And the man answers, "Practice, practice, practice." But I didn't have the slightest idea of how I had gotten to Carnegie Hall. I must've practiced myself right out of childhood. I did have a few specific memories, though. The earliest was my fourth birthday party. I was just about to blow out the candles on my cake when my brother stood right behind me and blew them out before I could. When I made a fuss about this, *I* was the one who got in trouble.

My father, who had been a semipro prizefighter, bought boxing gloves for my brother and me to settle our disputes. A few months later, my sister, Marjorie, was born—or, as I had been led to believe, purchased at the hospital. She was sleeping in her crib while my brother and I were boxing in an adjoining room. I threw a wild punch, and the glove flew off my fist, sailed across the room, through the open doorway, into the next room, hitting my baby sister on the head. She started crying and I got in trouble again.

That Christmas, my brother and I played our violins for a children's party at a hospital, but because I had been a bad boy that year, my parents stuffed my stocking with several lumps of coal. I didn't take it personally. Somehow I understood that it was *their* problem, and they were doing the best they could.

* * *

I could read music before I could read words, but I did know how to recite the alphabet backward. I had learned to read music with notes on wooden toy blocks. I had perfect pitch, but that didn't seem like anything special to me. All I did was memorize different tones, so that I could recognize the sound of A or B the same way I recognized the color orange or red.

People considered me a child prodigy because I had an advanced technique, but I had no real *passion* for the violin. I just didn't feel I had any options. Playing the violin was simply what I *did*. Mischa Goodman would keep yelling, "Violin up!" "Elbow in!" "Shoulder down!" "Wrist out!"—with jabs and slaps and punches to mark each particular spot. That was simply what *he* did.

Each week my brother and I would take the subway from Queens to Manhattan for our lessons at his studio in the Metropolitan Opera House. People in the train would stare at us with our violin cases, and we would do "owl eyes"—staring back until they looked away. I was fascinated by a blind man who played the accordion as his Seeing-Eye dog guided him through the subway cars. He sang "When Irish Eyes are Smiling," and passengers dropped coins into a tin cup attached to the dog's harness.

When I was five, my brother and I played at a concert in Mount Kisco, New York. While a virtuoso pianist was performing his solo, I managed to pull the curtain down on him. I was supposed to get paid $20 for my own performance, but they refused to give me the money. I would've been willing to accept punishment for my prank, but it was unjust not to pay me for my work, so I announced to my parents that I was going to run away from home, even though we weren't home yet.

We were still upstate, staying at a farm. My father packed some clothes and food in a bandana, tied it to the end of a broomstick, and slyly sent me on my way. My mother was frantic, but my father knew I had no place to go. After walking for almost an hour along strange dirt roads, I turned around and came back, defeated and dependent, but I still appreciated the way my bluff had been called.

I could recall getting fitted for my *Little Lord Fauntleroy* suit, which my mother had dutifully sewn, and being photographed in it. I could remember the day of the concert, running and sliding in the marble corridors of Carnegie Hall before the recital began. This musical Mecca held no special reverence for me. Then I was in a dressing room, tuning my violin and putting resin on my bow. Then backstage, peeking through the curtain.

Given a slight shove by Mr. Goodman, I almost tripped as I walked onstage. (A review in *Musical Courier* would report that I had "skipped engagingly." It was my earliest encounter with media distortion of the facts.) Then I was standing at the center of the stage, doing owl eyes at a bald man in the front row who was staring at me. I finally closed my eyes and began playing the Vivaldi concerto. And then came that itch in my left leg . . .

Now that I was *really* awake, I kept trying to recapture the sensation of my original zap. I would focus on that moment at Carnegie Hall again and again, as if to verify my sense of self. I had the innocence and curiosity of a newborn baby combined with the sophistication and skills of a six-year-old. I was proud that I could tie my shoelaces in the dark. I was amazed that there was extra skin on my elbows so they could bend. And I wondered whether God had *intended* for boys to button their shirts one way and for girls to button their blouses another way.

I was often late for school because I would constantly get distracted by my education. A trail of ants on the sidewalk could do it. I watched them meandering back and forth, and wondered if ants had to memorize stuff, or if individual ants ever got in trouble. Even though my mother always sent me off to school early, my teacher complained about my lateness. One time my mother followed me to school. She couldn't help but notice that I was walking all the way there by taking two steps backward for every three steps forward. How could I explain to her that I was only trying to exercise my willpower? I couldn't even explain it to myself.

At the age of seven, I saw my first movie, *Intermezzo*. It was also Ingrid Bergman's first movie. She fell in love with her violin teacher, and I fell in love with the title theme song. I couldn't fathom why it felt so good to hear a specific combination of notes in a certain order with a particular rhythm, but it gave me such pleasure just to keep humming that sweet melody over and over to myself. It was like having a secret companion. I couldn't wait to tell Mischa Goodman that I wanted to learn how to play "Intermezzo." But he obviously didn't share my enthusiasm.

"*Intermezzo?*" he sneered. "That's not right for you."

His words reverberated in my heart. *That's not right for you!* This was not merely a turndown of my request. It was a universal declaration of war upon the individual.

★ ★ ★

In 1940, my family moved from one section of Queens to another, from Sunnyside to Astoria. I saw my second movie, *Knute Rockne*, about the Notre Dame football coach, and Ronald Reagan, who starred as the Gipper, became my first role model. I didn't know anything about him except that he seemed so handsome and manly on the big screen.

And, once again, I fell in love with the background music. This time it was the Notre Dame school song: "Cheer, cheer for old Notre Dame! Wake up the echoes cheering her name!" I kept singing it to myself, with my own lyrics: "Cheer, cheer for old Notre Dame! You take the Notre, I'll take the Dame!" My parents said I could go to Notre Dame someday if I wanted to, but I told them I just liked the song, that's all. I didn't even *mention* it to Mischa Goodman.

A young bully lived in our apartment house, and I decided to do something about it. My mother had a fancy box of chocolates, so I took one of those little pieces of dark brown paper in which the candies nested, and placed it over my two front teeth so they appeared to be missing when I smiled. Holding in my hand a pair of bloody molars our family dentist had recently extracted, I went from door to door claiming that the bully had knocked my teeth out.

"You have a perverted sense of humor," one neighbor told me.

I assumed this was a compliment and thanked her politely. Then I looked up *perverted* in the dictionary. Unnatural? Abnormal? And *I* thought I had been providing a public service. But here I was in trouble again. My father spanked me with his leather belt, and I knew what my intention had been, but that only made him madder. It was ridiculous. The harder he hit me, the more I laughed, even while I was crying.

My father punished me in ways that might have traumatized another kid. If I ate with my fingers, he would make me eat off a plate on the floor like an animal. But I was lucky. I had been blessed with a sense of absurdity. Nevertheless, I tried to stay out of trouble at home. However, I continued to get in trouble at my new school. I got in trouble for not wearing a red necktie to the auditorium on assembly day. Then I got in trouble for *wearing* a red necktie because it was on a T-shirt. I also got in trouble for not bowing my head when they recited religious material.

One time there was this mean teacher whose gray hair was tinted blueish, so I drew a stick figure of her with colored chalk on the blackboard, giving her a patch of purple pubic hair. Another time, there was a student who got transferred to reform school for exposing himself, and I thought that wasn't fair. The next day, before the teacher came in, I stood in front of the class and unbuttoned my fly, only to reveal a *picture* of my pippy that I had drawn the previous evening as a self-imposed art–homework assignment. The whole class laughed at the way I was bending the rules of indecent exposure, and I got away with it.

If I were a kid who did those kinds of things today and got caught, I would undoubtedly be force-fed Ritalin through a Pez dispenser.

* * *

I embraced whatever bits of wisdom captured my fancy. My mother would say, "Nothing ventured, nothing gained," and I would take that as a personal omen. My father would mention "the law of supply and demand," and I would adopt that as a method of understanding all human behavior. But I was also intrigued with the way adults were always giving orders to kids that they would never give to other adults. At one family gathering, they were doing it again, but this time I was prepared.

"Paul, take that sweater off," one of my aunts said. "It's so hot in here."

"I can't. My shirt has no sleeves."

"Don't be ridiculous. Now take it off."

But I had already cut the sleeves off an old shirt at the shoulders, saving only the cuffs, which I left sticking out of the sleeves of the sweater I was now taking off, only to reveal that my arms were completely bare except for those cuffs.

One afternoon, when I was nine and my brother was twelve, we were alone in the apartment, getting ready to go to our aunt's house in Brooklyn for a big Passover dinner. Our parents were already there with our sister. Another relative, Aunt Evelyn, paid us a surprise visit. She just sat there in the kitchen with us for a while, acting sort of strange. Then she asked for the bread knife. I pointed out that there wasn't any bread since we only had *matzohs* for the holiday.

Nevertheless, my brother, not wishing to offend, got her the bread knife. Then Aunt Evelyn went to one of the bedrooms, stood in the doorway and, holding the knife in stabbing position, she beckoned us: "Come here,

I want to talk to you." My brother obediently started walking in her direction, but I ran out of the house, screaming, "Help! There's a murderer in my house! There's a murderer in my house!"

The neighbors sitting on the steps figured it must be another example of my perverted sense of humor, so they just ignored me. I ran to get the building superintendent, and he followed me back. The door was now locked, but the super used his shoulder as a battering ram and knocked the door right off its hinges. My brother and aunt were wrestling. The knife was on the floor, and his finger was bleeding.

The super subdued Aunt Evelyn and called the police. While a cop was holding her arms behind her back, I got brave and punched her in the stomach, saying, "You dirty murderer!" She looked at me, almost apologetically, and said, "It's all because of your Uncle Pete." Aunt Evelyn was my mother's sister, and Uncle Pete was my father's brother, but I didn't know they had ever met.

My brother and I took the subway from Astoria to Brooklyn. We were the only ones on that entire train whose aunt had just tried to murder them. My brother told me how Aunt Evelyn had ordered him to put his pippy in her mouth or she'd cut it off. We had never guessed that she was so crazy. We were supposed to call Uncle Pete's twin brother to pick us up at the subway station when we got to Brooklyn, but we were too scared. How did we know that he wasn't *also* in on the plot? So instead, we got off the train and took a trolley car to our aunt's house.

When we arrived, I began to spill out the whole scenario right there in the living room in front of all the relatives. They weren't sure whether this was just another sleeveless-shirt hoax that I was describing, but when I got to the part about Aunt Evelyn standing in the bedroom doorway holding the bread knife, there were looks of frozen horror on everybody's faces. My mother brought us upstairs to finish the rest of the story in private. Then my father gave my brother and me each a dollar bill.

"All right," he said, "now forget about it."

I took the dollar, but I didn't exactly forget about it.

* * *

Incredibly, the cops let Aunt Evelyn go free. My father brought me to school for a few days until they found her wandering around the streets, and this time she was hospitalized.

I became an expert eavesdropper in my own home. My parents had both come from puritanical backgrounds, but I was finally able to gather from their conversations that Uncle Pete had seduced Aunt Evelyn as a teenager, and that fellatio was included in their relationship. My father referred to it as "playing the skin flute." That was the closest that I ever came to understanding her motivation. But I did understand—without having the vocabulary to describe it to myself—that Mischa Goodman had one projection of me and Aunt Evelyn had another, but that neither projection had anything to do with me.

Although Aunt Evelyn was now hospitalized in a mental ward, I began to have dreams where all my *other* aunts—who were always naked, but they all had men's pippies—were chasing after me with bread knives. I eventually learned to tell when I was dreaming by flapping my arms like wings. If I could fly, then I would know it was a dream and I could go right on dreaming without being afraid, or maybe even change it to a better dream. Sometimes that worked, but other times I dreamed that I *wasn't* dreaming, that I really *was* flying, and it seemed perfectly natural. Then along would come a naked flying aunt with a bread knife and a dangling pippy, and that seemed perfectly natural too.

I developed a private ritual of lying on my side in bed at night and shaking my head against the pillow until I fell asleep. My mother took me to our family doctor to help me stop. He used to give me some kind of injection in the buttocks to help me stop separating my foreskin flap from my scrotum skin, and now I was grateful that he had no such treatment for my headshaking.

His prognosis: "He'll get over it."

When I confided in our family doctor that I wanted to stop playing the violin, he told me that it would be a sin to waste my God-given talent. But how could anyone else know what God meant for *me* to do? My God-given talent was to be a professional brat. At a concert, I would finish performing, then bow with my rear end to the audience, while Mischa Goodman sputtered with frustration. One day my brother and I went to his home for our violin lessons.

"Nice day for a murder," I announced to his neighbors.

I was trying to drive Mischa Goodman crazy.

Meanwhile, George and I were invited to play our violins at various events—from the 1939 World's Fair, where I witnessed television for the first time, to the dentist's office, where my brother innocently played "The Flight of the Bumblebee," which didn't exactly help take the patient's mind off the dentist's drill. Once my father brought us and our violins to a marathon dance at a ballroom where his friend worked. It made no sense to me that all these couples would be deliberately dancing themselves to exhaustion. I was glad nobody asked us to play there.

George and I did everything together. We practiced "cross-fire"— simultaneously emptying our bladders with careful aim so that the two streams of urine would meet in the air and spray before reaching the toilet. We played paddle tennis in the park, and the loser would have to shine the winner's shoes. He beat me every time. On the subway, when the train stalled between stops and there was silence, we would stand up like a pair of vaudevillians and recite jokes.

"Give me a pound of kidlies, please," I'd say.

"You mean *kidneys*, don't you?"

"I *said* kidlies, did'l I?"

We mined our jokes from a thick book, *2500 Jokes for All Occasions*. I tried to read through the entire collection, but ultimately I got bored. What good were jokes if they couldn't make you laugh? Then I discovered the world of comic books. *Detective Comics* with Batman and Robin the Boy Wonder. *Action Comics* with Superman. One superhero after another— Captain Marvel, Plastic Man, The Human Torch, Wonder Woman, The Flash, Sub-Mariner, Johnny Thunderbolt, Crimebuster—they all helped to sustain my spirit of adventure. Vicarious adventure was better than no adventure at all, and I came to associate the feel of a dime in my hand with the smell of a new comic book.

George and I performed a few times on a Saturday morning radio show, "The Horn & Hardart Children's Hour." Horn & Hardart ran the Automat restaurant chain. The older kids called it Horn & Hard-on. We all had to sing their theme song: "Less work for mother, just give her a hand. Less work for mother, and she'll understand. She's your greatest treasure, just make her life a pleasure, less work for mother, dear." But they never even gave us a free lunch. Ralph Edwards was the regular host of the show, but this was Ed Herlihy's debut. He called me "deadpan" on the air when I finished playing. I asked him what that meant.

"It's because you didn't smile," he said.

"This is radio," I reminded him. "They can't see me."

★ ★ ★

The radio had become my best friend. My favorite program was Edgar Bergen, with Charlie McCarthy and Mortimer Snerd. Charlie was the pretentious city slicker, wearing a top hat and monocle. Mortimer was his naïve, freckle-faced, buck-toothed country cousin. I wore a Charlie McCarthy T-shirt and I ate with a Charlie McCarthy teaspoon. I realized that there was something bizarre about featuring a ventriloquist on radio, but it didn't matter—they all *sounded* like different personalities. One time Bergen said, "Charlie, what are you doing?" And Charlie McCarthy replied, "Oh, nothing." But Mortimer Snerd interjected in his goofy, innocent manner, "Well, then how d'ya know when yer finished?" It was a veritable Zen koan from the mouth of a wooden dummy.

Lionel Barrymore, who played the crippled Dr. Gillespie in the original *Dr. Kildare* movies, had a program where he would sit in his own wheelchair, spouting maxims and dispensing homilies. In his authoritative, quavering voice, he once said, "Happiness is not a station you'll arrive at, it's the train you're traveling on." That single sentence immediately became my complete philosophy of life. But, a few decades later, I would read in *Hollywood is a Four Letter Town* by James Bacon:

> Lionel Barrymore once told me, as he sat in his wheelchair crippled with arthritis, that he would have killed himself long ago if it hadn't been for Louis B. Mayer: "L.B. gets me $400 worth of cocaine a day to ease my pain. I don't know where he gets it. And I don't care. But I bless him every time it puts me to sleep."

So happiness wasn't a radio station you'd arrive at, it was the wheelchair you were traveling on, and for Lionel Barrymore, it must have been an express trip all the way.

Every week, I would be delighted by two particular shows, Jack Benny and Fred Allen. I believed that Jack Benny actually went down to his money vault, and that Fred Allen actually visited Allen's Alley, and that they were both feuding in real life. When a photograph of them standing together appeared in the newspaper, a caption explained that the armed guards keeping them apart were not in view. I also believed, as Chiquita Banana sang, "You should never put bananas in the refrigerator—no-no, no-no!"

Bob Hope became instant folklore because he got away with telling dirty jokes on the radio, even though he was immediately cut off the air each time. "Meet me at the pawnshop," he would say to a lady, "and you can kiss me under the balls." Or she would ask him, "Do you have any meat for my dog?" And Hope would answer, "No, but I've got a bone for your pussy." Or he would say about an actress, "When she was a little girl she swallowed a pin, but she didn't feel a prick until she was eighteen."

I didn't need much sleep and listened to music on the radio almost all night, but softly so that it wouldn't wake my brother. I began to worry that the world was going to run out of beautiful melodies. In school, I would entertain myself by writing down song titles. My list totaled more than six hundred songs. While the other students were paying attention to the teacher, I would be reciting romantic lyrics to myself: from "My Ideal" (*Will I ever find the girl in my mind, the one who is my ideal?*); from

"Stardust" (*. . . and each kiss an inspiration*); from "Down in the Depths on the 90th Floor" (*Even the janitor's wife has a better love life than I*).

Instead of practicing the violin, I would read comic books. I would be standing in the bedroom with the door closed, violin in hand and a comic book on the music stand, but whenever I'd hear my mother approaching, I would quickly shove the comic book under my pillow and start playing the violin. Mischa Goodman wanted me to practice each piece ten times, marking X's on a sheet of paper to keep count. I hated practicing, so on the subway I would mark ten X's on a scrap of paper which I would then show to Mischa Goodman, and he would assure me that I was playing much better as a result.

But I kept hearing the voice of Mortimer Snerd asking, "How d'ya know when yer finished?" The answer finally came when Mischa Goodman died. I went into the subway with my violin and my mother's enamel measuring cup attached to my belt. I walked through the train playing the "Mendelssohn Concerto." With the money that passengers eagerly put into my cup, I bought potato chips, vanilla fudge with walnuts, and the sheet music for "Intermezzo," which I taught myself to play. I performed it for my parents. Then I put my violin in the closet and vowed never to play it again.

★ ★ ★

I simply *decided* to stop shaking my head at night when I went to summer camp, because I knew the other kids wouldn't be as tolerant as my brother, who was in a bunk for older boys. At home, one of my classmates used to force me to play his skin flute in the stairwell behind the mailboxes, and now at camp, when I confided to my counselor about that, he forced me to play *his* skin flute. I still didn't even know what sperm was *for*. The next day I asked my counselor if I was still eligible for the Clean Camper Award, and he chased me around a field until he caught me. Then he kept punching me on the arm.

I also got in trouble at camp for wearing my Charlie McCarthy T-shirt, because it had a tar stain that never came out in the wash. They wouldn't let me come to lunch unless I changed to another T-shirt. On the way back to my bunk, I was feeling weird. I noticed an apple core on the ground, but when I bent down to pick it up and throw it away, there was a *second* apple core right next to it. I was seeing double. Back at my bunk, I looked in the mirror. My left eyeball was all the way over to the left corner of my eye, and I couldn't move it back to the middle. No matter where I looked with my right eye, my left eye stayed in the corner. Now I was *really* in trouble. I ran all the way back to the mess hall with my left eye closed.

The camp director called my parents, and my brother and I were put on a train and sent back home. Our family doctor referred me to a specialist, who diagnosed my condition as bulbar polio—infantile paralysis—which was generally associated with the inability to use a limb. I was placed in a hospital, where the standard treatment consisted of applying hot compresses to a paralyzed arm or leg. They couldn't do that with my eye, but they kept me quarantined in the polio ward at the hospital anyway.

I was twelve years old and still believed that babies were purchased at the hospital. Ironically, it was there *in* the hospital that I found out where babies actually came from, and how they got there in the first place. Since I was the most mobile kid in the ward, I acted as a courier of comic books, bringing them from one bed to another, and it was while trading comics that I became informed about the bizarre practice of sexual intercourse.

The nurses were furious that I had been walking freely around the ward. They put me into a straitjacket so that I couldn't get out of my bed. That night, when everything was quiet but nobody was asleep yet, I said in a very loud whisper, referring to a comic-strip character, "Barney Google eats Pillsbury Farina." It worked. The other kids immediately got a case of hysterical giggles. But what could the nurses do? I was *already* in a straitjacket. Would they go so far as to put adhesive tape over my mouth?

The next day I got discharged from the hospital.

My paralyzed eye had to be exercised frequently at home. Several times each day my mother would patiently move a pencil horizontally in front of my left eye, over and over, while I would try to make the muscle work by following the path of the pencil, keeping my right eye closed. I couldn't fake this like practicing the violin. During that year, my left eyeball gradually moved toward the center.

Most of the time I wore a black patch over my good eye in order to strengthen my weak eye. Other kids called me Paul the Pirate. Eventually my left eyeball returned to its normal position, but the pupil remained larger, and the sight in that eye continued to be blurry. When I finally recounted to my classmates the details of my revised sex education—how the men's seeds impregnated the women's eggs—they thought I was making it up.

"Get outta here! *Eggs?*"

My new knowledge also got me in trouble when my brother and I did a joke for the relatives before a big family dinner.

"If your mother and father had a fight," he asked, "who would you stick up for?"

"I'd stick up for my father—he stuck it up for me."

And I got slapped in the face by one of my *sane* aunts.

My social skills were not well developed. While I was focused on the mystery of why we were here on earth, and the inconceivability of infinite time and space, everyone else seemed to be concerned with the details of daily living. I found it hard to communicate, yet I wanted to participate in their world. I sent away for the *Ethel Cotton Conversation Course*. When it arrived, I asked my standard question, "Is this what God intended?" The answer was no, and I returned the package. Instead, I eavesdropped on people talking, and I started to keep a list of handy clichés.

My favorite—a rhetorical question which I always took literally—was, "Whattaya gonna do?"

* * *

The Broadway movie theater was just a block away from our house. On the side of the building, the ladies' bathroom had a window that was usually open a few inches. I used to stand outside and peek in. Although I could see nothing but a pair of shoes on the floor of one particular stall, I kept indulging in voyeurism for its own sake.

Every Saturday afternoon, my brother and I would pack a lunch and go to the movies. For a dime, you could see a double feature, a news-reel, and twenty-four animated cartoons, plus a serial episode and the weekly race, with different stereotypes—a fat guy, a colored guy, a Chinese guy—running, riding a motorcycle, hijacking a hay-wagon, triumphing with slapstick speed over one obstacle after another. The whole audience screamed with excitement. And if the number you received when you bought your ticket matched the number of the first one to cross the finish line, you'd win a prize.

Occasionally a group of us guys would go to the Astoria Theater, which was further away but featured a live stage show between the movies. We would start clapping in the middle of a tap-dance act in response to a simple step, just to observe the applause spread through the audience.

After Errol Flynn was charged with statutory rape, we all went to see his latest movie and cheered when he appeared on the screen. Statutory meant only that the seventeen-year-old girl was underage—"jailbait"—but we didn't really consider it rape because it was voluntary.

Once a drunk lady sat next to me at the movies and started playing with my pippy, but the other guys sat behind us and heckled. Actually, I was relieved by their interruption, since I wasn't mature enough to ejaculate. When there was a circle jerk—a few of us would meet on the roof or at somebody's house—I pretended that I had an orgasm by gathering saliva in my mouth and emptying it into my hand when nobody was looking.

Meanwhile, my brother had obtained nude photos of movie stars like Rita Hayworth or Burt Lancaster, which we sold for seventy-five cents each. This was a long way from the time when we performed magic shows and charged a penny admission. When our parents were out, my brother and sister and I would examine each other's naked bodies. It was a form of sex education. George and I even had Marge sign a piece of paper promising to continue this practice in the future, when she would develop breasts and grow pubic hair. Although it was something to look forward to, we never held her to that agreement.

Marge and I were not really friends yet. She had a piano scholarship and practiced a lot. One winter, she found a Christmas tree, carried it up the elevated subway steps—she wasn't allowed to cross the street—dragged the tree past the change booth and down the other steps on our block. We never had a Christmas tree in the house before, but after all that trouble, my mother couldn't deny her the pleasure.

George and I had different approaches to leisure. I only read comic books, but he read the entire dictionary. I thought dancing was for sissies, but he bought a bottle of Brylcreem hair tonic and sent in the boxtop for a free copy of *Arthur Murray's Dance Book,* with diagrams of shoes, and arrows indicating how to do different dance steps. He tried to teach me the Fox Trot, but it was too mechanical for my taste. I thought dancing was just a poor substitute for sex.

One night, when I was dreaming about that drunk lady who played with my pippy in the Broadway Theater, I had my first nocturnal emission. Never again would I have to pretend that I ejaculated. Now I only had to fake conversation.

* * *

I had my own private religion, including my own personal prayer.

"Please, God," it began, "let's win and prevent all these wars." World War II was in progress. Novelty shops were selling rolls of toilet tissue with pictures of Hitler, Mussolini, and Hirohito on alternate squares, with the slogan *Wipe Out the Axis!* My prayer continued: "May all my loved ones live long, healthy, happy, complete lives, and may all *their* loved ones live long, healthy, happy, complete lives." Then, to win extra brownie points for courtesy, I would always add, "Excuse me. Please. Thank you, God," while making a circle with the thumb and forefinger of my right hand, the other fingers sticking out—this was also the symbol for ordering a Ballantine beer or a frozen Milky Way—and along with that gesture, I would wink at God just to keep it all on an informal, friendly basis.

According to my eclectic theology—a mixture of cultural superstition and health folklore—if you were eating a cookie and it fell to the ground, you could still pick it up and eat it without getting poisoned if you first touched it to your puckered lips and said, "I kiss it up to God." In rainy weather, if you wore galoshes over your shoes at the movies, it was bad for your eyes. If you sat on a toilet during an electric storm, lightning could strike you by coming up through the plumbing. If you bit your fingernails and swallowed them, it could cause appendicitis. My brother used to bite his fingernails, and my mother would apply a bitter-tasting liquid, gentian violet, to his nails. I developed a macho habit of spitting on the sidewalk instead, but my parents had no medicine to discourage me. Wherever I stood on the sidewalk, there would be a design of saliva spots left in that place.

Although I didn't consider myself Jewish, the bullies who picked fights with me did. I would sneak off to Hebrew School with my books hidden under my sweater. I challenged the rabbi on the ethics of circumcision. He had a stammer and said that "a *b–b–briss* is a c-c-covenant with G-G-God."

"A covenant should be *voluntary*," I argued.

"It b-b-began as a c-c-covenant," he said. "It b-b-became an ob-ob-obligation."

For my bar mitzvah, I rewrote the generic speech provided by the synagogue and thanked my parents for nurturing me through my illness. There was one point in the ceremony where my father was supposed to repeat what the rabbi said in Hebrew. "*B–b–baruch atoy adon-n-noy . . .*" My father innocently repeated what the rabbi said, complete with stutter. The congregation snickered, and you could almost see the steam coming out of the rabbi's ears as he chastised my father for making fun of him. Our relatives called out, "He didn't do it on purpose!" "He doesn't speak Hebrew!" "Leave him alone!"

Fountain pens were a traditional bar mitzvah gift, but ballpoint pens were new on the market, and I was given one which was guaranteed to last for six years. I figured that it would see me through the rest of junior high school and all through high school without running out of ink.

That's how naïve I was.

* * *

Attached to our kitchen ceiling, directly over the table, there was a rack with several horizontal lines of rope. It could be lowered by a pulley. My mother would hang wet laundry on those ropes with clothespins and bring the rack back up—but not when we were eating, or the clothes would drip on our food. Cockroaches would roam leisurely across the ropes. Once a cockroach lost its balance and fell *kerplunk* right into my split-pea soup.

We also had mice. And mousetraps. My task was to empty a trap whenever a mouse got caught. I didn't want to touch the dead mouse, so I would pick up the trap with a pair of pliers, release the spring with a screwdriver, drop the dead mouse into a paper bag with an apology, and throw the bag away in a trash can outside. If the mouse had been caught by the tail and was still alive, I would set it free in the basement.

In the middle of our rectangular-shaped apartment house, there was an open courtyard surrounding an oval-shaped garden, with tunnels on two sides that led to the sidewalk. There were stairway entrances at each inner corner of the building. I used to ride my bicycle around and around the border of the garden, singing—"Oh, I love the life I lead, and I lead the life I love"—over and over and over. I would always pedal slowly in case a neighbor was coming through one of the tunnels from the sidewalk.

"Stop going around in circles," a neighbor called out from her window. "You're making me dizzy."

One summer, at a field day on the local high school athletic grounds, there was a variety of competitive events, but only one really appealed to me—the slow bicycle race. After all, I had been inadvertently training for it, and was now in top form. You had to ride your bicycle as slowly as possible for about a hundred feet without turning or zigzagging. If your foot touched the ground you were automatically disqualified. Whoever came in last would be declared the winner.

The starting whistle blew. Fortunately I got off to a slow start. Now the trick was to remain behind. It was as if I had studied Zen in the Art of Slow Bicycle Riding. I *became* my bicycle. I was at one with the seat, the handlebars, the chain that drove the wheel. Pushing gently on the pedals, I gradually increased the distance between myself and the rest of the contestants until I was far enough behind them that it became obvious I would reach the finish line last. In an ordinary race, others could catch up to you, but here they would have to slow down.

Even though I hadn't crossed the finish line yet, I was so far behind now that it was inevitable I would win. The spectators were all cheering me on. There was no way I could lose, as long as I kept my balance. I felt absolutely exhilarated. But there was always the Unknown—that irrational, unpredictable, Aunt Evelyn factor—allowing you to take nothing for granted. Just when you thought you were in perfect harmony with the universe, Fate might suddenly intervene like a gigantic fist in the sky, punching at you through the clouds, as a disembodied voice boomed:

"Oh, yeah? *Pow! Pow! Pow!*"

So the only thing to do was savor the experience. Whether or not I came in last, I was *already* the winner of the slow bicycle race.

* * *

My mother used to walk right into the bathroom while I was taking a bath, and when I finally complained, she said, pointing to my groin area, "I'll stop coming in when you grow hair down there."

I became obsessed with pubic hair, it was so taboo. My brother and I would go to Brighton Beach and stroll around on the sand, sneaking glances at sleeping ladies in the hope of finding a few stray curlicues of that forbidden pubic hair peeking out from their various and sun-dried crotches. And if we spotted any, it felt as though we'd had a real productive afternoon.

We went to Steeplechase, a unique outdoor amusement park in Coney Island. To enter, you had to walk under the toothy smile of this tremendous joker face named George C. Tilyou. Then you'd stumble through a large rotating barrel, losing your balance and your change. There were all kinds of rides, games of chance or skill, and refreshment stands outside, plus an indoor arena with more rides.

There was one where you'd climb up a ladder, go down a spiral slide, and land on one of several revolving turntables. You had to keep your arms crossed to avoid getting wood-burn. On another ride, you started out in the center of this large round thing that rotated so fast you would be pulled to the side and held against the wall by centrifugal force even when the floor was lowered. You hoped you wouldn't throw up from the hot dog and malted milk and French-fried potatoes you'd eaten, because the vomit would only fly right back in your face, unless you turned your head at just the right instant. Timing was important.

There was a little theater at one end of the arena. You could sit in the audience, eat your lunch and watch, not actors, but regular people, who kept coming out of a door onto the stage, which was like a miniature fun house. They would have to walk across a wooden platform that jiggled and shook, struggling not to fall down. There was a one-inch-diameter hole in the floor which emitted a spout of air that would blow up a woman's skirt as she passed over that portion of the stage, and the audience would applaud.

Occasionally someone wouldn't be wearing panties or a bathing suit underneath, and there'd be a flash of her pubic hair. Then the audience would applaud with extra appreciation. Some women knew what to expect, and they would hold their skirts down, but for this contingency there was a dwarf dressed in a clown costume and wearing makeup that made him look hostile, waiting on stage for them.

He had an electric cattle prod, and he would buzz a woman in the buttocks so that her hands would instinctively go toward the shock, letting go of her skirt. Then the air spout would be effective again. Even though I was obsessed with pubic hair, I was offended by this particular method of revealing it. Once again, I asked myself, "Is this what God intended?" My parents had told me to act normal, but I was confused by what passed for normalcy.

The most popular ride was the Steeplechase Horses, which were like merry-go-round horses, except that they didn't travel rooted in a circle; they weren't impaled on a carousel. Rather, they moved individually on elevated tracks, up and down hills, all around the perimeter of the park, so that you could see the ocean, the beach, the boardwalk, the rides— the Tilt-a-Whirl, the Whip, the Parachute Jump. The Steeplechase Horses operated mechanically, but it seemed as if you could make them go faster by pelvic thrusts alone. When the ride ended, you had to walk down a passageway to an exit door, which turned out to be the entrance to that stage. This was the only way out, so you instantly became a captive performer.

After I rode the Steeplechase Horses, I came through the door and saw that the dwarf in the clown costume was standing at the edge of the stage with his back toward me, talking to someone in the front row. His electric cattle prod was leaning against the railing. I knew that I had to make a decision immediately. Time froze.

The left, more rational, lobe of my brain warned, "You must realize that if you turn his own electric cattle prod on him, it will definitely change the dynamics of this particular encounter and inevitably result in hostile vibrations." The right, more impulsive, lobe of my brain queried, "How can you resist such a temptation? You'll regret it for the rest of your life if you don't seize this opportunity right now. You'll never get a chance like this again." And, in that split second while time froze, the left and right lobes of my brain fused. Impulse and choice became the same process.

Having my retrospect in advance, I realized in a flash what I had to do in order to avoid regret. I picked up the electric cattle prod and buzzed the dwarf clown in *his* buttocks. He jumped away, just as he had made countless others jump away. The audience cheered and applauded wildly. Suddenly I was a hero—but not to the dwarf clown. He was fuming. He chased me off the stage, shaking his fist and cursing me out. He continued to run after me, around the cotton-candy stand and in between the Dodge'm Scooter Cars.

There was a certain dreamlike quality to all this—being chased around an amusement park by a dwarf in a clown costume because I had just buzzed him in the ass with his own electric cattle prod—so I began to flap my arms like wings while I was running, and since I didn't fly, I knew it wasn't a dream. This was reality.

It was, in fact, the most exciting ride in Steeplechase.

★　★　★

When my maternal grandparents came to live with us, my parents sacrificed their bedroom and slept in the living room on a convertible couch next to the piano. My brother, my sister, and I slept in the other bedroom. There was a lot of tension in the house. Marge almost lost her scholarship because it was so hard to concentrate. Whenever things got too tense, I would take our dog, Skippy, out for a walk. Once, he was squatting in the street, straining unsuccessfully at his stool because it was hanging from his anus by the cellophane from around a slice of salami he had eaten. I tore off a piece of newspaper in a trash can and extracted it for him.

Frank Sinatra replaced Ronald Reagan as my role model when he made a short film, *The House I Live In*, that was against prejudice. The lyrics of the title song summed it up: "All races, all religions, that's America to me. The right to speak my mind out, that's America to me." I had a new hero. I would sing his love songs to myself—"Saturday night is the loneliest night of the week" and "It was just a ride on a train, that's all that it was, but, oh, what it seemed to be." I even went to a masquerade party as Sinatra, wearing a large bowtie, padded shoulders, and pegged pants, crooning into my broom-microphone. I won first prize. From then on I continued to comb my hair like him.

My hair wasn't platinum blond anymore. Now it was light brown, though my mother called it "dirty blond." I began a search for the perfect hair tonic. I compiled a list of attributes from various ads—non-greasy, keeps hair in place, nonalcoholic, keeps hair well-groomed—and finally selected Wildroot Cream Oil. My father bought me a giant, barber-shop-size bottle, but the smell was so embarrassing that I used it only once.

That seemed to be my pattern. As a result of my search for the perfect candy, I bought twenty boxes of Holloway's Milk Duds, then lost interest after eating the first box. I hoarded the rest in my desk, but my mother was afraid they would attract ants, so I threw them away. Instead, I bought a can of chocolate-covered ants in a gourmet food store, but my mother wouldn't let me keep it in the refrigerator, not even while the can was still unopened.

My grandmother had very long gray hair, and she started using my Wildroot Cream Oil every day. It couldn't overpower the bitter smell of boiling senna leaves—an herbal laxative—that she prepared every day. My grandfather was always kicking the dog away from his legs. One time, as if for revenge, Skippy climbed onto the toilet, then the hamper, managing to extract my grandfather's false teeth from a herring jar on the bathroom widow sill. Then he hid under the couch with the false teeth in his mouth.

You could see this human-type smile on the dog's face, like some silly creature in an animated cartoon.

* * *

I always had some kind of part-time job. One was at a grocery store where, among other tasks such as delivering orders, I had to separate the good cherries from the moldy ones. I marveled at the blindness of Nature's force. The green mold didn't *know* what it was doing any more than the red cherries knew what *they* were doing. Another job was at a candy store in the front of our building. The family who owned it lived in the apartment right above the store. They made whiskey in their bathtub, and it was connected by a pipe to one of the soda faucets in the candy store.

My job there was to insert various sections of *The New York Times* into the main section. That's exactly what I was doing when I learned about the atomic bomb being dropped on Japan. I kept reading the headline over and over as I inserted the newspaper sections. I couldn't understand why an all-knowing, all-powerful God would allow such total devastation to happen to so many innocent civilians. And so I became an atheist at the age of thirteen. I was aware of the Japanese sneak attack on Pearl Harbor, but I knew nothing about Nazi concentration camps and genocidal ovens, or I would've become an atheist then.

My behavior didn't change, though. In fact, I was even *more* determined to be a moral person. That would show God—except I no longer believed that there was a God to *know* that I didn't believe in Him, a God that could think, *This is Me!*

In school, I had to write a report on a political candidate. I chose Vito Marcantonio, who was running for mayor of New York. I didn't know anything about him except that Frank Sinatra was supporting his campaign and sang at a fundraiser. Marcantonio was running on the American Federation of Labor ticket, but my teacher called him a Communist. He got very agitated and phoned my parents.

What I learned was that the Constitution didn't guarantee the separation of politics and culture. One of my favorite songs, "But Not for Me," included the phrase "more clouds of gray than any Russian play could guarantee," but now, on the radio, I heard an altered version: "more clouds of gray than any *Broadway* play could guarantee." Early tremors of the Cold War. My mother insisted that her family had come from White Russia, not Red Russia. My father threatened that if I ever became a Communist, he would kick me out of the house. I didn't even know what a Communist was. When my grandmother died, my father got drunk and poured the rest of her Wildroot Cream Oil hair tonic out the kitchen window. That was his style of catharsis.

* * *

There was a time when playing stickball seemed to be the most important thing in the world. The only equipment we needed was a tennis ball and a broomstick. The street served as our playing field, the sewer manhole covers were our bases, and the game stopped for traffic.

Later I graduated to sandlot baseball. I played right field for the Astoria Red Sox in the YMCA league. The guys on one team were all from Elmhurst or Jackson Heights; they were called the Elmjacks. The guys on another team were all Irish or Italian; they were called the Mickwops, until the Y made them change their name. There were a few Puerto Ricans on my team who did their infield chatter in Spanish, and the umpire complained that they were cursing him.

Long Island City High School didn't have a baseball team, but the local American Legion post wanted to sponsor a team with an automobile dealer. I tried out and played second base. Every Sunday morning, I became a living parody of a Norman Rockwell painting on the cover of *The Saturday Evening Post*. I would be wearing my American Legion baseball uniform (on the back it said "Universal Cars—Sales & Service"), riding my bicycle on my newspaper route, with my dog Skippy in the basket.

I wanted to be an FBI agent when I grew up. But for now I was the only member of my baseball team who brought a shoehorn to the games to help put on my spiked shoes.

My infield chatter was considered improper. Instead of chanting, "C'mon, baby, strike 'im out," I'd shout, "He couldn't get it up last night, so how's he gonna swing the bat now?" Although I always played my best, I didn't really care whether my team won or lost. I had to fake enthusiasm or disappointment. But I loved the adrenaline rush at that instant when you had to decide whether or not to swing at a pitched ball.

Once, during an especially tense moment in the bottom of the ninth inning, the score was tied, and I was at bat with a runner on second base. I couldn't resist breaking into a tapdance on home plate. Then I got a hit, which sent in the winning run.

It was the same with basketball. I had been fouled, and was about to take my free throw at a critical point near the end of the game. I bounced the ball a few times, took a deep breath, and started singing "Indian Love Call" in a falsetto voice. It drove the coach nuts, but then I sank the shot.

I played on a Police Athletic League team, and also a Catholic Youth Organization team where we would all stand in a tight circle before each game. Everybody would clasp hands, then separate and genuflect and pray before we trotted out to our positions on the court. Instead of making the sign of the cross, I would just scratch my chest and mumble gibberish.

Not only didn't I care if my team won, but I didn't have any school spirit in general. Nevertheless, I was elected president of the Student Court. My first official act was to subpoena the new principal for coming from a rival school. I also wrote, produced, directed, and starred in the senior play, about a teacher called Mr. Schnook. I had to defend my choice of that name when I was interviewed by a committee for membership in Arista, the high school honor society.

I explained that I called him Mr. Schnook "because I didn't want it to apply to any one *particular* teacher." They accepted me into Arista because I had a good record of extracurricular activity as well as excellent grades, even though I did an absolute minimum of homework and hadn't read a single book.

Whereas my high school was in the factory district at Queens Plaza, my college was in the business district in Manhattan. This branch of CCNY was on East 23rd Street, and the campus was on the ninth floor. In college, I continued to con my way through courses without reading any books, but it kept getting more difficult, and I had to compromise by reading everything in the textbooks that was in italics and taking notes on everything that the instructors *said* in italics.

I got all through high school and college doing book reports based on *Classic Comics*. You could read an entire novel in less than half an hour. Once, in a literature course, I gave an oral report on *Hamlet* based solely on the previous night's reading of the *Classic Comics* version, and I acted out the final scene of Hamlet stabbing himself.

"Farewell, Horatio," I said, "the rest is silence—*aarrggghh!*"

At home, we didn't have a TV set yet, and I felt culturally deprived when I heard other students talking about what Dean Martin and Jerry Lewis had done on their show the previous night. Stores actually closed on Tuesday evenings because customers were staying home to watch the Milton Berle show. Every Saturday, my whole family would take the car and visit another family to watch *Your Show of Shows* with Sid Caesar and Imogene Coca, until we finally got our own TV set.

* * *

I met my first girlfriend, Deedee, at the summer camp where we both worked as counselors. This was 1950, I was eighteen and extremely horny, but the sexual revolution had not yet occurred for either of us, so all we did every night was kiss and rub against each other's bodies with all our clothes on, then go to our separate bunks. In the morning our lips felt completely swollen.

Every week there was a campfire with a different theme, announced by a flyer on the bulletin board. One time, somebody changed "Hobo Campfire" to "Homo Campfire" and a few of the older boys came in drag. At the Gypsy Campfire, I got dressed up as a fortune teller, using a blown-up prophylactic as my crystal ball—well, at least it wasn't going to waste—and I was chastised by the camp director. My mistake had been to use a condom with a reservoir tip.

At the end of that summer, I went to the camp masquerade party dressed all in red with a white string tied to my head. For the campers, I was an unused firecracker. For the counselors, I was a used Tampax.

When Deedee told me that her previous boyfriend was a Negro, I was stunned to hear myself actually verbalize what I was feeling subconsciously.

"Did you kiss him on the lips?" I asked.

I had always thought that I was super-conscious, but despite my delusion of being really awake, I had somehow absorbed this combination of racism and sexism by cultural osmosis. It was so incongruous with what I believed that by simply uttering those words out loud, I was able to start demystifying the implications of my prejudice.

Maybe it *wasn't* really true that Negroes practice "bump Thursday." On that day each week, according to the folklore, Negroes would deliberately jostle white folks in the subway, on a bus, walking along the sidewalk, wherever, so that if it were to happen on a Wednesday, then you'd know it was only an accident.

★   ★   ★

My father originally had his own print shop. When the local Mafia representative came around for protection money, my father—who was a short man—grabbed the unwelcome visitor by his collar with one hand and held a wooden printer's mallet threateningly in his face with the other.

"I don't know who you work for," he said, " but I know *you*, and if anything happens to this place . . ."

Meanwhile, the International Typographical Union ran a campaign to unionize all print shops. My father was strongly pro-union, but he had a Negro assistant and the union wouldn't allow Negroes to become members. My father told the union he was willing to join, but insisted on keeping his assistant. That wasn't acceptable to them. So, although the Mafia didn't succeed in busting my father's print shop, the union did.

Now he worked in the composing room at the *Long Island Star-Journal*, setting up ads. However, national advertisers had developed a system whereby they supplied local newspapers with embossed mats, into which hot lead could be poured, and that would save—or lose—the job of setting it by hand. But the union was strong. They got a "reproduction" clause—nicknamed "bogus"—in their newspaper contract which fought off this automation by providing that even if a mat were used, the same ad also had to be set by hand.

With fine craftsmanship, my father would set up an ad, getting proofs and making corrections. Then, when it was finally perfect, it would be destroyed. The lead would be thrown into the Hell Box, and be melted down for use again. My father compared this to building a sand castle on the beach, only to see it washed away by the ocean, but to me it seemed like the ultimate alienation from work.

I became so obsessed with trying to decide what I wanted to do with my life that I took a leave of absence from CCNY to figure it out. In the morning I worked for a messenger service. The best thing about this job was that my boss's wife was an Armenian gourmet cook. Every day I would go to their house to pick up his lunch. Then I would stop in the park and sample each delicious temptation in the package, without leaving any evidence, before delivering it to him. This became my daily ritual. But one time I ate the *whole* dessert, and I hoped that my boss's wife wouldn't ask him how he liked it.

Every afternoon, I would go to a special branch of the library and read one vocational guidance brochure after another, but there was no category for Cultural Mutation. Even though humor was my religion, I had never seriously thought of stand-up comedy as a possible profession. Comedy clubs didn't exist yet, and there were virtually no role models for me.

My brother and I would go to the bandstand in Central Park every Labor Day weekend for a big show emceed by Milton Berle, but he told the same jokes every year. Even the same ad-libs. He would say to a voluptuous singer, "You look tired—go to my dressing room and rest." Other Borscht Belt comedians also did the same material year after year, condescending and boring. I kept hoping they would make me laugh, but instead I just felt insulted.

I returned to college, having decided to major in journalism and psychology, with a minor in draft dodging. I had an automatic deferment. Although I recognized this as a blatant form of elitism, I was not about to join the army and get sent to Korea just to demonstrate my spirit of equality. School was dull, filled with memorizing and regurgitating. One professor even announced precisely what the final exam would consist of.

He said, "Write down everything you can remember me saying this semester."

Between classes, I would either play basketball or read sex manuals in the library. I had the theory down quite well, but I never went out on a date to test it out. My greatest learning experience was in a social psychology course where I sat next to a female student. Our thighs kept rubbing together for the entire hour three times a week, and my pippy was in a constant state of arousal. We never verbally acknowledged that we were doing this. Once she was absent but I got an erection anyway. It was a stimulating object lesson in conditioned reflex.

★ ★ ★

One afternoon in the CCNY auditorium, there was a show put on by an entertainment troupe, the City College Service Organization. They had a professional guest comic, Morty Gunty, who did a routine about a guy who keeps repeating "trust me" to a girl as he proceeds to take liberties with her body. The audience was laughing, but I felt only annoyance. This humor was based on the approval of deceit, while I considered seduction to be the lowest form of rape. I realized then that I wanted to do stand-up comedy but still be true to my values, and I signed up for an audition.

Now all I needed was an act.

I had seen Victor Borge do comedy with the aid of a piano, while Jack Benny and Henny Youngman used their violins as props. I hadn't touched my violin for several years, but now I took it out of the closet. I did well in the audition, and began performing at hospitals and army camps.

My earliest routine took the form of a musical quiz. I would ask the audience, "In the Garden of Eden, what did Eve sing to Adam?" And then I'd play the opening bars of "Don't Sit Under the Apple Tree with Anyone Else But Me." My first political joke went like this: "Back in junior high school in a civics class, I learned that only Congress can declare war. But the reason Congress doesn't have to declare war on Korea is because it's only a *police action*."

I attached a red SOLD tag to the neck of my violin, and scotch-taped a large color photo of Marilyn Monroe onto the back. It was a rear view, but she was smiling at you over her shoulder. With one hand I would do *pizzicato* on the strings of my violin, and with the other I would make it appear as though I were plucking music from the strap of Marilyn's evening gown. Sometimes, I would play a few bars of music between jokes, accompanied by the sound of Mischa Goodman doing triple somersaults in his grave and yelling at me: "Violin *up*! Violin *up*!"

CHAPTER 2

THE FIRE HYDRANT
OF THE UNDERDOG

ALMOST THE ONLY THING I CAN REMEMBER FROM MY ENTIRE FORMAL EDU-
cation is a definition of philosophy as "the rationalization of life." For my
term paper, I decided to write a dialogue between Plato and an atheist. On
a whim, I looked up atheism in the phone book, and there it was: "Atheism
American Association for the Advancement of."

I went to their office for background material and met Woolsey Teller,
editor of *The Truthseeker*, the oldest freethought journal in the world.
(After his death, it would turn into an anti-Semitic and racist hate sheet.)
The AAAA sponsored the Ism Forum, where anybody could speak about
any "ism" of their choice.

I invited a few acquaintances from summer camp to go with me. The
forum was held on a Friday in a dingy hotel ballroom. There was a small
platform with a podium at one end of the room and heavy wooden folding
chairs lined around the walls. My favorite speaker propounded the Eleventh
Commandment: "Thou shalt not take thyself too goddamned seriously."

Making that maxim my unspoken theme, I got up and parodied the
previous speakers. The folks there were mostly middle-aged and elderly,
while I was a college senior, and they seemed to relish the notion of fresh
young blood in their movement.

My companions weren't interested in staying, though. Had I left with
them that evening in 1953, the rest of my life could have taken a totally
different path. Instead, I went along with the group to a nearby cafeteria,
where I learned about the New York Rationalist Society. A whole new
world of disbelief was opening up to me. On Saturday evening I went to
their meeting. The emcee was an ex-circus performer who entertained

his fellow rationalists by putting four golf balls into his mouth. He also recommended an anti-censorship tabloid called *Exposé*.

The next week I went to their office to subscribe and get back issues. I ended up with a part-time job, stuffing envelopes for a dollar an hour. My apprenticeship had begun. Lyle Stuart, the editor of *Exposé*, was the most dynamic individual I'd ever met. His integrity was such that if he possessed information he had a vested interest in keeping quiet—such as corruption involving a corporation in which he owned stock—this would automatically become top priority for publication in *Exposé*. He started a program to get jobs for the members of a tough street gang in his neighborhood, hiring three of them himself.

Lyle became my media mentor and my unrelenting guru. He and his wife, Mary Louise, were my flesh-and-blood role models. I had never seen such a loving couple, so filled with affection and respect and humor. I had never had any intimate friends before.

Lyle was working on a book, *The Secret Life of Walter Winchell*, and had published an article about the gossip columnist in *Exposé*. In order to ingratiate themselves with Winchell, thugs ambushed Lyle and beat him up; an ambitious attorney poured mimeograph ink over copies of *Exposé*; and *Confidential* magazine ran an article smearing Lyle. He decided to sue for libel. My assignment was to serve a subpoena on the publisher. I succeeded on my first try, and just stood there in his office.

"Okay, " he said, "it's served. What the hell are you waiting for, a *tip*?"

Exposé was dedicated to classical social and political muckracking, with articles on "Cancer Research" and "The Telephone Monopoly." But the name *Exposé* got confused with the slick scandal magazines that were flourishing—*Confidential* and its imitators, *Exposed*, *Whisper*, *Secret*—and so *Exposé* became *The Independent*.

One of my early responsibilities was to write ads for the books we offered, including *The American Sexual Tragedy* by Dr. Albert Ellis. Since his approach—rational hedonism—was so against the grain of mainstream culture, I asked to see any articles he had written that remained unpublished because they violated current taboos. He sent half a dozen pieces, which we published as a series in *The Independent*, and Ellis became a regular contributor. A few years later, Lyle Stuart would publish the Ellis columns in an anthology, *Sex Without Guilt*. He had become a book publisher on the basis of the money he'd won in the *Confidential* lawsuit.

I began writing a column, "Tomorrow's Leaders," for *The Independent*. I was getting college credit for working there, but in my final semester I failed a course, leaving me three credits short of a degree. I started to take it again in the summer, but had no motivation. One day I just decided to walk out of the class, and I never came back. I didn't care about graduating. Even if I had a diploma, I wouldn't have put it on my wall. And I didn't want a job where having a college degree was a prerequisite. I felt happier and more liberated than I'd ever been, but I had a difficult time explaining this to my parents. In fact, for a long time, I tried to make them believe that I had actually graduated.

*   *   *

Attorney Rowland Watts concluded a study of the injustices of the Military Personnel Security Program, whereby every draftee was required to sign a statement swearing that he didn't belong to any of the six hundred so-called subversive organizations that were listed. I wrote a feature story about it which Lyle ran on the front page of *The Independent*. Soon after, I received my draft notice, but that was probably just a coincidence, since my college deferment was over. I decided to challenge the constitutionality of the army Loyalty Program, because it was such a violation of freedom of assembly.

Originally I had planned to be a conscientious objector, challenging the constitutionality of the law that required CO's to believe in God, but someone else was already doing that. Ironically, I now expected to be waging a legal fight to get *into* the army. I went to the American Civil Liberties Union for help. I had never joined *any* group, so the ACLU attorney—who turned out to be Rowland Watts—was pleased. Since I wasn't trying to *hide* any subversive memberships, I would be an ideal test case. However, in preparing my statement, Watts suggested that I state that I was not a Communist. I refused.

"I'll tell *you* I'm not a Communist," I said, "but if I tell *them* that, then I might as well tell them that I don't belong to the Nature Friends of America—which is also on their list, as you know. I have to draw the line at the beginning or not at all."

He agreed, and we proceeded to prepare this statement:

> I am willing to certify that I have not engaged in any acts of sabotage, espionage, treason, or sedition, and I affirm my loyalty to the United States, and am willing to take the Serviceman's Oath. However, I refuse to further answer the questions on this "loyalty" certificate because I sincerely believe that such inquiry into my activities and associations is a serious invasion of privacy and violates the First Amendment.

Then came the waiting to be inducted. And the anxiety. I dreaded the possibility of involving anyone else, and I was afraid that my family would be traumatized by the investigation that would become an automatic procedure once I defied the system. Because of this anxiety, I developed a skin condition and picked at it with great diligence. As my apprehension grew, my face became highlighted by open sores.

At the army physical, I traveled along their conveyor belt of naked draftees, being inspected by one doctor after another, a specialist for every orifice. The rectum inspector had his own mantra: "Bend over and spread your cheeks." I asked, "What do you dream about at night?" He just sneered at me.

Now I was waiting on the final line. When I reached the desk I would have to announce that I refused to sign their loyalty pledge. My heart was throbbing. I kept reassuring myself that I was doing the right thing. Finally I was first in line, perspiring with panic. The sergeant sitting there looked at my sheaf of papers with all the medical and psychological data. Then he told me I was classified 4-F. They had rejected me because of my severe skin condition. I was free to go home. They were supposed to give me a subway token, but I didn't have the nerve to ask for it.

★   ★   ★

William M. Gaines was the head of Entertaining Comics, which published a line of crime and horror comics—plus *Mad*. Here was a comic book that poked creative fun at society in general and comic books in particular. What a kick to see Clark Kent going to a phone booth to change into his Superman outfit, only to find that Captain Marvel was already there. *Mad*'s mascot was Alfred E. Neuman, a gap-toothed, floppy-eared, dim-witted youngster whose total philosophy consisted of "What—me worry?"

His likeness was reproduced in college magazines and prison newspapers. On TV, Fred Astaire wore a rubber Alfred E. Neuman mask while dancing with Juliet Prowse to the tune of "Sophisticated Lady." In Florida, a practical joker matched his name up with a local girl, and the story landed on the society page.

Before he became Alfred E. Neuman, the kid had been kicking around for a long time in different forms. During the Depression, he was the most popular of the Gloom Chaser motto card series. Previously, on highway billboards advertising a patent medicine called Papaya, his face had appeared with the caption, "Have the Appetite of a Country Boy." He was also used in ads for Thom McAn safety shoes. His picture appeared in psychology textbooks as an idiot, and in biology textbooks as one who lacked enough iodine in his diet.

When Lyle Stuart subscribed to *Mad* with a fan letter, Bill Gaines wrote back, revealing that he had been a charter subscriber to *The Independent*.

Gaines signed his letter, "In awe." This led to their friendship, which led to a business relationship. Lyle accepted a position as general manager, and the office of *The Independent* moved downtown to what was unofficially known as the *Mad* building at 225 Lafayette Street.

We were on the seventh floor, right next door to the *Mad* office. The first time I met Bill Gaines, he was chasing his secretary around the room, trying to stamp FRAGILE on her forehead. Apparently this was a courtship rite, because they eventually got married. Since I was working for Lyle, I would also be doing things for *Mad*.

My first errand was to deliver a package to Bob and Ray while they were doing their morning radio show at WINS. They were just sitting there, relaxed and reading newspapers while a commercial was on. They had been preceded that night by the debut of Alan Freed—who invented the term *rock and roll*, acting it out as he banged the table and shouted along with the records he played. Bob and Ray were speculating about Freed's secret musical taste: "I'll bet he goes home and listens to André Kostelanetz."

I had also started to perform stand-up comedy in little out-of-the-way nightclubs under my new stage name—Paul Maul—wearing a bebop cap and using my violin in the act. I provided my own musical accompaniment for "This is Your Reincarnation," in which I honored the presence of an invisible worm that had been Sigmund Freud in a previous lifetime. In another bit, "Music to Masturbate By," I played a medley of songs such as Irving Berlin's "All Alone."

One club owner objected: "You gotta understand, people are having their *dinner* here, they don't wanna hear jokes about jerkin' off!"

I also got in trouble for satirizing Senator Joe McCarthy's anti-Communist crusade while people were eating. And, at the Five Spot, a jazz club on the Lower East Side, I was wondering aloud how the Virgin Mary felt when her period was late, and a somewhat tipsy man came out of the audience toward the stage.

"Hey, listen," he said, "I happen to be Catholic, and I don't appreciate your talking that way about the Holy Mother."

He looked like he wanted to punch me. I stood holding the microphone stand between us, ready to protect myself with it. "I'm sorry if I offended you," I said, "but don't you think you should consult your priest before you slug me?" The audience laughed, the guy realized where he was and went back to his seat. So this was comedy.

When Bill Gaines invited me to perform at the *Mad* Christmas party, it became the highlight of my career, to entertain this whole gang of artists and writers who were slicing through American piety with such vengeance and imagination. But then, on New Year's Eve, I was scheduled to perform for a big party at a nightclub in the Bronx. Everybody was boisterously drunk by the time the band stopped playing and I got introduced. I was just beginning to talk when somebody called out, "Get 'im off! We wanna dance!" Someone else yelled, "Yeah, we wanna dance!"

I could see myself from their point of view, and agreed completely. "You're right," I said. "Have fun! Happy New Year!" And I walked off the stage. I left the club without getting paid, welcoming the New Year in at midnight while sitting on a subway train with a bunch of inebriated strangers. My father thought I should've gone on with my performance, no matter what, and he called me a quitter. I figured maybe it was time for Paul Maul to get out of show business.

★　★　★

It was bad enough when the Boy Scouts officially sponsored a project to confiscate comic-book collections because they were reputed to breed polio bacteria. But then a psychiatrist, Frederic Wertham, wrote a book, *Seduction of the Innocent*, blaming the rise of juvenile delinquency on comic books, and hysteria really began to have a field day. There were newsstand boycotts and comic-book burnings. The Senate Judiciary Committee conducted special hearings to investigate the need for legislation to ban certain kinds of comic books.

The prime example developed out of an argument that artist Johnny Craig had with his wife. He came to the office late one night to let out his aggression in the form of a cover for *Crime SuspenStories*. It showed a man with an ax in one hand and the severed head of a woman in the other. Blood was dripping from her neck, her eyes were rolled back into her head, and her mouth was drooling saliva. Bill Gaines told Craig to eliminate the bleeding neck because it was just too gory. Later, when Gaines volunteered to testify at the hearings, Senator Estes Kefauver held up that very issue.

> KEFAUVER: This seems to be a man with a bloody ax holding a woman's head up which has been severed from her body. Do you think that this is in good taste?

> GAINES: Yes, sir, I do—for the cover of a horror comic. A cover in bad taste, for example, might be defined as holding the head a little higher so that the neck could be seen dripping blood from it, and moving the body over a little further so that the neck of the body could be seen to be bloody.

> KEFAUVER: You've got blood coming out of her mouth.

GAINES: A little.

KEFAUVER: And here's blood on the ax. I think most adults are shocked by that.

The senators tasted blood, and so did the press. Ultimately, to avoid government censorship, several publishers formed the Comics Magazine Association of America, which would require a stamp of approval on the cover of every comic book, guaranteeing that the contents were "wholesome, entertaining, and educational." Rather than risk the loss of distribution, publishers toned down their material to meet those subjective standards.

Lyle Stuart and Bill Gaines had initiated the association, yet now they wouldn't be allowed in it, for how could *Mad* possibly dilute its irreverence? Lyle suggested that they change it from a comic book to a magazine, so that it wouldn't be subject to the Comics Code. Gaines said that he didn't know anything about magazines, but Lyle assured him they could both learn together. Meanwhile, *Mad*'s editor, Harvey Kurtzman, was resigning because he had been promised the last third of every issue of *Pageant* magazine. Lyle talked Kurtzman out of leaving *Mad* and talked Gaines into publishing it as a magazine.

I flew to Florida with Lyle and Mary Louise for a vacation at her folks' ranch. It was the first time I had ever been on a plane. Now I was on a horse for the first time—clowning around by sitting backward—and didn't see a tree limb coming. It knocked me off the horse. We could hear Mary Louise calling Lyle, and when he saw that I wasn't injured, we both ran to the house. There was somebody on the phone for him.

When he picked it up and said, "Hello," a voice said, "Lyle?" He answered, "Yes." Then the other voice said, "Fuck you," and hung up. Lyle recognized the voice, laughed, and announced, "That was Bill." The phone rang again. This time Gaines said, "I'm in trouble." He told Lyle that Harvey Kurtzman was demanding 51 percent of *Mad*'s stock or he would quit. Kurtzman was waiting outside Gaines's office that very minute for a decision.

"Bill, listen to me and do exactly what I say," Lyle advised. "Call Kurtzman in, open the window behind you, and throw him out."

"I'm serious," Gaines said.

"*I'm* serious," Lyle said. "You have no choice here. Fire him *now*."

"If I do, what'll I do for an editor?"

"Hire Al Feldstein. He did a good job with *Panic*."

And that's exactly what Bill Gaines did, although it seemed strange, since Lyle had previously not been speaking to Feldstein. One afternoon,

Lyle passed Gaines and Feldstein together in the corridor. He greeted Gaines but ignored the confused Feldstein.

"Just because Lyle got you the job," Bill Gaines explained, "don't expect him to say hello to you."

★ ★ ★

I hadn't read my first complete book of fiction until I was twenty-one—*The Catcher in the Rye* by J.D. Salinger. I read it all in one night, identifying so strongly with the adolescent alienation of Holden Caulfield that I wrote a letter to Salinger, asking permission to use his character in a novel I planned to write. He gave the most appropriate response he possibly could—he completely ignored my request. His silence was so eloquent that for years I would continue to cringe with embarrassment at how incredibly naïve I had been.

Lyle lent me the second novel I read, *Johnny Got His Gun* by Dalton Trumbo, who had been an unfriendly witness before the House Un-American Activities Committee. "I shall answer in my own words," he testified. "Very many questions can be answered 'yes' or 'no' only by a moron or a slave."

As a result, he became a victim of the Hollywood blacklist and won an Academy Award for best screenplay under an assumed name. *Johnny Got His Gun*, originally published in 1939, was about a soldier so severely wounded that, with the aid of modern medical technology, he remained alive but without the senses of sight, hearing, smell, and taste. He had nothing left except the sense of touch and his consciousness. The book had a tremendous impact on me.

"There's a whole generation who never even heard of it," I said to Lyle. "Why don't *you* publish a new edition?" Which he did.

He also lent me *Kingsblood Royal* by Sinclair Lewis. It was about a white man who discovered that he had Negro blood. Lyle felt so strongly about the race issue that when he had been courting Mary Louise, he told her that he was part Negro. She passed the test and they got married.

They named their first child after me. But then Lyle called me, weeping, "Paul, our baby died." It was an incredible shock. Little Paul had lived for only six days, and our joy suddenly turned to sadness. There was absolutely nothing I could do except take care of the office while Lyle and Mary Louise went away. When they returned, he gave me the title of managing editor at *The Independent*.

★ ★ ★

The only freelance thing I'd ever sold was an idea to cartoonist Bil Keane, who had a syndicated feature, "Channel Chuckles." My cartoon showed two kids playing with toy guns. One was saying, "*Bang!* You're dead!" The other was saying, "*Bang!* You're Channel 2!" I got $5 for that. Then I had an idea that *Mad* bought. I wrote the script and Wally Wood did the artwork.

My premise was, "What if comic-strip characters answered those little ads in the back of magazines?" Orphan Annie would get Maybelline for her eyes. Dick Tracy would get a nose job. Alley Oop would get rid of his superfluous hair—only to reveal that he had no ears. But Al Feldstein wouldn't include Good Old Charlie Brown responding to the "Do You Want Power?" ad, because he didn't think the *Peanuts* strip was well known enough yet to parody. Nor would Popeye's flat-chested girlfriend, Olive Oyl, be permitted to send away for a pair of falsies.

Bill Gaines said, "My mother would object to that."

"Yeah," I said, "but she's not a typical subscriber."

"No, but she's a typical mother."

His mother would have objected to my final panel, which was also excluded from that spread, depicting a group of comic-strip bachelors—including air force pilot Steve Canyon, Dr. Rex Morgan, and detective Kerry Drake—who had sent for *Those Little Comic Books That Men Like* and were now all slobbering over these crude drawings of themselves performing sex acts that they were otherwise never allowed to enjoy. I sold a few other ideas to *Mad*, but when I suggested a satire on the pros and cons of unions, Feldstein wasn't interested in even seeing it because the subject was "too adult." Since *Mad*'s circulation had already gone over the million mark, Gaines intended to keep aiming the magazine at teenagers.

"I guess you don't wanna change horses in midstream," I said.

"Not when the horse has a rocket up its ass," Gaines replied.

I also sold a few sketches to the Steve Allen show. The first was about "Unsung Heroes of Television"—the one who pushed the isolation booth forward on *The $64,000 Question*; the one who erased the blackboard on *What's My Line?*; and the one who waited for the secret word to be said on *You Bet Your Life,* then dropped the duck down.

And I wrote a song lyric, "*Cosa Nostra*" ("Our Thing")—a romantic ballad with lines like, "I give you the kiss of death"—for which Steve Allen wrote a bossa nova melody, and he sang it on the show. But when I submitted a sketch making fun of psychiatry, his producer wouldn't consider it because Steve was going to a psychiatrist at the time.

Even Lyle Stuart edited me a couple of times at *The Independent*. I had been writing a new column, "Freedom of Wit." On one occasion Lyle objected to the use of the word *bogeyman* because he thought it would be offensive to Negroes. And then I wrote a column analyzing the sick-joke fad. Sample: "Mommy, Mommy, why do I keep walking around in circles?" "Shut up or I'll nail your *other* foot to the floor." But there was one example that Lyle wouldn't print: "Daddy, Daddy, why do all the other kids call me a queer?" "Shut up and keep sucking."

Meanwhile, censorship was becoming a futile process. Ed Sullivan wouldn't permit the bottom half of Elvis Presley to be seen undulating on his show, but young children across the country were practicing pelvic movements with their hula hoops that would bring a blush to the face of Elvis himself.

★ ★ ★

The word *greetings* had a negative association for me. That's how the telegram from Selective Service began—GREETINGS—before they told you to report for a physical. You had to register at age eighteen, and they could continue trying to induct you until you were twenty-six. So now I received another notice. The Korean War was over, but the peacetime draft lingered on. Since my own aborted attempt to challenge the Army Loyalty Program, somebody else had tested the law and the Supreme Court declared, 8 to 1, that it was unconstitutional, so now I wouldn't have to fight to get into the army, but to keep *out* of it.

I was determined to avoid the draft. I had a pathological resistance to authority. There was one regulation that every soldier had to keep a package of cigarettes in his inspection kit. What was the message? *There are no nonsmokers in foxholes! Do whatever we say!* I realized that I would probably end up in the brig for refusing to buy a lousy pack of cigarettes.

As the date of my army physical approached, my anxiety increased and I developed a nightly ritual of self-mutilation. I would stand in front of the bathroom mirror with a sewing needle, symmetrically gouging holes in the skin on my face and neck. A spiritual practice, I rationalized, strengthening my faith in the healing process. But the blood would flow and I would cry out softly, "I'm making myself ugly!"

It was an insane activity—I could acknowledge the insanity even while I was carrying it out—but if an aggravated skin condition had kept me out of the army previously, wait till they saw me *this* time. At my physical, I told the army psychiatrist exactly what I had been doing and why. They classified me 4-F again, reasoning that if I had gone to such an extent to make myself *seem* crazy, then obviously I must *be* crazy.

And they were right—because I *continued* to expand the scar tissue on my face, like some kind of masochistic junkie. My original self-preserving commitment had turned into a self-destructive compulsion. But one night, while creatively mutilating myself, I whispered to the mirror image: "What are you *doing?* The army *already* rejected you. This is *absurd!*" And suddenly I broke through this heavy habituation—*stopped*—just like that.

I must have been putting myself into some kind of trance every time I stood in front of that bathroom mirror, tattooing these designs on my face. Decades later I would read in *Omni* magazine about a study which concluded that cigarette smokers were not addicted to nicotine so much as the endorphins which were produced in response to tissue damage in the throat.

So even though I had convinced myself that I was participating in some archetypal rite of passage, I had merely gotten hooked on my own endorphines. But at least it kept me out of the army. My father was not at all pleased. He had been too young to enlist in World War I, but too old to enlist in World War II, and he still maintained a certain disappointment.

"Do you know what a 4-F means?" he asked. "It means that the army has classified you as physically, mentally, or morally deficient."

I couldn't argue with that.

★ ★ ★

A split had developed in the organization behind a freethought magazine, *Progressive World,* and Lyle Stuart proposed to the publishers—an elderly couple from whom the publication was, in effect, being stolen—that a lively *new* freethought magazine should be published, and that it could be launched with their mailing list.

"With you as the editor," Lyle told me. "You'll be perfect."

"Why do you say that?"

"You're the only one I know who's neurotic enough to do it."

America had a powerful tradition of alternative journalism that could be traced back, from contemporary periodicals—*The Independent,* I. F. Stone's *Weekly,* George Seldes's *In Fact*—to Brann's *Iconoclast,* published in the 1890s in Waco, Texas, all the way back to Benjamin Franklin and Tom Paine during revolutionary times. Now I was being given an opportunity to become part of this tradition. While I was contemplating the possibilities, I read an article in *Esquire* by Malcolm Muggeridge, former editor of *Punch,* the British humor magazine. He wrote:

> The area of life in which ridicule is permissible is steadily shrinking, and a dangerous tendency is becoming manifest to take ourselves with undue seriousness. The enemy of humor is fear and this, alas, is an age of fear. As I see it, the only pleasure of living is that every joke should be made, every thought expressed, every line of investigation, irrespective of its direction, pursued to the uttermost limit that human ingenuity, courage, and understanding can take it.

The moment that limits are set (other, of course, than those that are inherent in the human situation itself), then the flavor is gone. Humor is an aspect of freedom, without which it cannot exist at all. By its nature, humor is anarchistic, and it may well be that those who seek to suppress or limit laughter are more dangerous than all the subversive conspiracies which the FBI ever has or ever will uncover. Laughter, in fact, is the most effective of all subversive conspiracies, and it operates on *our* side.

The article was called "America Needs a *Punch*," and I took the implication of that title as my personal marching orders. This was before *National Lampoon* or *Spy* magazine, before *Doonesbury* or *Saturday Night Live*, *Politically Incorrect*, *The Daily Show*, *The Colbert Report*. I had no role models, and no competition, just an open field mined with taboos waiting to be exploded.

My goal was to communicate without compromise. My vision was a magazine of "freethought criticism and satire." Ironically, this concept was a leap of faith—there just *had* to be others out there who were also the only Martians on their block. If I was the only one, there would be no hope.

The name of the new magazine was suggested by Fred Wortman, a columnist for *Progressive World*. He was the personification of an old-fashioned village atheist. He wrote thoughtful, provocative, witty letters to the editor of his local paper in Albany, Georgia, cured himself of cancer with a grape diet, and was ecologically ahead of his time—instead of throwing away a used typewriter ribbon, he would re-ink it himself. Wortman wrote to me that *The Realist* might be a good name, and I recognized immediately that it was the appropriate one.

So there I was—the editor of *The Realist*. Now all I needed was a magazine. I found a quote from Groucho Marx: "Satire is verboten today. The restrictions—political, religious, and every other kind—have killed satire."

Then I began contacting writers and cartoonists, exchanging ideas and giving assignments, hoping to help bring satire back to life. I started with John Putnam, the art director at *Mad*. He designed *The Realist* logo, and also wrote the first column, "Modest Proposals," bylined John Francis Putnam. Although *Mad* staffers were not allowed to have any outside projects, Putnam was willing to risk his job to write for *The Realist*. Bill Gaines appreciated that and made an exception for him.

And then, late one extremely hot night in the spring of 1958, alone and literally naked, I was sitting at my desk in Lyle Stuart's office, preparing final copy for the first issue, to be dated June. In my opening editorial, I wrote:

I am nonpartisan in that I'm not a Democrat or a Republican or a Vegetarian. Not a Communist or a Fascist or a Prohibitionist. Not a socialist or a capitalist or an anarchist. Not a liberal or a conservative or a vivisectionist. Not Catholic or Protestant or Jewish. Not Unitarian or Buddhist or Existentialist. Not hip or square or round. Not even an American—in the sense that, as one book reviewer puts it, to call a man a South African just because he was born in South Africa is like calling a kitten a biscuit because it was born in an oven.

I was supposed to have everything ready for the printer the next morning. I felt exhausted, but there was one final piece to write. My bare buttocks stuck to the leather chair as I borrowed a satirical form from *Mad* and composed:

A CHILD'S PRIMER ON TELETHONS

See the tired man. He has been up all night. He is running a telethon. He wants the people to send money. It is for leukemia. That is a disease. Little children like you can catch it. Evil.

See the sexy girl. She is a singer. She doesn't know whether the telethon is for leukemia or dystrophy or gonorrhea. Her agent got her the booking. She needs the exposure. Notice her cleavage.

See the handsome man. He *does* know that it's for leukemia. You can tell. He is singing a calypso melody. Listen to the lyrics. "Give-your-money," he sings, "to-leukemia. Give-your-money, to-leukemia." Listen to the audience applaud. He is very talented.

See the sincere politician. He is running for reelection in November. He is against leukemia. He is willing to take an oath against it. That proves he is against it.

See the wealthy businessman. He is making a donation. He wants his company's name mentioned. Then we can buy his product. Then he will make profits. Then he can make another donation next year.

See the little boy. He has leukemia. Too bad for him. The nice lady is holding him up to the TV camera. Aren't you glad it's not you? But wouldn't you like to be on TV? Maybe you can fall down a well.

See the fancy scoreboard. It tells how much money they get. They want a million dollars. Uncle Sam has many millions of dollars. He cuts medical research funds by more than seven million dollars. Why? Because he needs the money for more important things.

See the mushroom cloud. That costs lots of money. It has loads of particles. They cause leukemia. Money might help to find a cure. That is why we have telethons.

See the tired man.

Steve Allen became the first subscriber to *The Realist*. He sent in several gift subscriptions, including one for controversial comedian Lenny Bruce, who in turn sent in gift subscriptions for several others. From this momentum the satirical wing of my readership would spread. And, out of three thousand *Progressive World* readers, six hundred subscribed to *The Realist*. That was the freethought wing. Edwin Wilson, director of the American Humanist Association, wrote in *Free Mind*:

> Those two facets of *The Realist* seem to complement each other. The social concern may prevent such nihilistic negativism as Ambrose Bierce represented. The humor, biting as it may be, may protect the polemics of the magazine from that complete certainty of an earlier type of reformer who was sure that by his deed the world assuredly would be saved.

The Realist had struck some kind of transcendent nerve. I heard from the Fortean Society and the Libertarian League, from psychics and secularists. Satirical troubadour Tom Lehrer wrote, "I anticipate, things being the way they are, that the magazine will expire before my subscription does, but I'll take my chances." And Charles Carver, author of *Brann and the Iconoclast*, wrote, "I am certain Brann would have relished *The Realist*. May the publication thrive!" The cover of his book had an illustration of Brann being shot in the back with a rifle. All I wanted to do was make people laugh.

★   ★   ★

The religious climate of the day was revealed by a stripteaser named Norma. Vincent Peel, and by evangelist Billy Graham telling a legislative committee that any censorship bill should "state just what parts of the female body must be covered in printed pictures." By the University of Colorado refusing to give campus status to the Student Committee for Freedom of Religious Dissent. And by the director of the National Catholic Welfare Conference suggesting that the human race find another planet rather than limit its population by birth control. Which inspired another child's primer for *The Realist*:

SEX EDUCATION
FOR THE MODERN CATHOLIC CHILD

This is a diaphragm. Women use it when they don't want to have a baby. That is very immoral. Why, you ask? Because it is artificial, that's why. But never fear. There are other methods to prevent conception. They are very moral. Why, you ask? Because they are natural, that's why.

This is brother's pajama bottoms. He had a nocturnal emission last night. What a shame. It woke him up. But see the semen stain. It has millions of dead sperms. They were killed the natural way.

This is sister's sanitary napkin. It doesn't look very sanitary anymore, does it? There is an ovum somewhere in that bloody mess. But it will never be fertilized. It will be flushed down the toilet bowl. That's the natural way too.

This is a baby. It was born dead. Every year in the USA, 136,000 infants are stillborn or die within a month. Now suppose their Mommies and Daddies had interfered artificially with the process of procreation. God's purpose would never have been achieved. Just think what a tragedy that would've been. But at lease some of the dead babies were baptized. That's the natural way.

This is a special calendar. It marks off menstrual periods. That's for the rhythm system of not having babies. A husband and his wife are in bed. They start to make love. Then they get out of bed. Because they have to look at the calendar. That's the natural way.

This is a husband and wife who want to have a baby. But the calendar says that the time is sterile. Lucky for them they have a calendar. It saves them from having unnecessary intercourse. So they stop making love. Unless they'd like to gamble on having an unwanted baby. That's the natural way.

This is a confessional booth. There is a screen in the middle. The person on one side is a priest. The person on the other side is a confessor. He is confessing that he has had evil thoughts. The priest tells him that to have an evil thought is evil. It is just as evil as committing the evil act that the evil thought is about. Priests never have evil thoughts themselves. They don't have to. They have an ample supply of other people's evil thoughts to draw upon.

This is the husband and his wife again. The ones who don't want to have a baby yet. Now the calendar says that the time is sterile. How convenient. Now they can make love without stopping. And without worrying. But they're good, consistent Catholics. And so they *are* worrying. Because they know that evil thoughts are evil. Their evil thought is to have intercourse but to avoid having a baby. They can't be *sure* they won't have a baby—that's why the rhythm system is moral—but the *intention* is there. Tomorrow they will go to confession.

When *The Realist* began, there were eighteen states with laws forbidding the sale of contraceptives. The pill had not yet been developed, but freelance journalist Harry Kursh gave *The Realist* an exclusive article about experimentation with a birth control pill. The human guinea pigs were women in Puerto Rico.

"When the birth control pill is finally reported on by scientists and made commercially available," he wrote, "it may prove to be the political and sociological atomic bomb of this age."

Meanwhile, when my mother read "Sex Education for the Modern Catholic Child," she said, "I've had three children, and you know more about birth control than I do." Twenty-six years later, the Pope would warn that the rhythm method of birth control could be "an abuse if the couple is seeking in this way to avoid children for unworthy reasons."

★ ★ ★

I was publishing what was considered to be the hippest magazine in America, yet I was still living with my parents. I was twenty-six years old, yet I was still a virgin. But I *had* become an expert at heavy petting. I even wrote a sex manual for adolescents titled *Guilt without Sex*. It was turned down by *Mad* but accepted by *Playboy*.

The night finally arrived when I would get laid for the first time. Because I had no place to take a girl, Bill Gaines gave me a key to his office and permission to use his convertible sofa. My date Joanie and I went to a rehearsal of the Steve Allen show to catch Lenny Bruce. At the time, Elizabeth Taylor was converting to Judaism so she could marry Eddie Fisher, and Lenny's opening line was a rhetorical question:

"Will Elizabeth Taylor be bat mitzvahed?"

Then Joanie and I went to the *Mad* building. Bill Gaines's office had original paintings of his famous horror characters hung around the walls— the Old Witch, the Crypt Keeper, the Vault Keeper—and there was also a framed portrait of *Mad*'s mascot, Alfred E. Neuman, watching over us while I lost my sexual innocence, just as he had been watching over a whole generation as they lost their cultural innocence. Joanie and I were rolling around on the carpet, kissing and groping and undressing each other. To open the convertible sofa now would interfere with our compulsive spontaneity.

I had read so much about Bartholin's glands, how they lubricate the vaginal cavity and take the friction out of intercourse, but now that I was *actually* putting *my* thing into *her* thing, now that I was sliding around inside another person's body after fantasizing about it for so many years, it occurred to me to flap my arms like wings to make sure I wasn't dreaming—but, since my weight was on my elbows, I couldn't carry out that particular reality check without losing my balance.

Joanie and I were beginning to reach that certain point in lovemaking where the voluntary is on the verge of becoming the *in*voluntary. I needed to get the condom which had been residing in my wallet beyond any possible estimated shelf life, so I stopped moving while I still could, and broke the silence with a strained yet noble whisper:

"I better put something on."

"Oh, that's okay," Joanie said. "You can fuck me without worrying."

I had never heard a girl say the word *fuck* before, and I was just a little shocked to hear it now, even though we were in the *middle* of fucking. As our spasms of pleasure mounted and began to overwhelm us, her reply remained in my awareness—*You can fuck me without worrying*—then suddenly my verbal ejaculation became as inevitable as my physical ejaculation, and I simultaneously surrendered to both, blurting out, in a voice that was not quite my own, "*What—me worry?*"

Even though I had been in the very throes of orgasm, I still could not resist responding to such a perfect straight-line.

★ ★ ★

I never knew where I would find new contributors to *The Realist*.

One night I woke up at three o'clock in the morning. My radio was still on, and a man was talking about how you would try to explain the function of an amusement park to visitors from Venus. It was Jean Shepherd. He was on WOR from midnight to 5:30 AM every night, mixing childhood reminiscence with contemporary critiques, peppered with characters such as the man who could taste an ice cube and tell you the brand name of the refrigerator it came from and the year of manufacture.

Shepherd would orchestrate his colorful tales with music ranging from "The Stars and Stripes Forever" to Bessie Smith singing "Empty Bed Blues." He shared philosophical insights like "Life is a series of resolutions and relapses." He edited several of his stream-of-consciousness ramblings into articles for *The Realist* under the title "Radio Free America."

One of Shepherd's regular features was the hurling of invectives. He would instruct listeners to put the radio on a windowsill. He'd whisper, "Now turn the volume all the way up," and then he would yell something that *sounded* ominous—"Shut up, you filthy *pragmatist*"—for the rest of the neighborhood to wonder whose family was quarreling with such unusual profanity.

Someone in my building was following those orders. It turned out to be a teenaged Nazi who liked Shepherd best when he talked about Nietzsche—all those unseen listeners heard his program through their own particular filters—and I published his article, "I Am a Nazi," to the dismay of many readers. It was the second time a teenager had appeared in *The Realist*. The first was an account of a petition to halt nuclear tests. Now, the teenaged Nazi called *that* "pacifist rot." He was also indignant about John Francis Putnam's "Modest Proposal" satirizing Nazi war memoirs.

Another writer, Robert Wilson, editor of the *Institute for General Semantics Newsletter*, gave himself a middle name, Anton, for his first published article in *The Realist*, "The Semantics of God," in which he posed this suggestion: "The Believer had better face himself and ask squarely: Do I literally believe 'God' has a penis? If the answer is no, then it seems only logical to drop the ridiculous practice of referring to 'God' as *he*." Wilson began writing a regular column, "Negative Thinking."

I was the entire office staff, and took no salary, but I did have to figure out how to continue publishing—paying the printer, the mailer, the writers, and artists—without accepting ads. So naturally I got involved with a couple of guys who had a system for betting on the horses. Although I lost all my savings, there was one blessing in disguise. At the racetrack, I bought a handicap newsletter, *The Armstrong Daily*, which included a clever column by Marvin Kitman.

I invited him to write for *The Realist* and he became our consumer advocate with an Independent Research Laboratory. His first report, "I Tried the Rapid-Shave Sandpaper Test," called the bluff of a particular advertising campaign when he described his personal attempt to shave sandpaper with shaving cream. He also wrote sardonic pieces such as "How I Fortified My Family Fallout Shelter," on the morality of arming yourself against neighbors who *didn't* have a fallout shelter.

Ultimately, I was able to subsidize *The Realist* with freelance magazine assignments and by performing stand-up at colleges in the guise of giving guest lectures. *The Realist* was now two years old and had a circulation of three thousand. Novelist Herb Gold mentioned in one of his books that I kept the subscriptions in a shoe-box, not realizing that his fictional tidbit was literally correct.

In my capacity as editor of *The Realist*, I could follow the impulse to satisfy certain curiosities that might otherwise have remained in limbo. When I heard a rumor that IBM employees were required to have their teeth capped by a company dentist, I checked into it. Their medical director replied, "We do not maintain dental services nor do we provide remedial dental care."

When it was reported that Bertrand Russell had just predicted he would die in June 1962 because he would then be ninety years old and that age "seems like a good time to die," I queried my favorite philosopher-activist about the accuracy of what seemed to be a very un-Russell-like bit of mysticism. He replied: "Your letter has astonished me. The prediction of my death was made in 1937 purely as a joke which I thought was obvious. I find, however, that astrologers and such have taken it seriously."

And when I heard that a TV drama by Rod Serling with a New York locale used a film clip of the Manhattan skyline with the Chrysler Building erased from the scene because the program was sponsored by the Ford Motor Company, I wrote to Serling, and he verified it, adding: "In a *Playhouse 90* script, I was not permitted to use a line of dialogue which read as follows: 'Have you got a match?' The reason for this, advanced by the agency, was that the sponsor was the Ronson Lighter Company, and that matches were 'competitive.'"

It was the banality of such fear that inspired a piece I wrote, "Monologue by a Miss Rheingold Loser." The winner of this beauty contest—sponsored in seven states by Liebmann Breweries, the maker of Rheingold Beer—garnered more votes than did both presidential candidates in those same states. My Miss Rheingold Loser confessed, "We all had to wear the same blue dresses and shoes, with white pocketbooks and gloves, so that none of us could take unfair advantage of individuality."

She praised permanent registration in certain bars, revealing ballot-stuffing in others, and concluded, "Far be it from me to get catty about the winner, but I heard that Boss Liebmann had decided on her at the original caucus." In that same issue, I published a critique of the FBI. Subsequently an agent was assigned to find out all he could about *The Realist* and its personnel. But he wasn't from the FBI. Rather, this "investigator" was from an advertising agency whose client, Liebmann Breweries, wanted to know who was *really* behind "Monologue by a Miss Rheingold Loser."

And there was the southerner who saw a Negro man kissing a Caucasian woman on his TV set. He wrote a nasty letter, threatening never to buy the sponsor's product again. Actually, the kinescope that had run on his local station was defective—the leading man was really white. So the sponsor flew an account executive there and held a private screening for that lone irate viewer. It was this climate of paranoia that spawned *The Realist*'s infamous TV Hoax.

I selected the most innocuous program on the air—*Masquerade Party*, where a panel had to guess which celebrity was wearing a mask. I picked an upcoming air date and suggested that readers "write a letter complaining about the offensive thing that was said on the program. Use your own wording. *But don't mention anything specific.*" I gave the addresses of the network and the sponsors. More than a hundred readers wrote. The theory was that each letter represented fifty thousand that were *not* sent. There was a panic at NBC, but in their official response they fought vagueness with vagueness:

> This is to acknowledge your critical appraisal of a recent *Masquerade Party* program. It is a matter of genuine concern to us that you found this program objectionable. We will most certainly note your sensitive expression of criticism and relay it to the Manager of our Continuity Acceptance Department.

Producers called people across the country, telling each one that he or she was the only person who had complained. When the hoax was finally revealed, an advertising executive predicted that I would be charged with malicious mischief. I could hardly wait.

* * *

The State Department was financing counterrevolutionary broadcasts to Cuba from a radio station on Swan Island in Honduras. Program content ranged from telling Cubans that their children would be taken away to warning them that a Russian drug was being added to their food and milk that would automatically turn them into Communists. Lyle Stuart was national treasurer of the Fair Play for Cuba Committee, which sponsored a trip to Cuba in December 1960, and he persuaded me to come along, all expenses paid.

Since I had never been to a prostitute, Lyle brought me to the Mambo Club, a combination bar and whorehouse in Havana, and left me there. I sat at the bar and asked for an orange juice. The bartender said he didn't have any. I asked for a soda. They didn't have that either. I settled for a frozen daiquiri which I didn't drink. A woman sat next to me and asked for a cigarette. I told her I didn't smoke. She asked if I would buy her a drink, so I did. Then we went out the back door to one of several small cottages. While we were sitting on the bed getting undressed, I kept asking political questions.

She finally said, "Are you a Communist?"

"No, I'm just curious."

She was the first Cuban I'd met who didn't have a strong sense of optimism. The revolution had ruined the prostitution business. She used to be thin and blonde for tourists. Now she was plump and brunette. "I bleached my *poosy*," she explained while washing my genitals in the tiny bathroom. Later, in the middle of performing fellatio, she stopped and looked up. "You *sure* you're not a Communist?"

"Even if I was, I wouldn't tell you *now*. You'd bite it off."

That night, there was a reception at the Presidential Palace for several hundred visitors from around the world. When Castro arrived in the main ballroom, he was surrounded by an eager, protoplasmic circle of admirers and well-wishers. He stood tall and handsome in their midst, uniformed but hatless. Mary Louise compared him to Marlon Brando's Zapata.

"If I were a homosexual," I remarked to her, "I could go for him."

"If *I* were a homosexual," she replied, "*I* could go for him."

The throng of people with Castro at the hub surged forward a few feet at a time toward the end of the ballroom and finally gave way to a line that formed to meet him, one by one. Some asked him to pose with them, which he did. A man with a camera stood on a plush chair for a better angle, but his wife, who was posing with Castro, yelled at him, "Max! Don't stand on that chair! This is a *palace!*"

I gave Castro a copy of *The Realist* and requested an interview. He told me to set it up with his secretary. Then a palace guard handed him a cablegram from Dwight Eisenhower—in the final weeks of his lame-duck presidency—calling off diplomatic relations with Cuba. I asked Castro for a statement.

"I do not think it is up to me to comment," he said, "since it is the United States that has broken relations. I will say only that Cuba is alert."

There was no official announcement at the Presidential Palace, but the news spread rapidly among the guests as Castro strode across the ballroom and departed.

I had brought Lawrence Ferlinghetti's *Coney Island of the Mind* to Cuba. Now I was in my hotel room, sitting on the bidet and reading his long poem, "I Am Waiting," while waiting in vain for a call from that secretary. But Fidel Castro obviously had more important things to do than answer my questions. In retrospect, I would like to have asked him, "Do you believe in term limits?"

★   ★   ★

I was becoming bad company. Campus bookstores were banning *The*

Realist. Students whose parents had burned their issues often wrote in for replacement copies, but I was publishing material that was bound to offend. For example, Madalyn Murray was a militant atheist who was challenging the constitutionality of compulsory Bible reading in public schools, and she concluded her article:

"I feel that Jesus Christ is at most a myth, and if he wasn't, the least he was, was a bastard, and that the Virgin Mary obviously played around as much as I did, and certainly I feel she would be capable of orgasm."

The Realist had become a central clearinghouse for bizarre news items sent in by readers. I reprinted unusual material from medical journals: on fracture of the penis; on the caloric content of semen; on objects found in the rectum, from a tennis ball to a frozen pig's tail. And I published this letter from a reader: "I found the article entitled 'Great Moments in Medicine,' concerning foreign bodies stuck in the rectum, thoroughly repellent. I trust that you know what you can do with your magazine."

The Realist had also developed a reputation as a haven for cartoons which could be published nowhere else. Our first cartoon, by Drury Marsh, was a reaction to the National Association of Broadcasters amending its TV code to ban the use of actors in "white-coat commercials." The revised ruling read:

> Dramatized advertising involving statements or purported state-ments by physicians, dentists, or nurses must be presented by ac-credited members of such professions.

The cartoon showed a man dressed like a doctor doing a cigarette com-mercial, then changing to his civilian clothes in a dressing room, going back to his own office and getting dressed like a doctor again, and finally telling a patient, "You're going to have to give up smoking."

An unsolicited comic strip arrived from editorial cartoonist Frank Interlandi. It showed a man walking along, spotting a poster of a mush-room cloud with the question, *If a Bomb Falls, What Would You Do?* He continued walking as his answer appeared in a thought balloon: "I'd shit!"

Interlandi wrote to me: "Actually, I did the cartoon with the intention of sending it to the syndicate, but when it came to putting the punchline in, I couldn't think of anything but 'I'd shit!' The more lines I tried the less funny it got, and the surer I was that the original line was the best and only one—it was a genuine reaction; the feeling of being helpless and returning to infantilism. But why do I have to explain a cartoon? Naturally I knew the syndicate would reject it, so they never did see it, but I wanted to see it printed and I thought of you."

At a convention of editorial cartoonists, several artists observed that Interlandi's drawing should have won a Pulitzer Prize, but they knew it couldn't. Nor would the *Village Voice* accept an ad including that cartoon, afraid of jeopardizing their second-class mailing permit. Ours was still pending.

A *New Yorker* artist who preferred to remain anonymous sent me a cartoon that he knew would also be rejected. The top half showed a guest on a TV talk show, saying, "Frankly I didn't give a *damn* about it!" The bottom half depicted a family watching the program at home. Now the TV guest was saying, "Frankly I didn't give a *bleep* about it!" Thought balloons indicated that the mother was thinking, "Fuck?" The father: "Piss?" The grandmother: "Shit?" And the son: "Crap?"

When the Cuban missile crisis occurred, Richard Guindon created his most popular cartoon for *The Realist*, which I put on the cover. It depicted a reclining nude woman, leaning on her elbow with her back to us—her buttocks fashioned a globe with latitudinal and longitudinal lines—as she faced a couple of faceless men, both naked except that one was wearing boxer shorts with stars and stripes while the other had a hammer and sickle tattooed on his chubby arm. The Kennedy-like American was gesturing toward the Khrushchev-like Russian and speaking to the Earth-woman: "It's his turn now and then me again."

That cartoon captured a certain feeling of powerlessness that permeated the country. Two Broadway stars—Orson Bean in *Subways are for Sleeping* and Anthony Newley in *Stop the World, I Want to Get Off*—had it framed on their dressing room walls, even while certain bookstores and newsstands were displaying that issue face down.

And political satirist Mort Sahl chastised me: "I think *The Realist* is probably the most vital publication in America, but I don't think the magazine should dissipate its time on *crudeness*. I don't mind telling you, that kind of thing is offensive to me. I don't think that both the United States and Russia are raping the world."

"Now you used the word *rape*," I said. "How do you know that the female representing the earth was not being submissive?"

"Or even seductive," Sahl said. "Well, I'll never know. I didn't see her face in that cartoon. You didn't emphasize that part, you know."

I published a cartoon by Mort Gerberg, depicting a Mother Goose character—the old lady who lived in a shoe and had so many children she didn't know what to do—speaking on the phone: "Dr. Burnhill?—Uh, you don't know me, but, uh, I've been told that you could, uh, perform a certain, uh, operation—" It turned out that there was an *actual* Dr. Burnhill, an obstetrician-gynecologist, who called me in distress after patients started bringing that issue of *The Realist* to his office.

Although I apologized to the doctor, every succeeding cartoon by Gerberg would include a character named Burnhill.

★ ★ ★

I had become friends with Paul Jacobs, a radical union organizer, who was commissioned by the Health, Education and Welfare Department to write a paper, "Keeping the Poor Poor," for presentation at a social workers conference and to be included in a book on poverty. His analysis was prefaced by a quotation in its original language, Portuguese. Translation: "If shit ever gets to have any value, the poor will be born without assholes."

In *The Realist*, I applied that proverb to the subject of abortion:

> A poor woman has to undergo an unsuccessful hassle to get permission for a therapeutic—that is, a legal—abortion, even though she contracted German measles from a syphilitic cousin who raped her and then stole all her money plus the secondhand toys of her eighteen children, then calmed her down with tranquilizers containing thalidomide. Whereas, a wealthy woman can avoid having an unwanted offspring under safe and sanitary conditions *simply because she decided* not to have a baby. Why, she might conceivably go so far some day as to achieve the ultimate status symbol by obtaining an abortion when she isn't even pregnant.

Actually, when abortion was illegal, women had no choice but to seek out back-alley butchers for a medical procedure. If there was a botched surgery and the victim went to a hospital, the police were called and they wouldn't allow the doctor to provide a painkiller until the patient gave them the information they sought.

There was an article in *Look* magazine that stated, "There is no such thing as a 'good' abortionist. All of them are in business strictly for money." But in the June 1962 issue of *The Realist*, I published an anonymous interview with Dr. Robert Spencer, a humane abortionist, promising that I would go to prison sooner than reveal his identity.

Dr. Spencer had served as an army doctor in World War I, then became a pathologist at a hospital in Ashland. He won the town's respect for going down into the shafts after a mine accident, and aiding miners to obtain Workmen's Compensation for lung disease. Now, at a time when five thousand women were killed each year by criminal abortionists who charged as much as $1500, his reputation had spread by word-of-mouth, and he was known as "The Saint." Patients came to his clinic in Ashland, Pennsylvania, from around the country.

I took the five-hour bus trip from New York to Ashland with my gigantic Webcor tape recorder. Dr. Spencer was the cheerful personification of an old-fashioned physician, and used folksy expressions like "by golly." He had been performing abortions for forty years. He started out charging $5, and never more than $100. He rarely used the word *pregnant*. Rather, he would say, "She was *that way*, and she came to me for help."

Ashland was a small town, and Dr. Spencer's work was not merely tolerated; the community *depended* on it—the hotel, the restaurant, the dress shop—all thrived on the extra business that came from his out-of-town patients. He built facilities at his clinic for Negro patients who weren't allowed to obtain overnight lodgings elsewhere in Ashland. The walls of his office were decorated with those little wooden signs that tourists like to buy. A sign on the ceiling over his operating table said KEEP CALM.

Q. Do you have any idea about how many actual abortions you've performed during all these years?

A. To be accurate, he replied, it's 27,006.

Q. Have medical people come to you, who would otherwise shun you?

A. Oh, yes, I've had medical people who bring me their wives, and I've had quite a few medical people send me patients.

Q. But they wouldn't perform the operation themselves?

A. No, they'd never perform it, and just exactly what their attitude would be, I don't really know. Some of them, I presume, were absolutely against it, because I've had ministers, and they'd bring me their daughters or their nieces.

Q. Have police come to you for professional services?

A. Oh, yes, I've had police in here, too. I've helped them out. I've helped a hell of a lot of police out. I've helped a lot of FBI men out. They would be here, and they had me a little bit scared—I didn't know whether they were just in to get me or not.

Q. What would you say is the most significant lesson you've learned in all your years as a practicing abortionist?

A. You've got to be careful. That's the most important thing. And you've got to be cocksure that everything's removed. And even the uterus speaks to you and tells. I could be blind. You see, this is an operation no eye sees. You go by the sense of feel and touch. The voice of the uterus . . . But the only thing I can see is hypocrisy, hypocrisy. Everywhere I look is hypocrisy. Because the politicians—and I've had politicians in here—they still keep those laws in existence, but yet, if some friend of theirs is in trouble . . .

That issue of *The Realist* included a reprint of an article from the *London Observer,* which began: "Three Roman Catholic theologians have expressed the opinion that, in times of revolution and violence, it is lawful for women, particularly for nuns, to take contraceptive pills and precautions against the danger of becoming pregnant through rape." On that same page was our Rumor of the Month: "So-called 'flying saucers' are actually diaphragms being dropped by nuns on their way to Heaven."

After my interview with Dr. Spencer was published, I began to get phone calls from scared female voices. They were all in desperate search of a safe abortionist. It was preposterous that they should have to seek out the editor of a satirical magazine, but their quest so far had been futile, and they simply didn't know where else to turn.

With Dr. Spencer's permission, I referred them to him. At first there were only a few calls each week, then several every day. I had never intended to become an underground abortion referral service, but it wasn't going to stop because in the next issue of *The Realist* I would publish an interview with somebody else.

A few years later, state police raided Dr. Spencer's clinic and arrested him. He remained out of jail only by the grace of political pressure from those he'd helped. He was finally forced to retire from his practice, but I continued mine, referring callers to other physicians who he had recommended. Occasionally I would be offered money by a patient, but I never accepted it. And whenever a doctor offered me a kickback, I refused, but I also insisted that he give a discount for the same amount to those patients referred by me.

Eventually, I was subpoenaed by district attorneys in two cities to appear before grand juries investigating criminal charges against abortionists. On both occasions I refused to testify, and each time the D.A. tried to frighten me into cooperating with the threat of arrest.

In Liberty, New York, my name had been extorted from a patient by threatening *her* with arrest. The D.A. told me that the doctor had confessed everything and they got it all on tape. He gave me until two o'clock that afternoon to change my mind about testifying, or else the police would come to take me away.

"I'd better call my lawyer," I told him.

I went outside to a public phone booth and called, not a lawyer, but the doctor.

"That never happened," he said.

I returned to the D.A.'s office and told him that my lawyer said to continue being uncooperative. Then I just sat there waiting for the cops.

"They're on their way," the D.A. kept warning me. But at two o'clock, he simply said, "Okay, you can go home now."

Bronx District Attorney (later Judge) Burton Roberts took a different approach. In September 1969, he told me that his staff had found an abortionist's financial records, which showed all the money that I had received, but he would grant me immunity from prosecution if I cooperated with the grand jury. He extended his hand as a gesture of trust.

"That's not true," I said, refusing to shake hands with him.

If I *had* ever accepted any money, I'd have no way of knowing that he was bluffing. The D.A. was angry, but he finally had to let me go.

Attorney Gerald Lefcourt (later president of the National Association of Criminal Defense Lawyers) filed a suit on my behalf, challenging the constitutionality of the abortion law. He pointed out that the district attorney had no power to investigate the violation of an unconstitutional law, and therefore he could not force me to testify. In 1970, I became the only plaintiff in the first lawsuit to declare the abortion laws unconstitutional in New York State.

"Later, various women's groups joined the suit," Lefcourt recalls, "and ultimately the New York legislature repealed the criminal sanctions against abortion, prior to the Supreme Court decision in *Roe vs. Wade.*"

Dr. Spencer never knew about that. He had died in 1969. The obituary in *The New York Times* acknowledged the existence of his abortion clinic. The obituary in the local paper in Ashland did not.

I continued to carry on my underground abortion referral service. Each time, though, I would flash on the notion that this was my *own* mother asking for help, and that she was pregnant with *me*. I would try to identify with the fetus that was going to be aborted even while I was serving as a conduit to the performance of that very abortion. Every day I would think about the possibility of never having existed, and I would only appreciate being alive all the more.

Pretending to be the fetus was just a way of focusing on my role as a referral service. I didn't want it to become so casual that I would grow unaware of the implications. By personalizing it, I had to accept my own responsibility for each fetus whose potential I was helping to disappear. That was about as mystical as I got. Maybe I was simply projecting my own ego.

In any case, by the time these women came to me for help, they had *already* searched their souls and made up their minds. This was not some abstract cause far away—these were real people in real distress—and I just couldn't say no. So I made a choice to abort myself every time.

For nearly a decade, that became my fetal yoga.

Postscript:

Before *Roe vs. Wade*, when abortion was illegal, I thought it would never be legalized in my lifetime. And then I thought abortion would never be i*l*legal again. So now, in 2012—fifty years after my interview with Dr. Spencer—it's disheartening to see the right-wing religious conservative movement that supposedly wants to keep government out of our lives, while simultaneously promulgating compulsory transvaginal probes in the process of trying to *re*-criminalize reproduction rights in my lifetime.

Things seem to be going backward. The Dinosaur Follies—better known as the Republican presidential primaries—suck so badly that the candidates have finally turned themselves inside out. Most despicable is the way they've all pandered to their fanatical anti-choice constituents.

My unofficial Campaign Pandering Award goes to Mr. Anti-Choice, Mitt Romney. He wants to destroy Planned Parenthood and to overturn *Roe vs. Wade.* And yet, in 1994, when he was running for the Senate, he came out in *favor* of choice for women. Freelance journalist Suzan Mazur has revealed that he admitted to Mormon feminist Judith Dushku that "the Brethren" in Salt Lake City *told* him he could take a pro-choice position, and that in fact he probably *had* to in order to win in a liberal state like Massachusetts.

While Romney believes that life begins at conception, Rick Santorum believes that life begins at foreplay. He has gone way beyond his frenzied position against women's right to abortion. He's also against birth control, even though that would *prevent* the need for an abortion. He claims that "contraception is *not* OK" and that it turns sex into "simply pleasure." He has also vowed to "ban all pornography"—or as I call it, "Masturbation Helper"—even though watching porn would *prevent* the need for contraception.

CHAPTER 3

LENNY THE LAWYER

IN 1960 I WAS A MISFIT AMONG MISFITS ATTENDING A COMEDY WORKSHOP in a Times Square rehearsal loft. A group of would-be stand-up comics met every week and tried to make each other laugh. There were two performers who did impressions. One was Vaughn Meader, whose specialty was John Kennedy; the other was David Frye, whose specialty was Richard Nixon. And so it became an attachment beyond ordinary political considerations that motivated Meader and Frye to root respectively for Kennedy and Nixon in the presidential campaign.

As vice president, Nixon had labored behind the scenes to establish Operation 40, by which the CIA covertly trained Cuban intelligence officers in exile here. Ironically, during the election campaign, Kennedy began advocating a plan to invade Cuba. Nixon couldn't reveal that the plan was already in effect, because Operation 40 was a secret organization. Furthermore, Nixon found himself in the schizophrenic position of attacking his own scenario whenever Kennedy articulated it, because it violated treaty commitments. In April 1961, Operation 40 would serve as the missing link between the White House and the CIA in in the Bay of Pigs invasion of Cuba.

During the campaign, I became disillusioned with Frank Sinatra, my early adolescent role model. At first I admired him for attempting to defy the Hollywood blacklist by hiring Albert Maltz to write a screenplay for *The Execution of Private Slovik*, based on a book about the army deserter. Maltz had been an "unfriendly witness" before the House Un-American Activities Committee, exclaiming, "I will not be dictated to or intimidated by men to whom the Ku Klux Klan, as a matter of Committee record, is an acceptable institution." But then, under pressure from Kennedy's father, Sinatra fired him. Ironically, Maltz had written that short film, *The House I Live In,* which originally inspired me.

When Kennedy won the election, Vaughn Meader seized the opportunity. He began to comb his hair with a flamboyant pompadour dipping across his forehead. He consciously regressed to the Boston accent he had previously tried so hard to lose. And he made a comedy album, *The First Family,* which broke sales records and turned him into a star.

As for David Frye, he would have to depend on his impressions of Kirk Douglas and Robert Mitchum.

★ ★ ★

The first interview in *The Realist* was with philosopher Alan Watts.

Q. Would you call yourself a Buddhist?

A. No.

Q. Would you care to enlarge on that?

A. I simply feel that a human being must always recognize that he is qualitatively more than any system of thought he can imagine, and therefore he should never label himself. He degrades himself when he does.

Q. What is Zen?

A. (Soft chuckling)

Q. Would you care to enlarge on that?

A. (Loud guffawing)

At one point Watts described beat writer Jack Kerouac as "a very warm, feeling, sensitive personality, but because he has no bones he doesn't sustain it. I mean, of course, Zen bones. Jack has Zen flesh, but no Zen bones yet." Kerouac responded: "Alan Watts, you can think as long as you want about my not having any Zen bones but nothing will stop it; you can think as far as you want but it won't fill anything."

The second interview was with Lenny Bruce.

Q. Could you be bribed to do only "safe" material from now on?

A. What's the bribe? Eternal life? A cure for cancer? $45,000,000? What's the difference what I take—I'd still be selling out.

Q. Do you think there is any sadism in your comedy?

A. What a horrible thought. If there is any sadism in my work, I hope I—well, if there is, I wish someone would whip me with a large belt that has a big brass buckle.

Q. What would you say is the role of a comedian?

A. A comedian is one who performs words or actions of his own original creation, usually before a group of people in a place of assembly, and these words and actions should cause the people assembled to laugh at a minimum of, on the average, one laugh every fifteen seconds—or let's be liberal to escape the hue and cry of the injured and say one laugh every twenty-five seconds—he should get a laugh every twenty-five seconds for a period of not less than forty-five minutes, and accomplish this feat with consistency eighteen out of twenty shows.

Now understand, I'm discussing comedy here as a craft—not as an aesthetic, altruistic art form. The comedian I'm discussing now is not Christ's jester, Timothy; this comedian gets paid, so his first loyalty is to the club owner, and he must make money for the owner. If he can upgrade the moral standards of his community and still get laughs, he is a *fine* craftsman.

The next interview was with Albert Ellis. We were discussing the Norman Vincent Peale version of "positive thinking" when we veered off onto a tangent:

A. No matter how often a person tells himself, "Every day in every way I'm getting better and better" or "Jesus loves me, therefore I am saved," if he keeps saying to himself, much louder and more often, "I'm really a shit; I'm no fucking good; I'll never possibly get better," all the positive thinking in the world is not going to help him.

Q. Incidentally, you may recall, a couple of issues back, a *Realist* correspondent said that one can express any thought without being boorish. Why—by his standards—do you deliberately make yourself out to be a boor?

A. Why should I live up to his, or for that matter any other individual's, standards? My own standard is that certain modes of expression, including the use of many of the famous or infamous four-letter words, are usually appropriate, understandable, and effective under certain conditions, and at these times they should be unhesitatingly used. Words such as fuck and shit are most incisive and expressive when properly employed.

Take, for example, the campaign which I have been waging, with remarkable lack of success, for many years, in favor of the proper usage of the word *fuck*. My premise is that sexual intercourse, copulation, fucking, or whatever you wish to call it, is normally, under all circumstances, a damned good thing. Therefore, we should rarely use it in a negative, condemnatory manner. Instead of denouncing someone by calling him a "fucking bastard" we should say, of course, that he is "an unfucking villain" (since *bastard*, too, is not necessarily a negative state and should not only be used pejoratively).

Q. Isn't the apparently inconsistent use of the word *fuck* due to the fact that it actually has two meanings? One, it means intercourse. The other, it means screw—you know, like in business—"I fucked him."

A. You're right. But since the word *screw* has the same two meanings, and since screwing is (in my unjaundiced view) equally enjoyable to fucking, I would want the usage to be "I unscrewed him," when we mean that I outwitted him or gave him a rough time.

Q. How about the famous army saying, "Fuck all of them but six and save them for pallbearers." There, fuck means kill.

A. Yes, and it is wrongly used. It should be "Unfuck all of them but six." Lots of times these words are used correctly, as when you say, "I had a fucking good time." That's quite accurate, since fucking, as I said before, is a good thing; and a good thing leads to a good time. But by the same token you should say, "I had an unfucking bad time."

Q. I can see this scrawled on subway posters: "Unfuck You!"

A. Why not? It's fuckingly more logical that way, isn't it?

The Ellis interview resulted in a number of subscription cancellations. I knew it would, but the alternative was to be a censor instead of an editor. I certainly didn't want to insult the readers' intelligence by resorting to asterisks or dashes, as other magazines did at the time. But my printer wouldn't even set that portion of the interview in type until I brought in a note from my lawyer. Usually Martin Scheiman—to whom I gave a measly $10 retainer fee every month—didn't see *The Realist* until after it was published. Now he wrote:

> I have examined the text of the interview with Dr. Albert Ellis that you plan to publish in the forthcoming issue of *The Realist*. It is

my opinion that the publishing and printing of that article will not contravene either the Federal or New York obscenity statutes. In so concluding, I am motivated by the facts that nothing in the article appeals to the prurient interests of the ordinary reader; the subject matter is presented from a scholarly point of view in connection with what purports to be a serious discussion of sociological interest; and Dr. Ellis enjoys the reputation of being an outstanding authority in the field of sexology.

* * *

Just when that issue was published, Lenny Bruce came to New York for a midnight show at Town Hall. He called me that afternoon, and we met at the Hotel America in the theater district, where he was staying with Eric Miller, a Negro musician who worked with Lenny in certain bits, such as "How to Relax Colored People at a Party."

Lenny would play the part of a "first-plateau liberal" trying to make conversation with Miller, playing the part of an entertainer at an otherwise all-white party. Lenny would spout one racial cliché after another. The *New York Journal-American* critic blasted him for "the insulting way in which he ridiculed races and creeds."

Miller lamented, "They just don't understand."

At that point in his career, Lenny was still using the euphemism *frig* onstage. Although the mass media were already translating his irreverence into "sick comic," he had not yet been branded "filthy." I handed him the new issue of *The Realist* with the Albert Ellis interview. He was amazed that I could get away with publishing it.

"Are you telling me this is legal to sell on the newsstands?"

"Absolutely. The Supreme Court's definition of obscenity is that it has to be material which appeals to your prurient interest."

Lenny magically produced an unabridged dictionary from the suitcase on his bed, and he looked up the word *prurient*.

"Itching," he mused. "What does that *mean*—that they can bust a novelty-store owner for selling itching powder along with the dribble glass and the whoopie cushion?"

"It's just their way of saying that something gets you horny."

Lenny closed the dictionary, clenching his jaw and nodding his head in affirmation of a new discovery. "So it's against the law to get you *horny*."

He asked me to give out copies of *The Realist* with the Ellis interview in front of Town Hall before his concert that night. Lenny brought a copy onstage and proceeded to talk about it. As a result, he was barred from performing there again. "They'll book me again," Lenny said. "They made too much money on that concert. I'd have more respect for them if they *didn't* ever book me again. At least, it'd show they were keeping their word." But he was right. They *did* book him again.

Lenny marveled at the similarity between what his mother had advised him—"Lenny, don't tell it like it should be, tell it like it is"—and what Alan Watts said in *The Realist* interview: "My philosophy is not concerned with what should be, but with what is." Lenny began talking onstage about the difference between what *should* be—"those bullshit standards we set for ourselves and never do live up to"—and what *is*.

★   ★   ★

When I decided to work at a summer camp again, I queried *Playboy* about writing an article on the social life of counselors, but the idea was rejected: "It is our feeling that the college man does not want to read very much about his own breed, but would rather fantasize about the urban executive world he is about to enter."

Playboy offered me a position on their editorial staff, but I would have to give up *The Realist* and move to Chicago. They asked me to think it over for a week, but I turned them down. I had been spoiled by my own freedom.

Then they came up with another offer whereby I would *not* have to stop publishing *or* leave New York. Hugh Hefner wanted me to moderate a new feature, the Playboy Panel. I accepted and said I would begin after the summer. They were anxious for me to get started, though, and kept calling me at camp, so I decided to leave that job in order to work for *Playboy*, and one morning, while the kids were having breakfast, this little counselor ran away from camp.

It turned out that I wouldn't be getting credit for doing the Playboy Panels. Instead, the moderator would be identified as *Playboy*. So I told Hefner that I was planning to have my name legally changed to Paul Playboy. The other thing about the Playboy Panel was that it wasn't really a *panel*. I had to interview each person separately, then follow up with questions to give the illusion of interplay, and finally weave all the material into a discussion until even I was convinced that we had all been sitting at a table together in the same room. *Playboy* supplied me with the names and phone numbers of the "panelists." The first panel was on "Jazz and Narcotics." Gerry Mulligan refused to participate.

He asked me, "Do I have to show my nipples?"

I told him, "Yeah, just one."

The second panel was "The Hip Humorists." Bob Newhart refused to participate because as a Catholic he was offended by *Playboy*. Mike

Nichols was on the panel, but not his partner, Elaine May, because this was, after all, a *men's* magazine. I flew to Milwaukee to interview Lenny Bruce. He was staying at the YMCA. I checked into my room, then called him and went to his room. We talked for a while before going out. As we were about to leave his room, he stood in the doorway.

"Did you steal anything?" he asked furtively.

I took my watch out of my pocket—since I didn't like to wear it on my wrist—and, without saying a word, placed it on Lenny's bureau. He laughed—one loud staccato "*Ha!*"—and kissed me on the forehead.

Lenny wanted to do a complete makeover of my wardrobe for *Playboy*, with before and after photos. He dressed sharply, but all I wore was sweatshirts and dungarees—this was before they called jeans.

"Dungarees," Lenny mused. "That name must've come from cowboys when their pants dragged along the cow dung in the pasture."

I had already interviewed Mike Nichols for the panel, and now I mentioned to Lenny that Nichols had put him down in my interview.

"He's just mad," Lenny explained, "because I balled his wife."

That evening three plainclothes police walked into his dressing room at the dinner club where he was working. They told Lenny that he was not to talk about politics or religion or sex, or they'd yank him right off the stage. The night before, a group of Catholics had signed a complaint about his act. The cops told him that he shouldn't say "son of a bitch" in his impression of a white-collar drunk. Lenny was nervous. That night, after he did two slightly toned-down shows, we went back to his room and took turns naming all the books we had *not* read—even though we both used references from them—from James Joyce to Harold Robbins, from Franz Kafka to Kahlil Gibran.

"People use *The Prophet* to get laid," Lenny said.

Critics had written about each of us that we were in the tradition of Jonathan Swift and Mark Twain, but neither of us had read any of their books. Coincidentally, though, we were both reading books by Nathanael West. I was reading *Miss Lonelyhearts* and Lenny was reading *The Dream Life of Balso Snell*. There was a line in the latter about an old actress with much-shaved armpits, which triggered Lenny to improvise on what eventually developed into a bit about a popular singer who used to flash her *un*shaved armpit to the audience.

We stayed up till morning, discussing such things as the subjectivity of humor. We talked about a rehearsal for the Steve Allen show, where the network had scheduled an appeal for funds to cure some disease. A little girl who was afflicted with it was supposed to walk toward her mother, who would be waiting with open arms at the center of the stage. The little girl wasn't at the rehearsal, but they had to know the camera angle, so a man on the staff hunched very low and walked toward the mother. Some folks thought that was funny, and others thought it was awful.

We talked about the "Lone Ranger." I told Lenny about the time my brother had played the violin in a concert given by the All-City High School Orchestra. They performed the "William Tell Overture"—which was the theme song of the Lone Ranger radio show—and kids in the audience started calling out, "Hi-yo, Silver, *aw a-a-a-a-y!*" Again, some folks thought that was funny, and others thought it was awful.

At breakfast in the YMCA cafeteria, a man sitting at our table told us how he had slapped his daughter because she wanted to see *Psycho*. He had seen it himself, and didn't want her to witness a kissing scene at the beginning between a partially disrobed couple. He didn't mention the violence in the infamous shower scene. The contradictions in that conversation would work their way into Lenny's performance that night.

I was fascinated by the way he played with ideas, and I became increasingly inspired by the way he weaved his targets—from teachers' low salaries, religious leaders' hypocrisy, cruel abortion laws, the double standard between illegal and prescription drugs—into stream-of-consciousness vignettes.

I was intrigued by the way he played show-and-tell with his audiences. When he heard "There is a Rose in Spanish Harlem" on the radio, he bought the record, came onstage with a phonograph, and played it. "Listen to these lyrics," he said. "This is like a Puerto Rican *Porgy and Bess*." And when Gary Cooper died, he brought the *New York Daily News* onstage to share a headline: "The Last Roundup!"

"I found this today," he would say, introducing his audience to a bizarre concept, as though it were as tangible as a record or a newspaper. Then, in each succeeding performance, he would sculpt and resculpt his findings into a theatrical context, experimenting from show to show like a verbal jazz musician, with a throwaway line evolving from night to night into a set routine. Audience laughter would turn into applause for the creative process itself.

"Please don't applaud," Lenny would request. "It breaks my rhythm."

Sometimes he would become so serious about what he was saying that the laughs wouldn't always come every fifteen to twenty-five seconds. I reminded him of his apparent inconsistency with that definition of a comedian's role.

"Yes, but I'm changing," he said.

"What do you mean?"

"I'm not a comedian. I'm Lenny Bruce."

Lenny encouraged me to start performing again, but without the Paul Maul stage name and without using my violin as a crutch. I began trying to memorize a long list of things that I could talk about, and the order they were in. Lenny told me to just go out on stage with a completely blank mind, but I wasn't ready for that yet. In December 1961, I opened at Art D'Lugoff's Village Gate in New York, making a logical jump from contraception to abortion during my performance:

> India has allocated 105 million dollars for birth control, but can you imagine the uproar there would be in *this* country? So don't tell me we're free from religious interference. I won't be satisfied until you can find an abortionist in the Yellow Pages. Until it's as socially acceptable as a nose job. Until people can start sending studio cards saying, "Good luck on your abortion." And don't say, "Well, that's different from birth control, that's murder." Because, when you talk about abortion being murder and birth control not being murder, what's your focal point? The moment of conception. Before, *si.* After, *no.* But this gets into all kinds of equivocal ramifications. Shouldn't a *douche* be ruled out? That's foul. It's a very tenuous thing. You're gonna have these rabble-rousers going around scrawling on signs in the subway: ZONITE IS A MURDERER!

Lenny couldn't come to my show because he was too busy getting arrested. His first bust had occurred in September, ostensibly for drugs—for which he had prescriptions—but actually because he was making too much money and the local officials wanted a piece of the action. Lenny was appearing at the Red Hill in Pennsauken, New Jersey, near Philadelphia. Cops broke into his hotel room to make the arrest, and that night an attorney and bail bondsman came backstage and told him that $10,000 was all it would take for the judge to dismiss the charges. Lenny refused. A lawyer friend, David Blasband, happened to witness this attempted extortion. The others assumed he was a beatnik, just hanging around the dressing room. That was on Friday. On Monday Lenny went to court and pleaded not guilty.

"Incidentally," he added, "I can only come up with $50."

The case was dismissed.

In October, Lenny was arrested for obscenity at the Jazz Workshop in San Francisco for playing a character who used the word *cocksucker* to describe a cocksucker. He got busted for aptness of vocabulary. The officers said they came because of an anonymous phone call the previous night, although the doorman insisted that there had been no complaints or walkouts.

"We're trying to elevate this street," a sergeant told Lenny. "I took offense because you broke the law. I can't see any way you can break that word down. Our society isn't geared to it."

Lenny replied, "You break it down by talking about it."

He was writing an autobiography—*How to Talk Dirty and Influence People*—which *Playboy* planned to serialize, then publish as a book, and they hired me as his editor. We hooked up in Atlantic City, where Lenny drove around in a rented car. We passed a sign warning CRIMINALS MUST REGISTER, and he started thinking out loud:

"Criminals must register. Does that mean, in the middle of the holdup, you have to go to the county courthouse and register? Or does it mean that you *once* committed a criminal act? Somebody goes to jail, and after fifteen years' incarceration, you make sure you get them back in as soon as you can by shaming anyone who would forgive them, accept them, give them employment—by shaming them on television—'The unions knowingly hired ex-convicts.'"

This kind of reaction was an instant amalgamation of Lenny's comedic, moralistic, and legalistic instincts. Indeed, a few years later, the ACLU would support a group of New Jersey citizens who were opposed to that criminal registration ordinance, because it could be used to harass people who had paid their debt to society and were attempting to build law-abiding lives for themselves. And so Lenny decided to dedicate his book: "To all the followers of Christ and his teachings; in particular to a true Christian—Jimmy Hoffa—because he hired ex-convicts as, I assume, Christ would have."

Lenny was taking Dilaudid for lethargy, and had sent a telegram to a New York contact, with a phrase—DE LAWD IN DE SKY—as a code to send a doctor's prescription. Now, in Atlantic City, Lenny got sick while waiting for that prescription to be filled. Later, while we were relaxing on the beach, I hesitatingly brought up the subject.

"Don't you think it's ironic that your whole style should be so free form, and yet you can also be a slave to dope?"

"What does that mean, a slave to dope?"

"Well, if you need a fix, you've got to stop whatever you're doing, go somewhere and wrap a lamp cord around your arm —"

"Then other people are slaves to *food*. 'Oh, I'm so famished, stop the car, I must have lunch immediately or I'll pass out.'"

"You said yourself you're probably gonna die before you reach forty."

"Yeah, but—I can't explain—it's like kissing God."

"Well, I ain't gonna argue with *that*."

Later, though, he began to get paranoid about my role.

"You're gonna go to literary cocktail parties, and you're gonna say, 'Yeah, that's right, I found Lenny slobbering in an alley—he would've been nothin' without me.'"

Of course, I denied any such intention, but he demanded that I take a lie detector test, and *I* was paranoid enough to take him literally. I told him that I couldn't work with him if he didn't trust me. We got into an argument, and I left for New York. I sent a letter of resignation to *Playboy* and a copy to Lenny. A few weeks later I got a telegram from him that sounded like we had been on the verge of divorce—WHY CAN'T IT BE THE WAY IT USED TO BE—and I agreed to try again.

* * *

In December 1962, I flew to Chicago to resume working with Lenny on his book. He was performing at the Gate of Horn. When I walked into the club, he was asking the whole *audience* to take a lie detector test. He recognized my laugh.

Lenny had been reading a study of anti-Semitism by Jean-Paul Sartre, and he was intrigued by the implications of an item in *The Realist*, a statement by Adolf Eichmann that he would have been "not only a scoundrel, but a despicable pig" if he hadn't carried out Hitler's orders. Lenny wrote a piece for *The Realist*, "Letter from a Soldier's Wife"—namely, *Mrs. Eichmann*—pleading for compassion to spare her husband's life. Now, onstage, giving credit to Thomas Merton's poem about the Holocaust, he requested that all the lights go off except one dim blue spot. Then he began speaking with a German accent:

> My name is Adolf Eichmann. And the Jews came every day to what they thought would be fun in the showers. People say I should have been hung. *Nein.* Do you recognize the whore in the middle of you—that you would have done the same if you were there yourselves? My defense: I was a soldier. I saw the end of a conscientious day's effort. I watched through the portholes. I saw every Jew burned and turned into soap.
>
> Do you people think yourselves better because you burned your enemies at long distance with missiles without ever seeing what you had done to them? Hiroshima *auf Wiedersehen*. [*German accent ends.*] If we would have lost the war, they would have strung Truman up by the balls, Jim. Are you kidding with that? Not what kid told kid told kid. They would just schlep out all those Japanese mutants. "Here they did; there they are." And Truman said they'd do it again. That's what they should have the same day as "Remember Pearl Harbor." Play them in unison.

Lenny was arrested for obscenity that night. One of the items in the Chicago police report complained: "Then talking about the war he stated, 'If we would have lost the war, they would have strung Truman up by the balls.'" The cops also broke open Lenny's candy bars, looking for drugs.

They checked the IDs of audience members, including George Carlin, who told the cops, "I don't believe in IDs." Then they arrested *him* for disorderly conduct, dragged him along by the seat of his pants, and hoisted him into the police wagon.

"What are *you* doing here?" Lenny asked.

"I didn't want to show them my ID."

"You schmuck," said Lenny.

Lenny and Carlin had similar points of view—for example, they were both outspoken about the decriminalization of drugs—and they were both self-educated, but their working styles were different. Lenny didn't write his material, it evolved onstage, whereas Carlin *did* write all his routines and then memorized 'em. Although both were unbelievers as far as religion was concerned, Lenny came from a Jewish background, and Carlin came from an Irish Catholic background.

"I guess what happens," Lenny told me, "if you get arrested in Town A and then in Town B—with a lot of publicity—then when you get to Town C they *have* to arrest you or what kind of shithouse town are *they* running?"

Chicago was Town C. Lenny had been released on bail and was working again, but the head of the vice squad warned the manager: "If this man ever uses a four-letter word in this club again, I'm going to pinch you and everyone in here. If he ever speaks against religion, I'm going to pinch you and everyone in here. Do you understand? You've had good people here. But he mocks the pope—and I'm speaking as a Catholic—I'm here to tell you your license is in danger. We're going to have someone here watching every show."

And indeed, the Gate of Horn's liquor license was suspended. There were no previous allegations against the club, and the current charge involved neither violence nor drunken behavior. The only charge pressed by the city prosecutor was Lenny Bruce's allegedly obscene performance, and his trial had not yet been held.

Chicago had the largest membership in the Roman Catholic Church of any archdiocese in the country. Lenny's jury consisted entirely of Catholics. The judge was Catholic. The prosecutor and his assistant were Catholic. On Ash Wednesday, the judge removed the spot of ash from his forehead and told the bailiff to instruct the others to do likewise. The sight of a judge, two prosecutors, and twelve jurors, every one with a spot of ash on their foreheads, would have all the surrealistic flavor of a Lenny Bruce fantasy. *Variety* reported:

> The prosecutor is at least equally concerned with Bruce's indictments of organized religion as he is with the more obvious sexual content of the comic's act. It's possible that Bruce's comments on the Catholic Church have hit sensitive nerves in Chicago's Catholic-oriented administration and police department.

On the fourth day of his trial, thirty girls from Holy Rosary, a Catholic college, dropped in on a tour of the court. Judge Ryan requested them to leave because of "the nature of the testimony."

Lenny said, "That was the thing that really did me in, in front of the jury."

Driving around Chicago, we passed a religious novelties store with a framed portrait of Pope John in the window. He was the first pope in history to smoke cigarettes. Lenny went in and bought the painting.

"I just know I could make him laugh," he said.

Later we stopped near a parochial school in the midst of dismissing a flock of young Catholic girls in their pristine uniforms. Lenny beckoned a pair of them to the car.

"Hey, c'mere," he said. "I got the real thing. Look!"

And he popped the pope up to the window. The girls giggled their way toward the car and examined the portrait of the pontiff.

"Their parents only warned them against taking *candy* from strangers," Lenny observed.

After the first week of the trial, he flew to Los Angeles—Town D—where he was promptly arrested on suspicion of narcotics possession. Years later, his arresting officer went to prison himself, for drug smuggling. Ralph J. Gleason wrote in the *San Francisco Chronicle*:

"A columnist who privately agreed once that Bruce might have been framed on his narcotics conviction, and that the case might be broken open if the cop-turned-smuggler angle were publicized, admitted he couldn't lead the crusade, because his paper wouldn't let him."

When the Chicago case resumed, Judge Ryan instructed Lenny's attorney to make a formal move for postponement. This the attorney did, but then the judge denied the motion, forfeited Lenny's bond, issued a warrant for his arrest, and asked the state's attorney to start extradition proceedings. Next day, the jury found Lenny guilty. The judge gave him the maximum penalty—a year in jail and a $1,000 fine—"for telling dirty jokes," in the words of one network newscaster.

A week later, the case against the Gate of Horn was dismissed, but it had become obvious that Lenny was now considered too hot to be booked in Chicago again. In San Francisco the jury found him *not* guilty of obscenity. Arresting officers admitted on the witness stand that his material didn't arouse their prurient interest. But in Chicago, Judge Ryan refused to permit that line of cross-examination by the defense. Nor would he allow the head of the vice squad ("I'm speaking as a Catholic") to take the stand, on the grounds that his testimony would be extraneous to the issue before the court.

"Chicago is so corrupt it's thrilling," Lenny said.

★   ★   ★

In less than two years, Lenny was arrested fifteen times.

"There seems to be a pattern," he said, "that I'm a mad dog and they have to get me no matter what—the end justifies the means."

In fact, it became an actual news item in *Variety* when Lenny *didn't* get arrested one night. While the Chicago verdict was on appeal, he was working at the Off-Broadway in San Francisco. The club's newspaper ads made this offer: "No cover charge for patrolmen in uniform."

Since he always talked onstage about his environment, and since police cars and courtrooms had lately *become* his environment, the content of Lenny's performances began to revolve more and more around the inequities of the legal system. "In the Halls of Justice," he declared, "the only justice is in the halls." But he also said, "I love the law."

Instead of an unabridged dictionary, he now carried law books in his suitcase. His room was always cluttered with tapes and transcripts and Photostats and law journals and legal briefs. Once he was teasing his ten-year-old daughter, Kitty, by pretending not to believe what she was telling him.

"Daddy," she said, "you'd believe me if it was on tape."

Lenny's jazz jargon was gradually being replaced by legal jargon. He had become intimate not only with the statutes concerning obscenity and narcotics but also with courtroom procedure, and his knowledge would be woven into his performances.

"Query," he would begin. "If a tape recording is my voice, are they using me to testify against myself, since it's my voice that would indict me?" But as club owners became increasingly afraid to hire him, he devoted more and more time and energy to the law. When he finally got a booking in Monterey, he admitted, "I feel like it's taking me away from my work."

Lenny lived way up in the Hollywood Hills. His house was protected by barbed wire and a concrete gate, except that it was always open. He had a wall-to-wall one-way mirror in his living room, but when the sun was shining you could see *into* the room instead of out. He was constantly hassled by police on his own property.

One evening in October 1963, we were talking while he was shaving, and four officers suddenly appeared, loud and obnoxious. He asked them to leave unless they had a search warrant. One of the cops took out his gun.

"Here's my search warrant."

Then Lenny and the cops had a discussion about the law—specifically, the rules of evidence—and after half an hour they left. Lenny tried to take it all in stride, but the encounter was depressing, and he changed his mind about going out that night. Later, when everything was quiet, we went outside and stood at the edge of his unused swimming pool. Dead leaves floated in the water. Lenny cupped his hands to his mouth.

"All right, you dogs," he called out. "Bark for the rich man!"

Thereby setting off a chain reaction of barking dogs, a canine chorus echoing through the Hollywood Hills.

One time we were walking around and passed a newsstand where, on the cover of *Newsweek*, there was a photo of Caroline Kennedy, the president's young daughter.

I commented, "She probably plays with herself with a bobby pin."

"What a great image," Lenny said. "Can I have that?'

"Sure. It's not even mine. I once knew a guy who told me his sister actually did that."

Lenny's genius was his ability to integrate imagery into a satirical context. That particular image became almost a throwaway line in his hot-lead-enema routine—inspired by the capture of U2 spy pilot Gary Powers—where Lenny talked about how he himself would never be able to withstand torture:

"I'll give away state secrets"—and, presaging decades-later revelations about the futility of torturing for information—"I'll even *make up* secrets— Caroline Kennedy plays with herself with a bobby pin—just don't give me that hot-lead enema!"

But Lenny's tragedy was that he was not being merely hypothetical. According to Sandy Baron, who played the title role in the Los Angeles and Broadway productions of *Lenny*, he had once turned in a drug dealer in order to save himself from going to prison, which would've been his equivalent of the hot-lead enema. But he continued to be tortured by his own secret awareness.

When he would say onstage, "Have a little *rach manus* [sympathy] for that guy behind bars who can't kiss and hug a lady for twenty years," he was talking about himself as much as to the audience.

"I am part of everything I indict," Lenny would say.

That was the closest he would ever come to a public confession.

★ ★ ★

When John F. Kennedy was assassinated, Lenny Bruce and I were both scheduled to do shows, and we each knew that our performance would be influenced by an acute awareness of the president's death. On Saturday evening, one day after Kennedy's assassination, I was supposed to perform at a fundraiser for the Committee to Aid the Monroe Defendants, a case which involved trumped-up kidnapping charges against civil rights activists.

"What are you gonna say?" Lenny teased me. "Tell 'em that Steve Allen said satire is tragedy plus time, and you want a postponement."

The benefit was held in a meeting hall at the headquarters of the Young Socialist League. They published a tabloid newspaper, *The Militant*. A doctored photo on the cover of *Life* magazine would soon feature Lee Harvey Oswald posing with a rifle in one hand and a rolled-up copy of *The Militant* in the other. The headline on the flyers for this event promised: LAUGH WITH PAUL KRASSNER! But it wouldn't be easy. This was an all left-wing audience, which had at first assumed that Oswald was a right-winger.

"Aren't you sorry," I began, "that it turned out to be one of *your* nuts instead of one of *theirs*?"

With that opening line, I was, in effect, acknowledging the single-assassin, left-wing, lone-nut theory. But I couldn't stop thinking about the intelligence-community lingo that Lee Harvey Oswald used to describe himself. "I am only a patsy," he shouted to reporters. It just didn't make any sense for a lone killer to say that. If it were true, he would have to be killed himself. And, on Sunday morning, nightclub owner Jack Ruby shot Oswald to death, live on TV, in a Dallas police station. For those who slept late, the scene would be repeated over and over again, throughout the day and evening, in spastic slow motion.

Lenny told me, "I know other comics who have worked for Jack Ruby. Dig this. They say he has a tattoo of a vagina on his upper arm, and whenever he flexes his muscle, the vagina dilates open."

Lenny was booked to perform at the Village Theater on the Lower East Side a week after the assassination. The whole country was still in a state of shock, and the atmosphere in the theater was especially tense that night. The show hadn't begun yet, but the entire audience seemed to be anticipating what Lenny would say about the assassination. Now he walked onstage. He removed the microphone from its stand. When the applause for his entrance subsided, he stood there in silence for a few seconds, milking the tension.

He finally whistled into the microphone, "*Whew!* Vaughn Meader is *screwed . . .*"

And there was an instant explosion of laughter. But Lenny was right. Meader had been scheduled for appearances on two TV shows—*Hootenanny* and *To Tell the Truth*—but he was canceled out of both during the week following the assassination, even though he had planned other material for *Hootenanny* and would not have appeared on *To Tell the Truth* as President Kennedy. Yes, Vaughn Meader was indeed screwed.

Ah, but not David Frye—*he* could do Lyndon Johnson.

★ ★ ★

Hanging around with Lenny was a true delight, except perhaps for the time that someone told him red cabbage was a fantastically healthy food and he ate a whole head of red cabbage in one sitting. In New York he was staying at a funky hotel in Greenwich Village. There was no television in his room, so a friend borrowed a TV set from the hotel lobby. They wanted to watch me on Les Crane's late-night call-in show.

Cartoonist Jules Feiffer and I were guests. The first call was from an anti-Semite. She wanted to know why there was a preponderance of Jewish guests. Later, in the middle of the show, Michelle Cole came to the station with a note from Lenny: "To offset the Jewish imbalance, I am sending my Hawaiian friend."

"I'd like to point out something," I said. "I don't consider myself Jewish. I equate religion with organized superstition. And anyone who thinks of Judaism as a race rather than a religion is accepting the Nazi tenets." I hesitated, sensing that my syllogism was somehow incomplete. "Therefore," I added, "Lenny Bruce is a Nazi."

Crane immediately pressed the little red panic button which—thanks to a five-second delay that was a feature of live tape—enabled him to eliminate the sound for the viewing audience. During a commercial, he explained why I got cut off.

"That's actionable, Paul."

"Of course it is, but can you possibly imagine Lenny Bruce suing me for libel because I called him a Nazi on television?"

One time we were fooling around with a tape recorder in his hotel room, and Lenny began spinning out a fantasy:

> I will confess to some experiences that I've had. Forbidden sights I have seen. The most beautiful body I've ever seen was at a party in 1945. I was in the bedroom getting the coats. The powder room door had been left intentionally ajar, and I viewed the most perfect

bosom peeking out from the man-tailored blouse above a tweed pegged skirt.

"You like what you see? They *are* nice, aren't they?" she said, caressing the area near her medallion.

"Yes, they are very nice."

"Would you like to touch them?"

"I'm—I'm—"

"You're shocked," she said, "aren't you?"

Indeed I was. Eleanor Roosevelt had the prettiest tits I had ever seen or dreamed that I had seen.

> "I've got the nicest tits that have ever been in this White House, but because of protocol we're not allowed to wear bathing suits, you know. I get a million offers for pictures, but being saddled with the Girl Scout coordinators has left me with only a blind item in a gossip column: *What Capitol Hill biggie's wife has a pair of lollies that are setting the Washington-go-round a-twitter?*"

Lenny's problem was that he wanted to talk onstage with the same freedom he exercised in his living room. That harmless little bit of incongruity about Eleanor Roosevelt would show up in his act from time to time. Murray Kempton, whose criticism was usually of a more political nature, said that it reminded him of *A Child's Christmas in Wales* by Dylan Thomas.

Poetic or not, it certainly didn't fall within the definition of hard-core pornography which the Supreme Court had ruled was not protected by the First Amendment. Nevertheless, Lenny was arrested in a Greenwich Village club, the Café Au Go Go, for giving an indecent performance, and at the top of the police complaint was "Eleanor Roosevelt and her display of tits."

Lenny's New York obscenity trial reeked with hypocrisy, as epitomized by one witness for the prosecution, *Daily News* columnist Robert Sylvester, who stated under cross-examination that he had used the very same taboo words in his private conversation for which Lenny was arrested.

"You have, in fact," asked the defense attorney, "used those words condemning censorship, have you not?"

Sylvester admitted, "I have."

Another witness, *National Review* correspondent Ernest van den Haag, supposedly an expert on contemporary community standards, testified that he had made a study of nightclubs even though he hadn't been inside one for twenty years.

An additional charge against Lenny was making "masturbatory motions" with his hand. Actually, he had gestured with a microphone, nowhere near his crotch, to bless the audience in papal fashion. At one point, attorney Ephraim London asked a witness who had been present at the performance, "Did you see Mr. Crotch touch his bruce?"

I wrote in *The Realist*:

> Henceforth and forevermore, we shall have had at that precise moment a meaningful new synonym added to our language.*"Mommy, look, there's a man sitting over there playing with his bruce." *"Beverly Schmidlap is a real bruceteaser." *"Kiss my bruce."

Ultimately, Lenny fired all his lawyers and defended himself. He was found guilty, even though the law stated that to be obscene, material must be *utterly without any* redeeming social importance; therefore, if *one single person* felt that Lenny's performances had *the slightest bit* of redeeming social importance—and there were several witnesses who so testified—then he should have been found not guilty.

He hadn't been able to get work in six months. Club owners were afraid to book him. He almost got an engagement in Philadelphia, but the deal fell through when the district attorney demanded that Lenny show up a couple of days early and take a Naline test to prove there was no morphine in his system—plus he was told to present his material in advance. CRIMINALS MUST REGISTER.

Lenny performed at a club in Westbury, but on his way to the parking lot after the first performance, a district attorney warned him, "If you do another show like the one you did tonight, I'll arrest you." Then the D.A. told the club owner, "If you let him go on, I'll pull your license."

Lenny went before the Court of Appeals seeking an injunction that would prevent district attorneys from arresting him in the future. The three-judge panel was headed by Thurgood Marshall, former chief counsel for the NAACP, who would later become the first black justice ever appointed to the Supreme Court. Lenny pleaded that he was like a carpenter whose tools were being taken away. He compared the denial of his rights to "a nigger who wants to use a toilet in Alabama."

"You're not a Negro, Mr. Bruce," said Judge Marshall.

"Unfortunately not, Your Honor."

And Lenny's request was denied.

A week later, he was due to be sentenced and, once again, he acted as his own attorney. In court, he wanted to borrow a wristwatch, because he planned to state for the record what time he began and ended his argument—"so that the judge can't close me out for taking too long." I didn't have my watch with me. I tried to borrow one from Jules Feiffer, who was sitting at the back of the courtroom, but he declined.

"Think how awful it would be," Feiffer said, "if the judge gave Lenny three years, and then I had to go and ask for my lousy *watch* back."

Lenny finally borrowed a watch, and he spoke for a solid hour. He did everything in this special one-time-only matinee performance short of applying burnt cork to his face, donning white gloves, getting down on his knees, and singing "Nobody Knows de Trouble Obscene," but his most relevant argument concerned the very obscenity statute which he'd been accused of violating.

As his legal homework, Lenny had obtained the legislative history of that statute from Albany, and he discovered that back in 1931 there was an amendment proposed, which *excluded from arrest* in an indecent performance: stagehands, spectators, musicians, and—here was the fulcrum of his defense—*actors*. The law had been misapplied to him. The amendment had finally been signed into law by then-Governor Franklin Roosevelt, despite opposition by the New York Society for the Suppression of Vice.

Lenny had complained that District Attorney Richard Kuh tried to do his act in court. A friend of mine who dated Kuh swears that he took her back to his apartment and played Lenny Bruce records for her. Maybe someday he would play for her the soundtrack album from the movie *Lenny*, with Dustin Hoffman doing Lenny's act on stage where he complains about the district attorney doing his act in court.

But now, before sentencing, Kuh recommended that no mercy be granted because Lenny had shown a "lack of remorse."

Lenny responded, "I'm not here for remorse, but for justice. The issue is not obscenity, but that I spit in the face of authority."

The face of authority spat back at Lenny Bruce that afternoon by sentencing him to four months in the workhouse.

"Where can I appeal?" asked Lenny.

"The court cannot act as counsel," replied the judge.

Then, in the press room of the Criminal Courts Building, reporters were interviewing Lenny. WNBC's Gabe Pressman asked, "Do you believe in obscenity?"

"What do you mean?" said Lenny. "Do I believe we should *pray* for obscenity?"

As we walked into the lobby, a man came up and said, "Listen, I have some stag films and party records that you might be interested in."

Lenny and I went for some pizza instead. Then we headed for his hotel room where, to help unwind from the day's tension, he played some old tapes, ranging from a faith healer to patriotic World War II songs. "Goodbye, Mama, I'm off to Yokohama, the Land of Yama-Yama . . ."

"Ignoring the mandate of Franklin D. Roosevelt," observed Lenny lawyer, "is a great deal more offensive than saying Eleanor has lovely nay-nays."

* * *

When Lenny finally completed his book, I sat in the *Playboy* office with their attorneys. They were anxious to avoid libel, so they kept changing or deleting the name of any person in his original manuscript who might bring suit, all the way to the end. Lenny had written:

> My friend Paul Krassner once asked me what I've been influenced by in my work.
>
> I have been influenced by my father telling me that my back would become crooked because of my maniacal desire to masturbate; by reading "Gloriosky, Zero" in *Annie Rooney*; by listening to Uncle Don and Clifford Brown; by smelling the burnt shell powder at Anzio and Salerno; torching for my ex-wife; giving money to Moondog as he played the upturned pails around the corner from Hanson's at 51st and Broadway; getting hot looking at *Popeye* and *Toots and Caspar* and *Chris Crustie* years ago; hearing stories about a pill they can put in the gas tank with water but "the big companies" won't let it out—the same big companies that have the tire that lasts forever—and the Viper's favorite fantasy: "Marijuana could be legal, but the big liquor companies won't let it happen"; Harry James has cancer on his lip; Dinah Shore has a colored baby; Irving Berlin didn't write all those songs, he's got a guy locked in the closet; colored people have a special odor.
>
> It was an absurd question. I am influenced by every second of my waking hour.

The false gossip items about Harry James and Dinah Shore were edited out of that paragraph, but for some unfathomable reason the one about Irving Berlin remained. In his manuscript, Lenny had mentioned an individual named Blow Job Betty, and the lawyers were afraid.

"You must be kidding," I said. "Do you believe anybody would actually come out and *admit* that she's known as Blow Job Betty?"

There was one incident which was omitted entirely from the book. Lenny had been working at Le Bistro, a nightclub in Atlantic City. During his performance, he asked for a cigarette from anyone in the audience. Basketball star Wilt Chamberlain happened to be there, and he lit a cigarette and passed it up to Lenny.

"Did you see *that*?" Lenny whispered to his microphone. "He nigger-lipped it!"

There were liberals who could accept Lenny's profane alternatives for sexual parts and functions, but weren't able to similarly discard their reaction to ugly racial and religious names—"Nigger!" "Kike!" "Wop!" "Chink!" "Sheenie!" "Spic!" "Mick!"—so Lenny would go onstage and play with the audience by combining those epithets in poetic cadences as though he were reciting poker hands, demystifying the words until they became nonsense.

(He did *not* walk up to a black man and shout "Nigger!" in his face, as the film *Lenny* would later depict, nor did he ever perform so zonked out that he wore only one shoe.)

Lenny and I had an unspoken agreement that there would be nothing in the book about his use of drugs. When I first met him, he would shoot up in the hotel bathroom with the door closed, but now he just sat on his bed and casually fixed up while we were talking. That's what we were doing one time when Lenny nodded out, the needle still stuck in his arm.

Suddenly the phone rang and startled him. His arm flailed, and the hypodermic came flying across the room, hitting the wall like a dart just a few feet from the easy chair in which I uneasily sat. Lenny picked up the phone. It was Blow Job Betty, calling from the lobby. She came up in the elevator and went down on Lenny. In front of me.

After a little while, Lenny said to her, "I wanna fuck you now."

"In front of *him*?" Blow Job Betty protested, gesturing toward me.

"Okay, Paul, I guess the interview's over now."

The next day, Lenny said to me, "I'm not usually an exhibitionist."

"That's okay," I replied. "I'm not usually a voyeur."

Anyway, the *Playboy* lawyers changed Blow Job Betty's name to Go Down Gussie.

"I hope there actually *is* somebody out there named Go Down Gussie," I told them, "and that *she* sues for invasion of privacy."

★   ★   ★

Playboy had dropped their Playboy Panel feature, switching to individual interviews, and I was taken off their payroll. Instead, I was invited to write a column, "The Naked Emperor," for *Cavalier*, a men's magazine that was beginning to publish underground writers and artists. They paid me $1,000 a month. My first column was a report on an auction of one-inch squares from the hotel bedsheets slept on by the Beatles during their first trip to America.

My second column was about Lenny Bruce. I went to the bank and deposited my check, withdrawing half of it in cash, a $500 bill. Lenny was alone in his hotel room on Christmas Day when I presented it to him. He was grateful, but I quoted his own line to him:

"There's no such thing as an anonymous donation," I said. "So maybe I should've just left it for you at the front desk."

"Yeah, but then I would've gone crazy trying to guess who it was from."

And, with a large safety pin, Lenny attached the $500 bill to the outside breast pocket of his dungaree jacket. Ironically, he had begun to dress like me.

In 1964, with Lenny's permission, I published his obituary in *The Realist*. Before the issue went to press, he called his mother and a few others to let them know it would only be a hoax. The point was that he couldn't get work and his work was his life so he might as well be dead. And if people regretted that they hadn't helped him, well, now they could have a second chance because he was still alive. The obituary evoked inquiries from newspapers, wire services, foreign publications, radio, and TV.

"What's the meaning of it?" one editor asked me. "There's a lot of excitement at the city desk."

"That *is* the meaning of it."

Some readers assumed that they had missed the news in their daily papers. Others assumed that it had been suppressed. One of Lenny's lovers, Gloria Stavers, the editor of *Sixteen*, a rock magazine, called me with understandable hostility, but we eventually became friends, and she took me to the Beatles concert at Shea Stadium. You could hardly hear them sing above the screaming of the crowd. One girl held up a sign: IT'S ALL RIGHT, JOHN—I WEAR GLASSES TOO.

When the obituary was published, Lenny and I sat in his hotel room, discussing it.

"This way," I said, "when you *really* die, my grief will be pure. I won't have to stop and think, 'Oh, shit, now I have to write an obituary.'"

"There's just one thing you're overlooking, Paul."

"What's that?"

"I may outlive you."

* * *

One time, Lenny literally lived out one of his own satirical insights.

He had talked onstage about the difference in sexual conditioning between men and women. A guy would fuck a chicken, mud, anything. If he got his leg chopped off in an automobile accident, he would still make a play for the nurse in the ambulance on the way to the hospital. If the guy's wife called him an animal, he would justify his act: "I couldn't help it—she had a cute ass."

Now Lenny was staying at the Swiss-American Hotel in the North Beach section of San Francisco. Nearby, Hugh Romney was working with a satirical troupe, The Committee, and distributing LSD in his spare time. He wandered around carrying a chromium lunch box that had green velvet lining, a thermos bottle filled with hot soup, and his dope supply in the inner lining. Lenny wasn't in his messy room on the second floor of the hotel, but Eric Miller was, so Romney left a couple of hits of acid there. Lenny had never tried LSD before, and Romney figured Lenny would just give it to someone else, not take it himself. He also left another hallucinogenic, DMT, with a note saying: "Please smoke this till the jewels fall out of your eyes."

Lenny returned, saw the package on his dresser, swallowed both hits of acid and smoked the DMT. He had never seen colors like this before in his life. He was standing on the low window ledge, talking to Miller with great animation, when suddenly he lost his balance and fell backward, through the window. It was an accident, but the instant he realized that he was *committed* to the fall, he called out in midair: "Man shall rise above the rule!" Then he hit the pavement below. Miller ran down to the sidewalk and tried to comfort him. Lenny's pelvis and both ankles had been broken, but he managed to ask a nurse if she would please give him some head.

When Lenny got out of the hospital, he became the Hermit of Hollywood Hills. Jerry Hopkins, a talent booker for the Steve Allen show, arranged for me to perform at the Steve Allen Playhouse, and Lenny, in one of his rare departures from the house, came to my show, both legs still in casts. At one point during my performance, I was talking about the importance of having empathy for other people's perversions. During the question-and-answer session with the audience that followed, Lenny stood up on his crutches and asked me to clarify what I meant by that.

"Well, I was in the subway once—it was rush hour and it was really crowded—and an elderly lady's buttocks kept rubbing against me, and I began to get aroused."

"You're *sick!*" Lenny yelled. The audience howled.

I said, "Thank you, Mr. President," and ended the show.

Groucho Marx was in the audience, and Hopkins introduced him to Lenny and me.

"That was very smart, the way you finished," Groucho said. "Besides, I was getting fidgety in my seat."

★ ★ ★

On October 2, 1965, Lenny visited the San Francisco FBI headquarters. Two days later, the San Francisco FBI sent a memo to the FBI director in Washington, describing Lenny as "the nightclub and stage performer widely known for his obscenity," and stating:

> Bruce, who advised that he is scheduled to begin confinement 10/13/65, in New York State as a result of a conviction for a lewd show, alleged that there is a conspiracy between the courts of the states of New York and California to violate his rights. Allegedly this violation of his rights takes place by these lower courts failing to abide by decisions of the U.S. Supreme Court with regard to obscenity.
>
> Bruce admitted that he has failed to exhaust his rights of appeal from the courts of either state, explaining that he has dismissed his attorney and is now a pauper. Further, he admitted that the Legal Aid Society locally refused to furnish him assistance and that several attorneys, whom he did not name, had refused to give any support to his contention that such a conspiracy as he described did, in effect, exist.
>
> Bruce advised that he had made no other attempt to make a similar complaint at any other FBI office. The foregoing is furnished for the information of the Bureau and New York.

On October 13—Lenny's fortieth birthday—instead of surrendering to the authorities in New York, he filed suit at the U.S. District Court in San Francisco to keep himself out of prison, and he got himself officially declared a pauper. He also asked the federal court to protect him from harassment by police in New York, Chicago, Los Angeles, and San Francisco, to determine how much money he had lost since his conviction in New York, and to order the police department there to pay him damages. Since his first arrest for obscenity in San Francisco, his earnings had plummeted from $108,000 to $11,000, and he was $15,000 in debt.

On May 31, 1966, Lenny wrote to me: "I'm still working on the bust of the government of New York State." And he sent his doodle of Jesus Christ nailed to the cross, with a speech balloon asking: *Where the hell is the ACLU?* Lenny hadn't identified with Christ's jester, but now he did seem to be identifying with Christ himself.

On August 3, while his New York obscenity conviction was still on appeal, he received a foreclosure notice on his home. Lenny died that day from an overdose of morphine. It was two years since I had published his fake obituary. Ralph J. Gleason began his column: "There had been rumors before, even the grisly put-on when *The Realist* ran his obituary. But this time, you knew it had to be true. Lenny Bruce was dead."

Lenny's death was on the cusp of accident and suicide. In his kitchen, a kettle of water was still boiling. In his office, the electric typewriter was still humming. He had stopped typing in mid-word—*Conspiracy to interfere with the 4th Amendment const*—constitutes *what*, Lenny? Where was Blow Job Betty when he needed her? Why didn't she wake him up with a phone call from the lobby of a hotel when he nodded out *this* time?

A week before, Lenny had told his girlfriend, comedian Maury Hayden (who later changed her name to Lotus Weinstock), "I'm gonna die this year."

She pleaded, "If I get you some raisin cookies, will you wait a year?"

But Lenny wasn't dissuaded by the promise of raisin cookies. Lotus recalled: "Lenny was half making plans to live, half to die. He didn't go searching for drugs till that last week. The drug that killed him, he wanted more of it at that point. He was really in a self-destructive mode. I think he surrendered. There was part of him that wanted to die. He couldn't bear the thought of being an old hippie. He may have played a part in it, but I don't think that he ever intended to—I think he wanted to take the pain away, and I think he was gonna go as far as he had to go to make the pain go away that day. He wanted to live and he wanted to end the agony too."

In a documentary about New York District Attorney Frank Hogan on WNET, a former assistant D.A., Michael Metzger, revealed that Lenny's seemingly paranoid complaint to the FBI was not exactly unjustified. He said that Lenny "was prosecuted because of his words. He didn't harm anybody, he didn't commit an assault, he didn't steal, he didn't engage in any conduct which directly harmed someone else. So therefore he was punished first and foremost because of the words that he used. It's wrong to prosecute anybody because of his ideas. It was the only thing I did in Hogan's office that I'm really ashamed of. We drove him into poverty and used the law to kill him."

Another former assistant D.A., Vincent Cucci, said, "It makes me, in retrospect, embarrassed to have been in an office that prosecuted with the vigor that Dick Kuh did prosecute the case for Frank Hogan. I would characterize Hogan's attitude about that case as hysterical. You couldn't look sideways. At one point he would not permit assistants to even sit in during the trial. He directed all assistants out of the courtroom, questioned each of them as to why they were there, and sent everybody on their way with the admonition that if anyone didn't like the Lenny Bruce prosecution, they could quit right then and there."

Four years after Lenny's death, the New York Court of Appeals upheld a lower court's reversal of his guilty verdict.

Twelve years after Lenny's death I found out the source of his final score. It was his own stepfather, Tony Viscarra. I sat there as Lenny's mother, Sally Marr, tried to comfort Viscarra.

"Don't feel bad," she told him, with true compassion. "Lenny would've done the same for you."

Lenny was buried in a Jewish cemetery in Los Angeles. At the funeral, his roommate and sound engineer, John Judnich, dropped Lenny's microphone into his grave before the dirt was piled on. Later, friends wanted to have a picnic on his plot, but the owner closed the premises.

He asked Lenny's mother, "Who's gonna clean up?"

In New York, I emceed a memorial service at Judson Memorial Church, where a religious fanatic carrying an American flag came up onstage and started preaching, while a woman sitting in a back pew was nursing a baby wearing diapers made of an American flag. Lenny would've enjoyed that.

And finally, there was a séance. A medium who had never seen him perform went into a trance, wobbling her head just like he used to wobble his. Was she actually going to *do* Lenny speaking?

> My generation saw a few of the freaks in the carnival—you know, Zip and Pip, the Onion-Head Boy, Lolly and Lulu, the Mongoloid, the Chinless Wonder, the Alligator Lady, and the guy who could typewrite with his toes. Our kids won't see any of those freaks, at least only a few of them. It's a shame. But we will see a few of them. Yeah, thank God for the Catholic Church there'll still be freaks— those thalidomide babies will grow up and get a good tie-in with the Barnum & Bailey sideshow. So they'll still see Zip and Pip and Flip and Mip. Yeah, that's what I *really* got busted for.
>
> And it's really strange. I know that the peace officer that busts me really doesn't even realize that, that's what he's busting me for. But here's how it ends. One day I'm going to get an order to appear in court. "Oh, shit, what it is *this* time?" But when I get there the courtroom will be all decorated, dig, with balloons and streamers and confetti, and when I walk in they'll all jump up and yell, "*Surprise!*" And there'll be all the cops that busted me, and the judges and the D.A.s who tried me, and they'll say, "Lenny, this is a surprise party for you. We're giving you a party because even after everything that happened, you never lost respect for the law."

But, no, the medium merely channeled a couple of messages from Lenny Bruce: "I'm very high now." And, "You can't live your whole life on applause."

Lenny's mother had brought his old faded dungaree jacket to the séance. That large safety pin was still there, pinned to the outside breast pocket.

In 1999, a documentary, *Lenny Bruce: Swear to Tell the Truth*, was nominated for an Academy Award, but as producer Robert Weide told me, prophetically, "If there's a documentary about the Holocaust, it will win."

"You don't think you have any chance at all?" I asked.

"The odds against my film winning are six million to one."

Lenny would really have appreciated that. Onstage, he had once held up an issue of *The Realist* with the headline, "Six Million Jews Found Alive in Argentina."

In May 2003, Robin Williams, Penn and Teller, Margaret Cho, Tom and Dick Smothers, First Amendment scholars, lawyers, and Lenny's daughter Kitty were among the signers of a petition addressed to New York Governor George Pataki. Referring to the 1964 obscenity conviction at the Café Au Go Go, it stated:

"A pardon now is too late to save Lenny Bruce. But a posthumous pardon would set the record straight and thereby demonstrate New York's commitment to freedom—free speech, free press, free thinking."

In July, Pataki was still giving this blatant no-brainer "serious consideration." Finally, in December, he granted the posthumous pardon. "Freedom of speech is one of the great American liberties," Pataki said, "and I hope this pardon serves as a reminder of the precious freedoms we are fighting to preserve as we continue to wage the war on terrorism." Lenny would have been simultaneously outraged and amused by the irony that the governor had pardoned him in the context of justifying the invasion of Iraq, which Lenny would have opposed.

★ ★ ★

When rock star/activist Bono received an award at the Golden Globes ceremony in 2003, he said, "This is really, really fucking brilliant." The FCC ruled that he had *not* violated broadcast standards, because his use of the offending word was "unfortunate" but "isolated and nonsexual." You see, it was merely an "exclamative" adjective. The FCC did not consider Bono's utterance to be indecent because, in context, he obviously didn't use the word *fucking* to "describe sexual or excretory organs or activities."

But the next year, in a duet with Janet Jackson during the halftime extravaganza at the Super Bowl, Justin Timberlake sang the lyric, "Gonna have you naked by the end of this song," and in what was defended as "a wardrobe malfunction," he exposed Janet Jackson's breast for 9/16th of a second. I had never seen the media make such a mountain out of an implant.

That incident served as an excuse to crack down on indecency during an election year. So, in 2004, the FCC reversed their own decision, contending that Bono's utterance was "indecent and profane" after all. But an appeals court reversed the FCC's reversal, and suddenly Bono was, once again, not guilty of indecency.

But in 2009—six days after Fox News anchor Shepard Smith shouted on the air, "We are America! I don't give a rat's ass if it helps [get information from suspected terrorists]! We do not fucking torture!"—a Supreme Court ruling reversed the reversal of the reversal. It was suddenly retroactively *un*acceptable for Bono to say, "This is really, really fucking brilliant."

But then in 2010 an appeals court struck down the FCC policy because barring the use of "fleeting expletives" violated the First Amendment and could inhibit free speech. A fucking brilliant decision. Thus, the reversal of the reversal of the reversal was reversed.

In 2012—another election year—the Supreme Court heard arguments on the constitutionality of an FCC action against the TV series *NYPD Blue* for showing partial nudity (the buttocks of actress Charlotte Ross), as well as those naughty-language cases. Conservative pundit Dennis Prager has characterized the fight over *fuck* as central to civilization's "battle to preserve itself."

As for Bono's casual use of such a hazardous word, in June 2012, the Court decided *not* to reverse the reversal of the reversal of the reversal of the reversal of his right to say *fuck* on the air. Otherwise, as a monument to political opportunism, former Governor Pataki might have revoked his posthumous pardon of Lenny Bruce. All I know is that when the little kids on my block are playing outside, they actually curse at each other by yelling, "*Bleep you!*"

CHAPTER 4

QUEEN JEANNE

IN THE COURSE OF PUBLISHING *THE REALIST*, I PORED THROUGH SO MANY newspapers and magazines that I hardly had any time left to read books, although I scanned a lot of nonfiction. I kept buying books and not reading them. Instead I practiced a kind of mystical bibliomancy. I would put my index finger into the pages at random and zero in on a particular passage. So, although I never read Aldous Huxley's novel *Antic Hay*, I happened to discover in it my favorite literary phrase—"excruciating orgasms of self-assertion"—and that began to serve as one more filter through which to perceive all human behavior.

When I attended my first literary cocktail party, I felt like a real impostor. And looked the part. I was the only guy there not wearing a tie. In *The Realist* I had revealed that beat-generation novelist Chandler Brossard was the ghostwriter of Norman Vincent Peale's advice column in *Look* magazine. Now I was being introduced to Brossard. "So *you're* the one," he said. "I could sue you." But, several drinks later, he admitted that not only had he written Peale's answers but he had also made up the questions.

I also met Joseph Heller there. His book *Catch-22* had recently been published, and he asked me if I had read it. "I'm in the middle," I said. The truth was, I hadn't *started* reading it. I didn't even have a copy.

In the next issue of *The Realist*, I publicly confessed my lie. Heller sent me a copy of the book with this note: "If you haven't read it yet, there's no hurry—you practically write *Catch-22* with every issue of *The Realist*." I asked him for an interview, and he accepted. Then, I didn't just read *Catch-22*, I *studied* it. And then I learned a fundamental lesson in advanced satire.

Q. I want to ask you about the use of exaggeration as a vehicle for satire. Do you think you may have exaggerated too much beyond the possibilities of reality?

A. Well, I tried to exaggerate in almost every case, gradually, to a point beyond reality—that was a deliberate intention, to do it so gradually that the unreality becomes more credible than the realistic, normal day-to-day behavior of these characters. Everything in *Catch-22* could possibly happen—nothing in there is supernatural—but it defies probability. But so much of what we do—without even thinking about it—so much of what is done in our day-to-day existence defies probability if we stop to examine it. And this is the effect I wanted to achieve, to make these characters seem more real in terms of their eccentricities carried to absurdity.

When Norman Mailer wrote his first novel, *The Naked and the Dead*, he used the euphemism "fug" for "fuck." At our first encounter in Lyle Stuart's office, I asked Mailer if it was true that when he met actress Tallulah Bankhead she had said, "So you're the young man who doesn't know how to spell fuck."

With a twinkle in his eye, he told me that he had replied, "Yes, and you're the young woman who doesn't know how to."

I saw Mailer again in 1961 at City Hall Park. We were among a thousand citizens committing civil disobedience of the law that we had to seek shelter during an air-raid drill. Umbrellas bearing the legend PORTABLE FALLOUT SHELTER were held up while we sang "America the Beautiful." As soon as the air-raid siren sounded, the police chief announced, "Officers, arrest those persons who do not seek shelter!" The cops seized those persons who were nearest to them. Then the all-clear sounded, and the rest of the crowd began to disperse.

When *The Realist* was originally launched, I had requested an interview with Mailer. He declined, and declined again, but in late 1962, after I published the Joseph Heller interview, Mailer called me. He was finally ready. We met at his house in Brooklyn Heights. Mailer sat in his chair, poised like a prizefighter. And I was his sparring partner.

Q. Is it possible that you have a totalitarian attitude toward masturbation?

A. I wouldn't say all people who masturbate are evil, probably I would even say that some of the best people in the world masturbate. But I am saying it's a miserable activity.

Q. Well, we're getting right back now to this notion of absolutes. You know—to somebody, masturbation can be a thing of beauty—

A. To what end? Who is going to benefit from it?

Q. It's a better end than [what you referred to as] the beauty of a bombing.

A. Masturbation is bombing. It's bombing oneself.

Q. I see nothing wrong if the only person hurt from masturbation is the one who practices it. But it can also benefit— look, Wilhelm Stekel wrote a book on autoeroticism, and one of the points he made was that at least it saved some people who might otherwise go out and commit rape.

A. It's better to commit rape than masturbate. Maybe, maybe. The whole thing becomes difficult.

Q. But rape involves somebody else.

A. Just talking about it on the basis of violence: one is violence toward oneself; one is violence toward others. Let's follow your argument and be speculative for a moment—if everyone becomes violent toward themselves, then past a certain point the entire race commits suicide. But if everyone becomes violent toward everyone else, you would probably have one wounded hero-monster left.

Q. And he'd have to masturbate.

A. That's true . . . But—you use that to point out how tragic was my solution, which is that he wins and still has to masturbate. I reply that at least it was more valuable than masturbating in the first place. Besides, he might have no desire to masturbate. He might lie down and send his thoughts back to the root of his being.

★ ★ ★

Mad magazine had moved to Madison Avenue, and *The Independent* had moved to Park Avenue South, but *The Realist* remained in the old *Mad* building. I rented a tiny apartment a couple of blocks away. The telephone there was an extension of my office number, so it rang in both locations simultaneously. I would answer by saying *"Realist"* during regular business hours and "hello" in the evening and on weekends. Somebody might call when I was still in bed, but I'd clear my throat and answer *"Realist"* alertly as though I were sitting at a desk. If the caller wanted me to check a subscription, I'd explain, "I'm sorry, but I'm not at the files right now. Let me call you back later."

I usually had lunch at a little diner where cops would cash their bribery checks. The owner specialized in "cheeserized" sandwiches. I met an actor there, Del Close, who would later become a teacher of improvisation. The first time I stopped by his apartment, I noticed that his bathtub was piled a few feet high with his collection of books.

"You may be filthy and unwashed," I said, "but at least you're well-read."

Although *The Realist* had become a healthy combination of entertainment and the First Amendment, I became increasingly frustrated that it wasn't more effective in serving people directly. Then I had dinner with George von Hilsheimer, who had been a child evangelist and was now a practicing humanist. He'd just spent a few weeks exploring public and private sources of support for a national expansion of child-care centers, and he was still in shellshock from dealing with bureaucracies. We were talking about Humanitas, an organization in Holland with twenty thousand volunteer social workers. He said he could live on $50 a week, and I guaranteed him a year's subsistence to launch an American version of Humanitas called People.

The Realist soon began to serve as an organizing tool for this domestic Peace Corps—a community of idealists with nothing to lose but their armchairs. With my *Playboy* salary, I was already supporting the free birth-control clinic; the Neighborhood Pilot Project, a remedial reading program run by John Davis and Aggie Dodd; the Lower East Side Action Project; and a judo center run by Larry and Michelle Cole. Now I made arrangements to do a benefit at Town Hall for People.

Meanwhile, I didn't have a steady girlfriend. I was lonely for my other half, but I didn't want to be celibate while I was waiting. Early one morning I was in bed with a girl I had met at a party, when the phone rang. It was her boyfriend, a lower-echelon Mafioso. I thought of them as Judy Jewish and Gary Gangster. He asked if I knew where she was. I told him no, even as she was cuddling next to me. He said he would check his source and call me right back. A few minutes later he did.

"You were seen with her last night. You spent the night with her. She didn't come home last night. You *punk!*"

He said that he was coming to my office—which is where he thought he was calling me—to talk about it. I told Judy Jewish she'd better leave, and I rushed to the office, but Gary Gangster was already waiting outside the *Mad* building, peering through the locked outside door into the lobby, expecting the elevator door to open and me to step out and open the door for him. Instead he saw me on the sidewalk coming toward him.

"What are you doing out here?" he said.

"Well, I came out just a minute ago, but you weren't here."

"I was calling you up because you didn't come out."

"Oh—I figured you had the address wrong, so I took a walk around the block."

"Let's go to your apartment."

"Don't you want to come up to my office?"

"I said, 'Let's go to your apartment.'"

"You don't expect to find her *there*?"

"She leaves traces wherever she goes. By the way, do you have a telephone at your apartment?"

"Oh, yeah, well, it happens to be the same number as my office, incidentally."

There was a certain tension between us while we were walking to my apartment.

"Tell me," he said, "do you have many friends who smoke Tareyton cigarettes?"

I suddenly realized what he meant by "she leaves traces." At the apartment, Judy Jewish was gone, but the bed was unmade and Gary Gangster couldn't help but notice the semen stain on the sheet. Which, of course, was no proof that it was *she* who had been there. However, the ashtray was filled with Tareyton cigarette butts.

"Do *you* smoke Tareytons?"

"No," I answered, "I don't smoke *any* cigarettes."

"I guess I caught you with your pants down, didn't I?"

He picked up the phone and dialed a number. He was calling her mother. "I found him," he said. "What should I do, throw 'im out the window?" I was scared that he might actually do it. He hung up the phone and I didn't know what to expect. I thought, *How could a realist have gotten himself into such an unrealistic situation?*

Gary Gangster and I proceeded to have a discussion.

"I got the *horns*," he yelled. "I gotta *do* something! It ain't *manly*!"

"Look, restraint itself can be a form of manliness."

"You know," he said, "I could arrange to have you killed while I was having dinner with your mother and father."

"Well, actually, they're not having too many people over to the house these days."

His low chuckle in response to that wisecrack marked a positive turning point in our conversation. He finally forgave me, and we shook hands. He borrowed $20, which we both knew I would never get back. He also asked for complimentary tickets to my show at Town Hall, and I said yes. But then he wanted to be staff photographer for *The Realist*, and I told him no. He said he understood, and we parted on friendly terms. And I vowed never to go to bed again with anybody who smoked cigarettes.

My performance at Town Hall was in January 1963. The audience was mostly *Realist* readers, looking each other over as though they were attending a Martian convention. Gary Gangster and Judy Jewish were there. I told my story about them, and I was relieved to see them laughing. From the stage, I introduced *Realist* writers and artists—who stood up so folks could compare them with their bylines—as well as the subjects of my interviews. When I introduced Joseph Heller, somebody else stood up, but since the audience didn't know what Heller looked like, they applauded.

"That's not Joseph Heller. This is right out of *Catch-22*."

Then I introduced Norman Mailer, and again somebody else stood up. This time it was a young woman.

"I'm a friend of Norman's," she called out. "He couldn't come tonight."

"That's the story of his life." It was a cheap shot, but I couldn't resist it. "He's writing another book about it."

* * *

When Jeanne Johnson was seventeen, her parents helped her run away to New York. Her mother gave her a green hide-a-bed, and her father—who was half Choctaw Indian—had all the floors done in linoleum that was supposed to look like wood. She lied about her age and got a job working for a book publisher. She had an affair and became pregnant when she was eighteen, but the relationship soured, and she went to Dr. Spencer for an abortion. She recalled:

> Now that I think back, I was lucky. It wasn't some guy who picks you up on the street corner and drives you to some undesignated spot and asks if you suck cock before he puts you under. It was Dr. Robert Spencer. He was a sunny little man with a red beret and red scarf and red cheeks who immediately understood that I was a child afraid and with not enough money to stay at the motel. So he gave me the keys to his office and told me I could stay there overnight. In the morning he found a nice couple to drive me back to New York.

Two years later, she left a wild party and went screaming through the streets. She thought she was being melodramatic, but the authorities assumed she was a mental case, and they put her in Bellevue for observation, her diaphragm firmly in place. An old friend, Norman Mailer, decided to do a good deed and get her out. Her parents signed the appropriate papers, and he became her legal guardian.

The night of my Town Hall concert, Mailer was busy meeting a deadline, so he sent Jeanne in his place. After the show, she came backstage and introduced herself. Most women then didn't extend their hand first, but she did, and her handshake was confident. She had a pixie haircut, darkish skin, a vulnerable smile, and she seemed to veer at you from an angle. She had the aura of a Moroccan princess who had been kicked out of clown school for being too silly.

The next week she came to *The Realist* for advance copies of the issue with the Mailer interview. She was also looking for a job—and I needed an office scapegoat. I still had more interviews scheduled, so I told Jeanne I wasn't sure yet. Then, a few days later, she called, using a Southern accent.

"I attended the University of Alabama where I majored in scapegoating." That did it. She was obviously qualified for the job.

Since *The Realist* office was near police headquarters, there were stores in the neighborhood that catered to their needs. When Jeanne saw a flyer in a store window promoting a groin holster, she talked the proprietor into letting her have it. The ad offered: "For the first time, a truly concealed holster that can be worn with leisure clothing! Ideal for all year round and especially warm weather. No jacket necessary; no outside shirt tails! Comfortable, convenient. Guaranteed. Used by peace officers everywhere."

The accompanying photo sequence showed a man wearing shorts reaching into his fly and withdrawing his pistol. The guarantee read: "I understand that if I am not fully satisfied with my holster I can return it within 10 days and receive a complete refund of the purchase price." Sure, if a purchaser was still alive. The cause of death might well have been a stuck zipper. This was a perfect item for *The Realist*, and Jeanne was a perfect Scapegoat.

She had excellent instincts. She persuaded me not to print a letter to the editor which gave instructions on how to perform an abortion on oneself, because it was too dangerous a procedure. She also was a superb bullshit detector. One time she was on the phone with a subscriber who said, "You have a lovely voice, you must be very beautiful."

"Actually, I'm deformed," she replied.

Later she was afraid that she might have indulged in cruel humor, but I insisted that the caller had asked for it. Her soulfulness was the basis of her irreverence. Watching the dwarf actor Michael Dunn at the Academy Awards on TV, she remarked, "I'll bet he doesn't rent *his* tuxedo."

Jeanne was the queen of her own yin-yang universe. She could fit a complete set of checkers—twelve red and twelve black—into her mouth, and yet maintain a total sense of dignity. Challenge was her middle name. She once climbed up the side of a building, through a window, into an apartment, and out the door, confessing that she was "guilty of breaking and leaving." She charmed my ass off.

Our relationship remained platonic, though, until she invited me to dinner at Norman Mailer's house, where she was living, and we kissed goodnight, tentatively at first—she was, after all, my employee—but then her tongue entered my lips and touched my heart. My Scapegoat would become my Scapemate. In Mailer's words, Jeanne and I "fell in together." But, as if to prove just how special our connection was, we waited two whole weeks before falling into bed. In those days, that was considered a long time.

Jeanne was still living at Mailer's house, but she would often stop by my little apartment in the morning on her way to work. I had a mattress on the floor and kept my clothes in a filing cabinet. I was working on the Lenny Bruce book at the time, and sometimes, while I transcribed his tapes, she would lay by my side, mimicking Lenny's impression of a flaky Cardinal Spellman as played by actor Hugh Herbert going, "Whoo-whoo-whoo!"

We would fight sometimes, but then make up, and the relief was always worth the tension. Usually, the disagreement was based on a misunderstanding. Once we were coming out of an Italian restaurant, and she was complaining about the service. Quoting from one of Lenny's bits about how *not* to act on a date—and mistakenly thinking that she had heard this particular routine—I said, "What'sa matter, you got the *rag* on?" In response, Jeanne punched me in the stomach. I was perversely impressed with the way she refused to play the role of a dependent female.

Another time, walking around Chinatown in the silent aftermath of an argument, a panhandler approached us. "Just give me one of your dreams," he said. It brought tears to our eyes. We went back to my tiny apartment and made love. That was the night our child was conceived. Jeanne realized a few weeks later that she was pregnant.

"I want this baby," she declared.

"So do I."

We decided to live together. Although we were both anarchistic enough not to want the government involved in our relationship, we decided to get married—but not legally. Since George von Hilsheimer was a minister, but not licensed in New York State, he could perform the ceremony. I called my parents with the news. My mother had always asked if any girl I went out with was Jewish, and now she was asking again.

"I told you," I teased her, "that I would never answer that question again, because it's irrelevant to me. But if you want to ask Jeanne directly, I'll put her on the phone."

I could almost hear my mother asking, "So, are you Jewish?" I assumed Jeanne might respond, "Are you kidding? I was the president of Junior Hadassah." Which was true, even though she *wasn't* Jewish. But instead, she said with a chortle, "Oh, no—I'm anti-Semitic," and made my mother laugh.

At that instant, I fell one step deeper in love with Jeanne. I had never known anyone who could dance on the edge with such spontaneity and grace. When she came to my parents' home for the first time, I told them about that time she had punched me in the stomach. "But it's different now," I added, sticking my stomach out to display my trust. And Jeanne punched me in the stomach again.

"You shouldn't have tempted me like that," she explained.

★ ★ ★

Through People, I was now supporting a day-care center, a bail fund, and a children's camp, inspired by A.S. Neill's Summerhill School in England, based on the notion that learning should be fun. George von Hilsheimer was supposed to run the camp in Rosman, North Carolina, but there were threats against the Negro kids, so on June 30, 1963—the day Jeanne had set for our wedding at Norman Mailer's house—von Hilsheimer and I were checking out another site in New Jersey.

I left him there so I could get back to help with wedding preparations, such as picking up the cake Jeanne had ordered with the words *At Last* decorating the top. Von Hilsheimer would be four hours late, and the ceremony had to be delayed. Meanwhile, guests were getting drunk, Jeanne's divorced parents were flirting with each other, and a telegram arrived from the architect warning that the balcony could only hold a limited number of people.

My father suggested that my uncle, who was a judge, could marry us, but I declined without bothering to explain that this would've made it legal. My father took Jeanne and me into the kitchen, went to the stove, and turned on the gas jet beneath a teakettle. "You have to always remember," he said, "that water doesn't boil unless you put a flame under it." Jeanne thought he was talking about sex, but I knew he was talking about anger.

Later, I asked Mailer if *he* had any advice about women for his new son-in-law.

"You're putting me on," he advised, gently jabbing me on the arm. As a wedding gift, he gave us a pair of marmoset monkeys. We named them Idiot and Delight.

Since Lenny Bruce was in San Francisco at the time, preparing for his trial, *Playboy* wanted me there to get him to write additional material for his book, so that's where Jeanne and I decided to go for our honeymoon. On the way, the pilot announced that he would have to make an emergency landing in Chicago. Jeanne pouted.

"I guess we didn't need to get round-trip tickets," she said.

In 364 out of 450 airplane crashes, the automatic recording devices found in the wreckage indicated that at least one of the crew members began to whistle in the last few moments aloft. I wasn't aware of that particular statistic, but I was holding Jeanne's hand and whistling "Tsena, Tsena." Special trucks were spreading foam on the ground, and we landed safely.

In San Francisco, we took a long walk to Lenny's hotel in North Beach. On the way, we stopped at a barbershop where three Oriental men—with a guitar, a violin, and a bass fiddle—were playing "Bei Mir Bist Du Schoen." The shop was closed, but they let us come in, sit down, and listen, as long as nobody wanted a haircut. We tried to bring Lenny there, but he was too deeply buried in his legal papers to take time out.

"I'm fighting for ten years of my life," he explained.

Jeanne recalled that meeting.

> Listening to Lenny's tapes, hearing his tales, I felt like his sister, because one can't really feel like his friend; *alone* is written all over his face. His room was a kind of warm, seedy place, home of the night people and a few young, apple-pie delicious dumb hookers. It had a communal feeling, and when everybody was awake, late in the afternoon, most of them seemed to be occupied doing errands for Lenny, who never seemed to have a shortage of things he wanted, needed, or fancied. He never seemed to wonder why these people wanted to help—he was too busy—but I wondered what these big-titted, tight-dressed, high-heeled girls got out of it.
>
> They didn't understand him, he certainly didn't look like he was successful, he was as down and out as the rest of them. He didn't lavish attention on them, he didn't even fuck them slow. What magic feeling, vibration, something special in our midst, or maybe he was somebody who just wanted something done and he knew who to ask for what, and there was great pride in taking his shoes to the shoemaker and doing a good job, just the way he liked it. Sometimes to see those broads sitting over a typewriter, slowly, painfully transcribing his tapes, with the mascara running down their faces, their dresses up to their crotches, their feet turned over

at the ankles in their red shoes, sweat pouring off with the effort of it all, they sort of reminded you of the man on crutches in *Greaser's Palace* who fell to his knees and said, "I can crawl again."

Lenny thought that prostitutes had a special insight, and he once hired a hooker to read his manuscript.

"If it's all the same to you," she said, "couldn't we just ball?"

Lenny said no, that wasn't what he paid her for. But he began his show that night with this opening line: "I've balled every waitress in this club." It might even have been true.

* * *

In Rosman County, North Carolina, there was a persistent rumor campaign that "those people [at Camp Summerlane] have six nigger families hidden up in them hills and are going to bring them out in September to integrate the Rosman High School." The mayor claimed that *The Realist* had a sexual promiscuity theme and was "unfit to be read by gentlemen." The sheriff agreed. The paper was atheistic, he said, and "we're mostly Baptist and pretty serious about it." And so it came to pass that a mob of serious Baptist gentlemen raped a children's summer camp.

Stones were thrown at kids and counselors in two canoes, an act which escalated into physical beatings, a knifing, a posse of armed men, rifle shots, a bullet-riddled bus, gasoline being thrown on the pond, then on the lake, with matches set to both. Nobody was killed, but there was an awful fear. Summerlane was evacuated at 7 o'clock the next morning, and the scared campers headed for New Jersey. They had never seen a lake on fire before.

While Jeanne was in New York, fielding calls from understandably hysterical parents who didn't know where their kids were, en route from North Carolina to New Jersey, I was at the *Playboy* mansion in Chicago, working on the Lenny Bruce book.

Dick Gregory was performing at the Playboy Club and invited me to his show. Two years previously, Negro comedians performed only in Negro nightclubs, and Gregory was no exception. But one evening the regular white comic at the Playboy Club in Chicago got sick, and Gregory took his place. It made *Time* magazine, and he was invited to perform on *The Tonight Show*, but he declined unless, after doing his stand-up act, he would be asked to sit down and talk with Jack Paar. The gamble worked, and Gregory became an instant celebrity, breaking through the color barrier with humor.

Although he was getting a lot of publicity in the mainstream press, he requested to be interviewed in *The Realist*. Eventually we became friends and fellow demonstrators. Now he was performing at the Playboy Club, not as a substitute comic but as a star attraction. They had to supply me with a jacket, and a tie that was decorated all over with bunny symbols. Gregory was already onstage.

"How could Columbus discover America," he was asking the audience, "when the Indians were already *here?*"

In his dressing room between shows, Gregory took out his wallet and showed me a tattered copy of his favorite poem, "If," by Rudyard Kipling. I laughed and he looked offended, until I explained that I was laughing because it was also *my* favorite poem, and "the unforgiving minute" was my favorite poetic phrase. Meanwhile, in New York, a young stand-up comic found out where Jeanne and I lived and tried to convince her that I should interview him for *The Realist*. His name was Bill Cosby, and he wanted to prove that a Negro comedian didn't *have* to talk about racism.

Jeanne and I finally left the old *Mad* building so that we could work together at home. We moved into a duplex brownstone on East 18th Street. The entire side of one building on that block featured a fading advertisement for a cleanser personified by the Gold Dust Twins, a pair of little Negro boys. It had originally been painted right on the bricks.

When Dick Gregory saw it, he said, "They ought to take that whole wall and preserve it in a museum somewhere."

In August, Jeanne and I went with some friends to the March on Washington. It was hot and crowded when we got there. Jeanne was a few months pregnant and extremely uncomfortable. All she really wanted to do was go to an air-conditioned movie. So, while Martin Luther King was delivering his most famous speech, we were alone in a theater, watching *Bye Bye Birdie*. Reverend King had a dream, but we were cool.

* * *

Jeanne was the personification of sauciness. At John Francis Putnam's outdoor Fourth of July party, she beckoned me into the bushes, pulled down her panties, and we screwed standing up, accompanied by fireworks and the smell of barbecue smoke.

Putnam wanted to give us a housewarming gift. He had designed the word FUCK in red-white-and-blue lettering emblazoned with stars and stripes. Now he needed a second word, a noun that would serve as an appropriate object for that verb. He suggested AMERICA, but that didn't seem right to me. It certainly wasn't an accurate representation of my feelings. I was well aware that I probably couldn't publish *The Realist* in any other country. Besides, a poster saying FUCK AMERICA lacked a certain sense of irony.

There was at that time a severe anti-Communist hysteria burgeon-
ing throughout the land. The attorney general of Arizona rejected the
Communist party's request for a place on the ballot because state law
"prohibits official representation" for Communists and, in addition, "the
subversive nature of your organization is even more clearly designated by
the fact that you do not even include your zip code."

Alvin Dark, manager of the Giants, announced that "any pitcher who
throws at a batter and deliberately tries to hit him is a Communist." And
singer Pat Boone declared at the Greater New York Anti-Communism
Rally in Madison Square Garden, "I would rather see my four daughters
shot before my eyes than have them grow up in a Communist United
States. I would rather see those kids blown into Heaven than taught into
Hell by the Communists."

So I suggested COMMUNISM as the second word, since the usual correla-
tion between conservatism and prudishness would provide the incongruity
that was missing. Putnam designed the word COMMUNISM in red lettering
emblazoned with hammers and sickles. Then he presented Jeanne and
me with a patriotic poster which now proudly proclaimed FUCK COMMU-
NISM!—suitable for framing. I wanted to share this sentiment with *Realist*
readers, but our photoengraver refused to make a metal plate, explaining,
"We got strict orders from Washington not to do stuff like this."

I went to another engraver, who said no because they had been visited
by the FBI after making a metal plate of a woman with pubic hair. So
instead of publishing a miniature black-and-white version of the poster in
The Realist, I offered full-size color copies by mail. And if the post office
interfered, I would have to accuse them of being soft on Communism.

The first person to buy a poster was an employee of Radio Free
Europe. After a few days, the security people took it off his office wall.
His employer explained that it was funny but he didn't want women to see
it. The FUCK COMMUNISM! poster was purchased by an Episcopalian priest,
a mayor, an astronaut, by college groups for mock political conventions, by
Norman Mailer, Terry Southern, and Joseph Heller, who sent posters out
as Christmas gifts. Chicago disc jockey Dan Sorkin kept one in the front
window of his home, just waiting for any Commie sympathizer to *dare*
criticize him. Somebody gave a FUCK COMMUNISM! poster to Gus Hall,
head of the Communist Party. He accepted it.

"People have been saying that to me for years," he laughed.

In London the head of the UN mission to Ethiopia spotted a *Playboy*
executive's poster and commandeered it for his office in Addis Ababa.
Playwright Arthur Cowan had one framed and shipped it to England
with instructions that it be installed in his Rolls-Royce. Country Joe

McDonald stuck one on his car bumper and almost got arrested by a confused traffic cop. Paul Jacobs brought a couple of posters to Washington and gave them to Secretary of Labor Willard Wirtz and Peace Corps Director Sargent Shriver, who kept the poster in a back room used it to beguile selected Peace Corps recruits.

One subscriber bought twenty-five posters and asked me to send them to, among others, J. Edgar Hoover, the John Birch Society, and 1964 presidential candidates Barry Goldwater and Lyndon Johnson—all with a personal note from me: "Dear So-and-So: A reader of ours thought you might get a chuckle out of the enclosed patriotic poster." Senator Goldwater's response to receiving a FUCK COMMUNISM! poster crystallized the generic spirit of political campaigns everywhere and forever:

"Your comments and suggestions mean a great deal to me," his form letter stated. "You may be sure that I will keep them in mind as the campaign progresses. I want you to know I appreciate your taking the time and trouble to write."

A couple who lived on a former ferry that was now docked at the houseboat community in Sausalito, California, stapled a FUCK COMMUNISM! poster to their floating home. One afternoon a sheriff's captain marched down the gangway, climbed up the ferryboat, tore the poster down, and ripped it to shreds. He proceeded to arrest the couple for "outraging public decency."

Newspapers reporting the arrest described the poster as a "blunt anti-Communist sign" and "a colorful attack on Communism," substituting asterisks or dashes for FUCK. A jury was finally selected, but when the bailiff removed three teenage girls from the courtroom to spare their ears, the defense moved for a dismissal. The judge refused to grant this motion, but charges were dismissed before the case came to trial. The district attorney said that he had received assurances that the incident was "an isolated case and repetition is unlikely."

At a midwestern college, one graduating student held up a FUCK COMMUNISM! poster as his class was posing for the yearbook photograph. Campus officials found out and insisted that the word FUCK be airbrushed out. But then the poster would read: COMMUNISM! So that was airbrushed out too, and the yearbook ended up publishing a class photo that showed this particular student holding up a blank poster.

Writer Robert Scheer was doing research for a booklet, *How the United States Got Involved in Vietnam*, to be published by the Fund for the Republic. He was frustrated because he wanted to witness firsthand what was going on in Southeast Asia, and they wouldn't send him. Since *The Realist* had already sold a couple of thousand FUCK COMMUNISM! posters at a dollar each, I made out a check for $1,900, the price of a round-trip airline ticket. Scheer traveled to Vietnam and Cambodia, then wrote his seminal report. He also wrote an article for *The Realist*, titled "Academic Sin," documenting the role of Michigan State University professors in the Diem dictatorship.

Proceeds from another poster—originally a *Realist* cartoon depicting an anthropomorphic deity buggering Uncle Sam, with the legend ONE NATION UNDER GOD—were used to bail the artist, Frank Cieciorka, out of jail after he was arrested for voter registration work in Mississippi.

★　★　★

In November, Dr. Spencer and his wife had Thanksgiving dinner with us. Jeanne told them how she had switched gynecologists mid-pregnancy because she wanted to have our baby the Lamaze way. It was not yet a trendy method. We warned our new obstetrician that if he delivered a boy, we weren't sure whether we would allow him to be circumcised.

When Jeanne was seven months pregnant, we went to a Happening at Café Au Go Go where nothing happened. She felt this was a ripoff, so she created her own Happening. She stood on the shoulders of Mort Gerberg and borrowed a huge, colorful Mardi Gras head that was hanging on a wall in the lobby. Later she noticed—in a calendar from a liquor store advising, "You don't have to wait till Christmas"—that Enrico Rastelli Day was coming. He was a famous Italian juggler. So we held our Christmas party on December 19th that year. And since the Mardi Gras head *looked* like Enrico Rastelli must have looked, it went on top of the tree.

On the afternoon of January 23, 1964, I had been planning to attend a conference sponsored by the Planned Parenthood Federation. Instead I ended up in a delivery room. Jeanne and I walked to the hospital, which was only a block away. She stopped to lean against a car while she had a contraction.

"Listen," I told her, "you don't have to go through with this if you don't want to." It was my way of being supportive.

Watching our baby being born was a profound and humbling experience. Jeanne was awake, alert, and laughing. She said that when the doctor brought forth the baby's head, it felt like a simultaneous climax and withdrawal. Our baby didn't even have to be slapped on the buttocks, because the trip through the birth canal was so quick there was no need to gasp for oxygen. She came out wailing. The doctor let us know indirectly that our baby was a girl.

"Well," he said, "you have one less decision to make."

We considered calling her Kay Sarah, as in *qué serà*, but instead we named her Holly, after the character Holly Golightly in *Breakfast at Tiffany's* by Truman Capote. Holly was, of course, breast-fed.

"I finally found out what tits are really for," Jeanne said.

Holly's shit smelled so sweet we wanted to bottle it, proud parents that we were. Three days after she was born, our monkeys had a litter of two, just like in the movies. Jeanne checked with the zoo and found out that it was extremely rare for marmosets to have offspring in captivity, and usually it would only be a single birth.

We named the twins Wit and Half-Wit. We also had a dog named Clit. Jeanne claimed that she was officially registered with the American Kennel Club as Clitoris Humphrey. One day, Clit was running around with Lenny Bruce's hypodermic in her mouth. Lenny tried to get it back, but Clit ran under the couch.

"C'mere, you freaky dog!" Lenny yelled. "You better bring me that this minute!"

While Lenny was staying with us, Holly had the hiccups, and Lenny did a running commentary, like a radio announcer:

"We're on the air. This is the fourteenth day of little Holly and her hiccuping. We've tried everything. We've got her tongue pulled out now. You sit with her for a while, Paul. God only knows. Poor little curly-headed darling."

When Jeanne was nursing Holly, Lenny averted his eyes. Jeanne teased him about his shyness.

"But," he said, "everybody knows that titties are dirty. That's why you can't show pictures of them."

"Except if they're in atrocity photos," Jeanne added.

Later, in his performance at the Café Au Go Go, Lenny said, "If a titty is bloodied and maimed, it's clean. But if the titty is pretty, it's dirty. And that's why you never find any atrocity photos at obscenity trials, with distended stomachs and ripped-up breasts."

That night, Lenny got busted for obscenity again.

* * *

Lyle Stuart had originally helped me find a printer for the FUCK COMMUNISM! posters. They were supposed to say, at the bottom in small print, "Additional Copies Available from the Daughters of the American Revolution." I wasn't afraid of a lawsuit, figuring that the D.A.R. would have to *acknowledge* the FUCK COMMUNISM! posters before they could *disclaim* them, but Mary Louise Stuart suggested that I change it to "Mothers of the American Revolution" and I liked that better.

John Francis Putnam designed a patriotic Mothers of the American

Revolution letterhead, which appeared to be the stationery of a pressure group, so I could use it as a means of getting information that might otherwise be held back from *The Realist*. The first such opportunity was inspired by this news item: "Catholic travelers on Trans-World Airlines may eat meat on Fridays and on other days of abstinence under a special dispensation granted the airline by the Holy See in Rome."

Mothers of the American Revolution wrote to every airline: "We would like to know if the Vatican has granted special dispensation to Roman Catholics traveling on [your airline] in regard to abstaining from eating meat on Friday—and if not, why not?"

Typical response: "We are happy to report that Japan Air Lines passengers are granted a dispensation from the law of abstinence so that on Fridays and all other days when that law pertains, Catholics may partake of any meat courses served on board JAL flights. I hope we may have the pleasure some day of welcoming the ladies of your organization aboard a Japan Airlines Jet Courier."

Mothers of the American Revolution also wrote to every cigarette-paper company to find out how they felt about manufacturing a product that was used for illegal purposes.

★ ★ ★

When I had been working for Lyle Stuart, Ralph Ginzburg was preparing *An Unhurried View of Erotica*. I recommended that Lyle turn down the opportunity to be copublisher, which he did. Nevertheless, he guided Ginzburg through the book's publication—finding him a typesetter, a printer, a distributor, a mailing house, and when the post office seized Ginzburg's mailing piece, Lyle sent attorney Martin Scheiman to Washington to obtain release of the mailing.

One day, Lyle was giving Ginzburg help on his ad campaign.

"I'm publishing a book by Albert Ellis called *Sex Without Guilt*," Lyle said. "When you book some of your radio and TV things, could you suggest him as a fellow guest?"

"But the topic will be pornography."

"Ellis is a pornography expert. He's testified in many trials."

"I can't do that," Ginzburg said. "What's in it for me?"

Thus did Ralph Ginzburg make Lyle Stuart's permanent shit-list in a single bound. Years later, on the basis of his mail-order book success, Ginzburg went on to publish *Eros* magazine. He wrote to the postmaster of Intercourse, Pennsylvania: "After a great deal of deliberation, we have decided that it might be advantageous for our direct mail to bear the postmark of your city."

The response: "I acknowledge receipt of your recent letter concerning the bulk mailings. I must inform you that our office is very small and our equipment and facilities are limited. So, in view of this, I feel we are not able to handle mail in such a volume."

Ginzburg made the same request to the postmaster of Blue Ball, Pennsylvania, and received essentially the same response. *Eros* was, however, granted a bulk-mailing permit from Middlesex, New Jersey. In five months more than five million subscription invitations were mailed.

Ginzburg went on trial for obscenity, and the jury found him guilty. I had become the moderator of a weekly Speak-Out at the Village Vanguard and, before Ginzburg went to prison, I invited him to be a panelist one night when the subject was "What's Wrong with Prurience?" A few days later, Lyle called me.

"Is it true that you invited Ralph Ginzburg on some panel?"

"Yes."

"That's all I wanted to know." In the background, I could hear Mary Louise say, "Tell him he's on my list."

I was very upset. On her *list?* I thought we were *family*. And yet I hadn't exactly *acted* with any sense of family. I rationalized that I was being true to the principle of the First Amendment. After all, Ginzburg was going to be put behind bars for what he had *published*.

"It's like Al Capone," Lyle said. "He murdered people, but he went to jail for tax evasion."

When I invited Ginzburg to be on the panel, I knew Lyle and Mary Louise might feel betrayed by me, although I didn't expect our relationship to end so abruptly. There was no further discussion. For eleven years they were my closest friends, but now I had failed their loyalty test. I felt devastated. I had never been rejected like this before.

* * *

In 1965, I met Joan Baez at a conference, Democracy on the Campus, at the University of Pennsylvania. She had come there only to speak, but was requested to sing. Nobody had a guitar, so she sang a capella. After her first song, a student stood up.

"I would suggest that we continue the meeting," he said. "We have serious problems and this music is irrelevant."

Baez responded, "I think you're quite wrong. Without these songs the civil rights movement in the South would have been in desperate straits. But I'll sing just one more, and then you can get on with your serious problems."

The audience joined her in "We Shall Overcome."

Back in New York, she came with me when I spoke at CCNY. Later she called and invited me to accompany her on a vacation in Canada. There had been nothing sexual between us, and I didn't know if there would be, but that was a moot point. I was married and had a baby daughter, and Baez knew it. "I can't," I said. Jeanne was listening in on our conversation on the upstairs phone, unhappy that I had even been *invited*.

"Why don't you take *me* on a vacation?" Jeanne said.

I wasn't sure whether she was talking to me or to Joan Baez.

It began to seem as if Jeanne and I were deliberately conspiring to kill the magic between us, to chop up our bond of total trust into cheap little power games. Ultimately we could each focus on one specific act that epitomized the path of our self-destruction.

For me, there was the time that Jeanne came into my office, sat on my lap, and started kissing me. "C'mon," I said, "I'm trying to write." What a pretentious fool I was. I had probably *become* a writer just so a pretty lady like Jeanne would come sit on my lap and kiss me, but now I was so busy pricking pomposity that I had become a pompous prick in the process. Years later, I told Jeanne how bad I felt about that.

She responded, "I thought *I* was being insensitive," which only made me feel *worse* retroactively.

For Jeanne, there was the time, in an attempt to get closer again, that I suggested that we get a babysitter for Holly that evening so we could go out, have dinner, and then attend the Broadway production of *Marat/Sade*, which she had wanted to see.

"No," she said, "you're supposed to clean your room tonight."

How could a pair of zany romantics like us have developed into this strange and petty parent-child relationship? We kept separating and getting back together again. I really wasn't used to fighting. Jeanne attributed her anger to taking birth-control pills for the first time. I had even published an article by chiropractor Jack Soltanoff about the physical and emotional side effects of the pill.

We fought over my being such a pack rat—saving piles of newspapers and magazines and documents, boxes filled with clippings and correspondence and manuscripts. We fought over the way I dressed—wearing a T-shirt to Times Square. We fought over the way I handled money—when I lent a nurse $400 for an abortion, Jeanne was convinced that I'd never get it back. The nurse not only returned the $400 but she also brought a floppy yellow lion for Holly, which became her favorite doll. She named him Lenny and took him everywhere.

Once, while I was out, Jeanne got a call warning her that the cops were on their way to arrest me for abortion referrals. I didn't smoke marijuana, but she smoked an occasional joint, and when I got home, she told me that she had hidden the stash in her vagina—which inspired my all-time worst play on words: "What's a nice joint like that doing in a girl like you?" But the warning call had been a false alarm. Another time, an abortion referral call woke us up at three o'clock in the morning.

While I was giving the caller the information she wanted, Jeanne said, "Tell her to call tomorrow. She'll be just as pregnant in the morning."

When I got off the phone, I said, "I was just trying to have a little compassion for her. She'll sleep better knowing there's a doctor she can go to."

"How about having a little compassion for *me?*"

In addition to all the abortion referral calls, there was a continuous invasion of Jeanne's privacy while I was publishing *The Realist* from our home, so I finally rented a small apartment a few blocks away to use as an office. But the first time I came home, the door was locked from the inside, and Jeanne wouldn't let me in. I had no idea what she was so angry about. *Those fucking birth-control pills!* I didn't know what to do.

I went to a phone booth and called Norman Mailer, but his assistant said he was working against a deadline and couldn't be disturbed. I really needed to handle this myself. By now Jeanne had braced a bookcase against the door. I punched through a pane of glass in the door, stuck my hand in and unlocked the door, then pushed it open, wedging my way in, but knocking over the bookcase. It came crashing down near where Holly was standing, and Jeanne became hysterical.

"You tried to kill the baby!" she yelled.

She got a bread knife and threatened to stab me if I didn't get out of the house. But this was not my crazy aunt. This was my soul mate. Holly was holding on to Lenny the Lion and screaming as she watched all this. I told Jeanne I would leave as soon as she put the knife down, because I didn't want Holly to think that this was the way to get people to do things. Jeanne finally threw the knife on the floor. Then she started crying and punching me on the shoulder. Finally we talked.

She had found a mushy letter to me from Sheila Campion, which I hadn't thrown away because I never threw *anything* away. While Jeanne and I were temporarily separated, Sheila and I had a one-night stand. When Jeanne and I got back together, I had already hired Sheila as *The Realist*'s new Scapegoat. I told her that there would be nothing sexual between us again, *but Jeanne had no way of knowing that.* Suddenly I understood this whole explosion from *her* point of view. She could *only* have concluded that Sheila and I were screwing around in our cozy little love nest in the guise of an office. Jeanne must've been incredibly hurt.

"I've slept with other people too," she said.

I could only blame myself. I had even said in an interview that Jeanne and I were "not ready for *honest* adultery." But when she told me *who* she had slept with—two of my closest friends, Lenny Bruce and Paul Jacobs—it really hurt. Jeanne shared the details, from Lenny asking her if it would offend her if he propositioned her, to "Lenny *directed* me. He'd say, 'Okay, now put this leg up here against the bedpost.' He was like a Fellini of the bedroom."

"When were you with him?"

"The last time you were in Chicago."

"*What?* You mean you were fucking Lenny while I was interviewing Mort Sahl?"

Eventually I confronted them. Paul Jacobs acknowledged what had happened, and we embraced, but Lenny refused to admit anything.

"Look," I told him, "I'm not mad. I just wanted you to know that I *know.*"

"What is this Lone Ranger shit?" he insisted.

"Okay, you don't have to say anything to me. Just tell Mike Nichols." Lenny ignored my sarcasm. "I guess you'd deny it even if I had walked in on you," I said, reflecting a concept from his own act. "I know, I know—you were just giving her artificial respiration."

★ ★ ★

Jeanne and I continued to live under the same roof, but after three years of marriage, the pain finally began to outweigh the pleasure, and we broke up. She was such a responsible and creative parent that we agreed it was better for Holly to stay with her, but I could see Holly anytime.

I moved into a loft on Avenue A. It was the size of a basketball court, and I installed a backboard-and-basket on the wall. I would get a large trampoline and a telephone with a thirteen-foot cord attached to the receiver so that I could jump up and down while talking on the phone. I bought a vibrating recliner chair for me and a rocking horse for Holly.

Jeanne wanted to try for reconciliation, but I refused. Only in retrospect would I realize how stubborn I had become. And how I had treated our marriage vows like elephant shit. I would be particularly haunted by the memory of one night when Jeanne had awakened me.

"I was dreaming that you were being mean to me," she said.

I could have comforted her. We could have delved into the dream. Obviously it had importance for her. Jeanne's dreams were part of her reality. But all I said was, "You woke me up to tell me *that?*" Thereby being mean to her and making her dream come true. I had wanted to liberate communication around the world, but I didn't even know how to talk with my own wife.

CHAPTER 5

MY ACID TRIP WITH GROUCHO MARX

WHEN IT CAME TO DRUGS, I WAS REALLY PURITANICAL. I DIDN'T EVEN USE any *legal* drugs. I never took aspirins or sleeping pills or tranquilizers. I never smoked cigarettes, and I never drank coffee or liquor. I had no socially acceptable vices. But I became influenced by the material I published in *The Realist*.

In 1962, John Wilcock wrote a column titled "What People are Talking About that *Vogue* Won't Admit to." Under "Names to Drop," he included: *Tim Leary*—a young Harvard professor who's been experimenting with non-addicting, consciousness-changing drugs, because the sensible and unsecretive way he's been handling his research might mean the first major breakthrough in the official wall of prejudice and therefore the possible availability in the future of such drugs for anyone who wants them.

In 1964, I ran a front-cover story by Robert Anton Wilson titled "Timothy Leary and His Psychological H-Bomb." He wrote:

> The future may decide that the two greatest thinkers of the 20th Century were Albert Einstein, who showed how to create atomic fission in the physical world, and Timothy Leary, who showed how to create atomic fission in the psychological world. The latter discovery may be more important than the former; there are some reasons for thinking that it was made *necessary* by the former.
>
> Nuclear fission of the material universe has created an impasse which is not merely political but ideological, epistemological, metaphysical. As Einstein himself said, atomic energy has changed

everything but habits of thought, and until our habits of thought also change we are going to drift continually closer to annihilation. Timothy Leary may have shown how our habits of thought can be changed.

When that issue of *The Realist* was published, Leary invited me to visit him at the Castalia Foundation, his borrowed estate in Millbrook, New York. The name Castalia came from *The Glass Bead Game* by Herman Hesse, and indeed, the game metaphor permeated our conversation. Leary talked about the way people are always trying to get you onto *their* gameboards. He discussed the biochemical process "imprinting" with the same passion that he claimed he didn't believe anything he was saying, but somehow I managed to believe him when he told me that I had an honest mind.

"I have to admit," I said, "that my ego can't help but respond to your observation."

"Listen," he reassured me, "anybody who tells you he's transcended his ego . . ."

Leary and his research partner, Richard Alpert, were about to do a lecture series on the West Coast. At the University of California in Berkeley, there was an official announcement that the distribution only of "informative" literature—as opposed to "persuasive" literature—would be permitted on campus, giving rise to the Free Speech Movement, with thousands of students protesting the ban in the face of police billy clubs.

Leary argued that such demonstrations played right onto the game boards of the administration and the police alike, and that the students could shake up the establishment much more if they would just stay in their rooms and change their nervous systems. But it wasn't really a case of either-or. You could protest *and* explore your thirteen-billion-cell mind simultaneously.

In the original edition of this book, I included a story that, during the mass imprisonment of Free Speech Movement demonstrators, a Bible, which had been soaked in an acid solution, easily made its way into their cells. The students just ate those pages up, getting high on Deuteronomy, tripping out on Exodus.

However, in 2004, at the fortieth anniversary of the FSM, I met one of its original founders—my old friend, Michael Rossman. He had asked several of the participants who were arrested whether my report was true, only to conclude that it was a false rumor. This was the last time I saw Michael before his death, but I promised that I'd retract the story, and now I've kept that promise. But, I admit, I really *wanted* to believe that an acid-soaked Bible had been smuggled into the jail.

★ ★ ★

I confessed in the December 1964 issue of *The Realist* that "I'm still too chicken to try LSD should the occasion ever arise." But I became intrigued by the playful and subtle patterns of awareness that Leary and Alpert manifested. If their brains had been so damaged, how come their perceptions were so sharp? I began to research the LSD phenomenon, and in April 1965 I returned to Millbrook for my first acid experience

I was thirty-three years old, and I'd never been high. Leary was supposed to be my guide, but he had gone off to India. Alpert was supposed to take his place, but he was too involved in getting ready to open at the Village Vanguard as a sort of psychedelic comedian-philosopher. However, he did reassure me that my memory wouldn't be affected.

So my guide was Michael Hollingshead, the bald-headed British rascal who had first turned Leary on. Our start was delayed for a few hours, and I made the mistake of raiding the refrigerator while waiting. Finally we went to an upstairs room and ingested tasteless, colorless, odorless liquid, pure Sandoz LSD. Then my trip began with a solid hour of what Hollingshead described as "cosmic laughter."

The more I laughed, the more I tried to think of depressing things—like American atrocities in Vietnam—and the more uproarious my laughter became. The climactic message I got was: IT'S VERY FUNNY! I felt an obligation to share this tremendous insight in *The Realist* with one giant headline and nothing else on the front cover. But, no, I couldn't do *that*. I debated the matter with myself, finally concluding that even though I tried to live by this universal truth, I wouldn't jeopardize the magazine by *flaunting* it like that.

"Well, the least you can do," my lunar self said, "is inform your readers that no matter how serious anything in *The Realist* may appear, you will always be there between the lines saying IT'S VERY FUNNY!"

I was laughing so hard that now I had to throw up. The nearest outlet was a window. I stuck my head out and had a paranoid flash that this was actually a guillotine and that Hollingshead was about to be my executioner. But I knew in my heart that I could trust him so I concentrated instead on the beautiful colors of my vomit as it started moving around on the outside ledge like an ancient religious mosaic coming to life. Napalm was burning someone to death in Vietnam that very moment, but I was alive, and that's really what I was laughing at, the oneness of tragedy and absurdity.

On the stereo, the Beatles were singing the soundtrack from *A Hard Day's Night,* and I began weeping because Jeanne and I had seen that film together. At this point we were temporarily separated, but I began to have *reverse* paranoia—that she was doing nice things for me behind my back—and I had an internal hallucination that she had not only helped *plan* for that particular record to be played but, moreover, in doing so, she must have collaborated with a guy she considered an asshole in order to please me. What a fantastic thing to do! She had always complained of my associations with assholes, yet now she had obviously worked *with* the one who had arranged for this acid trip. Filled with gratitude, I felt compelled to call her up, but I held back because I also convinced myself that she had *planned* for me to call her up *against my will*. So I figured I would call her up but I would also assure her that I was calling of my own free will. I argued with myself about this for a while, as the dial on the downstairs pay phone became the inanimate object of my megalomania and changed into Dali's limp clock in *The Persistence of Memory*.

I sat there, immobilized, unable to call until I could rationalize that as long as I *knew* that she had programmed this telephone call, and as long as I went through the *process* of deciding to call, it would be acceptable to my warped sense of independence. The coin slot was as squiggly and vibrating as my vomit, though. How was I ever going to get a dime into *that*? But then I took out a dime, and *it* was also squiggly and vibrating. My dime fit into the coin slot perfectly. I called collect, and the operator asked my name.

"Ringo Starr," I said.

"Do you really want me to say that?"

"Of course, operator. It's a private joke between us, and it's the only way she'll accept a collect call."

That wasn't true, but when the operator told Jeanne that there was a collect call from Ringo Starr, she *did* accept it immediately. I explained why I was calling.

"Paul," she said, "you're thanking me for something I didn't *do*."

And I was so sure that we had communed.

I visited with Dick Alpert for a while. He was soaking his body in a bathtub, preparing his psyche for the Village Vanguard gig. He had taken three hundred acid trips, but there I was, a first-timer, standing in the open doorway, reversing roles and comforting *him* in his anxiety about entering show business.

"It's only an audience," I reassured him. "What can they do to you? If they don't laugh, it doesn't make any difference. What do you have to lose?"

When I told my mother about taking LSD, she was quite concerned. She warned me, "It could lead to marijuana."

* * *

The CIA had originally envisioned using LSD as a means of control, but millions of young people became explorers of their own inner space. Acid was serving as a vehicle to help deprogram themselves from a civilization of sadomasochistic priorities. While the nuclear family was exploding, extended families were developing into an alternative society.

What had happened to me as a child at Carnegie Hall was now occurring throughout the culture. A mass awakening was in process. There had always been a spirit of counterculture, taking different forms along the way, and just as the beatniks had evolved from the bohemians, the hippies were now evolving from the beatniks. There were subcommunities developing across the country. And the antiwar movement sprouted like weed.

The CIA's scenario had backfired.

San Francisco became the focus of this pilgrimage. A whole new generation of pioneers was traveling westward, without killing a single Indian along the way. In January 1966, on one of my trips to the West Coast, folks all over the Bay Area were ingesting LSD in preparation for the Acid Test at the Longshoreman's Hall, organized by Ken Kesey and the Merry Pranksters. The ballroom was seething with celebration, thousands of bodies stoned out of their minds, undulating to rock bands amid balloons and streamers and beads, with a thunder machine and strobe lights flashing, so that even the Pinkerton guards were contact high. Kesey asked me to take the microphone and contribute a running commentary on the scene.

"All I know," I began, "is that if I were a cop and I came in here, I wouldn't know where to begin . . ."

> My next stop was determined by a press release from the campaign headquarters of Robert Scheer, who was running for Congress in Oakland: Usually informed sources reported today that an outlawed left-wing psychedelic splinter within the Scheer campaign will caucus with Paul Krassner 2 a.m. Saturday night, at the Jabberwock. These authoritative sources reported that Krassner, who has just returned from Washington, will deliver a preview of the State of the Union Message for 1966.

At this coffeehouse caucus, I displayed a headline from the *San Francisco Examiner*: "Pope Will Do 'Anything' for Peace." It was a proper introduction to the state of Lyndon Johnson's union, and I asked a rhetorical question: "Would the pope perform an abortion on Luci Baines Johnson if it would bring about world peace?"

Scheer's increasingly broad support was based mainly on his reputation as a spokesperson for opposition to the war in Vietnam, but the California Democratic Committee wanted him to drop his platform plank to legalize abortion. Conversely, a psychiatrist on the Board of Directors of the Society for Humane Abortion had also been active on the Vietnam Day Committee, but to avoid giving offense, the Society translated that to "anti-war groups" in their brochure.

Ostensibly, there was a conflict between antiwar and pro-dope, so Scheer pleaded to the acid culture, "[Secretary of Defense] McNamara hasn't dropped out yet." Nevertheless, legalization of marijuana was one of Scheer's platform planks, although he said he wouldn't smoke it himself as long as it was illegal. I in turn announced that I wouldn't *stop* smoking pot until it *was* legal. Stew Albert of the Vietnam Day Committee had introduced me to Thai stick in 1965, and I became a toker.

"Now I know why there's a war going on in Southeast Asia," I said. "To protect the crops." That quote was enough to land my picture on the front page of the *Berkeley Barb*.

But my mother was right. LSD *did* lead to marijuana.

* * *

When Tim Leary got arrested in Texas for possession of pot, the notoriety of his research in Millbrook spread. Law enforcement in nearby Poughkeepsie, led by Assistant District Attorney G. Gordon Liddy, raided the estate. In the summer of 1966, Leary and his associates ran a two-week seminar on consciousness expansion, culminating in a theatrical production of Hermann Hesse's *Steppenwolf* legend that weaved its way around the Millbrook grounds and buildings. Leary invited Liddy and members of the grand jury that indicted him, but none showed up.

For this occasion I drank my LSD with orange juice. Walking along the porch leading to the front doors of the Millbrook mansion, I passed a series of psychedelic Burma-Shave signs: *What . . . Is . . . Is . . . Within*. On the floor inside, the Holy Bible and *Scientific American* lay side by side like the proverbial lion and lamb. The event was a costume party. Musician Charlie Mingus was dressed as a sultan; novelist Alan Harrington had on a football uniform; playwright Sidney Kingsley was wearing a nightgown and beads. I had turned a pair of white pants into a makeshift straitjacket. Acid researcher Ralph Metzner told me I resembled an embryo.

Someone else said, "You're making fun of the crazy game, aren't you?"

"No," I replied, "I'm just a projective test."

In the kitchen, a man with a headache was about to take an aspirin.

"Wait," said Leary, "I'll be your guide." He returned to his conversation with a reporter from *Look* magazine. "Someday people won't ask what book you're reading," Leary said. "They'll ask which level of consciousness you're in contact with."

"Yeah," I interrupted, "but just like people lie about the books they read, they'll fake levels of consciousness too."

The *Look* reporter asked me, "Is Leary putting me on? He told me that everyone here is on LSD."

"Of course he's putting you on," I said. "Only the children are on LSD. Can't you tell by the way they're acting?"

Meanwhile, Shane Mage, a professor of Marxian economics, was walking around looking rather manic and carrying a fruit bowl that contained a couple of crushed cigarette packages which he was *stirring* rather joyfully. Somehow I was confident that he had a perfectly valid rationale for his behavior.

When I later interviewed Tim Leary, I mentioned his eating steak when we had dinner in New York. He had this response:

> I feel that part of me is mammalian and does demand and need animal fiber. In my plan for the future, there will be some carnivorous activity. We will be food-conscious, and we'll pay respect to the rights of the other species; as a matter of fact, starting next week, we're going to have animals on this property here in Millbrook. Some of these animals we will raise to slaughter, but we will not kill these animals until we know them well and have had LSD sessions with them, until we have seen that they have produced offspring. We will then preserve their offspring.

In *Esquire*, artist Ed Sorel lifted part of that quote from *The Realist*, and he caricatured Leary and a cow jumping over the moon together.

Leary and I became friends. He told me about prominent people whose lives had been changed by taking LSD—actor Cary Grant, director Otto Preminger, think-tanker Herman Kahn, Alcoholics Anonymous founder Bill Wilson, *Time* magazine publishers Henry Luce and Clare Boothe Luce. Of course, it wasn't so difficult to drop out when you had such a stimulating scene to drop *into*. But on the day that he announced the formation of a new religion, the League for Spiritual Discovery (LSD), I signed up as their first heretic.

Dick Alpert and I also became friends. We enjoyed what he called "upleveling" each other with honesty. On one occasion, we were at a party. I was particularly manic and he pointed it out, choosing an eggbeater as his analogy. I appreciated his reflection and calmed down.

On another occasion, Alpert, onstage at the Village Theater, was sitting in the lotus position on a cushion, talking about his mother dying and how there seemed to be a conspiracy on the part of relatives and hospital personnel alike to deny her the realization of that possibility. He also talked about some fellow in a mental institution who thought he was Jesus Christ. I teased him about having discussed his mother openly but concealing the fact that the man who thought he was Christ was his *brother*—death obviously carrying more respectability than craziness. At his next performance, Alpert identified the man as his brother.

★ ★ ★

LSD became illegal on the afternoon of October 6, 1966, and in San Francisco the event was publicized with the Diggers' "Prophecy of a Declaration of Independence":

> When in the flow of human events it becomes necessary for the people to cease to recognize the obsolete social patterns which had isolated man from his consciousness and to create with the youthful energies of the world revolutionary communities to which the two-billion-year-old life process entitles them, a decent respect to the opinions of mankind should declare the causes which impel them to this creation.
>
> We hold these experiences to be self-evident, that all is equal, that the creation endows us with certain inalienable rights, that among these are: the freedom of the body, the pursuit of joy, and the expansion of consciousness, and that to secure these rights, we the citizens of the earth declare our love and compassion for all conflicting hate-carrying men and women of the world.

The blossoming counterculture—encompassing sex, drugs, and rock 'n' roll—was at its core a spiritual revolution, with religions of repression being replaced by disciplines of liberation, where psychotropic drugs became a sacrament, sensuality developed into exquisite forms of personal art, and the way you lived your daily life demonstrated the heartbeat of your politics. There was an epidemic of idealism. Altruism became the highest form of selfishness.

The underground press was flourishing around the country, and the first psychedelic paper was the *San Francisco Oracle*. They interviewed me on one of my visits.

> **Q.** I was an atheist before I took LSD. Now I have an understanding of what is meant by God instead of just putting it down.

A. Now wait, I never put God down any more than I put Santa Claus down.

Q. Did your atheism change after LSD in any qualitative way?

A. No, no, how could it change? There was a different God I didn't believe in? People were very Christian before Christ ever existed, if he did. People were very humanistic before Humanism was ever organized. People were very loving before LSD was ever discovered. I dug defecating before I ever knew it was a Zen thing to do. So, what I'm saying is, awareness existed before LSD.

But there *was* an ecological renaissance in progress. While hundreds of thousands of gallons of milk were being dumped daily by farmers in twenty-five states, the Diggers were feeding their community at no cost. Standing in their rented garage, the Free Frame of Reference, I asked how they felt about charitable gestures.

Emmett Grogan responded, "Why don't you give us $10 and find out?"

I had heard of the Diggers' reputation for burning money, so I gave Grogan a *one*-dollar bill. He held it up, singing, "Paulie gave us a *dollar*. Paulie gave us a *dollar*." Then he touched it to a candle, and I watched my dollar bill burn. I had to put this into perspective. We were, after all, burning over a billion dollars every month to force Vietnam into seeking what we considered their proper destiny. Grogan placed the unburned corner of the dollar in the hand of an eight-year-old Negro boy who was hanging around the garage with his friends.

"Here," said Grogan, "bring this home to your mommy and ask her about poverty—and she'll slap your face."

The kid asked, "How can you do a stupid thing like that, burning a dollar bill?"

"You have another level to go," Grogan said.

I wasn't impressed. There were those who felt that if minority groups would only take LSD they'd stop aspiring to white middle-class values. But the desire to avoid rat bites might well have transcended white middle-class values. Ironically, the Diggers were spawned by a curfew that grew out of racial unrest. People had to be indoors if they weren't doing something specific. So the Diggers started making food for each other, cooking and eating in Golden Gate Park's Panhandle.

Not even the National Guard could make them go away. But it was still a compromise. To stand on a street corner—*waiting for no one*—that was the real goal, inspired by beat poet Gregory Corso's play, *Standing On a*

Street Corner. The Diggers had a strong theatrical bent, and they actually performed Corso's play *on* a street corner for passing pedestrians.

Hustling bruised food that would otherwise be thrown away at four o'clock in the morning and peeling a potato for the first time in your life at four o'clock in the afternoon were merely extensions of theater. Which helped explain the great tomato fight the Diggers had with a bushel of tomatoes given to them for the purpose of eating, not splattering.

The Diggers ran the Free Store, also known as the Trip Without a Ticket. All the clothing and other merchandise were donated. Nobody paid anything except the changes they went through. One afternoon a patron got caught shoplifting, and consequently she was aided in her selections by the clerk. I devoted an entire issue of *The Realist* to "The Digger Papers," and gave the Diggers forty thousand free copies.

Emmett Grogan was one of the most skillful bullshit artists I'd ever met. He bragged that he had coined the aphorism, "Today is the first day of the rest of your life." Actually, it was Gregory Corso. Grogan told me that the Diggers had slaughtered a horse to protest an execution at San Quentin. That was absolute horseshit.

When he came to New York, Grogan told me that Norman Mailer had complained to him that "LSD will make everybody pacifists," and that he replied, "C'mere, I'll bite your nose off." I foolishly printed that without first checking with Mailer, who denied having the conversation. I compounded that error in a show at the Village Theater, when someone in the audience asked me if Mailer had ever taken acid.

"No," I replied. "He's afraid that his cock would fall off."

Mailer was furious with me. He called Leary and Alpert "cunts on deodorant."

When a stage version of Mailer's novel, *The Deer Park*, was produced, I was invited to the opening night party. Strange energy abounded, from the cameo appearance of Woody Allen to the fight between journalist Pete Hamill and boxer Jose Torres. Somebody (not me) had invited a few grizzled street people to come up. They wore seedy overcoats and were dipping their bare hands into the punch bowl. I wrote about all this for my monthly society column in *Ramparts* as if it were the third act of his play, titled "The Deer Party."

I intended it as an affectionate piece, but Mailer called it "smarmy" and stopped speaking to me for a year. I had crossed the line, treating a friend like a media object.

★　★　★

When I was growing up, it was a sexual thrill just to get a quick glimpse of a girl's bra strap through the sleeve of her blouse. Now girls danced topless in the park. Bouncing bare breasts were definitely on the front lines of the sexual revolution. On December 31, 1966, the Sexual Freedom League invited me to their New Year's Eve Orgy in San Francisco. The party was for couples only, so I went with my friend, Margo St. James.

She was a member of the Psychedelic Rangers, who went around late at night painting fire hydrants in Day-Glo colors. A former hooker, she later launched a prostitutes' rights organization, COYOTE, an acronym for Call Off Your Old Tired Ethics. She turned the finest trick of her life when she spun prurient interest around on itself to spread the message of the first Hookers Convention. The official poster featured an illustration of a woman fingering her clitoris, with the slogan, "Our convention is different—we want *everybody* to come!"

Flo Kennedy, a radical black attorney, gave the keynote speech at the convention, titled "What is this Shit?" She asked why the FBI was orchestrating a "national campaign of busting prostitutes while everyone else is sucking their way to success *anyway*?" Then she answered her own question. "It's a control mechanism—of hookers, of veterans—of all victims. The government must maintain guilt as a tool of oppression over those whom they niggerize. Migrant farmers are brought in illegally, then they're on the defensive and can't fight for their rights."

Now, Margo was wearing one of her Christmas gifts, a brand-new nun's habit, and the cab driver gave her a rose. After we were admitted to the orgy site, because she had guests that evening, she gave me the rose and returned home. The party was in a large theatrical studio, with 150 people dancing in the nude. Behind the closed curtains on the stage there were fifteen small mattresses for those who wished to screw.

A few loners stood around backstage, playing with themselves as they ogled couples playing with each other. I sat on a chair, in the studio, conspicuous because I was fully dressed, sniffing my rose like a harmless voyeur. Then a naked girl sat down next to me. She had been dancing.

"Those guys out there," she complained, "they shouldn't just *automatically assume* they're gonna have intercourse with their dance partner of the moment."

"But," I asked, "in effect, aren't you cockteasing?"

"No. It's okay to hug when you're dancing close, but if a guy starts to kiss me or put his tongue in my ear, I tell him not to. Or if he begins to get an erection, then I tell him we'd better stop dancing. It's only fair. You have to draw the line somewhere."

At 11 PM, a league official announced that somebody had been smoking an illegal substance, and since the orgy, albeit legal, was especially vulnerable to a police visit, the smoker was endangering the other guests and should kindly leave. Three-quarters of the party left. By then I had taken off all my clothes so that I could fade into the crowd. A girl sitting next to me started stroking my knee. "You're very neighborly," I said. At 2 AM we went onstage and started making love on one of the mattresses. Suddenly the curtain opened. They were closing the theater. I looked up and saw a man who was sweeping the auditorium.

"Did we get the part?" I asked.

On New Year's Day, Margo St. James became *The Realist* Nun. She decided to wear her nun's habit when she drove me to the airport. She looked authentic, from the Mammy Yokum button-up shoes to the rimless granny glasses. However, she was wearing nail polish, the button under her collar read *Chastity is Its Own Punishment*, and her pubic hair was trimmed in the shape of a heart.

At the airport we kissed goodbye—bodies grinding, tongues wiggling, hands groping—as the waiting passengers watched in utter disbelief. I was wearing my dungaree jacket and looked like a Hell's Angel reject. They must have thought that Margo was from some particularly progressive order of nuns. She gave me a farewell pinch on the ass as we departed.

"Give my regards to Father Berrigan," I called out.

Naturally, I wrote about that incident in *The Realist*. Paul von Blum, an instructor at Golden Gate College, reprinted that account as part of the final exam for his political science class, assigning the students to write an essay about it, "particularly in terms of some of the ideas we discussed in our class when we dealt with the role of symbols and images."

On another occasion, Margo masturbated me in a porn movie theater while wearing her nun's outfit. Patrons were shocked more by us than by what was on the screen. The incident wasn't mentioned in any final exam, though.

★ ★ ★

Tim Leary had told me about the use of acid by Herman Kahn, director of the conservative Hudson Institute and author of *On Thermonuclear War*.

"Herman is not just a war planner," Leary said, "he's a civil-defense planner. Herman's claim is that he is one of the few highly placed Americans who's willing to gaze with naked eyes upon the possibilities of atomic warfare and come up with solutions to this horrible possibility. Perhaps his LSD sessions have given him this revelation and courage. And even his phrase, 'spasm war,' which to the intellectual liberals sounds gruesome, is a powerful, cellular metaphor describing an event which the very phrase itself, 'spasm war,' might prevent."

Now Herman Kahn had a request. He wanted me to guide him on a tour of the Lower East Side. When we met, his assistant, Anthony

Wiener, was there—he had been the conduit for CIA funding of the MK-ULTRA project, which used LSD in behavior-modification experiments with unaware subjects. Now Wiener was recommending a film, *The War Game*, to Herman Kahn.

"How does it scan?" asked Kahn.

"It scans beautiful," Wiener said, about to leave us. "But you really ought to see it, Herman. You're in it."

"Why? I saw *Dr. Strangelove*. I was in that."

I brought Kahn to Tompkins Square Park and told him about the police attack on hippies there. Kahn's point of view was that of one who attempts to create an objective scenario as the basis for his predictions of the future, such as, "The hippie dropout syndrome is delaying the guaranteed annual wage."

I told him that the CIA was running opium dens around Cambodia. He wasn't surprised, he said, because they smoke dope and show affection with equal openness. In his capacity as a human think tank, Kahn had been present when a Laotian general was briefing John Kennedy in the White House.

"The trouble with your people," complained the exasperated president, "is that they'd rather fuck than fight."

"Wouldn't you?" replied the general.

Kahn and I stopped in a bookstore.

"I'll show you the books I bought," I said, "if you'll show me the books you bought."

"You know," he replied, "when I was three years old, I said to a little girl, 'I'll show you mine if you'll show me yours'—and she wouldn't do it—now you'll print that because I was frustrated as a child I want to blow up the world."

He had purchased a collection of poetry by Allen Ginsberg, a book on Russian economics, a John Hersey novel, short stories by Isaac Singer, and *LSD and Problem Solving* by Peter Stafford and B.H. Golightly. Then I took him to the Underground Head Shop, where he bought a poster that warned, CHICKEN LITTLE WAS RIGHT!

* * *

The office of *The East Village Other* was across the street from *The Realist*. I dropped by one time when the editors—Walter Bowart, Alan Katzman, and Dean Latimer—were discussing a book, *Morning of the Magicians*. They were intrigued to learn that LSD released serotonin in brain receptors. They wondered if it was in nonchemical substances, and learned that serotinin could be found in bananas, inspiring them to launch the great banana hoax. The *Berkeley Barb* picked up the story, then the Underground Press Syndicate—and finally the mainstream wire services—spread it around the country.

It quickly became public knowledge that you could get legally high from smoking dried banana skins. In San Francisco, there was a banana smoke-in, and one entrepreneur started a successful banana-powder mail-order business, charging $5 an ounce. Agents from the Bureau of Narcotics and Dangerous Drugs headed for their own laboratory, faithfully cooking, scraping, and grinding thirty pounds of bananas according to the recipe in the underground press. For three weeks, the Food and Drug Administration utilized an apparatus that "smoked" the dried banana peels.

The *Los Angeles Free Press* in turn promoted yet another hallucinogenic—pickled jalapeño peppers, anally inserted. All over Southern California, heads were sticking vegetables up their asses. And, at a benefit for the Diggers, I mentioned onstage that the next big drug would be FDA. Sure enough, *Time* magazine soon reported that there would be "a super-hallucinogen called FDA." Silly me, I thought I had made that up.

When *Time* decided to do a cover story on the hippies, a cable to their San Francisco bureau instructed researchers to "go at the description and delineation of the subculture as if you were studying the Samoans or the Trobriand Islanders." It was a proper anthropological approach.

For example, at the Summer Solstice celebration in Golden Gate Park, the same hippies who ridiculed Lyndon Johnson's call for a national day of prayer were now imploring the sun to come out at 5 AM. Although they had given up trying to influence the administration, they were still trying to influence the universe.

★   ★   ★

In May 1967, *An Evening with God* was held at the Village Theater in celebration of the Pentecost—a benefit for Reverend James McGraw's *Renewal*, a Christian magazine—with Dick Gregory, Tim Leary, Malcolm Boyd, Harvey Cox, Len Chandler, and myself—"Speaking of the Devil," according to the poster. I was to be their token nonbeliever.

The night before, I had been in bed with Sandy, Norman Mailer's assistant. While we were making love, there was an evangelist on the radio providing a strangely appropriate background. He was talking about the importance of having "a firm God" and about "sliding your finger into any passage in the Bible." It was funny until he claimed that six million slaughtered Jews in Nazi Germany were doomed to Hell because they had never accepted Jesus Christ as their savior, yet Adolf Eichmann went to Heaven because he had converted to Christianity a couple of days before he was executed. Sandy made the most religious statement that whole night.

"I'm so glad I have a cunt," she said. It was a celebration of life.

At *An Evening with God*, I told that story and invited the women in the audience—including several nuns—to repeat Sandy's chant after me as a congregational response. "All right, now everybody—*I'm so glad I have a cunt.*" There was only laughter and booing. "I'm sorry, I didn't mean to offend you with such crudity. Okay, please repeat after me: *I'm so glad I have a vagina.*" But they still didn't respond. "You mean you *aren't* glad?"

I concluded my talk at *An Evening with God*: "I stand before you as an atheist, doing what men of the cloth should be doing. A couple of decades ago, Joe Louis said, 'God is on our side.' Now Muhammad Ali is saying, 'We're on God's side.'"

Then I burned, not my draft card, but a Photostat of it. That way I would be able to continue burning my draft card over and over again. In fact, I burned Photostats of my draft card at campuses in a dozen states.

"What can the authorities do," I asked a courtroom filled with students at Harvard Law School—"send me a Photostat of a subpoena?"

* * *

True to its amorality, the Mafia had reportedly financed the printing of a poster showing the faces of Lyndon Johnson and Hubert Humphrey superimposed on the bodies of Peter Fonda and Dennis Hopper riding their motorcycles in *Easy Rider*. Now the Mafia was getting into the business of distributing LSD. A friend asked me to test a capsule, so I decided to take it at Expo in Montreal. I had been invited to speak at the Youth Pavilion and also to give my impressions, on Canadian TV, of the United States Pavilion—a huge geodesic dome engineered by Buckminster Fuller.

Before entering the United States Pavilion—which was guarded by marines who had gone to Protocol School—I ingested the acid. I began the CBC interview—saying, "It's really beautiful, with all these flowing colors; you don't see them, but I do"—and ended up burning a Photostat of my draft card. "Now, the reason I'm doing this," I said, "is because we get hung up on symbols. People will be more upset about this than about the fact that *children* are being burned alive."

The marine lieutenant called his captain. When the interview was finished, the captain told me it was against the law to burn my draft card. So I took out my draft card and showed it to them.

"But he *burned* it," the marine insisted. "I *saw* him, sir. He *burned* it."

"I burned a *Photostat* of my draft card," I explained. "So I lied on television. That's not a crime. People do it all the time."

"It's also against the law to make a *copy* of your draft card," the captain said.

"Well, I destroyed the evidence."

I knew that political demonstrations were barred at Expo, but I had managed to smuggle one in. The interview was labeled an "incident," and there was a heated argument between the U.S. Information Agency and CBC, but the incident was already on tape, so now it had become a free-speech issue. It would be shown on TV that night and become front-page news in Montreal papers the next day.

Just as I was leaving the United States Pavilion, a band struck up a fanfare, and I made the mistake of projecting my own feelings, and suddenly I was convinced that LSD had been sprayed into the air, that *everybody* was tripping, that peace and love were breaking out all over the world *at that very moment*. As I was walking along, I started smiling at people and waving to them, and they were smiling and waving back. But then a core of reality came to the surface, the force of my own feedback made me turn around, and I saw that those same people were now *pointing* at me. What an asshole!

Still blushing, I found a phone booth and called up my friend in New York. "Well, you can tell the Mafia that I don't approve of their methods *or* their goals, but their acid is pretty powerful."

It was the Summer of Love.

★ ★ ★

While visiting Los Angeles in 1967, I was a guest on the Mort Sahl show. He had a blackboard on which he wrote "We Demand Faith in the Future." He wanted to have a mock trial on his program as a preview of the Vietnam War Crimes Tribunal, and he asked me to act as a defense attorney for Lyndon Johnson, Dean Rusk, and Robert McNamara. I agreed to do it and said that I would have them plead not guilty by reason of insanity.

I was also a guest on the Joe Pyne show. Phil Ochs offered to drive me there. We had become friends when he asked for permission to write a song, "The Ballad of William Worthy," based on an article in *The Realist* by Worthy, an award-winning journalist whose passport had been revoked.

Joe Pyne held up a copy of *The Realist* and called it "a filthy, avant-garde, left-wing rag." He asked me, "Why do you feel compelled to print the most obscene words in the English language every month?"

"Well," I replied, "why do *you* feel compelled to underline a few words in a magazine that contains twenty or thirty thousand words?"

"Does your magazine cater to homosexuals?"

"Why, Joe? Did you find something that appeals to you?"

"Well, this caught my eye here. You printed a cartoon about a homosexual act."

The cartoon, by Bud Handelsman, depicted a man sitting at a huge desk, speaking on the telephone: "I'm very sorry, but we of the FBI are powerless to act in a case of oral-genital intimacy unless it has in some way obstructed interstate commerce."

"Joe, that's also a *heterosexual* act."

But he wouldn't let me read the caption out loud to allow the audience to decide for itself.

"Why are you for the repeal of abortion laws?" he asked.

"Because I don't think that a woman should have to bear an unwanted child as punishment for an accidental conception."

"Do you edit your magazine because you were an unwanted child?"

"No, Daddy."

Pyne tried to give me a hard time about a photo I had reprinted from the *Reader's Digest* showing Jimmy Durante standing behind a little disabled boy as though he were dry-humping him.

> PYNE: I won't give this man's name, but he's probably one of the most beloved stars in all of the history of entertainment, and some time ago he posed for what obviously was an Easter Seal picture with a crippled child on crutches—a child that looks to be about maybe a year and a half—and the—whatever information there was about that picture has been cropped and Krassner has put on the top: "Soft-Core Pornography of the Month," and below indicates that the man is a child molester. And this is what I mean about how [*glancing at me*] how this man can take everything that is decent and—and worthwhile—and twist it into something that is—Marquis de Sade looked like a Boy Scout compared to you.
>
> KRASSNER: Well, let me just explain that. The beloved movie star you're talking about is—
>
> PYNE: Don't mention his name, please?
>
> KRASSNER: —obviously not a child molester, we all know that. The point of this whole feature—continuing feature called "Soft-Core Pornography of the Month"—is simply to point out that obscenity exists only in the mind of the beholder, and that people can take a tender scene like that and find something dirty in it, if they wish.
>
> PYNE: Where do you say all that, Mr. Krassner? All you say is

"Soft-Core Pornography of the Month" on the top, and then you say "Peterofilia in the *Reader's Digest*" on the bottom.

KRASSNER: It's pedophilia, Joe. Well, do you think for a moment that anybody's going to take that seriously, and think we're actually accusing that beloved movie star—

PYNE: Well, I have such respect for this man that I take it seriously . . .

Then he began making vicious references to the scar tissue on my face. "Well, Joe, if you're gonna ask questions like that, then let me ask *you*: Do you take off your wooden leg before you make love with your wife?"

Pyne had lost his leg as a marine in World War II. Now his jaw literally dropped, the audience gasped, the producers averted their eyes and the atmosphere became surrealistic as Pyne went through the motions of continuing the interview. One feature of his show was the Beef Box, a podium with a microphone, where members of the audience could ask questions or make comments. One after another, his loyal fans understandably lambasted me. Then Phil Ochs was standing at the podium.

"Isn't it true," Pyne asked me, "that the man that is now in the dock is known to you as one of the leaders of the hippie revolution?"

"No, he's known to me as a folksinger."

"Uh-huh. Mr. Ochs, are you a hippie?"

"No."

"Do you play for the hippies, mostly?"

"No, I play for everybody."

Pyne had been put off balance by my question. He even called the *next* guest Mr. Krassner. When that interview was concluded and the guest made the mistake of trying to embrace him, Pyne shoved him away and made threatening karate gestures. The show was over, and Pyne walked off the set, hair mussed, loosening his tie. On his way out of the studio, he passed by me, sitting in an aisle seat in the audience.

"Son of a bitch put his hands on me," he muttered. "That I don't like."

When Ochs and I left, I told him about a pro-choice rally where 150 people marched from Times Square to St. Patrick's Cathedral. The tail end of the parade started first, so that the single-letter cards they carried, which had been arranged to read LEGALIZE ABORTION, came out backward, NOITROBA EZILAGEL. As they rounded a corner, you could see only the BAEZ portion.

"Must be folksingers," a bystander observed.

★ ★ ★

There was a concert in Pittsburgh, with the Grateful Dead, the Velvet Underground, the Fugs, and me. There were two shows, both completely sold out, and this was the first time anybody had realized how many hippies actually lived in Pittsburgh.

Backstage between shows, a man sidled up to me.

"Call me Bear," he said.

"Okay, you're Bear."

"Don't you recognize me?"

"You look familiar, but—"

"I'm Owsley."

Of course—Owsley acid! He presented me with a tab of Monterey Purple LSD. Not wishing to carry around an illegal drug in my pocket, I swallowed it instead. Soon I found myself in the lobby talking with Jerry Garcia. As people from the audience wandered past us, he whimsically stuck out his hand, palm up.

"Got any spare change?"

Somebody gave him a dime, and Garcia said, "Thanks."

"He didn't recognize you," I said.

"See, we all look alike."

In the course of our conversation, I used the word "evil" to describe somebody.

"There are no evil people," Garcia said, just as the LSD was settling into my psyche. "There are only victims."

"What does that mean? If a rapist is a victim, you should have compassion when you kick 'im in the balls?"

I did the second show while the Dead were setting up behind me. Then they began to play, softly, and as they built up their riff, I faded out and left the stage. Later, some local folks brought me to a restaurant which, they told me, catered to a Mafia clientele. With my long brown curly hair underneath my Mexican cowboy hat, I didn't quite fit in. The manager came over and asked me to kindly remove my hat. I was still tripping. I hardly ate any of my spaghetti after I noticed how it was wiggling on my plate.

I glanced around at the various Mafia figures sitting at their tables, wondering if they had killed anybody. Then I remembered what Jerry Garcia had said about evil. So these guys might be executioners, but they were also victims. The spaghetti was still wiggling on my plate, but then I realized it wasn't really spaghetti, it was actually worms in tomato sauce.

The other people at my table were all pretending not to notice.

* * *

Each tablet of Owsley White Lightning contained three hundred micrograms of LSD. I had purchased a large enough supply from Dick Alpert to finance his trip to India. The day before he left to meditate for six months, we sat in a restaurant discussing the concept of choiceless awareness while trying to decide what to order on the menu.

In India, he gave his guru three tablets, and apparently nothing happened.

Alpert's postcard beckoned, "Come fuck the universe with me."

Instead, I stayed tripping in America, where I kept my entire stash of acid in a bank vault deposit box.

LSD was influencing music, painting, spirituality, and the stock market. Tim Leary once let me listen in on a call from a Wall Street broker thanking him for turning him onto acid because it gave him the courage to sell short. Leary had a certain sense of pride about the famous folks he and his associates had introduced to the drug.

"But," he told me, "I consider Otto Preminger one of our failures."

I first met Preminger in 1960 while I was conducting a panel on censorship for *Playboy*. He had defied Hollywood's official seal of approval by refusing to change the script of *The Moon Is Blue*. He wouldn't take out the word *virgin*.

At the end of our interview, he asked, "Ven you tronscripe dis, vill you vix op my Henglish?"

"Oh, sure," I replied quickly. "Of course."

"Vy? Vot's drong viz my Henglish?"

I saw Otto Preminger again in 1967. He was making a movie called *Skidoo*, starring Jackie Gleason as a retired criminal. Preminger told me he had originally intended the role for Frank Sinatra.

Skidoo was pro-acid propaganda thinly disguised as a comedy adventure. However, LSD was not why the FBI was annoyed with the film. Rather, according to Gleason's FBI files, the FBI objected to one scene in the script where a file cabinet is stolen from an FBI building. Gleason was later approved as a special FBI contact in the entertainment business.

One of the characters in *Skidoo* was a Mafia chieftain named God. Screenwriter Bill Cannon had suggested Groucho Marx for the part. Preminger said it wasn't a good idea, but since they were already shooting and that particular character was needed on the set in three days, Groucho would be playing God after all. During one scene, Preminger was screaming instructions at him.

Groucho yelled back, "Are you drunk?"

I had dinner with him that evening. He was concerned about the script of *Skidoo* because it pretty much advocated LSD, which he had never tried, but he was curious. Moreover, he felt a certain responsibility to his young audience not to steer them wrong, so could I possibly get him some pure stuff and would I care to accompany him on a trip? I did not play hard to get. We arranged to ingest those little white tablets one afternoon at the home of an actress in Beverly Hills.

Groucho was especially interested in the countercultural aspects of LSD. I mentioned a couple of incidents that particularly tickled him, and his eyes sparkled with delight. One was about how, on Haight Street, runaway youngsters, refugees from their own families, had stood outside a special tourist bus—guided by a driver "trained in sociological significance"—and they held mirrors up to the cameras pointing at them from the windows, so that the tourists would get photos of themselves trying to take photos.

The other was about the day that LSD became illegal. In San Francisco, at precisely two o'clock in the afternoon, a cross-fertilization of mass protest and tribal celebration had taken place, as several hundred young people simultaneously swallowed tabs of acid while the police stood by helplessly.

"Internal possession wasn't against the law," I explained to Groucho.

"And they trusted their friends more than they trusted the government," he said. "I like that."

We had a period of silence and a period of listening to music. I was accustomed to playing rock and roll while tripping, but the record collection at this house consisted entirely of classical music and Broadway show albums. First, we listened to the "Bach Cantata No. 7."

"I'm supposed to be Jewish," Groucho said, "but I was seeing the most beautiful visions of Gothic cathedrals. Do you think Bach *knew* he was doing that?"

"I don't know. I was seeing beehives and honeycombs myself."

Later, we were listening to the score of a musical comedy, *Fanny*. There was one song called "Welcome Home," where the lyrics go something like, "Welcome home, says the clock," and the chair says, "Welcome home," and so do various other pieces of furniture. Groucho started acting out each line, as though he were actually *being* greeted by the clock, the chair, and the rest of the furniture. He was like a child, charmed by his own ability to respond to the music that way.

There was a bowl of fruit on the dining room table. During a snack, he said, "I never thought eating a nice juicy plum would be the biggest thrill of my life."

Then we talked about the sexual revolution. Groucho asked, "Have you ever laid two ladies together?" I told him about the time that I was being interviewed by a couple of students from a Catholic girls' school. Suddenly Sheila Campion, *The Realist*'s Scapegoat, and Marcia Ridge, the Shit-On—she had given herself that title because "what could be lower than a Scapegoat?"—walked out of their office totally nude.

"Sorry to interrupt, Paul," said Sheila, "but it's Wednesday—time for our weekly orgy."

The interviewers left in a hurry. Sheila and Marcia led me up the stairs to my loft bed, and we had a delicious threesome. It had never happened before and it would never happen again.

At one point in our conversation, Groucho somehow got into a negative space. He was equally cynical about institutions, such as marriage—"legal quicksand"—and individuals, such as Lyndon Johnson, whom he referred to as "that potato-head."

Eventually, I asked, "What gives you hope?"

He thought for a moment. Then he just said one word: "People."

I told him about the sketch I had written for Steve Allen, "Unsung Heroes of Television," with the man whose job it was on *You Bet Your Life* to wait for the secret word to be said so that he could drop the duck down, and Groucho told me about one of his favorite contestants on the show.

"He was an elderly gentleman with white hair, but quite a chipper fellow. I asked him what he did to retain his sunny disposition. 'Well, I'll tell you, Groucho,' he says, 'every morning I get up and I *make a choice* to be happy that day.'"

Groucho was holding onto his cigar for a long time, but he never smoked it, he only sniffed it occasionally. "Everybody has their own Laurel and Hardy," he mused. "A miniature Laurel and Hardy, one on each shoulder. Your little Oliver Hardy bawls you out—he says, 'Well, this is a *fine mess* you've gotten us into.' And your little Stan Laurel gets all weepy—'Oh, Ollie, I couldn't help it. I'm sorry, I did the best I could.'"

Later, when Groucho started chuckling to himself, I hesitated to interrupt his reverie, but I had to ask, "What struck you funny?"

"I was thinking about this movie, *Skidoo*," he said. "I mean some of it is just plain ridiculous. This hippie inmate puts a letter he got, which is soaked in LSD, into the water supply of the prison, and suddenly everybody gets completely reformed. There's a prisoner who says, 'Oh, gosh, now I don't have to be a rapist anymore!' But it's also sophisticated in its own way. I like how Jackie Gleason, the character he plays, *accepts* the fact that he's not the biological father of his daughter."

"Oh, really? That sounds like the ultimate ego loss."

"But I'm really getting a big kick out of playing somebody named God like a dirty old man. You wanna know why?"

"Typecasting?"

"No, no—it's because—do you realize that irreverence and reverence are the *same thing?*"

"Always?"

"If they're not, then it's a misuse of your power to make people laugh." His eyes began to tear. "That's funny," he said. "I'm not even sad."

Then he went to urinate. When he came back, he said, "You know, everybody is waiting for *miracles* to happen. But the whole *human body* is a goddamn miracle."

He recalled Otto Preminger telling him about his own response to taking LSD and then he mimicked Preminger's accent: "I saw *tings*, bot I did not zee myself." Groucho was looking in a mirror on the dining room wall, and he said, "Well, I can see *my*self, but I still don't understand what the hell I'm *doing* here . . ."

A week later, Groucho told me that members of the Hog Farm commune who were extras in the movie had turned him on with marijuana on the set of *Skidoo*.

"You know," I said, "my mother once warned me that LSD would lead to pot."

"Well, your mother was right."

When *Skidoo* was released, Tim Leary saw it, and he cheerfully admitted, "I was fooled by Otto Preminger. He's much hipper than me."

* * *

I met Otto Preminger again in 1969, when we were both guests on *The Merv Griffin Show*, guest-hosted by Orson Bean.

Deadpan comedian Jackie Vernon was also a guest on the show. He reacted to my long hair. "Why don't you take a bath?" he said. Nobody had ever asked me that on network TV before. Later, I would have a Monday-morning-quarterback session with George Carlin, who applied a kind of aikido to life as well as to comedy, turning negative energy into positive energy.

He suggested, "You should've said, 'Why, thank you, Jackie, I hadn't considered that.'"

But when it happened on TV, I was caught off guard and just kept silent. So did the audience. The tension was broken by Preminger.

"Dot iss duh seekness ov our society, dis stereotypical ottitood."

Then the audience applauded, and we went to commercial.

Over dinner, Preminger told me that his father was the equivalent of the attorney general in Austria before Hitler's conquest. And he said that someday he wanted to direct a film about Julius and Ethel Rosenberg.

"They were lynch victims of the Cold War," he said. "The law says spies can be executed during *wartime*. If Eisenhower had commuted their sentences to life, a less hysterical review of their case could later have resulted in their freedom."

Black Panther Eldridge Cleaver went underground to avoid being tried for a shootout in Oakland, and I mentioned on the show that I had interviewed him, which wasn't true, although Stew Albert was in fact trying to arrange such an interview. That week, a pair of FBI agents showed up at my loft. They wanted to know where Eldridge Cleaver was. I refused to let them in.

"Why should I cooperate with you?" I asked. "The FBI continually hassles people who haven't broken the law."

"Come on, now. That's the FBI. We're individuals."

"I don't believe it—this is just great—here's the FBI warning me about the danger of guilt by association."

★   ★   ★

In 1971, during an interview with *Flash* magazine, Groucho Marx said, "I think the only hope this country has is Nixon's assassination." Yet he wasn't subsequently arrested for threatening the life of a president. In view of the indictment against Black Panther David Hilliard for using similar rhetoric, I wrote to the Justice Department to find out the status of their case against Groucho, and received this reply:

> Dear Mr. Krassner:
>
> Responding to your inquiry, the Supreme Court has held that Title 18 U.S.C., Section 871, prohibits only "true" threats. It is one thing to say that "I (or *we*) will kill Richard Nixon" when you are the leader of an organization which advocates killing people and overthrowing the Government; it is quite another to utter the words which are attributed to Mr. Marx, an alleged comedian. It was the opinion of both myself and the United States Attorney in Los Angeles (where Marx's words were alleged to have been uttered) that the latter utterance did not constitute a "true" threat.
>
> Very Truly Yours,
> James L. Browning, Jr.
> United States Attorney

It would later be revealed that the FBI had published pamphlets in the name of the Black Panthers, advocating the killing of cops, and that an FBI file on Groucho Marx had indeed been started, and he actually *was* labeled a "national security risk." I phoned Groucho to tell him the good news.

"I deny everything," he said, "because I lie about everything." He paused, then added, "And everything I *deny* is a lie."

* * *

The last time I saw Groucho was in 1976. He was speaking at the Los Angeles Book Fair. He looked frail and unsmiling, but he was alert and irascible as ever. He took questions from the audience.

"Are you working on a film now?"

"No, I'm answering silly questions."

"What are your favorite films?"

"*Duck Soup. Night at the Opera.*"

"What do you think about Richard Nixon?"

"He should be in jail."

"Is humor an important issue in the presidential campaign?"

"Get your finger out of your mouth."

"What do you dream about?"

"Not about you."

"What inspired you to write?"

"A fountain pen. A piece of paper."

Then I called out a question: "What gives you the most optimism?"

I expected him to say "people" again, but this time he said, "The world."

There was hardly any standing room left in the auditorium, yet one fellow was sitting on the floor rather than take the aisle seat occupied by a large Groucho Marx doll.

CHAPTER 6

THE PARTS LEFT OUT
OF THE KENNEDY BOOK

JOHN F. KENNEDY HAD A REPUTATION FOR BEING A REAL WOMANIZER. Sweet young models asked not what their country could do for them as they were frisked by Secret Service agents—in a lingering fashion—because the president was a busy fellow and had no time for foreplay. Early in 1962 I began hearing stories about JFK, ranging from a Newport socialite who bore twins by him, to a blonde showgirl who landed in a helicopter on the White House lawn.

Then I heard a rumor that he had been married previous to Jackie Kennedy, and I got a tip that there was a genealogy that actually listed the alleged previous marriage. I decided to check it out as a matter of routine procedure, and sure enough, *The Blauvelt Family Genealogy*, published in 1957, had the following listing on page 884, under Eleventh Generation:

> (12,427) DURIE (Kerr) MALCOLM (Isabel O. Cooper [her mother] 11,304). We have no birth date. She was born Kerr, but took the name of her stepfather. She first married Firmin Desloge IV. They were divorced, and she married, third, John F. Kennedy, son of Joseph P. Kennedy, one time Ambassador to England. There were no children of the second or third marriages.

That rumor had now become the basis of a valid news report. I called up the White House for the first time in my life.

"May I speak to President Kennedy, please?"

"Who's calling the president?"

"Paul Krassner of *The Realist* magazine in New York City."

"The president is in conference right now."

"Can I speak to [Press Secretary] Pierre Salinger?"

"I'm sorry, he's tied up right now."

"How about [Salinger's assistant] Andrew Hatcher?"

"Mr. Hatcher isn't here right now. Is there anybody else who could help you?"

I settled for a lower echelon employee and asked about the genealogy.

"Well, it's completely untrue."

"Could you elaborate on that at all?"

"You want a real statement, don't you?"

"I suppose so."

"This is not for publication, but for guidance. There are three mistakes in that. One is that she was never married to the president. The second is that they have the two husbands in the wrong order. And the third is that since 1947 she's been married to a Mr. Thomas Shevlin. She's been living in Palm Beach and Long Island."

"Is there any reason that it's not for publication? Because, you know, the rumor has been going around. It's the most frequently asked question at the *Daily News* Information Bureau."

"You just can't say 'Mr. Salinger said' or you can't say 'The White House said' either. But you can go on and quote what I just gave you. You could say 'A reliable source said.'"

I learned that supporters of Barry Goldwater had been systematically spreading the rumor, but Goldwater told friends that *he* believed the Democrats were behind it in order to discredit the Republicans.

The wedding between Durie Malcolm and John Kennedy was supposed to have taken place in Oyster Bay in March 1947. The compilers of the genealogy wouldn't speak to me, but I finally reached Durie Malcolm by phone. She had nothing to say though. She had married her third—or fourth—husband, Thomas Shevlin, on July 11, 1947. On their marriage certificate, where it called for the number of times previously married, she wrote only *one* and listed Fermin Desloge.

When word got out that *The Realist* was going to publish the item, I was contacted by newspapers, magazines, wire services, radio and TV news departments, and various foreign correspondents. Syndicated columnist Drew Pearson had been ready to run it a year earlier. Instead, his assistant, Jack Anderson, sent a confidential memo to all editors who carried the column.

He told me, "I thought it might be wise, for the White House to acknowledge the rumor and to squelch it at this point."

I published the genealogy excerpt together with the White House denial in the March issue. *The New York Times* sent a reporter to my office to make sure that *The Realist* had gotten into the mail and onto the newsstands. Later, the night city editor of the *Times* sent a messenger to pick up a copy of the *Daily News* as soon as it hit the streets, because there was a rumor that the *News* was going to break the story, and if it did, then the *Times* would too, but the *News* didn't, so the *Times* didn't either.

Newsweek sent over a pair of researchers who interviewed me for two hours. "We've been waiting for somebody to break this story," said one. I asked, "Why didn't *you* break it?"—and the answer was one word: "Fear." A *Time* magazine researcher told me, "If anybody picks up this story from *The Realist*, then *Time* will jump in with both feet."

In September, *Parade*, a Sunday supplement to seventy papers, carried an item about the rumor after receiving twelve thousand inquiries. A few weeks later, *Newsweek* broke the story, with a reprint in advance by *The Washington Post*. The *Newsweek* report stated: "The story first appeared in a beatnik Greenwich Village magazine of slight circulation, *The Realist*."

The next issue of *Time* carried a two-page article, which stated: "In the absence of forthright denials, the story—and the rumors—grew. Last March, *The Realist*, a shabby Greenwich Village periodical, published the fact of the Blauvelt genealogical entry as an 'expose.'"

Between the *Newsweek* and *Time* articles, AP dispatched the story and it became front-page news. The *New York Post* headline: "JFK Wed Before? White House Says No." The *Times* carried a long article, mentioning that *The Realist* had "published the text of the entry." The following paragraph appeared in the Monday night "early bird" edition of the *Times* but was cut out of all succeeding editions:

> Some members of the far-flung family do not believe Mr. Blauvelt [deceased compiler of the genealogy] was in error. James Blauvelt told a member of *The New York Times* Washington Bureau that some of the family believed Howard Ira Durie [who assisted in the compilation] had been "paid off" by the Kennedys.

The *News-Bulletin*, published by the Cinema Educational Guild, stated:

> We have received a number of letters from old friends of the Kennedy family in Massachusetts and Cape Cod. Several of the letters distinctly verified the marriage, all of them stating that it made Rose, Jack's mother, very unhappy. However, she looked upon the marriage as just "one of Jack's youthful escapades," which she was sure "wouldn't last long"—and it didn't . . . In conversation with a close friend, John Bersbach, Durie's first husband, expressed full knowledge of her marriage with Kennedy.

When the genealogy-denial story hit the newspapers, it also broke on radio and TV. A Washington commentator on the *Huntley-Brinkley Report* added that NBC had the story for a long time but had the good sense not to use it. Actually, there was a memo on the bulletin board in the NBC newsroom ordering broadcasters not to carry the story in any form until it broke in some other medium or on some other network.

* * *

The executive committee of the Free Speech Movement on the Berkeley campus had been debating whether it would be appropriate for Mario Savio to lead protesting students in to occupy the Administration Building.

Barbara Garson announced, "I don't believe in the cult of personality, but if you've got one, use it."

At the final sit-in of the Free Speech Movement in December 1964, Marvin Garson, Barbara's husband, was noticeably missing. He had gone to Dallas to work for Mark Lane, who was investigating a possible conspiracy behind the assassination of John F. Kennedy. In the February 1965 issue of *The Realist*, I published Lane's claim that the bullet had really been fired from in front of the president's limousine because the doctors first said that the bullet hole in the throat was an entrance wound. He implied that there was chicanery when the federal pathologists later developed the wound-from-the-rear theory.

Meanwhile, in the memorial market, a John F. Kennedy salt-and-pepper shaker set went on sale. The pepper was in a china rocking chair; the salt was in a removable china figure of the president sitting in the rocking chair, with three holes in his back for pouring out the salt.

Four months after Kennedy was killed, his former press secretary, Pierre Salinger, called William Manchester to tell him that the family was authorizing him to write a book on the assassination. Manchester had not been their first choice. He would be playing a sloppy third to historians Theodore White and Walter Lord, dangling somewhere between the making of a president and the sinking of the *Titanic*. Bobby Kennedy made the official announcement in March 1964. He didn't mention an agreement giving him and Jackie Kennedy power to approve the manuscript.

Lyndon Johnson and Marina Oswald, widow of the alleged assassin, refused to grant interviews to Manchester, but Jackie submitted to ten hours of intimacy with his tape recorder. Two years later she would insist on cutting material that was too personal for publication. Bobby sent a telegram to Evan Thomas, editor in chief at Harper & Row, suggesting that the book "should neither be published nor serialized."

Thomas wrote to Kennedy advisers, asking for help in revising the manuscript, which he felt was "gratuitously and tastelessly insulting" to Johnson. Bennett Cerf of Random House read an unedited manuscript and said it contained "unbelievable things that happened after the assassination." Jackie filed a lawsuit.

She proclaimed, "Anyone who is against me will look like a rat, unless I run off with Eddie Fisher."

And indeed, the case was settled out of court in January 1967. Harper & Row made the requested deletions. So did *Look* magazine, which had purchased serialization rights for $665,000.

However, *Stern*, a German magazine with foreign serialization rights for the book, refused to make the deletions. *Look* described the last night of President Kennedy's life in a Texas hotel, but *Stern* went into detail about the special mattress that had been installed for his back problem. It was a double bed with a single mattress. Jackie had to sleep in another room. But why should American readers be denied the irony of what Lee Harvey Oswald and John Kennedy had in common—that on the night before one allegedly killed the other, neither had slept with his wife?

Then, in the middle of serialization, even *Stern* yielded to Jackie's lawyers and agreed to omit certain passages that she found unbearably offensive. The public's curiosity became even more aroused. This was a job for *The Realist*. I set about the task of obtaining the missing portions of Manchester's book.

Finally, on a brisk Saturday afternoon in February 1967, I took a long walk west to my printer in Greenwich Village. I was both exhilarated and frightened, but my only alternative would've been not to publish, and that was a totally unacceptable alternative. I delivered the following manuscript:

THE PARTS LEFT OUT OF THE KENNEDY BOOK

An executive in the publishing industry, who obviously must remain anonymous, has made available to The Realist *a Photostat copy of the original manuscript of William Manchester's book,* The Death of a President. *Those passages which are printed here were marked for deletion months before Harper & Row sold the serialization rights to* Look *magazine; hence they do not appear even in the so-called "complete" version published by the German magazine* Stern.

At the Democratic National Convention in the summer of 1960, Los Angeles was the scene of a political visitation of the alleged sins of the father upon the son. Lyndon Johnson found himself battling for the presidential nomination with a young, handsome, charming, and witty adversary, John F. Kennedy.

The Texan in his understandable anxiety degenerated to a strange campaign tactic. He attacked his opponent on the grounds that his father, Joseph P. Kennedy, was a Nazi sympathizer during the time he was United States Ambassador to Great Britain, from 1938 to 1940. The senior Kennedy had predicted that Germany would defeat England, and he therefore urged President Franklin D. Roosevelt to withhold aid. Now Johnson found himself fighting pragmatism with pragmatism. It did not work; he lost the nomination.

Ironically, the vicissitudes of regional bloc voting forced Kennedy into selecting Johnson as his running mate. Jack rationalized the practicality of the situation, but Jackie was constitutionally unable to forgive Johnson. Her attitude toward him always remained one of controlled paroxysm.

It was common knowledge in Washington social circles that the Chief Executive was something of a ladies' man. His staff included a Secret Service agent, referred to by the code name *Dentist*, whose duties virtually centered around escorting to and from a rendezvous site—either in the District of Columbia or while traveling—the models, actresses, and other strikingly attractive females chosen by the president for his not at all infrequent trysts. "Get me that," he had said of a certain former Dallas beauty contest winner when plans for the tour were first being discussed. That particular aspect of the itinerary was changed, of course, when Mrs. Kennedy decided to accompany her husband.

She was aware of his philandering, but would cover up her dismay by joking, "It runs in the family." The story had gotten back to her about the late Marilyn Monroe using the telephone in her Hollywood bathroom to make a long distance call to *New York Post* film-gossip columnist Sidney Skolsky.

"Sid, you won't believe this," she had whispered, "but the Attorney General of our country is waiting for me in my bed this very minute—I just had to tell you."

* *

It is difficult to ascertain where on the continuum of Lyndon Johnson's personality innocent boorishness ends and deliberate sadism begins. To have summoned then-Secretary of the Treasury Douglas Dillon for a conference wherein he, the new president, sat defecating as he spoke, might charitably be an example of the former; but to challenge under the same circumstances Senator J. William Fulbright for his opposition to Administration policy in Vietnam is considered by insiders to be a frightening instance of the latter. The more Jacqueline Kennedy has tried to erase the crudeness of her husband's successor from consciousness, the more it has impinged upon her memories and reinforced her resentment.

"It's beyond style," she would confide to friends. "Jack had style, but this is beyond style."

When Arthur Schlesinger, Jr. related to her an incident that he had witnessed firsthand—Mr. Johnson had actually placed his penis over the railing of the yacht, bragging to onlookers, "Watch it touch bottom!"—Mrs. Kennedy could not help but shiver with disgust. Capitol Hill reporters have observed the logical extension of Mr. Johnson boasting about his six-o'clock-in-the-morning forays with Lady Bird, to his bursts of phallic exhibitionism, whether it be on a boat or at the swimming pool or in the lavatory.

Apropos of this tendency, Drew Pearson's assistant, Jack Anderson, has remarked: "When Lyndon announces there's going to be a joint session of Congress, everybody cringes."

It is true that Mrs. Kennedy withstood the pressures of publicized scandal, ranging from the woman who picketed the White House carrying a blown-up photograph supposedly of Jack Kennedy sneaking away from the home of Jackie's press secretary, Pamela Turnure, to *The Blauvelt Family Genealogy* which claimed on page 884, under Eleventh Generation, that one Durie Malcolm had "married, third, John F. Kennedy, son of Joseph P. Kennedy, one time Ambassador to England."

But it was the personal infidelities that gnawed away at her—as indeed they would gnaw away at *any* wife who has been shaped by this culture—until finally Jackie left in exasperation. Her father-in-law offered her one million dollars to reconcile. She came back, not for the money, but because she sincerely believed that the nation needed Jack Kennedy, and she didn't want to bear the burden of losing enough public favor to forestall his winning the presidency.

Consequently, she was destined to bear a quite different burden—with great ambivalence—the paradox of fame. She enjoyed playing her role to the hilt, but complained, "Can't they get it into their heads that there's a difference between being the First Lady and being Elizabeth Taylor?" Even after she became First Widow, the movie magazines would not—or could not—leave her alone.

Probably the most bizarre invasion of her privacy occurred in *Photoplay*, which asked the question, "Too Soon for Love?"—then proceeded to print a coupon that readers were requested to answer and send in. They had a multiple choice: "Should Jackie (1) Devote her life exclusively to her children and the memory of her husband? (2) Begin to date—privately or publicly—and eventually remarry? (3) Marry right away?"

Mrs. Kennedy fumed. "Why don't they give them some *more* decisions to make for me? Some *real* ones. Should I live in occasional sin? Should I use a diaphragm or the pill? Should I keep it in the medicine cabinet or the bureau drawer?" But she would never lose her dignity in public; she had too deep a faith in her own image.

★ ★

American leaders seem to have a schizophrenic approach toward each other. They *want* to expose their human frailties at the same time that they do *not* want to remove them from their pedestals. Bobby Kennedy privately abhors Lyndon Johnson, but publicly calls him "great, and I mean that in every sense of the word." Johnson has referred to Bobby as "that little shit" in private, but continues to laud him for the media.

Gore Vidal has no such restraint. On a television program in London, he explained why Jacqueline Kennedy would never relate to Lyndon Johnson. During that tense flight from Dallas to Washington after the assassination, she inadvertently walked in on him as he was standing over the casket of his predecessor and chuckling. This disclosure was the talk of London, but did not reach these shores.

Of course, President Johnson is often given to inappropriate response—witness the puzzled timing of his smiles when he speaks of grave matters—but we must also assume that Mrs. Kennedy had been traumatized that day and her perception was likely to have been colored by the tragedy. This state of shock must have underlain an incident on Air Force One which this writer conceives to be delirium, but which Mrs. Kennedy insists she actually saw. "I'm telling you this for the historical record," she said, "so that people a hundred years from now will know what I had to go through."

She corroborated Gore Vidal's story, continuing: "That man [Johnson] was crouching over the corpse, no longer chuckling but breathing hard and moving his body rhythmically. At first I thought he must be performing some mysterious symbolic rite he'd learned from Mexicans or Indians as a boy. And then I realized—there is only one way to say this—he was literally fucking my husband in the throat. In the bullet wound in the front of his throat. He reached a climax and dismounted. I froze. The next thing I remember, he was being sworn in as the new president."

[Handwritten marginal notes: *1. Check with Rankin—did secret autopsy show semen in throat wound? 2. Is this simply necrophilia, or was LBJ trying to change entry wound from grassy knoll into exit wound from Book Depository by enlarging it?*]

The glaze lifted from Jacqueline Kennedy's eyes.

"I don't believe that Lyndon Johnson had anything to do with a conspiracy, but I do know this—Jack taught me about the nuances of power—if he were miraculously to come back to life and suddenly appear in front of him, the first thing Johnson would do *now* is kill him." She smiled sardonically, adding, "Unless Bobby beat him to it."

* * *

Barbara and Marvin Garson had moved from Berkeley to New York City, but she wouldn't allow him to smoke marijuana in the house, so he had to go elsewhere. On one particular occasion, he was turning on with Kate Coleman, an old friend from the Free Speech Movement, and later the Yippies. She was now a researcher at *Newsweek*. When Vice President Hubert Humphrey visited their offices, she refused to shake his hand, calling him a "war criminal."

It was really good dope. Marvin was practically tripping as he rambled on about the Kennedy assassination and the Manchester book. The controversy over Jacqueline Kennedy as censor tantalized his imagination as it had mine. Since I was unable to obtain the actual portions deleted from *The Death of a President*, I had decided to write them myself, trying to imitate William Manchester's style.

I started with a news item from *The New York Times*, which had been brought to my attention by Bob Abel, who was listed in *The Realist* as "Featherbedder." I remembered exactly where I had left that clipping—on the sofa in my loft, because I didn't have a bulletin board. The report was about Lyndon Johnson claiming that Joseph Kennedy was a Nazi sympathizer.

Next I began improvising on stories that White House correspondents knew to be true but which had remained unpublished, peeling off layer after layer of verisimilitude, getting closer and closer with each new paragraph to some unknown core at the center of this apocryphal onion. And then Marvin Garson called.

He had written up his stoned rap and thought maybe I could use it in *The Realist*. He proceeded to read it to me over the phone. When he came to that scene of what must be spelled neckrophilia, I screamed out loud– *"Yaaagghh!"*—an utterly spontaneous reaction to my having just stumbled upon an astounding metaphorical truth.

With Marvin's permission, I boiled his five typewritten pages down to one paragraph, so that I could attempt to nurture the incredible in a context of credibility. During the period I was writing the piece, I began spreading a rumor about the crucial scene so that underground gossip would build up and, when it finally appeared in print, there would already be a certain degree of familiarity.

I talked about it onstage at the Village Theater, and I mentioned it to friends on the phone. One of those I told was Terry Southern. A week later he called back and asked if I wanted him to write it up for *The Realist*. I said I had already done so, but he obviously had his own version of that infamous scene in mind and, not wanting to waste his creativity, he eventually molded it into a short story, "The Blood of a Wig."

My printer, Don Chenoweth, had been going for his doctorate in clinical psychology, but he went into the printing business instead. A socialist intellectual, he specialized in civil rights, pacifists, and radical periodicals and leaflets. He often disagreed with material in *The Realist*. I once offered him the same opportunity typesetters had during an early phase of the Cuban revolution—to state his disagreements in boldface type at the bottom of each column—but he never took me up on it. He did much of the typesetting himself, and he took the manuscript of "The Parts Left Out of the Kennedy Book" home with him that Saturday evening.

On Sunday morning his phone call woke me up. He tried to persuade me not to publish the material, but I had already done my soul-searching, and any decision to be made at this point would have to be his. So, he insisted that I find another printer. On Sunday evening, his wife, a law student, called to ask how I would feel if Jackie Kennedy were to commit suicide as a result of what I published. On Monday morning he called and suggested that I could be charged with incitement to the assassination of Lyndon Johnson. His wife had consulted her professor of constitutional law, and he argued that even liberal Supreme Court Justice Hugo Black would finally be forced to draw the line concerning freedom of the press.

Chenoweth asked me, "What do you think is the worst thing that can happen to you if you publish this?

"I don't know. I guess I could be assassinated?"

He assured me that I would automatically go to prison for criminal libel. He urged me to consult an attorney. Martin Scheiman had committed suicide a few months previously, and I hadn't been up to "replacing" him, but now I sought out a constitutional lawyer, Ernst Rosenberger, sent him a copy of the manuscript, asked whether he thought I should publish it, told him I would publish it regardless of *what* he thought, and asked if he would defend me anyway. He said yes.

But first I had to find a new printer. It wasn't easy. One after another refused to typeset the material. Even the company that printed the Communist *Daily Worker* turned down the job. Bob Abel tried to convince me to publish an issue *without* "The Parts Left Out of the Kennedy Book," so as not to interrupt *The Realist*'s continuity, but I was determined to find a new printer.

I finally found one in Brooklyn and, in April, after a two-month delay, the May 1967 issue went to press, featuring "The Parts Left Out of the Kennedy Book" as our cover story. Every issue of *The Realist* had a slogan, such as "The Fire Hydrant of the Underdog." The slogan for this issue was "Irreverence is Our Only Sacred Cow." And an editor's note requested, "When canceling your subscription, please be sure to include your zip code."

* * *

In 1965, I had been invited to moderate a symposium about "The Style of the Sixties" at Princeton University. On the panel were Günter Grass, Allen Ginsberg, and Tom Wolfe. I had a slight disagreement with Wolfe. He said that an artist ought not to get involved in any causes, and I said it was okay as long as responsibility to oneself and the audience wasn't compromised in the process. As if to confuse my point, I thrust myself into a bizarre situation. Günter Grass gave his opening statement in German, and the audience applauded. Then an interpreter, Albert Harrison, translated it to English, and the audience applauded even louder.

"Thank you, Günter Grass," I said, "and thank you, Albert Harrison, for translating Mr. Grass's bar mitzvah speech." The entire audience started hissing me in unison. One big, loud, long, disapproving *ssssssssssss*... Finally I said, "For two months I've been hearing rumors that God is dead. I'm very much relieved to see he only sprung a leak." And the hissing stopped.

Tom Wolfe would write that I looked like "a manic troll."

And so I was a little surprised to be invited back to the Princeton Symposium in 1967. It took place on the weekend that the issue of *The Realist* with "The Parts Left Out of the Kennedy Book" was due to hit the newsstands. I found myself on a panel with Evan Thomas, editor of *The Death of a President* for Harper & Row.

He passed me a note: *The passage you quote from Manchester was never in the manuscript.* I asked how he could have seen *The Realist* already. He told me that their lawyers had obtained a Photostat of our galley proofs. I was in no position to complain since I had pretended to obtain a Photostat of *their* manuscript. I offered him a copy of the actual issue.

He grimaced and said, "No, thanks."

That night I shared my dormitory bed with a young woman I met at the symposium. In the morning I rushed off to catch the bus back to New York. I just had to actually *see* that issue on the newsstands. My excitement was mounting. But first I stopped by to see Jeanne and Holly at their apartment.

When I kissed Jeanne hello, she said, "I smell pussy."

I had been in such a hurry to leave Princeton that I didn't even wash my face. How insulting to Jeanne. A sense of personal shame now tainted the editorial pride that I felt in publishing the Kennedy piece. On the way to my loft I stopped at a bookstore, and there it was—a pile of *Realists*—and people were already *arguing* about whether these were *actual* omissions from the Kennedy book.

One fellow said, "It doesn't make any difference whether it's true or not, because that's really where they're *at*."

I figured that Harper & Row had no grounds to sue *The Realist*. Nor did *Look* magazine, although their legal staff had certainly discussed the possibility. "Criminal fraud," spouted Editorial Chairman Gardner Cowles, but they didn't sue me. It was extremely unlikely that Jackie Kennedy or Lyndon Johnson would bring suit, if only because they would have to concede that what I had published was *believable*.

Indeed, one of LBJ's favorite jokes was about a popular Texas sheriff running for reelection. His opponents had been trying unsuccessfully to think of a good campaign issue to use against him. Finally one man suggested spreading "a rumor that he fucks pigs." Another protested, "You know he doesn't do that." "I know," said the first man, "but let's make the son of a bitch *deny* it."

William Manchester was probably the only one in a position to sue.

Then came a phone call: "This is Bill Manchester."

"Yes, sir."

"My attorneys told me not to call you, but I wanted to talk to you."

"Well, here I am."

"Let me ask, did you talk to any of my people?"

"Only to Evan Thomas, but that was after the fact."

"Look, the late president meant a great deal to me."

"I'm aware of that. We all show our loss in different ways."

"I know you didn't write that article. I've read *The Realist* before, and I know you're a moral man."

"It's irrelevant whether I wrote it or not, because it was my *decision* to publish it, so the moral *responsibility* is mine."

"That's true. But what was the purpose?"

"To satirize certain things about the assassination—its aftermath, the hypocrisy, the exploitation, the cover-up, the quest for power."

"Was it necessary to include that introduction?"

"Well, I had to establish verisimilitude. When Jonathan Swift wrote his *Modest Proposal*, he didn't say, 'Hey, folks, I'm only kidding. I don't really mean that we can solve both the famine and overpopulation problems by eating newborn babies.' It wouldn't have had the same impact."

"That's very abstract. Look, your readers are mostly intelligent, literate people, correct?"

"I suppose so."

"They'll know that what you published isn't true. But other people are going to pick up this issue and they might believe it."

"And then what? Then what?"

"Are you working on your next issue yet? Could you mention something to the effect—I know I shouldn't ask—"

"I really respect you. Why did your attorneys tell you not to call me?"

"I'll find that out in ten minutes."

"Give 'em my regards. I'm not making any actual commitment, but I appreciate your man-to-man confrontation, and I really will consider—"

"I'll be looking forward to your next issue."

"So will I."

In Hollywood, an attorney made several wagers with friends about the authenticity of the article. He wrote to Manchester, who replied: "The material in *The Realist*, as described to me by my attorneys, is pure fabrication and was never in my manuscript." I couldn't understand why Manchester was now implying that he hadn't read the issue himself. I wrote a letter, reminding him of our talk.

He wrote back: "You and I never had a telephone conversation. Indeed, I believe that such a conversation would have been impossible. My telephone number is unpublished and is used for personal purposes, and until today I did not know your number. Of course, I would never have called you."

Later on, Truman Capote told me that I had been the victim of a hoax myself. He claimed that the phone call I'd gotten, ostensibly from William Manchester, had actually been faked by Richard Goodwin, a speechwriter for Bobby Kennedy who was involved in the Harper &

Row manuscript battle and had a reputation for mischief. According to Capote, Goodwin made a tape of our conversation which he supposedly replayed for Kennedy intimates at the drop of a crown. According to Goodwin, however, the call was made by an eighteen-year-old hippie.

* * *

The most significant thing about "The Parts Left Out of the Kennedy Book" was its widespread *acceptance*—if only for a moment—by intelligent, literate people, from an ACLU official to a Peabody Award–winning journalist to members of the intelligence community who knew that sort of thing actually *does* go on.

Daniel Ellsberg told me, "Maybe it was just because I *wanted* to believe it so badly."

Except for the call from "Manchester," I never admitted to perpetrating a hoax. I insisted to those who called—and the phone rang continually with requests for verification—that they would have to decide for themselves if I had published an authentic document. One caller claimed that he could determine, by feeding the article into a computer, whether Manchester had written the portions I published.

Several individuals queried that final arbiter of truth, the Playboy Adviser. One reader "went out and bought the original *Death of a President* just to see if your parts would fit into the book—they did. Amazing!"

I got a call from a San Francisco radio talk show host, Joe Dolan, who asked me on the air to confirm his belief that I had published a "literary forgery." When I refused, he went into such a rampage I could practically hear the veins on his temples pulsating.

Finally, he shouted, "Why did you publish it?"

I answered calmly, "To separate the men from the boys."

He hung up. It was on Dolan's show that Mark Lane told how he had been on the same London TV program on which Gore Vidal described the incident which had been deleted from the text of the Manchester book—that Jackie Kennedy, during the transfer of her husband's body from Dallas, had moved to the rear of the plane where she saw Lyndon Johnson leaning over the casket and chuckling.

Consequently, I received a call from Ray Marcus, a critic of the Warren Commission report. He had discovered a chronological flaw in my article. How could Manchester leave something out of his book which was itself a *report* of something that he'd left out of his book? Marcus deduced that *The Realist* must have been given the excerpts by a CIA plant in order to discredit *valid* dissent on the assassination.

I received this letter from Gore Vidal:

Dear Paul,

You remain forever my role model, but . . . I do wish you'd get that story straight. I never said a word on British TV about LBJ chuckling, etc. I did chat with Mark Lane *before* I went on. He was spinning theories. I recalled that someone—Goodwin?—had told me that Jackie had gone back to the presidential suite on the plane to find him, alone, chuckling. That's it. The coffin was in the luggage compartment and anyone who got in there would have been frozen to death. Anyway, (1) I never went public with this story, but Mark Lane had me in headlines as having got it from Jackie—all untrue; (2) If it was Goodwin who told me, he is, as source, permanently tainted.

Buona fortuna,
Gore

A London scholar wrote: "The body of JFK was supposedly in a casket. Therefore, short of lifting out the corpse, an act of inverted parafellatio would be physically impossible."

George Lincoln Rockwell, head of the American Nazi party, called. "You got balls of steel," he said. "For a Jew, you shoulda been a Nazi." (It reminded me of the teenage Nazi I had once published in *The Realist*. "Suppose I were a Jew," I said. "If your dreams came true, I guess you'd have *me* thrown into the oven too, wouldn't you?" He pondered a minute. "No," he replied, "I like you. I'd merely have you undergo sterilization.")

And a note, signed William Blake, stated: "May I call to your attention a remark I made 174 years ago when I marred Heaven and Hell: 'Everything possible to be believed is an image of truth.'"

Look magazine ordered two hundred copies of that issue of *The Realist*, but when an employee of Harper & Row tacked it onto a bulletin board, he was suspended for four weeks without pay. An editor at *Holiday* magazine threatened to beat me up.

Bob Scheer, who was now managing editor of *Ramparts*, complained that I had destroyed faith in the veracity of *The Realist* so that articles like the one on CIA involvement in the murder of Malcolm X would no longer be taken seriously. But *Ramparts* editor Warren Hinckle sent a telegram reading, simply, BRILLIANT DIRTY ISSUE. There were several anonymous death threats, and this letter from a producer of the TV series *I Spy*:

It was my misfortune to have read the article about the Manchester book in the May edition of *The Realist*, which is laughingly known as a magazine. Not only do I reject that article as pure fabrication, but I am convinced that only a diseased and perverted mind could conjure up such rubbish. I trust that someone will put an end to your sick and perverted brain and thus stop you from sowing the seeds of lies in the brains of the American public. Hopefully, another sick human being will put a bullet in your throat and end your short, unhappy life.

A close friend of Manchester's vowed to work very hard to cost *The Realist* its second-class mailing privilege. A man sputtering with anger called Lee Leonard on NBC radio and swore he would make a citizen's arrest of me. One man decided to start a petition to put *The Realist* out of business. I asked for one so that I could sign it too.

A lawyer complained to the local police precinct, and a lieutenant visited my office. I explained the concept of obscenity as appealing to the prurient interest of the reader. He agreed that I hadn't violated any law—"but don't you think editors should have *some* standards?"

"Well, everybody has *standards*," I said, "even the Hell's Angels."

"What magazine do *they* publish?"

A plainclothes officer from another precinct also came by. His visit was the result of an anonymous letter to the mayor which had been channeled to the chief of detectives. He asked if I had any psychedelic posters. They were for his son, who had a rock-and-roll band called Orange Moose. *The Realist* was removed from newsstands in Cambridge, and when an attempt was made to give out free copies at a Boston love-in, police confiscated them.

The *McGill Daily*, an undergraduate newspaper in Montreal, asked for permission to reprint the piece. I said okay, if they wouldn't take anything out of context, and I warned them that they'd most likely get in trouble. The reprinting turned into a catalyst for a student power struggle that made the front page of Canadian newspapers, which described me as a "professional agitator." I was invited to speak at McGill and other campuses, and to appear on several radio and TV programs.

One interviewer asked, "Do you really condone necrophilia?"

"Oh, sure," I answered, "but only between consenting adults."

* * *

When Walt Disney died in December 1966, I remembered two things that he had said. One was, "I love Mickey Mouse more than any woman

I've ever known." In 1945, Aldous Huxley was a consultant on the filming of *Alice in Wonderland*, and there were rumors that Huxley had turned him on with magic mushrooms. A year later, Disney said, "If people would think more of fairies, they would forget the atom bomb."

There was an urban myth that his body had been frozen, although it was actually cremated. Somehow I had expected Mickey Mouse and Donald Duck and all the rest of the gang to attend the funeral, with Goofy delivering the eulogy and the Seven Dwarves serving as pallbearers.

After his death, I went to Disneyland with a couple of friends, one a lawyer whose dog jumped into the car as we were leaving his home. Dogs weren't allowed in Disneyland. Neither were male humans who had long hair or beards, except for musicians, so the Beatles and Jesus Christ would not have been permitted to enter Disneyland unless they were performing there.

We bluffed our way in with the dog by convincing a ticket-taker that the manager had given us permission earlier on the phone inasmuch as the dog was needed to guide my friend with impaired eyesight. Inside, we continued to fake it by explaining that the dog had already been cleared by the ticket-taker, until a large man with a small walkie-talkie approached us, offering a choice of putting the dog in the Disneyland kennel or leaving altogether. My friend complained that this exception to their rule had been arranged two weeks ago, and he asked to speak to the chief of security.

"I *am* the chief of security."

"Just the man I want to see."

Of course, the canine in question was not a Seeing Eye dog, not even a German shepherd. There was no metal brace for the owner to hold onto, just a rotting, knotted leather leash. And the dog was an old bloodshot-eyed basset hound that kept stumbling all over the ground looking for a place to pee. Apparently, no dog had ever previously peed in Disneyland, not even Pluto.

We decided to leave. But we were entitled to a refund. So, while the others waited at the gate, I was escorted to a building called City Hall. Inside, a woman was requesting that her lost child be paged over the loudspeaker, but she was refused because this wasn't considered an emergency. I asked an administrator if there had been any special ceremony when Walt Disney died.

"No, we kept the park open. We felt that Mr. Disney would have wanted it that way."

"Well, wasn't there *any* official recognition of his passing?"

"We did fly the flag at half-mast for the rest of the month."

Disney's death occurred the same year as *Time* magazine's famous "Is

God Dead?" cover, and it occurred to me that Disney had indeed served as the Creator of that whole stable of imaginary characters who were now mourning in a state of suspended animation. Disney had been *their* Intelligent Designer, and he had repressed all their baser instincts, but now that he had departed, they could finally shed their cumulative inhibitions and participate together in an unspeakable Roman binge, to signify the crumbling of an empire.

I contacted Wally Wood and, without mentioning any specific details, I told him my general notion of a memorial orgy at Disneyland. He accepted the assignment and presented me with a magnificently degenerate montage.

Pluto is pissing on a portrait of Mickey Mouse, while the real, bedraggled Mickey is shooting up heroin with a hypodermic needle. His nephews are jerking off as they watch a combination bed and cash register where Minnie Mouse is fucking Goofy. The beams shining out from the Magic Castle are actually dollar signs. Dumbo the elephant is simultaneously flying and shitting on an infuriated Donald Duck. Huey, Dewey, and Louie are peeking at Daisy Duck's asshole as she watches the Seven Dwarfs groping Snow White. The prince is snatching a peek at Cinderella's snatch while trying a glass slipper on her foot. The three little pigs are humping each other in a daisy chain. Jiminy Cricket leers as Tinker Bell does a striptease and Pinocchio's nose gets longer.

In real fake life, Mickey Mouse was a convict in a chain gang when he met Pluto. In World War II, his name was the password for the D-Day invasion. Snow White warned military personnel about the dangers of venereal disease. And although Wally Wood revealed no genitalia, he nonetheless unleashed the characters' collective libido and demystified an entire genre in the process, and the Disneyland Memorial Orgy served as a centerspread in the issue featuring "The Parts Left Out of the Kennedy Book."

The black-and-white centerspread became so popular that I decided to publish it as a poster. The Disney Corporation considered a lawsuit but realized that *The Realist* was published on a proverbial shoestring, and besides, why bother causing themselves further public embarrassment? They took no action against me, and the statute of limitations finally ran out. Meanwhile, the poster was pirated—painted in black-light Day-Glo colors, supposedly copyrighted in my name (spelled wrong) and widely distributed—without paying Wally Wood any royalties. I didn't sue the pirated poster, but the Disney people did, and that case was settled out of court.

(In 2005, a new, copyrighted, digitally colored edition of the original poster by a former Disney employee, became available at paulkrassner.com.)

In Baltimore, the Sherman News Agency distributed that issue with the Disneyland Memorial Orgy removed. One employee said that the

Maryland Board of Censors had ordered this—that it was the only way *The Realist* could be sold in that state but there *was* no such Maryland Board of Censors. Sherman's had merely taken what they considered to be a precaution. I was able to secure the missing pages, and offered them free to any Baltimore reader who had bought a partial magazine.

In Oakland, an anonymous group published a flyer with *The Realist* logo on top, reproducing the last few paragraphs of "The Parts Left Out of the Kennedy Book," along with a few sections of the Disneyland spread—adding, *Now on sale at DeLauer's Book Store, Your East Bay Family News and Book Store.* The flyer was distributed in churches and elsewhere. The police would have moved in for an arrest had it not been for my West Coast distributor, Lou Swift, who asked them not to act until they got a *complete* issue of *The Realist* and could see the material in context.

In Chicago, a bookstore owner and my distributor—Chuck Olin, who actually ran an ice cream company—were charged with selling and distributing obscene material. Specifically, the complaint was about the Disneyland Memorial Orgy, but local reporters told me that the charge was actually a smoke screen to attack *The Realist* for publishing the Kennedy piece. Theoretically the charges couldn't stick.

The centerspread certainly didn't arouse prurient interest. I tried to imagine a prosecutor telling a jury how they might get horny because look what Goofy and Minnie Mouse were doing, but even if it *did* arouse prurient interest, the rest of *The Realist* was certainly not *utterly* without redeeming social value. However, a judge there found the issue "to be obscene."

The charge against the distributor was dismissed, based on his lack of knowledge of the contents. The ACLU sought a federal injunction restraining authorities from interfering in any way with local distribution of *The Realist*. Other dealers were afraid to sell that issue, and in fact were warned by police not to sell it. I went on a late night Chicago radio program, inviting the police to arrest me. Unlike the bookseller and distributor, I would plead not guilty. Nothing happened, except that a woman who was listening to her car radio had pulled over to the side of the road, and a police officer questioned her.

"I thought you were a prostitute," he explained, "here for the Furniture Show."

★ ★ ★

The circulation of that issue of *The Realist* reached 100,000, plus an estimated two or three million in pass-on readership. In the next issue, I revealed details of the hoax, and concluded:

The ultimate target of satire should be its own audience.

Analogy: Several years ago, there was a French-&-Italian film, *Seven Deadly Sins*, consisting of seven vignettes, one for each sin—greed, lust, avarice, pride, Dopey, Sneezy, Bashful—and at the end of the seventh sin, the narrator told us that we were going to see the *eighth* sin. On the screen were all the images that we have been conditioned to associate with the intimations of sin—sailors, girls, an opium den—and then the narrator explained that the eighth sin was the desire to *see* sin.

The audience groaned its disappointment with a spontaneity that served only to underscore the narrator's point.

So, a reader sees the headline on that issue of *The Realist* and says: "The parts left out of the Kennedy book. *Oh, boy!*" Then reads it. Voluntarily. And says: "The parts left out of the Kennedy book. *Arrrggh!*"

What did you expect? What did you want?

Whether my motivation—to share this outrageous apocrypha with you—stemmed from hostility or affection, is as much a matter of subjective interpretation as was Jackie Kennedy's projection of what Lyndon Johnson did to her husband's corpse on that flight from Dallas. For all we know, it might have been an act of love.

In 1980, David Lifton wrote in *Best Evidence: Disguise and Deception in the Assassination of John F. Kennedy*: "Here was evidence that someone had altered the President's body prior to the autopsy; evidence that the autopsy report, the source of crucial information about the number and direction of shots, actually described a body no longer in the same condition as it had been immediately after the shooting. If this FBI report were true, the conclusions of the Warren Commission were erected on sand."

The thrust of his thesis was that there had been an actual surgical alteration of President Kennedy's neck wound.

In 1992, Charles Crenshaw—one of the doctors who treated Kennedy's gunshot wounds at the Parkland Hospital in Dallas in 1963—wrote in *JFK: Conspiracy of Silence*, that "there was no doubt" that the president was shot, not from the back by one "magic bullet," but from the front by two bullets, one entering the neck and the other the right side of his head. Although Dr. Crenshaw had personally supervised the placement of Kennedy's body in a casket, it arrived at Bethesda Naval Hospital "zippered in a gray body bag inside a different coffin," and the condition of the cranium "had substantially changed during a period of six hours and over a distance of 1500 miles. Great effort had been made to reconstruct the back of the president's head, and the tracheotomy (an incision at the front of the throat) had been enlarged and mangled . . ."

But *we* know what *really* happened, don't we?

My favorite response to "The Parts Left Out of the Kennedy Book" came from Merriman Smith, the UPI correspondent who always ended White House press conferences with the traditional "Thank you, Mr. President." He wrote in his syndicated column:

> One of the filthiest printed attacks ever made on a President of the United States is now for sale on Washington newsstands. The target: President Johnson. This is the May edition of a so-called magazine which says it is entered as second class mail. One newsstand owner says sales of this particular issue have been "quite active."
>
> This reporter is not embarked here on any defense of Johnson politically or personally, nor, for that matter, is this to suggest the need for greater respect for the presidency. These are matters that have been dealt with extensively in other forums.
>
> Certain unadorned facts, however, do stand out in the open circulation, mailing and other forms of distribution of this sort of slime: If a magazine of major national standing tries to use the same sort of language, federal action to stop it would be almost certain. The language referred to is not conventional hell or damn profanity—it is filth attributed to someone of national stature supposedly describing something Johnson allegedly did. The incident, of course, never took place . . .

So, not only did a sheriff deny that he had fucked a pig, but now there was an official denial that Lyndon Johnson had fucked the corpse of John F. Kennedy in the throat wound in order to fool the Warren Commission. LBJ's favorite joke had come home to roost.

CHAPTER 7

THE RISE AND FALL
OF THE YIPPIE EMPIRE

Two days after Lyndon Johnson was sworn in as president, the war in Vietnam began to escalate, and there developed a horrible ritual that was broadcast throughout America every Thursday on the evening news. It was the body count: so many "American dead"; so many "Vietnamese dead"; so many "enemy dead." Just abstract numbers.

I was invited to speak at antiwar demonstrations on campuses around the country, where students could be heard chanting: "Hey, hey, LBJ! How many kids did you kill today?"

Blacks were getting involved in the antiwar movement—"No Vietnamese ever called me nigger!"—and so was organized labor—"No Vietnamese ever froze my wages!" The United States was spending $2 million every day, and all they had to show for it was that lousy body count. Our language was becoming perverted in order to mask our behavior. Dead Vietnamese children were called *collateral damage*. Concentration camps were called *strategic hamlets*. Torturers were called *counterinsurgency experts*. Today, they indulge in *enhanced interrogation techniques,* a euphemism for a euphemism.

In May 1965, Jerry Rubin helped organize the first Vietnam Day Teach-In at the Berkeley campus of the University of California. He invited me to emcee. It was an outdoor rally, the largest such protest in American history, with a peak audience of thirty thousand. Simultaneous rallies were being held in London and Tokyo. The press called it a "carnival" and a "picnic." Berkeley professor Eugene Burdick described it as an "ideological circus" in a letter to the *San Francisco Examiner*. He wrote that there would be "comedians, folksingers, ministers, serious commentators, and silly commentators."

"Now I'm one of your silly commentators," I announced, "and I thought I'd have a little audience participation here because Burdick said there will be 'thrills of horror, gasps of partisan shock, laughter, and the low bellow of the true believer.' Now, if you'd join in with me in a few of these, I'll read them off, okay? Let's have first some thrills of horror. Let's hear it up here now." The audience bellowed out a bizarre sound that represented thrills of horror. "That's the way. Now let's have a gasp of partisan shock." The audience took its cue and let out a mass gasp. "That's good, that's good. Very good. All right, now let's see if you can come up with some extremist laughter." They did. "That's good. All right now, this one is a real challenge. I want the low bellow of the true believer." The audience came through with the lowest bellow I'd ever heard.

Shocking facts, from speaker after speaker, boomed over the public address system that afternoon. Normal Mailer took a different approach. He concluded his speech:

> They will print up little pictures of you, Lyndon Johnson, the size of postcards, the size of stamps, and some will glue these pictures to walls and posters and telephone booths and billboards—I do not advise it, I would tell these students not to do it to you, but they will. They will find places to put these pictures—upside down. Silently, without a word, the photograph of you, Lyndon Johnson, will start appearing everywhere, upside down. Your head will speak out—even to the peasant in Asia; it will say that not all Americans are unaware of your monstrous vanity, overweening piety, and doubtful motive. It will tell them that we trust our president so little, and think so little of him, that we see his picture everywhere upside down.

The crowd gave Mailer a standing ovation, but the next day the *San Francisco Chronicle* stated that he had received "light applause." It was this very difference between what people were experiencing on the street and the way it was being reported in the mainstream media, that nurtured the growth of the underground press. Mailer handed me the manuscript he had just read and said, "You want this for *The Realist?*"

The next month I published his complete speech with a photo of Lyndon Johnson upside down on the cover. There had just been a water shortage in New York, and immediately above that photo, in place of *The Realist* logo, I reprinted a Department of Water Supply, Gas, and Electricity poster, which read: DON'T FLUSH FOR EVERYTHING. The magazine's name was in small print at the bottom of the page. If I had been living in China and published a picture of Mao Tse-tung upside down, even *accidentally*, I would have been executed. This was the paradox of America—that we had the freedom to criticize so openly those unspeakable horrors being committed by the government in the name of the people.

The post office held up the mailing of that issue, but it was for purely bureaucratic reasons. They thought that I had changed the name of the magazine from *The Realist* to *Don't Flush for Everything* without filing a proper application form first.

At another outdoor rally at the Berkeley campus in October, Ken Kesey walked up to me and continued a conversation that we had never begun. There was a rumor that the Merry Pranksters were going to invite the Hell's Angels to a big bash in La Honda, so a group of these bikers showed up, they were befriended, and started hanging around. It was a strange alliance. Who could have predicted Day-Glo swastikas? So, when the Vietnam Day Committee invited Kesey to speak, the Pranksters and the Angels painted a bus together and made toy ack-ack guns to shoot at the enemy aircraft flying over the rally.

Kesey was the penultimate speaker. I introduced him, he took the stage, played a few bars on his harmonica between his words, which consisted essentially of warning the crowd that we should love our neighbors, that the march following the teach-in wasn't going to *change* anything, and that wars had been fought for ten thousand years.

"Just look at the war," he advised, "turn your backs and say 'Fuck it!'"

Ironically, this was the antithesis of the message of all the previous speakers, and fifteen thousand marchers were chafing at Kesey's bit. The next evening, at an indoor event, I borrowed a harmonica and did a parody of his talk. He stood up in the audience and shouted, "I object," then walked to the front of the auditorium, jumped onto the stage, and proceeded to defend his position.

★ ★ ★

There was a rumor that *yellow submarine* was an underground name in England for the capsule that LSD came in, but when a reporter asked the Beatles if "Yellow Submarine" was a drug song, the answer was, "You have a dirty mind." The reporter might also have asked if it was a political song, because a revolutionary change in the style of protest was brought about in the fall of 1966, when a few hundred individuals marched across New York City on a sunny Saturday afternoon, from Tompkins Square Park to the Gansevoort Pier, and launched a six-foot yellow submarine in the Hudson River. It was filled with bread, balloons, wine, and "messages of love, desperation, peace, and hope to all the people in the world from us."

The Workshop in Non-Violence built their yellow submarine for $51.73, as opposed to the cost of a Polaris submarine, $108,284,620—but the Polaris could obliterate sixteen major cities with nuclear missiles carrying more explosive power than was fired by both sides in all of World War II. So now the very nature of antiwar rallies was evolving into something else.

The influence of flower children was brightening up the movement. Demonstrations were becoming more playful. And yet there were those in the Old Left who looked disdainfully at this parade of folks trying to spread joy as an alternative to horror: "You're not offering any alternatives. You're just being positive."

By 1967, the seasons began to be measured by antiwar demonstrations— Spring Mobilization, Vietnam Summer—but the peace movement was still hung up on respectability. At a coalition conference in Washington, a motion to go on record as encouraging draft resistance was voted down, but a resolution *was* passed to support the antidraft movement in Puerto Rico. At a rally in San Francisco, demonstrators were warned to keep off the grass on the same field where football was played.

In New York, a hippie was wandering around the Sheep Meadow in Central Park, where an antiwar rally was in progress. He had a loaf of whole grain bread, and was looking for others to share it with, when he was approached by somebody with an American flag in one hand and a can of lighter fluid in the other. "Would you hold this?" The hippie held the flag while the stranger set it on fire.

This public destruction of a symbol became the impetus for a *pro*war march. Ironically, the American flags carried by flower children in the prowar parade were torn to pieces by patriots, along with the punching, stomping, and tarring-and-feathering of a bypasser who happened to be guilty of needing a haircut.

Armed Forces Day was a week later. It had been designated Flower Power Day by the Workshop in Non-Violence. The plan was to confront the official parade. The rallying cry: "Zap the military with love—blow their minds, not their bodies!" There had been meetings to decide on tactics. Someone offered to donate a thousand paper airplanes, but the idea was vetoed because it would mean littering.

Another idea was to chain male and female protesters together. "According to a New York City regulation," the plotter explained, "men and women can't be put in the same paddy wagon, so the cops would have to march us down Fifth Avenue." There was a call for volunteers who would spring ecstatically from the spectators and put flowers into the rifle barrels. But this planning had all been *before* the civilian brutality of the previous week. Now we were in Central Park, scared to leave its safety for unknown dangers lurking on Fifth Avenue.

Abbie Hoffman was in the group. "What is this?" he said. "We're huddled together like in a fuckin' *ghetto*, afraid to watch a fuckin' *parade*."

We decided to confront the parade, but a police captain approached one individual and said, "I'm gonna have to give you a summons for holding a meeting without a permit."

"We're merely holding a conversation, officer. And why are you singling *me* out?"

"You seem to be leading the meeting."

Although I was there as a reporter covering this event for *The Realist*, at that moment I took another step over the line separating my roles as an observer and a participant.

"Excuse me, officer, but *I* was leading that meeting. You'd better give me a summons too." I looked around. "Who else was leading the meeting?"

Hands went up. "I was." More hands went up. "I was." "I was." "I was." It turned out that about fifty people were leading the meeting.

"I'm not gonna give you a summons, but the *next* time you hold a meeting—"

"You mean," I interjected, "the next time we *don't* hold a meeting."

"You'd better have a permit."

"I'm sorry, officer, we can't continue this meeting any longer without a permit."

Then this horde of pacifists and hippies left the area, followed by a division of police. We passed the statue of Alice in Wonderland and her friends playing around a giant mushroom. We romped past, while some remained to present flowers to the Mad Hatter. The cops ordered them off, *surrounding* Alice as if they were guarding a fortress.

The Armed Forces Day parade began its way down Fifth Avenue. The marines marched by, and we chanted, "Get a girl, not a gun." The Navy marched by, and we sang "Yellow Submarine." Green Berets marched by, and we shouted, "Thou shalt not kill!" The Red Cross marched by, and we applauded. A missile rolled by, and we called out, "Shame!" Military cadets rode by on horseback, and we advised, "Drop out now!" The Department of Sanitation swept past, and we cheered.

When the parade was over, I left with Hoffman. Our paths had crossed at various meetings and events, but we'd never really hung around together. Now, over soup, he was telling me about the time he had brought a FUCK COMMUNISM! poster to a symposium on Communism, and how he had been influenced by *The Realist*.

I asked, "Do you think it's an ego trip for me to be concerned about whether the readers think I'm on an ego trip?"

"That's because you're Jewish," he laughed.

"I don't think of myself as Jewish. I'm an atheist. I mean *Christ* was Jewish."

"When I was at Brandeis," Abbie said, "I asked this professor, 'How come in one part of the Bible, Jesus says to God, *Why hast thou forsaken me?* But in another part of the Bible, Jesus says to God, *Forgive them for they know not what they do?* And the professor says, 'You gotta remember, the Bible was written by a lot of different guys.'"

★ ★ ★

Abbie Hoffman tempered his fearlessness with a gift for humor that was sharp and spontaneous. On a particularly tense night on the Lower East Side, we were standing on a street corner when a patrol car with four police cruised by. He called out, "Hey, fellas, you goin' out on a double date?" These were the same cops from the Ninth Precinct that he liked to defeat at the pool table.

I had become friends with Abbie and his wife, Anita. When CBS News wanted to film an acid trip at their apartment on St. Mark's Place, being propagandists, we agreed to do it. As a joke, I suggested to CBS that they ought to pay for the LSD because I was curious to see whether they would charge the expense to entertainment or travel. Blaming my suggestion, they changed their corporate mind, expressing fear that the trip would now be "staged." But we took the acid anyway—Abbie, Anita, a Digger named Phyllis, and me and we watched CBS on television. Every commercial seemed to be trying to sell us what we were already on. Abbie was having a rambunctiously good time.

"Fuck the revolution!" he shouted.

When Abbie and Anita walked into the living room naked, Phyllis and I figured it was time to leave. But just then a phone call came about some trouble at the Ninth Precinct. We decided to walk over there and check it out. However, I had raided the refrigerator, and I was feeling slightly nauseated. Abbie promised that if I did throw up outside, he and Anita and Phyllis would all circle around me to block the view of curious pedestrians.

"That's community," he added with a mischievous tilt of his head.

I told him, "You're the first one who's really made me laugh since Lenny Bruce died."

"Really? He was my *god.*"

At the Ninth Precinct we learned that a few black kids had been arrested for smoking marijuana in Tompkins Square Park. Blacks and Puerto

Ricans in the neighborhood couldn't quite understand why white middle-class folks wanted to drop out of a society that *they* were still trying to drop *into*. The lack of understanding bordered on hostility, but Abbie wanted to indicate that there *could* be solidarity between hippies and blacks, so he insisted on getting arrested too. The cops refused to oblige his request, and Abbie just stood there in the lobby. Captain Joseph Fink beckoned to me.

"Paul, do you think you can persuade Abbie to leave?"

"Abbie's his own man," I replied.

Abbie could see us talking from where he was standing, in front of a display case filled with trophies. He kicked backward with his boot, breaking the glass as though there were an emergency. It was a moment of transcendental meditation.

"*Now* you're under arrest!" Captain Fink yelled.

So Abbie finished that particular acid trip behind bars, but he was there because of a purely existential act, and this would remain his favorite arrest. At six o'clock that morning, I called artist Richard Guindon, who was temporarily in London. I had an idea for the cover of the next *Realist*. It would be that bandaged fife-and-drum corps trio from *The Spirit of '76*, only now they would be a Vietcong, a black man, and a female hippie. Guindon had to base his illustration on memory, since he couldn't find a copy of that classic painting in any British library. After all, England had *lost* the first American Revolution.

★ ★ ★

Phil Ochs had said, "A demonstration should turn you on, not turn you off."

Inspired by the sight of Allen Ginsberg wearing his Uncle Sam hat with Gandhi pajamas and declaring the end of the war with a Hindu chant, Ochs wrote a song, "The War Is Over," and helped organize a War Is Over rally in Los Angeles. There was a teach-in at the Cheviot Hills Park. Muhammad Ali was signing autographs, but only on draft cards. Thousands of us marched to the Century Plaza Hotel where the Supremes were serenading LBJ. The demonstrators sat down in the street facing the hotel. The riot police lived up to their name, using tear gas and billy clubs to chase protesters into a grassy field, even beating people in wheelchairs.

At a follow-up rally in New York, we ran through the streets with noisemakers and flags, skittering between cars against the afternoon traffic to make it difficult for the cops trying to follow us. We spread the news about the end of the war, pouring into office buildings, restaurants, and bars, swarming down the aisles of movie houses and legitimate theaters.

This was Wednesday and the matinee performers were building carefully toward their scheduled dramatic climaxes.

"The war is over!" we shouted. "The war is over!"

We had brought theater into politics and now we were bringing politics into the theater. Audiences resented this intrusion into their arena, but street theater was becoming the name of the protest game, and counter-cultural activists had become the players.

Jim Fouratt, a gay activist who helped organize the Central Park Be-In, had an idea for a piece of seminal street theater, which Abbie Hoffman proceeded to put into action. A group of hippies went to the Stock Exchange, armed with $200 in singles, which were showered onto the floor from the visitor's gallery. Stockbrokers weren't used to seeing real money there, and they immediately switched from screaming "Pork Bellies!" to diving for dollars. It was a trick we had borrowed from the CIA—you don't have to manipulate the media if you can manipulate the events which the media cover. Outside, reporters were given facts about Wall Street and the war.

Ed Sanders was another expert practitioner of street theater. He was a poet, editor of *Fuck You: A Magazine of the Arts*, proprietor of the Peace Eye Book Store, and leader of The Fugs, a name inspired by Norman Mailer's euphemism for "fuck." There was an apocryphal music store that kept The Fugs' albums in their classical section, under the misimpression that they were The Fugues.

When antiwar activist Dave Dellinger asked Jerry Rubin to be project director of the October 1967 demonstration at the Pentagon, Jerry moved from Berkeley to New York, Keith Lampe introduced Jerry to Abbie, and Ed Sanders teamed up with them to organize, not just a rally, but an *exorcism* of the Pentagon. The idea had originated with Allen Cohen, editor of the *San Francisco Oracle*, and painter Michael Bowen, after they read in *The City in History* by Lewis Mumford about the Pentagon being a baroque symbol of evil and oppression.

When LSD became illegal, the psychedelic *Oracle* became politicized, and the radical *Berkeley Barb* began to treat the drug subculture as fellow outlaws. So now there was to be an event in the nation's capitol that would publicly cross-fertilize political protesters with hippie mystics. The plan was simple—to defy the law of gravity. It was decided to hold a special ceremony which would levitate the Pentagon a hundred feet.

We applied for a permit, then revealed to the media that Pentagon officials wanted to limit levitation to twenty-two feet, because that was the height of their ladders, so they'd still be able to pull the building down. But later they insisted on restricting it to no more than three feet above the ground, and the press accurately reported that.

In order to build up further public interest in the event, we staged preliminary pranks that were bound to get media coverage. Abbie invented an imaginary new drug, a sexual equivalent to the police tear gas, mace. It was christened Lace—supposedly a combination of LSD and DMSO—which when applied to the skin would be absorbed into the bloodstream and act as an instantaneous aphrodisiac. Lace was actually Schwartz Disappear-O from Taiwan. When sprayed, it left a purple stain, then disappeared.

A press conference was called at Abbie and Anita's apartment where Lace could be observed in action. I was supposed to be there as a reporter who got accidentally sprayed with Lace from a squirt gun. To my surprise, I would put down my pad, take off my clothes, and start making love with a beautiful redhead who had also gotten accidentally sprayed, along with another *deliberately* sprayed couple, right there in the living room, while the journalists took notes. I was really looking forward to this combination media event and blind date. Even though the sexual revolution was at its height, there was something exciting about knowing in advance that I was guaranteed to get laid—although I felt somewhat guilty about attempting to deceive fellow reporters.

But there was a scheduling conflict. I was already committed to speak at a literary conference at the University of Iowa on that same day. So, instead of being accidentally dosed with Lace, I was assigned by Abbie to purchase cornmeal in Iowa, which would be used to encircle the Pentagon as a pre-levitation rite. I was supposed to be a rationalist, but it was hard to say no to Abbie. In Iowa, novelist Robert Stone drove me to a farm.

I told the farmer, "I'd like to buy some cornmeal to go."

"Coarse or fine?" he asked. I glanced at Stone for guidance.

He shrugged and said, "Since it's for a magic ritual, I would definitely recommend coarse."

"Coarse, please," I said to the farmer.

"How many pounds?"

"Uh, thirteen, please."

The farmer smiled and said there was no charge. And so I flew back to New York with a thirteen-pound sack of coarse cornmeal properly stored in the overhead rack. Meanwhile, there were stories about Lace in the *New York Post,* the *Daily News,* and *Time* magazine, including the promise that three gallons of Lace would be brought to Washington, along with a large supply of plastic water pistols, so that Lace could be sprayed on police and the National Guard at the Pentagon demonstration.

The guy who substituted for me in that accidental sexual encounter with the beautiful redhead at the Lace press conference ended up living with her. Even though I had never met her, I was jealous. Somehow I felt cheated.

I was among some thirty people arrested at a demonstration protesting the appearance of Vice President Hubert Humphrey at the Diamond Ball, so named because of the presence of a South African diamond king. The cops had been pushing us along the sidewalk toward the corner, but there was a red light.

I shouted, "There are cars coming! We have to wait!"

I was charged with "loud and boisterous conduct, and refusing to move when told to by an officer." I got busted for *stopping* at a red light. Among those arrested was a group dressed as Keystone Kops who were clubbing each other. All the arrestees were white, except for one black man who was in whiteface. The police took Polaroid pictures of each arrestee side by side with their arresting officer.

I asked mine, "Where do you wanna go after the prom?"

This was the same night that the Emergency Civil Liberties Committee was having its annual Tom Paine Dinner. All the radical attorneys in town were there, and it became a matter of decreasing seniority as to who was going to have to leave in the middle of the affair and spend the next several hours schlepping around night court.

After a half-dozen lawyers declined, the buck stopped at Bill Schaap, who had no one else to pass it to. He insisted that he had never handled a criminal matter alone. They told him it was just an arraignment. Next morning, when the clerk called the first arrestee—me—several spectators jumped to their feet and cheered. I was embarrassed. The judge banged his gavel and shouted, "Clear the courtroom!" Schaap gulped, then apologized to the judge.

The assistant district attorney had told Schaap, "Look, I don't want to try Krassner. If he will say that he was at the Diamond Ball as a journalist, I will throw his case out on First Amendment grounds." Schaap relayed the offer to me, but I declined. "I can't do that," I explained. "It wouldn't be fair to the others. And besides, it's a cop-out, because I *was* there as a demonstrator." The case was ultimately thrown out for lack of evidence, but in court the judge warned us, "Next time, don't tempt fate."

I mumbled, "Since when is freedom of assembly tempting fate?"

"C'mon, Paul," Schaap nudged me. "This is my first case. Don't blow it for me."

* * *

In December 1967, Stop the Draft Week failed to stop the draft but succeeded in raising consciousness. A police bus took away those who had volunteered to be arrested, and they made V signs with their fingers through the windows. In return, I made the V sign for the first time.

Abbie, Anita, and I decided to take our first real vacation, in the Florida Keys, where we rented a little house on stilts. I brought a stash of LSD to Florida, and we went on an acid double date—Abbie and Anita, me and a dolphin—at the Seaquarium in Miami.

Anita observed, "It looks like hippies have been using dolphins for their role models as pioneers of a leisure economy."

I was having a delightful nonverbal encounter with one particular dolphin. I would run to my left, and the dolphin would swim in the same direction. Then I would run back to my right, stop short, run to my left again, then back to my right, and the dolphin would swim in perfect synchronization. We resembled that scene in the Marx Brothers movie *Duck Soup* where Harpo mimics Groucho's motions in a nonexistent mirror. Finally it was time to leave for a movie, and I had to say goodbye to my new dolphin friend.

"By the way," I asked, "what are you always smirking about?"

The dolphin replied—and I'm willing to concede that this might have been my own acid projection—"If God is evolution, then how do you know He's finished?" It was obviously a male chauvinist dolphin.

We had planned to see *The Professionals* with Burt Lancaster and Lee Marvin—Abbie said, "That's my favorite movie"—but it was playing too far away, and a hurricane was brewing, so instead we saw the Dino De Laurentiis version of *The Bible*. Driving home in the wind and the rain, we debated the implications of Abraham being prepared to slay his son because God told him to do it. I dismissed this as blind obedience. Abbie praised it as revolutionary trust.

This was the week before Christmas. We had bought a small tree and spray-painted it with canned snow. Now, we were still tripping as the hurricane reached full force, and the house was shaking.

"Hey," Abbie shouted, "this is pretty fuckin' powerful acid!"

We watched Lyndon Johnson on the news. The TV set was black-and-white, but LBJ on LSD was purple and orange. His huge head was sculpted into Mount Rushmore. "I am not going to be so pudding-headed as to stop our half of the war," he was saying. And the heads of the other presidents—George Washington, Thomas Jefferson, Abraham Lincoln and Theodore Roosevelt—were all snickering to themselves and covering their mouths with their hands so they wouldn't laugh out loud.

That dolphin was right. The political system could evolve into a compassionate governing body; the economic system could evolve into a humane process; and progress itself could evolve into a balance of decentralization and the global village. But for now, all we knew was that we would have to go to the Democratic convention in Chicago the next summer to protest the war in Vietnam and help speed up the process of evolution just a little.

That evening I followed a neighborhood crow down the road, then continued walking to town by myself to use the telephone. First I called Dick Gregory, since it was his city we were planning to invade. He told me he had decided to run for president, and he wanted to know if I thought Bob Dylan would make a good vice president.

"Oh, sure, but to tell you the truth, I don't think Dylan would ever get involved in electoral politics."

Gregory would end up with assassination researcher Mark Lane as his running mate. Next, I called Jerry Rubin in New York to arrange for a meeting when we returned. The conspiracy was beginning.

★ ★ ★

On the afternoon of December 31, 1967, several activist friends were gathered at Abbie and Anita's apartment, smoking Columbian marijuana and planning the Chicago action. Our fantasy was to counter the convention of death with a festival of life. While the Democrats would present politicians giving speeches at the convention center, we would present rock bands playing in the park. There would be booths with information about drugs and alternatives to the draft. Our mere presence would be our statement.

We needed a name, so that reporters could have a *who* for their journalistic *who-what-when-where-and-why* lead paragraphs. A couple of months earlier, the Diggers had organized a parade in San Francisco to declare "The Death of Hippie." Instead, they wanted to be called "free Americans." It never quite caught on. Nobody was out there yelling, "Get a haircut, you filthy free American!"

But, whereas the Diggers wanted to avoid all the attention brought about by the media, we sought to utilize the media as an organizing tool. I felt a brainstorm coming on. I went into the bedroom so that I could concentrate. I paced back and forth, juggling titles to see if I could come up with words that would make a good acronym. I tried Youth International Festival. YIF. Sounds like KIF. Kids International Festival? No, too contrived. Back to YIF. But what could make YIP? Now *that* would be ideal, because then the word Yippie could be derived organically from YIP. "Yippie" was a traditional shout of spontaneous joy. We could be the *Yippies*! It had just the right attitude.

"The Yippies" seemed like the most appropriate name to signify the radicalization of hippies. What a perfect media myth that would be. And then, working backward, it hit me. *Youth*—this was essentially a movement of young people involved in a generational struggle. *International*—it was happening all over the world, from Mexico to France, from Germany to Japan. And *Party*—in both senses of the word. We would *be* a party and we would *have* a party.

So that became our immediate consensus. We would be the Youth International Party and we would be called the Yippies! The name provided its own power of persuasion. The Yippie logo was designed by Judy Lampe, using a particular style of Japanese lithography she had studied. Yippie was simply a label to describe a phenomenon that already existed—an organic coalition of psychedelic dropouts and political activists.

There was no separation between our culture and our politics. In the process of cross-pollination, we had come to share an awareness that there was a linear connection between putting kids in prison for smoking marijuana in this country and burning them to death with napalm on the other side of the globe. It was the ultimate extension of dehumanization.

That evening we watched *The Smothers Brothers Comedy Hour* on TV. Judy Collins sang Randy Newman's song "I Think It's Gonna Rain Today," and I started weeping at a line in the lyric, "human kindness overflowing." Then we all went to a New Year's Eve party. On the way, I rubbed some fresh snow into Jerry Rubin's bushy hair, singing the commercial jingle, "Get Wildroot Cream Oil, Charlie." It was a Yippie baptismal rite.

* * *

I paid the rent for an office in Union Square, run by Nancy Kurshan and Walli Leff, and we held open meetings every week at the nearby Free University. In February 1968, a few of us Yippies attended a college newspaper editors' conference in Washington, D.C. Senator Robert Kennedy happened to get off the same train that we were on. He had both come out *against* the bombing in Vietnam and voted *for* Johnson's supplementary budget to subsidize the war. Then he announced that he would not run against Lyndon Johnson for the Democratic nomination.

Now, here was Kennedy, talking to an aide in the train station. Abbie, Jerry, and I stood there, looking like the psychedelic Three Stooges. This particular encounter crystallized the difference in personality of the Yippie leaders. Jerry was the left brain of the Yippies, and Abbie was the right brain. Jerry was ogling Robert Kennedy. "Look how tan he is," Jerry said. "What an opportunity. We've gotta *do* something." Abbie, on the other hand, didn't hesitate a second to devise any tactic. He simply followed his impulse.

"*Bobby*," he roared, from six yards away —"*you got no guts!*"

The senator flinched ever so slightly.

As for me, two years previously I had sent reprints of an article from Dave Dellinger's *Liberation* magazine—"American Atrocities in Vietnam" by Eric Norden—to the president and every senator and member of Congress. Bobby Kennedy was the only one who at least had responded. Now I was tempted to thank him, but I didn't feel comfortable approaching him, especially on the heels of Abbie's outburst.

This was not Cuba. We were not a dozen bearded revolutionists hiding out in the Sierra Maestra. This was America, obsessed with the media, and that would be the Yippies' battleground. We started with the underground press. Liberation News Service, an alternative equivalent to the establishment wire services, sent out the Yippies' first press release, a manifesto signed by a variety of countercultural artists, writers, and musicians.

Then, early in March, publicist Michael Goldstein secured a plush conference room at the Americana Hotel in New York City, ostensibly for the purpose of announcing Judy Collins's new album, but the event had also been arranged to serve as a setting for the Yippies to officially proclaim their existence at an overground press conference. On this occasion, in order to emphasize the cultural over the political, Abbie and Jerry decided not to speak.

Judy Collins declared, "We will be going to Chicago for the children."

I said, "Bobby Kennedy announced he wasn't going to oppose Lyndon Johnson by seeking the nomination for president because he doesn't want to split the Democratic Party, but human life is more important than the Republican and Democratic parties put together."

A reporter asked me why the Yippies weren't supporting Eugene McCarthy. I explained that although there was no Yippie party line, it was our policy not to support any candidate. Then I criticized the McCarthy Clean-for-Gene campaign.

I said, "Allen Ginsberg wouldn't even be allowed to ring anybody's doorbell unless he agreed to shave off his beard."

The reporter asked, "Would you cut off your hair if it would end the war?"

Before I could answer, Ginsberg popped up and asked the reporter, "Would you let your hair *grow* if it would end the war?"

Later, in the thickly carpeted corridor of the Americana, several Yippies held an impromptu contest to follow up that line of questioning, concerned with exactly how open to self-sacrifice one might become in the pursuit of peace. Ed Sanders won, with this criterion: "Would you suck off a terminal leper if it would end the war?"

Meanwhile, the reporters had a *who* for their lead paragraphs. A headline in the *Chicago Daily News* summed it up: "Yipes! The Yippies are Coming!" The myth was already becoming a reality. Yippie chapters were forming on campuses, and Yippies across the country were beginning to find out what to call themselves.

★ ★ ★

After the assassination of John Kennedy, impersonator Vaughn Meader dropped out of comedy. He moved to San Francisco and become a late-blooming flower child. He returned to New York in 1968, and attended a few Yippie meetings. We invited him to play Bobby Kennedy at our counter-convention. But then, in mid-March, Kennedy announced that he was going to run for president after all.

Furthermore, Kennedy said that he would have "great reservations" about supporting LBJ if he won the nomination and the Republicans nominated a candidate who wanted to reduce the American military in Vietnam. As a by-product of Bobby Kennedy entering the race, the enthusiasm of Yippie leaders became replaced by doubt, and there was serious talk about calling off Chicago. Were the Yippies being co-opted by Kennedy?

On March 31, Meader asked me for a tab of LSD. That evening, President Johnson went on TV and announced that he would not seek reelection. My phone rang immediately. I answered, "I accept the nomination." It was Vaughn Meader calling. In the middle of tripping, he had just seen Johnson's announcement, and he couldn't tell whether it was an acid hallucination or an April Fool's Eve joke. But it was true—LBJ was out of the race. This was a further setback, but not only for the Yippies.

Lenny Bruce whistled from the grave, "*Whew!* David Frye is *screwed.*"

In April, Martin Luther King was assassinated. As attorney general, Bobby Kennedy had approved the FBI's wiretapping of King's phone. Now, as senator, he provided an airplane for King's widow. In June, on the night that Kennedy won the Democratic nomination in the California primary, *he* was assassinated. Kennedy had been on *The Tonight Show*, telling Johnny Carson that cigarettes kill more people than marijuana, and I was ready to believe that Sirhan Sirhan was a hired gun for the tobacco lobby.

On Tom Hayden's bedroom wall, there was now a pair of framed telegrams, one inviting him to Martin Luther King's funeral, the other inviting him to Robert Kennedy's funeral. Kennedy's death served to re-energize the Yippies' plans for going to the Democratic convention. The new front-runner, Vice President Hubert Humphrey, would never disavow Lyndon Johnson's war in Vietnam the way Kennedy had. Humphrey would hang himself with his own umbilical cord. I assigned artist Richard Guindon to create such an illustration.

Meanwhile, *Life* magazine was preparing to publish a profile of me. I had posed for photos parodying their style—playing basketball in the midst of my incredibly sloppy loft—and now their photographer was capturing my image as I lay on the floor of the airport writing a check for my ticket. The Yippies were flying to Chicago to try and get a permit for the revolution. Since I had no identification, the airline wouldn't accept my check, so the *Life* photographer bought my ticket with his credit card.

In Chicago, we were in the office of Mayor Richard Daley's assistant, Deputy Mayor David Stahl, in a futile attempt to obtain permits to sleep in the park, set up a sound system, and march to the convention center.

Stahl asked me, "What are you guys *really* planning to do at the convention?"

I said, "Didn't you see *Wild in the Streets?*"

In that movie, based on a short story in *Esquire*, teenagers put LSD into the water supply and took over the government, reducing the voting age to fourteen. This may have been one reason the Daley administration thought that the Yippies were actually planning to put LSD into the water supply.

"*Wild in the Streets?*" Stahl repeated. "We've seen *Battle of Algiers.*"

In that black-and-white documentary-style movie, a guerrilla woman wearing a burka walks freely through a security checkpoint and plants a bomb in a café. The camera pans around to show the innocent face of a child eating an ice-cream cone who is among those innocent citizens about to be blown up.

(In a Black Panther trial, the prosecution showed the jury *Battle of Algiers* to indicate the Panthers' state of mind, and the defense showed them *Z*, about a police state, to indicate the prosecution's state of mind.)

What was to happen on the summer of '68, then, would be a clash between *our* mythology and *their* mythology. Abbie remained in Chicago to organize for the event. Jerry said, "I feel like Fidel Castro when he left Che Guevara in the jungles of Bolivia." I continued to be a media spokesperson for the Yippies. If you gave a good quote, they would give you free publicity.

"Do you plan to live in tents?"

"Well, some of us will live intense, and other will live frivolously."

"Why don't you go to the Republican convention in Miami?"

"What, during the off-season?"

"Do the Yippies have a party line?"

"Yeah, we're gonna roll a ball of string all the way from New York to Chicago, and that'll be our party line."

"Suppose the war in Vietnam ends—then what will happen to the Yippies?"

"We'll do what the March of Dimes did when the polio vaccine was discovered—we'll switch to birth defects."

I objected when Abbie came up with "Kill your parents!"—but Jerry eagerly latched on to it. I knew it was only a metaphorical slogan, not supposed to be taken literally. Still, Abbie had two children by his first marriage—he didn't want them to kill *him*—and Jerry was *already* an orphan. A photo of Jerry made the cover of the *National Enquirer* with this headline: "Yippie Leader Tells Children to Kill Their Parents!"

A reporter for the *CBS Evening News* interviewed Abbie and me. Abbie said, "I'm prepared to win or die." That never got on the air. The reporter asked me, "What do the Yippies actually plan to do in Chicago?" I smiled. "You think I'm gonna tell *you?*" That portion of my answer was used to end Walter Cronkite's segment on the Yippies, but my follow-up sentence—"The first thing we're gonna do is put truth serum in the reporters' drinks"—was omitted. They had beaten me at my own game.

* * *

Before the birth of Yippie, Abbie had been using the Diggers' name to describe himself and other local community organizers. Emmett Grogan demanded that he stop. This was symbolic of the fierce rivalry between them. Even though Grogan had lent Abbie a pile of Digger leaflets in a spirit of cooperation, he resented Abbie for imitating the Diggers, from opening a Free Store on the Lower East Side to burning a dollar bill at a rally.

Grogan snarled, "You're a fuckin' copycat. The Diggers were burning money a couple of fuckin' *years* ago!"

I had told the Diggers of a conference at a campground in Denton, Michigan, sponsored by Students for a Democratic Society. They arrived in the middle of Tom Hayden's speech and were so disruptive that SDS accused them of being CIA. Grogan climbed onto a table and delivered a loud, mean-spirited, more-radical-than-thou rap. Then he jumped off the table and shoved it toward the audience—just a prop in his theater of cruelty.

I didn't expect to see this kind of hostility. Originally I was charmed by the gentleness of Digger pranks. Peter Berg had conned two reporters—one from *Time* and one from *The Saturday Evening Post*, both wearing hippie garb—into interviewing each other as manager of the Free Store.

When Abbie re-enacted Grogan's gesture on another occasion, over-throwing a table during his own speech, that only made Grogan cling more adamantly to his proprietary attitude. When he learned that Abbie had compiled a booklet, *Fuck the System*, he assumed it was based on the Digger leaflets, and he exploded with rage. At 3 AM he took a cab to Abbie and Anita's apartment. Grogan knew that Abbie was in Boston and spoke with him on the phone. He then proceeded to rape Anita in order to get even with Abbie. To compound the despicable nature of that act of revenge, he later boasted about it in his autobiography, *Ringolevio*, written in third person:

> Emmett got himself a can of something from the refrigerator and watched the movie [on TV] and talked with Anita for a while, before he took what he had to take, to show Abbot Hoffman how something "free" could be stolen and how it felt to have it taken.

When Anita told Abbie what happened, he got into an old-fashioned fistfight with Grogan, like a couple of street kids in a time warp. Nobody won. I asked Anita if she would prefer that I not write about the incident.

"Naturally, no one likes to be identified as a victim," she said, "so I'm not fond of discussing this, but I certainly see no reason to protect Grogan."

★ ★ ★

The Mad Scientist was neither mad nor scientific. Actually, he had been active in theater. However, when he took LSD for the first time in a lighting booth where he watched a production of *Cyrano* he had directed, he decided to leave the theater for the streets. In May 1968, he was in Paris with a suitcase full of hashish. He had been tangentially political before, but now he found himself in the middle of a citizens' revolt.

Barricades were being erected with the same cobblestones that had been dug up in the original French Revolution. The physical experience of being there served to radicalize him. None of his friends was a chemist, but somehow they had learned to make hash oil. Meanwhile, he was feeling a cultural force from America—the Yippie myth had crossed the Atlantic—and he decided to go to Chicago.

On the weekend before the convention, the Mad Scientist went strolling through Lincoln Park, asking, "Do you know Abbie Hoffman?" Eventually, he asked Abbie himself, and before you could say "hidden laboratory," there was one. The lab consisted of long tables, spread out with hundreds of packages of Bugler tobacco. The hash oil was cut with pure grain alcohol, put in atomizers, and sprayed on the tobacco, which was then rolled into joints, placed back in the packages, and given away as Yippie cigarettes.

I warned Abbie that smoking tobacco could be harmful to his lungs, but he said, "Don't worry. In the future, we're all gonna grow gills."

For those who preferred a healthier version, the hash oil was mixed into jars of honey. This was strong stuff. The Fugs were completely fugged up. Ed Sanders described the grass he was walking on as "a giant frothing trough of mutant spinach egg noodles." Tuli Kupferberg took a taste, and friends had to carry him by the armpits back to the apartment where he was staying.

"They're delivering me," he explained.

I swallowed two tablespoons of honey and stayed in the park. I was on my knees, holding on to the grass very tightly so that I wouldn't fall *up*. We so-called Yippie leaders were zonked out of our minds. Sam and Walli Leff were driving us around Chicago when we realized that we were being followed by another car. It was like being in a slow-motion chase scene. But could this merely be paranoia as a side effect of the hash oil?

I suggested that we go the wrong way down a one-way street. Then, if the other car was *still* following us, we could be sure that they *were* following us. We stopped in front of a guy sitting on a bench. I got out and told him that we thought we were being followed. We would drive around the block, and if he saw that this other car was in fact following us, he should give us a signal.

So we circled the block, the other car followed us, the guy on the bench gave us a signal, and we continued on, figuring that the two men who were tailing us were cops and now they had to wonder what this guy had just accomplished that he was signaling us about, and should they maybe follow *him* instead?

The previous day, we had been refused service at a restaurant. I told the manager, "You're about to have your first Yippie sit-in," and they finally served us. Now we stopped there again, shook hands with the manager, and told him there were no hard feelings, even as he was being put on the suspect list by the cops who were following us. We also stopped at an art-supply store where we had been treated rather rudely, and got *them* listed as accomplices too. Finally we parked. So did the cops. We got out and walked back to their car. They tried to appear nonchalant.

"Hey," Abbie asked, "are you guys following us?"

"That's right."

"Are you federal or local?"

"We're plainclothes officers with the Chicago Police Department. You're under twenty-four hour surveillance."

"Wow," I said, "three shifts, just for us!"

"No, we're short on manpower. We're on two twelve-hour shifts."

"Well," I said, "it's an honor just to be nominated."

We introduced ourselves and shook hands with the cops. Their names were Herbie and Mac. We offered them official Yippie buttons, but they said, "No, thanks, we're on duty." I explained that if we happened to lose them in a crowd, we'd be able to spot them more easily if they were wearing Yippie buttons, so they accepted the buttons and pinned them on their jackets.

But this kind of communication is a two-way street, and now the cops asked *us* if we were planning to eat soon, because they had been following us for a while, and now they were getting sort of hungry. Although we had terminal dry mouth from the hash oil, maybe lunch would stimulate our salivary glands. We asked the cops to recommend a good restaurant since we were new in Chicago.

"Well," Herbie said, "the Pickle Barrel in Old Town has pretty good food."

"And," Mac added, "their prices are quite reasonable."

"Okay, what's the best way to get there?"

"Follow us."

This was indeed a rare and precious moment. We obediently got back into our car and followed the cops. I thought they were going to try and shake us, but we managed to never lose sight of them. It was as if someone had pushed the rewind button and now our slow-motion chase scene seemed to be running backward. I expected to see the cops stop at the art-supply store, and the restaurant, and then a guy sitting on a bench would give them a signal—but instead we just followed them straight to the Pickle Barrel.

We sat at separate tables.

★ ★ ★

On the Saturday before convention week, officers were placed at every pumping and filtration plant to prevent the Yippies from putting LSD into the water supply, even though it was known that five tons of acid would be necessary for such action to be effective.

In the evening we were reminded that sleeping in the park would not be allowed, even though Boy Scout troops had been permitted to do so. We were given an eleven o'clock curfew. Allen Ginsberg played the role of a pied piper and safely led the troops out with the power of chanting: "*Ommmmmmm . . . Ommmmmmmm . . . Ommmmmmm . . .*"

On Sunday afternoon, Bob Fass was standing on a makeshift stage in Lincoln Park, preparing to introduce the MC-5, a band from Detroit. Fass's free-form show on Pacifica station WBAI in New York, "Radio Unnameable," helped orchestrate the nights there, serving as a central clearing house for community events, problems, and solutions.

Now his mouth was so dry from hash-oil honey, he could hardly talk, so he just stood there and smiled, but the audience—also having tasted from the honey pot—just sat on the grass and smiled back at him. It was Fass who said, "A Yippie is a hippie who's been hit on the head with a police billy club." Now, suddenly, the cops were about to act out his definition by using force to prevent the concert from continuing. Stew Albert was the first casualty. He got his skull smashed.

I screamed at the cops, "You're not supposed to attack us until eleven o'clock!"

After Stew's head was stitched and bandaged, we went to a Western Union office and sent a telegram to the United Nations, requesting them to send in a human rights unit to investigate violations in Chicago. First Malcolm X, and then the Black Panthers, had planned to take their case to the UN. Stew had served as a liaison between the Yippies and the Panthers.

A week before the Democratic convention, the Peace and Freedom party had held their convention in Ann Arbor, Michigan. Panther leader Eldridge Cleaver was nominated as their candidate for president, although Jerry Rubin was turned down as his running mate. Cleaver wanted to come to Chicago, but he was on parole and couldn't get permission to leave California. Fellow Panther Bobby Seale flew to Chicago in his place.

Robert Pierson, a local biker who had become Jerry Rubin's bodyguard, tried to persuade Jerry to arrange for Bobby Seale to lead a march from Grant Park to Lincoln Park. Whose conspiracy was this anyway?

Jerry told Stew, "Bob Pierson is really getting militant."

"It's too dangerous," Stew replied. "Just try not to hurt his feelings."

In Lincoln Park, Seale gave his standard pro-gun rap. "If a pig comes up to us and starts swinging a billy club, and you check around and you got your piece, you got to down that pig in defense of yourself! We're gonna barbecue us some pork!"

* * *

Although the Yippie leadership had a male image in the media, in reality so much of the behind-the-scenes work was done by women—Nancy Kurshan, Anita Hoffman, Walli Leff, Judy Clavir, Ellen Maslow, Anne Ockene, Kathy Streem, and Judy Lampe.

The leadership was all white, except for Jerome Washington, who was black. We had bonded at the October demonstration in Washington, where we were both pissing on the Pentagon building. As a Yippie organizer, he worked behind the scenes and was able to get permission from the Blackstone Rangers, the largest street gang in Chicago, for the antiwar movement to come to their city. He told me, "We could never have come if they hadn't okayed it. They really owned those streets."

Another unheralded Yippie organizer was known as Super-Joel. His grandfather was Mafia boss Sam Giancana, but Super-Joel had dropped out of the family business. Instead, he let his hair grow long and distributed

LSD. The intelligence division of the Chicago Police Department warned Giancana that Super-Joel shouldn't hang around with me. The cops were telling the Mafia that *I* was a bad influence. Super-Joel was arrested at the convention. He yelled and gave the cops the finger through the caged door at the back of the paddy wagon. Super-Joel got arrested three times during the convention. He was just another anonymous Yippie now.

"If it wasn't for acid," Super-Joel told me, "I with my Sicilian ancestry and you with your Jewish ancestry, we would never have become such close friends."

And he kissed me. But that was okay. It meant love now, not murder.

Abbie, Anita, and I were staying at the apartment of a friend, whose landlord freaked out. I learned later that he was sitting on the front steps of his building, holding a .32 caliber revolver, waiting to shoot Abbie or me.

I had taken a quick flight to speak at the University of Kansas, then returned to Chicago, going directly to the temporary office of the *Ramparts Wall Poster* to deliver my article. Writer Art Goldberg offered to drive me to the apartment from there. Because we both had long hair, a cop stopped us and searched the trunk. He asked for Art's driver's license, and when he saw the name Goldberg, he said, "We'll get you all in the oven yet."

It was during this delay that other police arrested the landlord with the gun. My life had been inadvertently saved by an anti-Semitic cop.

Abbie, Anita, and I moved into the apartment of my new girlfriend, Beverly Baysinger. On Monday of convention week, Beverly and I were walking in the park, holding hands and being followed by Herbie, the plainclothes cop who had been assigned to me. He now called himself Hawkeye and had taken to wearing a red cap so that I'd be able to spot him in a crowd in case we lost each other. Hawkeye even offered me half of his sandwich, which I accepted.

"My wife put some LSD in it," he said.

On Tuesday evening we all attended an Unbirthday Party for President Johnson at the Coliseum, with Ed Sanders serving as emcee. The atmosphere was highly emotional. Dick Gregory recited the Preamble to the Declaration of Independence with incredible fervor. Fists were being upraised in the audience as he spoke, and I thrust my own fist into the air for the first time.

Phil Ochs sang "I Ain't Marching Anymore," and the place went absolutely wild. As individuals in the crowd started burning their draft cards, others joined in this spontaneous combustion. The audience of five thousand wouldn't stop cheering. The standing ovation was an incredible emotional release. They were still cheering even after Phil left the stage.

As we embraced, he said, "That was the most exciting moment of my career."

When it was my turn to speak, I told the true story of a journalist who had once interviewed LBJ, and after the formal question-and-answer session was over, the president told him, "You know, what the Communists are really saying is, 'Fuck you, Lyndon Johnson,' and nobody says, 'Fuck you, Lyndon Johnson,' and gets away with it!" I paused. "Well, when I count three, we're all gonna say it—*and we're gonna get away with it!* Are you ready? One . . . two . . . three . . ."

And, from the Yippies and the Mobilization-Against-the-War and the Clean-for-Genes, it came at me like an audio tidal wave—thousands of voices shouting in unison, "*FUCK YOU, LYNDON JOHNSON!!!*"—a mass catharsis reverberating from the rafters.

I told Ochs, "That was the most exciting moment of *my* career."

That night, across the street from the Hilton Hotel, where many delegates were staying, there was an outdoor teach-in on Michigan Avenue. A Peace Corps veteran related how that idealistic organization had turned into "an arm of the State Department." Peter, Paul and Mary sang "If I Had a Hammer." And the crowd continued chanting: "*Fuck you, LBJ! Fuck you, LBJ!*" It wasn't exactly "*Ommmmmmm,*" but you could dance to it.

The teach-in was replaced by a mob scene the next night, when Hubert Humphrey was nominated. Ironically, LBJ had dropped out of the race because Eugene McCarthy won the New Hampshire primary, but Humphrey hadn't even *entered* a single primary. So now Michigan Avenue became a Roman arena for the delegates up in their balconies at the Hilton. By voting for Humphrey, they had turned their thumbs down on us.

Protesters planned to march to the Amphitheater the next day, but since sadistic violence had been building up from the beginning, some decided to remain in the park for sanctuary. There were restrictions on where we could march, but Dick Gregory had told me he was going to get around that rule by inviting *everybody* to come to his house, which just happened to be on the other side of the Amphitheater.

Several years previously, he told me that I had been the first white person who was a guest in his home. I had watched TV with his children, and we all laughed at the Clairol commercial which asked, "Is it true that blondes have more fun?" Now, the FBI planned to "neutralize" Gregory by alerting the Mafia to his verbal attacks on the crime syndicate.

The violence reached a peak on Wednesday during speeches in Grant Park. The *Chicago Tribune* would later report that Bob Pierson—the police provocateur posing as a biker who had volunteered to act as Jerry Rubin's bodyguard—was "in the group which lowered an American flag"—the incident which set off what the government's *Walker Report* would describe as "a police riot." In *Official Detective* magazine, Pierson wrote:

> One thing we were to do was defile the flag. The American flag in the park was taken down, then rehung upside down. After this had been photographed, a group of us, including me, were ordered to pull it down and destroy it, then to run up the black flag of the Viet Cong. I joined in the chants and taunts against the police and provoked them into hitting me with their clubs. They didn't know who I was, but they did know that I had called them names and struck them with one or more weapons.

Because of media omnipresence, our chant became, "The whole world is watching! The whole world is watching!" But Walter Cronkite left unchallenged Mayor Daley's assertion that the beating of protesters on the street was necessary because there had been an assassination threat against the candidates.

★ ★ ★

Marvin Garson had originally suggested that the Yippies nominate an actual pig as *our* candidate for president. When word of this reached the authorities, they put an armed guard on the pig in the zoo.

Keith Lampe asked William Burroughs, "What do you think of this idea—we're running a pig for president?"

Burroughs replied, "Well, that's a pretty good idea, but it would be more interesting if you ran a tape recorder."

Meanwhile, a certain competitiveness had developed between Abbie and Jerry. Abbie bought a pig, but Jerry thought Abbie's pig wasn't big enough, mean enough, or ugly enough, so Jerry went out and bought a bigger, meaner, uglier pig, which was released at City Hall.

The Yippies had been infiltrated by ego involvement.

Abbie wanted to spread a rumor that he had been killed by the Chicago police so there might be a riot in his name. Instead, he got arrested for having the word *FUCK* printed on his forehead with lipstick, an idea borrowed from Lenny Bruce, who had once printed *FUCK* on *his* forehead with strips of paper towel from a courthouse bathroom, in order to discourage photographers from taking his picture. Abbie might have gotten away with it if only he hadn't tipped his hat to the police who were sitting in their car across the street from the house where we were staying, waiting for us to start the day. They followed us to a restaurant, where they asked Abbie to take off his hat, and when he did, they told him he was under arrest.

"It's the duty of a revolutionist to finish breakfast," he replied, but the cops disagreed with his premise. They handcuffed him and proceeded to drag him out of the restaurant, forcing me to eat the rest of his breakfast.

Jerry wanted to obtain press credentials, gain entry to the convention hall, and run down the aisle protesting when Hubert Humphrey got the nomination. "Jerry," I warned him, "they'll shoot you before you ever get to the podium." He shrugged and asked rhetorically, "What's my life?" Instead, he got arrested for inciting to riot while he was walking out of a restaurant.

Nor was I immune to this infectious egomania. While I was walking away from the park, a young National Guardsman ordered me to halt, but I just kept on walking, not looking back, fantasizing that he might stick his bayonet through my back, which would certainly have received much coverage in the media, although, ironically enough, he wouldn't have even known who I was. But he didn't stab me, and I wandered onto Michigan Avenue, where the battle was building up.

Newsweek correspondent Don Johnson signaled me. "You better get off the street," he warned. "The cops are looking for you."

"But I'm not *doing* anything."

He laughed. "Did you forget what you wrote?" Johnson, who is black, quoted a line from my piece in the *Ramparts Wall Poster*: "The Yippies are a community of voluntary niggers."

"Yeah," I said, "but it's not *really* the same. We can just cut our hair anytime we want."

I asked if it was relevant to refer to him as black when I wrote about this. "Now more than ever," he said.

Six black youths had been killed outside the Republican convention in Miami. And just before the Democratic convention, a seventeen-year-old Indian was shot to death by the police, who insisted that he had drawn a gun first. The Yippies held a memorial for him. There was also a rally to protest the invasion of Czechoslovakia by Russian tanks. This confused those who were convinced that we were being financed by the Communist Party.

I was disappointed that my idea for the Yippie Olympics never reached fruition. There was an area in the park with an athletic field, and we were going to have a race around the track with contestants running backwards. There would have been a marathon high jump—contestants getting high, then jumping up and down for as long as they could. There also would've been a sugar-cube hunt and a joint-rolling contest.

At Abbie's request, I stood in the park and declared the Yippies dead. I announced that "Yippie was merely a slogan to bring together the New Left and the psychedelic dropouts. The Yippies never really existed."

Nevertheless, there would soon be a soft drink on the market named

"Yippie!" I got a call from a TV quiz-show researcher wanting to know the name of the pig that had been the Yippie candidate for president. I made a point of watching that particular show. The contestant, an air force pilot, didn't know the correct answer—Pigasus. A question in one of the Trivial Pursuit games would ask what members of the Youth International Party were called; the correct answer was, of course, "the Yippies."

Another question was, "Who first suggested putting LSD into the Chicago water supply?" And the answer was—*me*. An episode of *It's Garry Shandling's Show* revolved around the publication of an old photo of his mother sitting nude on Abbie Hoffman's shoulders. Jerry Rubin appeared in a cameo spot on *Saturday Night Live*, selling "revolutionary wallpaper." And an episode of *Barney Miller* would show a police inspector looking at an arrestee's record and muttering, "A Yippie, huh?" He then read from the rap sheet: "Making bombs, inciting to riot . . ." That's disinfotainment.

Richard Nixon defeated both Hubert Humphrey *and* Pigasus in the 1968 election, and David Frye became a born-again impressionist. Although the nation had a new Republican president, a certain horrifying ritual continued as a bipartisan policy. My daughter, Holly, then four, was sitting on my lap one evening as I watched the CBS News, and there was Walter Cronkite, matter-of-factly reciting that week's body count.

"Daddy," Holly asked, "is that happening in our universe?"

It was Thursday again.

CHAPTER 8

BURNING BRAS AND BRIDGES

WHAT WAS LIFE LIKE AFTER YIPPIE? THE TREND WAS TOWARD AFFINITY groups. My affinity group was not very together. We didn't know what actions to take. The London Bridge was being dismantled and shipped across the Atlantic Ocean, and there was some joking about blowing it up after it was rebuilt in Arizona. We also considered breaking the windows of glazier shops around New York. But first we would have to steal a quantity of wristwatches with second hands so that we could practice synchronizing them.

Actually, I was asked by antiwar activist Walter Teague to go on a more serious mission to Canada, to help arrange for an unofficial prisoner-of-war exchange. I was stopped and searched at the airport in Montreal. They found a card in my pocket bearing data about Ventnor Avenue. It was from a Monopoly game. I had found it on a subway train.

"What's this for?" asked a customs official.

"It's a deed. I'm a property owner."

They let me go. I was just too silly to fit their profile of a terrorist.

At the meeting, everyone was being obsequiously respectful of the representative from North Vietnam. Someone asked how the negotiator, Madame Ti Binh, would get to Canada from Paris.

"She's gonna walk across the water," I said.

There was an awkward silence until the Vietnamese man walked over, smiling, and embraced me.

"I like you," he said. "You're crazy."

The tension was relieved, and the others felt it was okay to laugh.

Back in New York, Ben Morea and Tom Neumann of Black Mask, an anarchist group in New York whose members were all dressed in black, became the nucleus of an SDS street chapter named "Up Against the Wall Motherfuckers," borrowing it from a line in a LeRoi Jones poem, "Up against the wall, motherfucker, this is a stickup!"

Whereas Black Mask had once issued a leaflet criticizing Tim Leary for being counterrevolutionary by advocating LSD, the Motherfuckers' urban commune started taking acid and changed their position. They began to wear beads—all black beads at first, and later a variety of colors. They appointed themselves watchdogs of the Lower East Side, following police around to make sure they didn't hassle citizens. Their red headbands were a precursor to the Guardian Angels' red berets a decade later.

When Bill Graham converted the Village Theater to the Fillmore East, the Motherfuckers demanded one free night a week. I accompanied Motherfucker Tom Neumann to a meeting with Graham, who asked, "What exactly do you want to do?"

"Bomb! Shoot! Kill!" Neumann explained.

I was embarrassed by this and added, "We thought you might like to contribute to the United Jewish Fund."

One night at the Fillmore East, the Living Theater participated in a benefit for the Columbia student radicals. But this was not the usual audience for their production of *Paradise Now*. Some folks in the audience were burning dollar bills *before* the actors chanted, "I cannot live without money." They were undressing *before* the actors chanted, "I am not allowed to take my clothes off." Joints were being passed around openly *before* the actors chanted, "I am not allowed to smoke marijuana." Suddenly, the Motherfuckers seized the stage to act out the leaflet they had distributed:

> Tonight the people return the theater to themselves. Originally our demands were modest, one night a week for the people of the FREE community. Bill Graham (who, within the archaic legal frames, was technically in control of the theater) refused our demands. Now we take what is ours anyway. The theater now belongs to the people, including Bill Graham. *We must preserve this liberated territory. Now!*

Graham came onstage and shouted, "You'll never take this building by force! You'll have to kill me!"

Naturally, folks in the audience called out, "Kill him! Kill him!" This was more than the Living Theater had bargained for. "Burn it down!" they screamed. "Burn it down!"

A riot could break out any minute. Journalist Michael Thomas wrote:

> And Paul Krassner, laughing, because that's what he does best, was standing backstage in this denim outfit he wears, like a love-soiled

prison guard, saying how he was scheduled to speak after the Living Theater, but he'd rather take his chances at the Apollo Theater in Harlem on the anniversary of the assassination of Martin Luther King while wearing a George Wallace button.

I did go onstage, though, and found myself arguing with the Motherfuckers about the Hare Krishnas.

Motherfucker Ben Morea shouted, "There's no place for religion in the revolution!"

"Bullshit," I shouted back. "Tell it to the Buddhist monks and nuns who set fire to themselves!"

Speaking of which, when I interviewed Woody Allen in 1965, our session concluded this way:

Q. Are you concerned about the population explosion?

A. No, I'm not. I mean, I recognize it as a problem which those who like that area can fool around with. I doubt if there's anything I can do about the population explosion, or about the atom bomb, besides vote when the time comes, and I contribute money to those organizations who spend their days in active pursuit of ends that I'm in agreement with. But that's all. And I'm not going to set fire to myself.

Q. But do you agree with the motivation of the Buddhist monks who set fire to themselves in Vietnam?

A. I don't think so. No, I think that they don't know what they're doing. I think they're nuts. That's not the answer. When all is said and done, it's not the answer. When you're home at night and you say to yourself, "Tomorrow morning I'll get up at eight o'clock and set fire to myself," there's something wrong. I wouldn't do it that way.

I can see dying for a principle, but not that way. At the very minimum, if you are going to die for something, you should at least take one of them with you. Go back to the Jews in Germany. If you have a loaded gun in your home, and the state comes to get you, you can at least get two or three of them.

I'm not opposed to violence as a course of action in many instances. Sometimes passive resistance is fine, but violence in its place is a good and necessary thing. But setting fire to yourself is not the answer. With my luck, I would be un-inflammable.

Anyway, Bill Graham, having a keen sense of community, ultimately gave the Motherfuckers their free night at Fillmore East. Each week a band would play, and then the Motherfuckers would do a commercial for the revolution.

★ ★ ★

Howard Rasmussen was not his real name. Actually, he was an FBI agent working in their New York office. One day in October 1968, he was reading *Life* magazine. He saw those photos of me—playing basketball in my loft, lying on the floor of an airport—accompanying a complimentary article. Then he sat down at his typewriter, creatively trying to choose every word so carefully that it would reek of credibility, as he composed the following letter to the editor of *Life* on plain stationery:

Sirs:

Your recent issue (October 4th), which devoted three pages to the aggrandizement of underground editor (?) Paul Krassner, was too, too much. You must be hard up for material. Am I asking the impossible by requesting that Krassner and his ilk be left in the sewers where they belong? That a national magazine of your fine reputation (till now that is) would waste time and effort on the cuckoo editor of an unimportant, smutty little rag is incomprehensible to me.

Gentlemen, you must be aware that *The Realist* is nothing more than blatant obscenity. Your feature editor would do well to read a few back issues of *The Realist*. Try the article in 1963 [*sic*] following the assassination of President Kennedy, which describes disgusting necrophilism on the part of LBJ. To classify Krassner as some sort of "social rebel" is far too cute. He's a nut, a raving, unconfined nut.

As for any possible intellectual rewards to be gleaned from *The Realist*—much better prose may be found on lavatory walls. If this article is a portent of things to come in *Life*, count me out, gentlemen, count me out.

Howard Rasmussen
Brooklyn College
School of General Studies

Before he could be permitted to mail the letter to *Life*, he was required to send a copy of it to FBI headquarters in Washington, along with this memorandum:

The 10/4/68 issue of *Life* magazine contained a three page feature on Paul Krassner, editor of *The Realist* and self-styled "hippie." Krassner is carried on the RI [Round-up Index] of the NYO [New York Office].

Bureau authority is requested to send the following letter to the editors of *Life* on an anonymous basis. It is noted that the *Life* article was favorable to Krassner.

Howard Rasmussen was merely doing his job, writing that poison pen letter, but is *that* how taxpayers' money was supposed to be spent? I had broken no law. The return memo—approved by J. Edgar Hoover's top two assistants, Kartha DeLoach and William Sullivan—was addressed to Mr. Floyd and Mr. Shackelford at the New York office. It stated:

> Authority is granted to send a letter, signed with a fictitious name, to the editors of *Life* magazine. Furnish the Bureau the results of your action.
>
> NOTE: Krassner is the Editor of *The Realist* and is one of the moving forces behind the Youth International Party, commonly known as the Yippies. Krassner is a spokesman for the New Left. *Life* magazine recently ran an article favorable to him.
>
> New York's proposed letter takes issue with the publishing of this article and points out that the *The Realist* is obscene and that Krassner is a nut. This letter could, if printed by *Life*, call attention to the unsavory character of Krassner.

Life magazine never published Howard Rasmussen's letter to the editor. However, they did publish *this* letter:

> Regarding your article on that filthy-mouthed, dope-taking, pinko-anarchist, pope-baiting, Yippie-lover: cancel my subscription immediately!
>
> Paul Krassner
> *The Realist*

There were Howard Rasmussens all over the place. One memo tried to smear Tom Hayden with the worst possible label they could invoke—"FBI informer." The FBI distributed a caricature depicting Black Panther leader Huey Newton "as a homosexual," and ran a fake "Pick the Fag" contest, referring to Dave McReynolds as "Chief White Fag of the lily-white War

Resisters League" and "the usual Queer Cats—like Sweet Dave Dellinger and Fruity Rennie Davis."

The FBI always took pains to instruct agents to "insure mailing material utilized and paper on which leaflet is prepared cannot be traced to the Bureau." In that context, "Bureau authority was received for New York to prepare and mail anonymously a letter regarding [an individual's] sexual liaison with his step-daughter (Age 13) to educational authorities in New Jersey" where he was a teacher.

In 1969, the FBI's previous attempt at mere character assassination of me escalated to a slightly more literal approach. This was not included in my own Co-Intel-Pro (Counter-Intelligence Program) files but, rather, discovered elsewhere by Sam Leff. At the Chicago convention, Leff had erased the line between anthropologist and activist. Later, as a Yippie archivist, he investigated a separate FBI project calculated to cause rifts between the black and Jewish communities.

He found this: Julius Lester had allowed a black teacher to read an anti-Semitic poem on his program over WBAI in order to showcase an artistic expression of the outrage behind that point of view. As a result, the station was picketed. The FBI reprinted the poem on a flyer with the photo of a picketer holding a placard reading DO NOT USE JEWS FOR SCAPEGOATS.

This leaflet was "aimed at individuals of Jewish background active in the New Left and who, until recently, gave open sympathy to Lester's revolutionary ideas." Then the FBI produced a WANTED poster featuring a large swastika. In the four square spaces of the swastika were photos of Jerry Rubin, Abbie Hoffman, Mark Rudd of SDS, and myself. Underneath the swastika was this message:

LAMPSHADES! LAMPSHADES! LAMPSHADES!

New York radio station WBAI recently featured programs under the tutelage of black revolutionary Julius Lester of the *Guardian* and Leslie R. Campbell, sometime teacher at JHS 271, from which it appeared that the only solution to Negro problems in America would be the *elimination* of the Jews. May we suggest the following order of elimination? (After all, we've been this way before.)

* All Jews connected with the Establishment.
* All Jews connected with Jews connected with the Establishment.
* All Jews connected with those immediately above.

* All Jews except those in the Movement.
* All Jews in the Movement except those who dye their skins black.
* All Jews (Look out, Jerry, Abbie, Mark, and Paul!)

Once again, this flyer was approved by the FBI director's top aides:

> Authority is granted to prepare and distribute on an anonymous basis to selected individuals and organizations in the New Left the leaflet submitted . . . Assure that all necessary precautions are taken to protect the Bureau as the source of these leaflets.

> NOTE: NY advised that Julius Lester, a revolutionary Negro writer for the *Guardian*, had recently featured one Leslie Campbell, a teacher at a Brooklyn high school, during one of his regular broadcasts over radio station WBAI. During the broadcast, Campbell read a poem which contained anti-Semitic statements. This and other broadcasts by Lester have resulted in organized picketing at WBAI and much comment in the press.

> NY suggested a leaflet be prepared, captioned: "Wanted: by Julius Lester" and containing pictures of several New Left leaders who are Jewish. This leaflet would refer to this broadcast and suggests facetiously the elimination of these leaders. Station WBAI is an ultra-liberal organization which has attacked the Bureau, as well as other Government agencies in the past. NY's proposal would lend fire to this controversy surrounding WBAI and also create further ill feeling between the New Left and the black nationalist movement as Lester is a spokesman of this latter group.

And, of course, if some overly militant black had obtained that flyer and "eliminated" one of those "New Left leaders who are Jewish," the FBI's bureaucratic ass would be covered: "We *said* it was a facetious suggestion, didn't we?"

Ironically, Julius Lester would later convert to Judaism. Oh, yes, and one other thing. It turned out that J. Edgar Hoover himself was a raving, unconfined nut.

*   *   *

In February 1969, a group of Yippies were busy rolling innumerable joints—the contents paid for by Jimi Hendrix—and wrapping each one in a flyer wishing the recipient a Happy Valentine's Day and containing facts about marijuana. More than 200,000 arrests for pot-smoking were made the previous year, and Mayor John Lindsay had just petitioned Governor Nelson Rockefeller to raise the penalty from one to four years for possession.

The Valentine joints were sent to various mailing lists—teachers, journalists—and to a specific individual only because he was listed in the phone book as Peter Pot. One local newscaster who displayed one of these joints was visited by a pair of narcotics agents on camera while he was still delivering the news—a TV first.

On Valentine's Day, I was scheduled to be on *The Tonight Show*. I had been invited by Orson Bean, who was the guest host. He was an old friend I had gotten to know at meetings of the Summerhill Society, which he attended even while starring in a hit play on Broadway. Eventually, he started a Summerhill-type school in New York, which Holly attended. The essence of Summerhill was that learning should be fun. When Orson had substituted for Johnny Carson on a previous occasion, he arranged for Summerhill founder A.S. Neill to be flown in from England as a guest on the show.

For my appearance, I wore a black Mexican cowboy hat that Abbie had given me and a bright orange shirt that Anita had embroidered with an Aztec design of an owl. I had developed a certain psychedelic *macho*. I especially enjoyed tripping while being interviewed on TV—from a marijuana brownie for Mike Douglas to magic mushrooms for Tom Snyder—and so, one hour before *The Tonight Show* began taping, I swallowed that week's withdrawal of an LSD tab from my bank vault. By the time Orson introduced me, the acid was coming on strong.

"Greetings," said Ed McMahon, as though he were from Selective Service.

While we were shaking hands, his face became a melting rainbow. I was tempted to just stand there and admire him, but instead I sat down and surrendered to spectator conversation with Orson. I was telling him about those marijuana joints that thousands of individuals had received in the mail that day from a mysterious source.

"Now," he interjected, "you've taken LSD, haven't you?"

I had an instant paranoid flash that my trip was *showing*, but I realized that he was referring to the past in general, not to that particular moment. I said yes, and the audience booed.

Orson asked, "Why do you think they responded that way?"

"Because they're predisposed."

Later, he asked me about "The Parts Left Out of the Kennedy Book." There I was, privately peaking on acid, and Orson Bean was questioning me on network TV about my most notorious achievement. Of course, we couldn't discuss the specifics of presidential necrophilia, but since it had been such an outrageous hoax, he asked if I hadn't shown disrespect for the readers.

"No, no," I answered, "it was *respect* for them. I didn't want to deprive them of the pleasure of discerning for themselves whether they were responding to truth or satire. In order to believe what I'd written, they would first have had to believe that the leader of their country was crazy."

The audience had no idea what we were talking about.

A progressive nun was scheduled to follow me on the show. She had arrived at the studio with another progressive nun. During the commercial, Orson whispered to me, "I'll bet she and her friend are eating each other out in the Green Room." And we laughed. I had always wondered what the hosts on talk shows whispered to the guests. When the nun came out, she wasn't dressed in clerical garb, just regular clothes.

At one point I asked her, "Did your order achieve the right not to wear a habit through protest marches, you know, carrying placards and chanting slogans like, 'Up against the wall, Mother Superior'?"

Ed McMahon quickly answered, "No, Paul."

The next day I was visited by a pair of narcotics agents who had seen the show. I told them that the Mafia must have sent out all those marijuana joints in order to discredit the Yippies. And a viewer wrote to NBC complaining that I had worn a shirt with the internal diagram of a uterus.

In the movie *I Love You, Alice B. Toklas*, Peter Sellers' marijuana brownies caused an immediate reaction, but in real life it takes a couple of hours. So, when my friend Bridget Potter booked me on *The Mike Douglas Show* in Philadelphia, I ate a pot brownie at Penn Station in New York, and it came on concomitantly with the end of a two-hour train ride. During the show, I didn't remove my Mexican cowboy hat.

"Do you always wear that hat?" Douglas asked.

"Except when I take a shower."

"Don't you think that's impolite?"

I opened my dungaree jacket and displayed a black sweatshirt with white lettering—*Cosa Nostra*—below which there was a montage of a revolver, a hypodermic needle, a whiskey bottle and glass, a limousine, a prostitute's leg in a net-stocking, a hand grenade, a dagger, and a machine gun. Underneath was the slogan WE AIM TO PLEASE.

"Wearing my hat is only a *symbol* of impoliteness to you," I explained. "If I were a professional criminal, I'd be here in my pin-striped suit, shiny black shoes, shirt, and tie. I'd be wearing an ostentatious pinky ring, and my hair would be neatly trimmed. But I could've arranged to have your mother killed, and I'd *still* have all the acceptable symbols of politeness."

"I see what you mean," said Mike Douglas.

★ ★ ★

In September 1968, I covered the protest of the Miss America Pageant in Atlantic City. There were a few hundred women there. On the boardwalk, demonstrators were holding a special ceremony. Icons of male oppression were being thrown into a trash barrel—cosmetics, a girdle, a copy of *Playboy*, high-heeled shoes, a pink brassiere—with the intent of setting the whole mix on fire. But there was an ordinance forbidding you to burn *anything* on the boardwalk, and the police were standing right there to enforce it.

So there was no fire, but that didn't matter. The image of a burning bra became inextricably associated with women's liberation. It was certainly a metaphorical truth.

Robin Morgan helped organize that event. We had been close friends since our Yippie days. Robin, her husband, Ken Pitchford, and I had shared dinners and acid trips, conversations and conspiracies, but early in 1970 she told me that I would no longer be welcome "as a brother" in her home unless I quit as film critic for *Cavalier*, because it was by definition a sexist magazine. I couldn't believe it. I was being purged from my own extended family. It was irrelevant that my column enabled me to support my daughter, or that Robin herself worked for Grove Press, which some feminists considered to be a sexist publisher.

Then, while Jeff Shero—editor of *Rat*, the most volatile underground weekly in New York—was visiting his hometown, Austin, Robin became part of an all-female collective that took over the paper. Eventually, she became the editor of *Ms.* magazine. Jeff changed his name to Nightbyrd and launched a mail-order business selling drug-free powdered urine. Just add water, stir, and you're ready to pass a drug test.

Meanwhile, I got fired by *Cavalier* magazine. They declined to publish a particular column—my review of *M*A*S*H* as though it were a Busby Berkeley musical called *Gook Killers of 1970*—ostensibly on the grounds of bad taste, but I learned that three wholesalers had told the publisher they were pressured by the FBI and would refuse to distribute *Cavalier* if my name appeared in it.

On top of that, my name was on a list of sixty-five "radical" campus speakers, released by the House Internal Security Committee. The blacklist was published in *The New York Times*, and picked up by newspapers across the country. It might have been a coincidence, but my campus speaking engagements stopped abruptly.

* * *

In 1969, I met Jada Rowland, who was an actress in the soap opera *Secret Storm*. Although I fell in love with Jada, I hated soap operas. They were the ultimate creation of a value system that was the antithesis of my own. Their main function was to program viewers into becoming greater consumers by manipulating them to identify with the lives of other people who didn't even exist. One viewer even sent a letter warning Jada that her "husband" was seeing another woman.

Still, within that corrupt context, Jada maintained a sense of integrity. Once, the script called for her to put down her young daughter by referring sarcastically to her imagination, and Jada refused to say the line.

We only had a two-night stand, but remained friends. I had presented her with a brass sculpture of a multi-armed Hindu demigod embracing his mate, whose legs were wrapped around him. As a symbolic gesture of my unrequited romance, Jada gave me a gift that she had made, a papier-mâché Donald Duck with eight arms and a tag attached, bearing the message, "Daisy Duck has been freed by Women's Liberation."

When Richard Avedon invited me to be included in a collection of his photos of countercultural people, I accepted on the condition that Jada and I would pose together, and we could choose the pose. What we had in mind was a send-up of the *Two Virgins* album cover, where John Lennon and Yoko Ono stood nude, holding hands.

We would be standing naked with our arms around each other. Jada would be holding a patriotic drinking mug with stars and stripes, and she would have arrows pointing to her breasts and crotch. I would be holding a small American flag, and I would have an erection. If *Two Virgins* was about anatomy, this would be about physiology. Jada was willing to risk losing her $1000-a-week job to participate in this photo shoot just for the fun of it.

"I think it was my idea," she recalls, "to do a take-off on Lennon and Ono. I was on one of my rants, objecting to the fact that the penis could never be seen erect and that there was a certain hypocrisy in their pretended 'innocence' as it seemed to me that they must have known that everyone just wanted to see the tits of the girl who stole the Beatle away."

I had ingested a capsule of THC powder before the photo session. Jada and I were now standing before the camera, and the only thing missing was my erection. I had heard that THC powder was actually an elephant tranquilizer. I would soon find out if that was true. Avedon asked what music to play during the session. I asked for the Beatles' "Hey Jude," but he didn't have it. He played my second choice, Bob Dylan singing "Lay, Lady, Lay," and I began to kiss Jada.

"This is obscene," she whispered.

"No," I whispered back, "it's very pure. But you're right, it *is* kind of goal-oriented."

As she remembers, "What was 'obscene' in my view was that I wasn't in love or in lust with you, so giving way to your request that I kiss you so you could get a hard-on seemed obscene. I felt both uneasily guilty, as I became aware that I was taking advantage of your fondness for me in order to be photographed by Avedon, and quite uncomfortable that you were taking advantage of the situation in order to kiss me. Those were the only 'obscenities' in my eyes."

We continued kissing. Dylan was now asking the musical question, "Why wait any longer for the world to begin?" My penis rose to the occasion, and the crew cheered us on.

I signed a release, assuming that the photo would never be seen because the publishing of an erection was so taboo. However, in 1999—three decades later—my bluff was called. A $75 book of photos by Avedon and Doon Arbus, titled *The Sixties*, was published. A review in the *Los Angeles Times* mentioned that I looked "sheepish" and "sustained an erection." Little did they know. On the back cover of the book, there's a photo of Abbie Hoffman, holding a toy rifle in one hand and giving the finger with the other. He is smiling broadly, sticking his tongue out, and on his forehead the word FUCK is written in lipstick.

★ ★ ★

In August 1969, wearing my new yellow leather fringe jacket for the first time, I was on my way to Woodstock among a half-million others, walking past newsstands with headlines shouting about a mysterious mass murder in Beverly Hills, in sharp contrast to the Festival of Music and Love.

The Hog Farm had been hired to provide security. At this event, security meant cream pies and seltzer bottles. Hugh Romney planned to wear a Smokey the Bear costume to warn people about putting out fires.

Woodstock looked like the vision the Yippies originally had of Chicago. I wandered around this gathering of the tribes. Tom Law was leading a group in yoga exercises. I warned him, "If the government finds out you can get high just from breathing, they're gonna ban oxygen."

The political contingent was encamped in a huge red-and-white-striped tent christened Movement City. In the afternoon, a mimeograph machine was churning out flyers proclaiming that the outdoor concerts should be free. At night, several festival-goers were busy unscrewing the metal-wire fencing that had been put up during the day. Yippie Roz Payne was among them. She helped take down the NO TRESPASSING sign and changed it into a sign that read PEOPLE'S BULLETIN BOARD.

On an afternoon when Abbie, Roz, and I took a stroll down Merchants Way, which led to the stage that was still being constructed, they took down the MERCHANTS WAY sign and put up a sign that read HO CHI MINH TRAIL. Lights had not yet been strung up along the path, and as it got darker, we kept walking and stumbling until we got lost in the woods. After a couple of hours, we saw a light through the trees, realized that we were right back where we started, and we laughed ourselves silly.

Abbie would get serious later on, though, ebbed on by his sense of justice and fueled by the tab of White Lightning that we had each ingested. During a break in The Who's performance of *Tommy*, he went up onstage with the intention of informing the audience that John Sinclair—manager of the MC5 and leader of the White Panther Party—was serving ten years behind bars for giving two joints to a narc; that this was really the politics behind the music.

"I think this is a pile of shit," Abbie shouted, "while John Sinclair rots in prison."

"Fuck off," Peter Townshend yelled. "Fuck off my fucking stage!"

He immediately transformed his guitar into a tennis racket and smashed Abbie on the head with a swift backhand. He assumed that Abbie was just another crazed fan.

When The Who played at Fillmore East the previous month, a plain-clothes cop rushed onstage and tried to grab the mike. He intended to warn the audience that there was a fire next door and the theater had to be cleared, but he was able to do so only after Townshend kneed him in the balls. Now, as Abbie fled from his bad trip, Townshend warned the audience, "The next person that walks across the stage is going to get killed." The audience laughed. "You can laugh, but I mean it!"

Inadvertently, I ended up with a political mission of my own at Woodstock. For a while, I was hanging around the Press Tent, which later turned into the Hospital for Bad Trips.

A reporter from the *New York Daily News* asked me, "How do you spell braless?"

I replied, "Without a hyphen."

He pointed out two men with cameras who were from the Criminal Intelligence Division of the army. And a journalist who knew someone with a source in the White House told me how the Nixon administration had assigned the Rand Corporation think tank to develop a game plan for suspending the 1972 election in case of disruption. I decided to mention this at every meeting I attended, every interview I did, every campus I spoke at, and every radio show that I was a guest on.

A year later, the story was officially denied by Attorney General John Mitchell. He warned that whoever started that rumor ought to be "punished." I wrote to him and confessed, but he never answered my letter. Actually, investigative journalist Ron Rosenbaum was able to trace the "rumor" back and discovered that I was the fifth level down from the original White House source.

Oh, yeah, and my yellow leather fringe jacket was stolen from the Movement City tent.

★ ★ ★

FBI files indicated that the government wanted to indict twenty individuals for conspiracy to cross state lines for the purpose of inciting a riot at the Chicago convention, but the grand jury wouldn't go along with such a wholesale indictment, so the list had to be narrowed down. They removed Kathy Boudin of SDS. Although they were hesitant to indict Bobby Seale for lack of evidence, he was a prize, and they were willing to trade two white Yippies for him, so Wolfe Lowenthal and Robin Palmer were both *un*indicted.

Super-Joel's indictment was dropped when an attorney for his grandfather, Mafia godfather Sam Giancana, managed to persuade them that not only did Super-Joel come from "a socially prominent family" in Chicago but also that he was mentally incompetent to stand trial. Stew Albert and I were taken off the list because they were afraid that we might use a freedom-of-the-press defense—if we had crossed state lines with merely the *intent* of getting a story, it wouldn't matter even if we incited people to riot once we were there.

The indictments were finally narrowed down to eight. Jerry Rubin said it was like winning "the Academy Award of protest." I felt like a disc jockey who hadn't been offered payola. At a fundraising party on Abbie and Anita's rooftop, Ed Sanders, Bob Fass, and I linked arms and formed a mini–chorus line doing the two-step and singing, in *nyah-nyah* fashion, "We weren't indicted! We weren't indicted!"

After the Great Conspiracy Trial began in 1969, I visited Chicago for Thanksgiving. I had never seen Abbie scared before. He didn't even finish his lunch in a restaurant because he was afraid of being late for court. Jerry said, "It's the duty of a revolutionist to finish lunch," and stayed. Dave Dellinger had already finished eating, but remained while Jerry ate, as an indication of a united front. I stayed too, but I wouldn't have been allowed in court anyway, because I was due to be a witness.

I was scheduled to testify in January 1970. On the evening before, Abbie coached me with a chronology of Yippie meetings, but trying to memorize all those dates and places made me nervous. It was like being unprepared for an important history exam. And Abbie gave me mixed messages. On one hand, he told me, "There's nothing you can do to help us, you can only harm us." On the other hand, he told me, "I want you to give the judge a heart attack."

I assured him, "I'll do my best." I didn't sleep much that night.

I had brought a stash of LSD with me, but things were too tense for an acid party. Instead, I decided to take a tab of acid before I took the witness stand—call me a sentimental fool—but it wasn't merely to enhance the experience. I had a more functional reason. My purpose was twofold.

I knew that if I ingested three hundred micrograms of LSD after eating a big meal, I was very likely to throw up in court. That would be my theatrical statement on the injustice of the trial. Also, I wouldn't need to memorize so much information that way. I had to psych myself up, to imagine it actually happening. The prosecutor would ask, "Now where did this meeting take place?" And I would go, "*waughhhhhppp!*"

They couldn't charge me with contempt of court because they wouldn't know I had done it on purpose. The judge would say, "Bailiff, get him out of here!" But just as he was dragging me away, I would get one more projectile off, onto the judge's podium—"*Waughhhhhppp!*" And, although there would be no photographic record of this incident because cameras weren't allowed, courtroom artists would capture my vomit with green and gold charcoal crayons for the eleven o'clock news.

Next day at lunch, while the others were passing around a chunk of hash, I took out a tab of LSD. Abbie said, "What's that, acid? I don't think that's a good idea." Jerry said, "I think he should do it." I swallowed it despite what *both* of them said. The acid really began to hit while I was waiting in the witness room. A few volunteers were watching film footage of Dave Dellinger pleading with a crowd at the convention: "Stay calm! Stay calm!"

I said, "Boy, when the jury sees this, it'll really be clear that Dave was doing anything *but* trying to start a riot."

The volunteers laughed. "Are you kidding?" said one. "They're never gonna allow that to be admitted as evidence."

Then suddenly I was thrust into the middle of a *Looney Tunes* cartoon. It happened at the precise moment that I was escorted into the court by Tom Hayden and Jerry Rubin—or, as I perceived them, Tom and Jerry. The furniture started dancing merrily.

Judge Julius Hoffman looked exactly like Elmer Fudd. I expected him to proclaim, "Let's get them pesky wadicals!" The court clerk looked exactly like Goofy. It didn't matter that a Disney character was making a guest appearance in a *Looney Tunes* cartoon—one learns to accept such discrepancies in a dreamlike state. Now I was being instructed by Goofy to raise my right hand and place my left hand on a Bible that was positively vibrating.

"Do you hereby swear," asked Goofy, "that the testimony you are about to give in the cause now on trial before this court and jury shall be the truth, the whole truth, and nothing but the truth, so help you God?"

The truth for me was that LSD—or any other catalyst for getting in closer touch with your subconscious, whether it be meditation, Zen, yoga, Aikido—served as a reminder that choices are being made every moment. So naturally I assumed that Goofy was offering me a choice.

"No," I replied.

Although I hadn't planned to say that, I realized it was a first in American jurisprudence. Ordinarily, the more heinous a crime the more eagerly will a defendant take the oath. However, my refusal to swear on the Bible was a leap of faith. Everything was swirling around in pastel colors, but there was still a core of reality I was able to grasp, and somehow I managed to flash back to a civics class in junior high school when we had studied the Bill of Rights in general and the First Amendment in particular. Now I found myself passing that lesson on to Goofy.

"I believe in the constitutional provision for the separation of church and state," I said, "so I will choose to affirm to tell the truth."

"Let 'im affirm," said Judge Fudd—begrudgingly, it seemed to me, as if to say, *Let 'im resort to the goddamn Constitution!* "Administer the affirmation, Mr. Clerk."

Goofy repeated the oath: ". . . and nothing but the truth?"

"Yes."

"This you do under pains and penalties—"

Elmer Fudd interrupted: "Listen to the last part before you say 'yes.'"

"If I am going to tell the truth," I said, "I am going to tell the truth no matter what the penalties are."

Goofy repeated the oath and continued, "Under pains and penalties of perjury?"

"Yes."

Defense attorney William Kunstler looked exactly like the Wise Old Owl. The prosecutor looked exactly like the Big Bad Wolf. I felt exactly like Alice in Wonderland. The Wise Old Owl was questioning me about the original Yippie meeting.

Q. Do you know Jerry Rubin?

A. Yes, I do.

Q. And which one is Jerry Rubin at this table?

A. The man trying to hide behind Mr. Dellinger.

Q. Can you identify Abbie Hoffman at this table?

A. (Pointing) He looks familiar. Yes, I would say that would be Abbie Hoffman.

ELMER Fudd: Would it be or is it?

ALICE in Wonderland: It definitely is. It would be him too, but he is. The Wise Old Owl continued.

Q. Do you know any of the other defendants at the defense table?

A. Well, I know all of them.

Q. You know all of the others?

A. I mean, I've only met a few since I learned they were defendants.

Q. Which of those few?

A. Well, I had never met John Froines before. I had never met Lee Weiner before.

Q. But the rest you have known before, is that correct?

A. I had never met Bobby Seale, or don't we count him anymore?

Q. Well, we count him even though he is not here.

I held back from saying, "Yes, he is." I had seen only artists' charcoal renditions of the missing defendant on TV newscasts, shackled to his chair with a gag taped over his mouth, and that was the image that I was now hallucinating—a generic courtroom sketch superimposed in front of the defense table. His attorney was ill, so he wanted to defend himself, but Elmer Fudd disallowed that, and he ultimately removed Seale from this trial.

The Wise Old Owl asked me who was at the original Yippie meeting.

Q. Can you identify Anita Hoffman?

A. Yes, the young lady who is standing.

Q. What about Nancy Kurshan?

A. The young lady who is *now* standing.

THE Big Bad Wolf: I object to this, Your Honor.

ELMER Fudd: Yes, I think it is inappropriate that the spectators here be identified by witnesses.

THE Wise Old Owl: Your Honor, they were at the meeting. He has just stated they were at the meeting. I am asking him to identify them.

ELMER Fudd: He hasn't been identifying them. They stood up when their names were mentioned. He hasn't gone down there and identified them.

ALICE in Wonderland: Do you want me to go down there and identify them?

ELMER Fudd: No, I don't want you to do anything but to answer questions properly.

THE Wise Old Owl: Your Honor, I am going to object to his not being able to identify these two women. If they had been men, they would probably be indicted here as defendants because they have been in every one of the meetings. They have been stated by witness after witness as being present.

THE Big Bad Wolf objected.

ELMER Fudd: "If they had been men, they probably would have been indicted here," and anything else that followed these words, are stricken from the record and the jury is directed to disregard them. I will say that if there is anyone else that this witness identifies, I would ask them not to wave back at the witness.

ALICE in Wonderland: Now, look, I'm a man and I wasn't indicted.

THE Big Bad Wolf: May we have that comment stricken, Your Honor?

Later, the questioning—about a backstage conversation at a benefit for the Yippies and *The Seed,* Chicago's underground paper—took on an aura of the Marx Brothers meet Abbott and Costello.

Q. Who was there?

A. Abbie Hoffman was there. Jerry Rubin was there. Nicholas von Hoffman from *The Washington Post* was there . . .

Q. Now, would you state who said what at that meeting?

A. Yeah, Jerry said that we ought to make the formal application to the city of Chicago for the permits, that we ought to do that the very next day. Do you want the specific details of the conversation?

Q. Yes. Go ahead.

A. Well, we proceeded to—

THE Big Bad Wolf: Who said what?

THE Wise Old Owl: Mr. Foran has suggested that you state who said what to whom as you can recall it.

ELMER Fudd: I approve of the suggestion.

THE Wise Old Owl: I approve of it myself, Your Honor.

ALICE in Wonderland: Is everybody through approving?

THE Wise Old Owl: Everybody has approved.

ELMER Fudd: The witness has been told that before, however. It is not an original thought of Mr. Foran's.

ALICE in Wonderland: Mr. Hoffman suggested—

ELMER Fudd: Is it Mr. Hoffman or Von Hoffman? Which was it? There were two there, weren't there?

ALICE in Wonderland: Oh, that's correct.

ELMER Fudd: You have mentioned a Von Hoffman, Nicholas.

ALICE in Wonderland: That's right, but now—

ELMER Fudd: Which one is talking now?

ALICE in Wonderland: Now I said Mr. Hoffman.

ELMER Fudd: Now it is Mr. Hoffman.

ALICE in Wonderland: That's correct.

ELMER Fudd: There was no Von in there? I thought you said Von Hoffman of *The Washington Post* was there, didn't you, in response to Mr. Kunstler's inquiry?

ALICE in Wonderland: That's correct.

ELMER Fudd: Well, then, there was somebody there.

ALICE in Wonderland: Yes, and now I am talking about Mr. Hoffman.

ELMER Fudd: Now you are talking about Mr. Abbot Hoffman.

ALICE in Wonderland: Abbie. Abbie.

ELMER Fudd: All right. I want to place the various Hoffmans or Von Hoffmans who were at that—I don't want anybody to be confused about the Hoffmans.

THE Wise Old Owl: "Von" is of the German nobility, Your Honor, and Mr. Hoffman has never been of the German nobility.

ELMER Fudd: Oh, is that what the "Von" means?

THE Wise Old Owl: That's what the "Von" means.

ALICE in Wonderland: I never call him Mr. Hoffman anyway. Abbie. Abbie said that—excuse me, did Your Honor say something?

ELMER Fudd: Go ahead and say what was said, if you ever get around to it—just like Mr. Foran said, who said what to whom. Go ahead, if they said anything. If they said nothing, you don't have to say anything.

ALICE in Wonderland: Abbie said, "Let's get it done as quickly as possible."

THE Wise Old Owl: Was that as far as you can recall the extent of the conversation?

ALICE in Wonderland: Oh, no. I just didn't want to bore the judge.

ELMER Fudd: Oh, I'm very much interested. You're not boring me. Besides, you're obligated to answer even if you bore the court. You must answer.

THE Wise Old Owl: Don't be misled by the judge's expression . . .

During recess, I started fiddling around with a gavel that was on the witness stand, and the bailiff took it away from me. I recalled when Jerry got busted in New York for marijuana, and Abbie and I got the giggles in court because someone had changed the motto on the wall behind the judge to read IN GOD WE RUST. And I recalled when Abbie got busted in New York for throwing a bag of blood at a demonstration, but I testified that I had flashed the V sign to him and he was simply returning it. The judge asked me what the V sign meant, and I explained that it had different meanings—it could mean *hello* or it could mean *victory*.

"Well," asked that judge, "what did it mean to you on this occasion?"

"It meant, *Hello, victory.*"

Recess was now over and the Chicago Conspiracy Trial resumed. Although I felt myself being sucked into some kind of psychic whirlpool, I was still able to speak with lucidity. But then, as the questions continued, I became increasingly nonlinear about the dates and locations of various meetings. I had really wanted to throw up, but now I didn't feel the slightest bit queasy.

> **Q.** Mr. Krassner, I call your attention to approximately nine PM on the night of August 7, 1968, and ask if you can recall where you were.
>
> **A.** August 7, I was in Chicago.
>
> **Q.** Where were you at that time, if you can recall?
>
> **A.** August 7. What time of day was this?

ELMER Fudd: Nine o'clock.

> **Q.** Nine PM, approximately nine o'clock at night.
>
> **A.** Nine o'clock at night, Auguest 7. That would have been—what day of the week was that?
>
> **Q.** I don't know myself. It's a Wednesday.
>
> **A.** Oh, I was confusing with the previous thing. August 7. That was the day that

ELMER Fudd: The question is, where were you?

My mind went blank. At the defense table, Abbie was mouthing the word *Chicago* and the marshal moved to prevent him, as if we were on a TV game show and he had to warn Abbie, "No coaching from the audience."

ALICE in Wonderland: In Chicago.

ELMER Fudd: That is a big city.

> **Q.** Do you remember what place you were at?
>
> **A.** Oh, you mean—
>
> **Q.** I didn't hear you.

ELMER Fudd: Nobody else did. He didn't say anything.

Q. That explains it. Do you know at what place in Chicago you were on August 7 at approximately nine PM?

A. That was the time—wait. I'll have to phrase this—let's see.

Q. Is your memory exhausted as to where you were at the time?

A. Specifically, yes.

ELMER Fudd: You don't remember where you were, is that it? He hasn't said he doesn't remember where he was.

Q. Well, I will ask him. Do you remember where you were at that time?

A. See, I'm having a difficult time associating that particular date in my memory with the event of where I was.

Q. Well, is your memory exhausted as to where you were on that particular day, that particular time?

A. Yes. It's—yes.

Q. Do you remember when you came to Chicago?

A. It was August 21.

Q. I call your attention to August 24, the evening of that day. Do you recall where you were then?

A. Tuesday—that's a Tuesday, right?

Q. That would be a Saturday night.

A. At the Coliseum. There was an Unbirthday Party for Lyndon Johnson.

Q. You are a week ahead of yourself.

A. I'm sorry.

Q. This is Saturday, the 24th.

A. Oh, I thought we were into the convention week already. I am sorry.

Q. Well, I will withdraw that question for a moment, and I will show you—

Me in my Little Lord Fauntleroy suit.

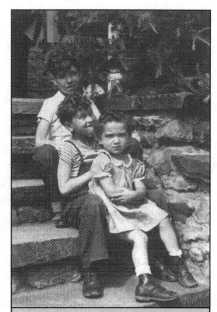

Here I am snuggled between my brother, George, and my sister, Marge.

My parents. The original caption by my mother read "The awakening of love—ahem!"

My brother and me, ready for a violin duel.

Two views of Paul Maul, with functional prop.

Here I am performing as myself at a benefit for the *Los Angeles Free Press* (*Van Pelt*)

Discussing *The Realist's* patriotic poster at the Radical Humor Conference.

Lyle Stuart and me. Lyle was the most important influence on me as a journalist.

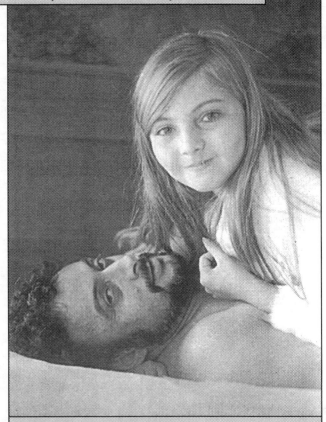

Lenny Bruce and his daughter, Kitty. Lenny was the most important influence on me as a satirist.

Jeanne Johnson and me, on our wedding day. *(John Francis Putnam)*

With our daughter, Holly.

Hanging around with comedian Bobcat Goldthwait before performing at a "Stop Contra Aid" concert. *(Deirdre Walpare)*

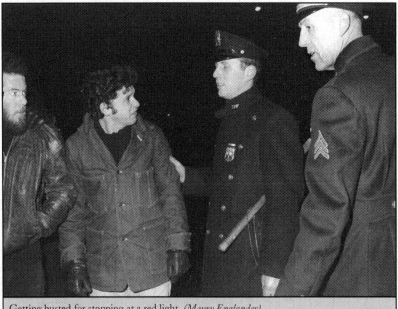

Getting busted for stopping at a red light. *(Maury Englander)*

Celebrating the Summer of Love at Golden Gate Park in San Francisco. *(Lisa Law)*

Burning a Photostat of my draft card during "An Evening with God" at the Village Theater in New York. *(James McGraw)*

Abbie Hoffman and me conspiring. *(Roz Payne)*

With Orli Peter, after living alone for eighteen years. *(Perry Garfinkel)*

Mae Brussell, the queen of conspiracy research. *(Barbara Brussell)*

Antiwar activist Rennie Davis (LEFT) had become a devotee of "the Perfect Master," who was then fifteen years old. I challenged him to a debate at Millennium '73 in the Houston Astrodome, "Resolved: that Guru Maharaj Ji and the Divine Light Mission serve to divert young people from social responsibility to personal escape." The moderator was Berkeley Barb editor Ken Kelley. Rennie ignored me when I referred to his guru as "the Perfect Masturbator."

Wavy Gravy introduced me on graduation day at Pacific High where I delivered the commencement address. David Crosby had rented this alternative school in the Santa Cruz mountains for Wavy to be able to recover from his third spinal fusion. In 1973, students were taken to the UN conference on the environment in Stockholm.

On top of the world with my daughter, Holly, at our secret mountain hideout in Oregon. *(Annie Leibovitz)*

Ken Kesey had thrown the *I Ching* to determine the fate of the entire universe, but Holly, through sheer mental power, caused one of his coins to remain on edge. Kesey was forced to accept an uncertain future. *(Annie Leibovitz)*

Old friends reunited to celebrate the twenty-fifth anniversary of Jack Kerouac's novel, *On the Road*. (FROM LEFT TO RIGHT) Allen Ginsberg, Tim Leary, myself, Abbie Hoffman, and William Burroughs. *(Jerry Aronson)*

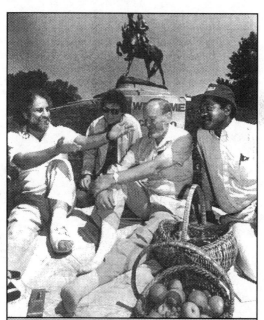

Picnicking in Grant Park, for the twentieth anniversary of the Democratic convention in Chicago. (FROM LEFT TO RIGHT) Abbie Hoffman, myself, Dave Dellinger, and Bobby Seale *(Associated Press/Wide World)*

Chatting with musician Richie Havens, at the rally preceding a march to shut down the Nevada nuclear bomb test site in April 1992. *(Lisa Law)*

Lindsay Wagner and me, at an American Heroes conference. She was the star of "The Bionic Woman."

Matt Groening, creator of "The Simpsons," and me at a "Freedom to Read" event at Small World Books on the Venice Beach boardwalk.

With my producer, Scott Kelman, and John Densmore, former drummer for The Doors. *(Jay Green)*

With Peter Bergman and Harry Shearer for the "Peter, Paul, and Harry" show. *(Jay Green)*

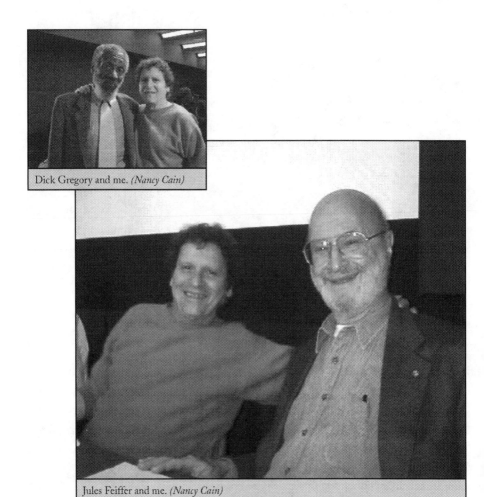

Dick Gregory and me. *(Nancy Cain)*

Jules Feiffer and me. *(Nancy Cain)*

My mother and me. *(Bart Friedman)*

With Nancy Cain, my favorite biological quirk. *(Jody Sibert)*

Holly, Dan, and Talia.

Watching my granddaughter conducting invisible music.

ELMER Fudd: May I suggest that you may not correct the answer of the witness.

THE Wise Old Owl: He is obviously confused, Your Honor. He was a week ahead.

ELMER Fudd: He is not confused.

THE Wise Old Owl: I thought he was confused.

ELMER Fudd: You simply corrected his answer by saying he is a week ahead of himself. Let the witness testify. Now, if you want to withdraw the question, I will strike the answer.

THE Wise Old Owl: Your Honor, it was obvious he was confused as to the week.

ELMER Fudd: No, it isn't obvious at all. If you want to withdraw the question, you may.

THE Wise Old Owl: I don't want to withdraw the question, but I don't want to let an answer which the witness is obviously confused about get before the jury who has heard exactly when the Coliseum was.

ELMER Fudd: You have said that twice now. He hasn't said he is confused. You have said he is confused.

THE Wise Old Owl: All right. I will withdraw the question, Your Honor, to save time.

THE Big Bad Wolf: One of the ways you test the credibility of a witness under the law, Your Honor, is with his memory.

THE Wise Old Owl: Now, I will call your attention to Sunday, August 25, at approximately 4 PM on that day. Do you know where you were?

ALICE in Wonderland: Sunday, August 25. May I respond to his comment about credibility and memory?

ELMER Fudd: No. Just answer this question if you can. If you can't answer the question, you may say, "I can't answer it."

A. Well, I was upset by what he said, and that affects my answer, see.

You are pretending that this is not an emotional situation . . .

Cross-examination by the Big Bad Wolf was brief:

Q. Where were you on Friday the 23rd?

A. Friday the 23rd. I think I was speaking—

THE Wise Old Owl: I don't think I asked him anything about that date, Your Honor. That is outside the scope of the direct examination.

THE Big Bad Wolf: We can test his memory.

ELMER Fudd: He said he came to Chicago on August 23. I have a note of it.

ALICE in Wonderland: No, I said the 21st. On the 23rd, I went to the University of—I went to Kansas. I spoke there before the National Students Association.

Q. Then you came back to Chicago the next day?

A. I flew back on the plane with Allard Lowenstein, yes.

Q. How old are you?

A. I am thirty-seven.

Q. Thirty-seven. You will be thirty-eight in April?

A. That is the way it goes chronologically.

Q. No more questions.

* * *

When my testimony was completed, in order to get centered, I asked myself, "All right, now why did you take LSD before you testified?"

"Because," I answered myself, "I'm the reincarnation of Gurdjieff."

This was slightly confusing, inasmuch as I didn't believe in reincarnation—I thought it was the ultimate ego trip—and besides, I had never even *read* anything by Gurdjieff. Then I flashed back to a conversation with Dick Alpert during my first visit to Millbrook. I had been curious about Tim Leary.

I asked, "Do you think Tim ever gets so involved he forgets he's playing a game?"

"Well, you know, he's an old Irish Catholic boozehound, and he tends to get caught up in his own game sometimes, but Tim's a very skillful game player, and he knows what he's doing."

"Well, who would you say—among all the seekers you've ever known of—who would you say was always aware of playing a game, even the game of playing a game?"

Alpert thought for a moment and then said, "Gurdjieff." So that's why I had taken the LSD, because the Chicago trial was just another game. But not to Abbie. He was furious. He felt, understandably, that I had been totally irresponsible.

"You were *creamed* on the stand!" he shouted. "You were *mean* to the judge!" I couldn't explain to him that somehow my original courtroom scenario had been short-circuited. Try as I might, I just hadn't been able to vomit. "You're not a *leader*," Abbie yelled. "You're a fuckin' *social gadfly*. You're not an *organizer*. You don't urge people to *do* things. You never make *demands*. That's what organizing *is*."

From Abbie's point of view, I was guilty of self-indulgent betrayal. As penance, he wanted me to turn *The Realist* into a Yippie organ. I refused, and Abbie broke off our friendship.

Ten months later, I would notice a little ad in the movie section of the paper—*The Professionals* was playing at the Charles Theater on Avenue D—so I ripped it out and mailed it to Abbie.

Apparently, that gesture broke the ice. Bob Fass called me and said that Abbie and Anita would like to have dinner with me, and so we celebrated a much-needed reconciliation.

The Conspiracy Trial defendants had been found guilty, but that verdict was overturned by a judge who had been appointed by Lyndon Johnson.

* * *

The original American Revolution was fought over taxation without representation, and that's what was happening all over again. In 1970, the War Resisters League in New York planned a demonstration at City Hall Park, and asked me to serve as emcee and to burn a blowup of a tax form, because so much tax money was financing the Vietnam War.

When I set fire to the huge tax form, reporters shouted at me: "Do you pay *your* income taxes?"

"That's irrelevant," I shouted back. "I'm not doing this as an individual. I'm doing it as a symbolic act."

The truth was, I hadn't paid my taxes for the first five years of *The Realist*. Then an accountant, Don Wilen, volunteered to prepare my back taxes, and he even got me a refund. I managed to pay my taxes every year since then. When the protest rally ended and I was walking away, Ben Silver of CBS News caught up with me.

"Excuse me," he said. "They were all yelling at you there, but I wonder if I can get you for just a minute, and you might answer that question."

"Okay," I said, and the camera was turned on.

"You've just burned that replica of a tax form," he said. "Have you paid *your* taxes?"

"Yes, and I would like to confess right here on network television that I'm a mass murderer, because so much of the tax money I pay to the government goes to the Pentagon for just that purpose. I pay taxes and that money has gone for dropping napalm on children in Vietnam."

My statement never got on the air.

* * *

While on a hiking trip in the Sierras with Margo St. James and a couple of friends, I considered moving to San Francisco to give my life a new beginning. There was a waterfall near our campsite, and I wanted to luxuriate in it, but the pond leading to the waterfall was painfully cold. I knew that only if I could take this plunge, would it serve as my commitment to moving. It had to be done immediately. I practically tore off all my clothes, counted to three, and ran screaming into the waterfall.

We spent that evening in the Sierra Nevada, on futurist-philosopher-poet Gary Snyder's land. The last time I'd seen him, we were on WBAI discussing countercultural trends. Now he was building his non-electric dream-house with the aid of his meditation students and electric tools. I ingested a tab of LSD to enhance the change my consciousness was already undergoing. Just as the acid was coming on strong, Snyder asked each guest to pump the water one hundred times. I could do *that* all right. Keeping count would be the hard part.

Later, we all sat around a campfire, making our own music and telling Native American legends. Snyder recited a poem by Robert Duncan. I imprinted on one particular concept: "If the possibilities are infinite, that means in both directions . . ."

That night, I had a dream about my brother, George. It took place in summer when we were kids. An aunt who was a health fanatic used to take us to Brighton Beach very early every morning. Then she would force us into the freezing cold ocean, completely naked. She brought along old newspapers for us to roll back into as we hit the shore, before we got dressed again. Although my brother was three years older, I was the one who decided to rebel against this bizarre practice, just as I was the one who decided to give up the violin.

George went to the High School of Music and Art, but he really liked math and science—he even brought his slide rule along on dates—and he shocked the family by turning down a scholarship at the Julliard School of Music. He wanted to be an electronics engineer, not a concert violinist, and he went to the University of Michigan as a graduate student. Our mother insisted that he mail his laundry back and forth to New York in a light metal case she had purchased for that specific purpose.

After he left, we drifted apart, and I began to develop a friendship with my sister Marge. She became a legendary music teacher at Boys & Girls High School. At the onset of the space program, George became a government engineer. His proposal to launch and lead a space electronics group was accepted, and they designed the first communications satellite built in the United States.

He coauthored a textbook, *Introduction to Space Communication Systems*—five thousand copies were printed, but more were sold overseas, especially to Russia, than in this country. He worked with the seven original astronauts, and on Project Horizon, a thirteen-person secret task force headed by Wernher von Braun.

It was such a secret project that George had to fly there, pretending to be a paratrooper who would jump last, but never did. Nor did he tell his wife, Judith. Each day on the phone, she would ask him about the weather in Washington, and each time he'd make up a weather report. Eventually he became an executive at a company that was selling helicopter components to the Pentagon.

"How do you feel about what's going on in Vietnam?" I asked.

"I think we should continue what we're doing there," he replied.

My heart sank with disappointment. George was certainly not an evil person, yet he was making money off the very war against whose inhumanity I was still protesting. He had a top secret security classification, while I was on an FBI list of radicals to be rounded up in an emergency. His security clearance was in continuous jeopardy because of my activities, with the FBI interviewing his neighbors. I found myself wondering why we had gone off in such opposite directions. What had turned him cynical, and me self-righteous?

Then I remembered a childhood incident which made me realize the part that *I had* played in his development. I had borrowed a dime and then pretended it never happened, making him cry. I was experimenting with the misuse of power. Now, a few decades later, I could no longer escape my responsibility.

As soon as I returned home from my California trip, I sent George a long letter with an apology and a dime attached. He appreciated the gesture and wrote a very honest letter in return. He had once told me, "My job is to make myself replaceable," but now he realized that he had become "part of the rat race." He accepted my apology and the dime, and he didn't even ask for any interest on the loan.

I also remembered that while I was peaking on acid, Gary Snyder mentioned that he knew someone from the Rand Corporation who had "an important story to tell." I contacted Snyder to follow up on that vague lead. The individual turned out to be Daniel Ellsberg, who, with Tony Russo, would leak the Pentagon Papers to *The New York Times* and *The Washington Post*. Ellsberg told me that if they hadn't published the material, he would have offered it to the *Los Angeles Free Press*.

* * *

He called himself One-Legged Terry, having had his right leg gobbled up by a machine at a kibbutz in Israel. Previously, he had taken LSD on a postwar visit to Dachau; fought with the Israeli Army; and was sympathetic to the Arab cause. He managed to smuggle into the United States a chunk of hashish inside a piece of cloth wrapped around what was left of his thigh. He was confident that nobody at customs would have the audacity to say, "I beg your pardon, sir, but I'm afraid we'll have to search your stump."

Terry told me that when he was in the hospital, it was the lyrics of Bob Dylan's songs that helped him to recuperate. And now he was teaching Hebrew to Dylan. One afternoon in 1970, Terry called me and said, "Bob Dylan wants to meet you." I walked over to Dylan's studio on Houston Street, trying not to plan our conversation, yet thinking I might start off by referring to a folksinger who was a mutual friend—"You know Happy Traum, don't you?"—but then I tried to block even *that* out of my mind.

When I got to the studio, Dylan and I shook hands, and *he* said, "You know Happy Traum, don't you?"

I had just come from seeing Holly, and I told Dylan how she insisted on calling her fingers "toes," and her toes "fingers." He in turn told me how his son wanted to be called "daddy" and insisted on calling Dylan "son." In the middle of this conversation, Dylan suddenly stopped.

"This isn't an interview, is it?"

"No, it isn't."

"Because, Bob Dylan—that's somebody who's waiting for me out in the car."

When Terry and I began talking about Cuba, Dylan picked up his guitar and started strumming a Latin-American riff for our soundtrack.

One evening, Terry moderated a radio panel, and Dylan came along to the studio. The panelists were Jewish Defense League founder Meir Kahane, Arab-American spokesperson Mohammed Medhi, Abbie Hoffman, and me. I suggested that the Gypsies were also entitled to a homeland, perhaps an empty supermarket. At the end of the two-hour discussion, everybody summed up their position.

I summed up mine in three words: "Nyah, nyah, nyah."

Later, Dylan said to me, "Hey, you didn't say very much."

"No, but it's all that'll be remembered." To my surprise, I was wrong. Twenty-two years later, an editorial in *Direct Marketing News* would state:

"How odd it is that the very people who are helping to keep Haitian refugees out of our country are offended over Japanese slurs against African-Americans. Satirist Paul Krassner once concluded a radio debate with a remark that could serve in any number of ethnic contexts. 'It's important to realize that we're talking about value judgments,' Krassner said. 'Not only may Jews not be the chosen people, but people may not be the chosen species.' A good thing to keep in mind."

Of course, Dylan didn't say very much himself. When I had asked why he was taking Hebrew lessons, he answered, "I can't speak it." He was a true minimalist.

Now, at the radio station, I pointed an imaginary microphone at him and asked, "So how did you feel about the six million Jews who were killed in Nazi Germany?"

"I resented it," he replied.

"I'll miss these little dialogues. I'm gonna move to San Francisco."

"Oh, yeah? Well, if you see Joan Baez, would you tell her that I'd like to do a benefit with her again some time?"

Eric Christiansen was also at the radio station, just observing. The son of a union organizer, he had read *The Realist* when he was ten years old. Now he was the program director at KSFX, ABC's FM station in San Francisco. We discussed the possibility of my doing a regular show when I moved there. I was skeptical about how much freedom I would have, but Station Manager John Turpin promised me, "You'll be surprised." There was a rumor that he was a Black Panther. On his office wall in San Francisco, there was a poster of Angela Davis, certainly not official ABC interior decorating policy.

Meanwhile, Stewart Brand had asked Ken Kesey to edit *The Last Supplement to the Whole Earth Catalog*, and Kesey said he would do it if I would coedit it with him. Brand called and asked me.

Without hesitation, I said, "Yes, yes, yes, yes, yes."

In a letter of confirmation, he wrote: "For two prime origins of the *Catalog* to help finish it is nice. Even tidy."

I figured that I'd be able to start my radio show in San Francisco immediately after *The Last Supplement*, since we would be working on that project in nearby Palo Alto. But first I had to do an audition broadcast in New York on WPLJ. I chose as my guests Vietnam Veterans Against the War and a radical rock group, Elephant's Memory. I even read a commercial for a film.

"I haven't seen it myself," I added, "but if it's really good, your friends will tell you."

Anyway, I got the job.

★　★　★

Eldridge Cleaver was still on the lam. He had gone from Cuba to Algeria. Tim Leary had been in prison for seven months, then escaped with the aid of the Weather Underground. Now Leary and his wife Rosemary were Cleaver's guests. I was scheduled to be a host on *Free Time*, Channel 13's answer to network talk shows. Among the guests on my first program was Marilyn Sokol, pretending to be Leary's mother.

"Welcome to the show, Mrs. Leary. That's a lovely coat you're wearing. What kind of fur is it?"

"Oh," she replied, "it's made of Algerian camel hump."

I had a little button in my ear, through which the producer kept telling me to inform the viewers that I was actually interviewing an actress. I felt like a contrary Joan of Arc, *ignoring* this voice that was buzzing around in my head. I just didn't want to condescend to viewers who might not be aware that this was a put-on.

Finally, the producer's exasperated voice said, "Paul, are you gonna say anything or not?"

I shook my head *no* as unobtrusively as possible, realizing that my first show would be my last. But that was okay, because I was leaving New York anyway. A group of ministers were now providing abortion referrals, so I could leave that service behind.

The last issue of *The Realist* that I would prepare before moving featured a "Report from Algiers" by journalist Jonah Raskin. I assigned artist Robert Grossman to do the cover illustration—a parody of the ad campaign for *Bob and Carol and Ted and Alice*—a caricature of Leary, Cleaver, and their wives, all in one bed, with the caption, "Tim and Rosemary and Eldridge and Kathleen," followed by the movie's slogan, "Consider the possibilities."

But that sense of togetherness disappeared just as *The Realist* hit the newsstands. Cleaver had put Leary and Rosemary under house arrest at gunpoint. Leary said, "Chromosome damage meets Black Panther. That means trouble." Cleaver, in his diatribe against Leary, called hippies "silly psychedelic freaks." And so, as a commitment to my culture, I decided that my radio name would be Rumpleforeskin.

There were about 160 cartons in my loft. For several weeks I went through each box, throwing stuff away, saving an occasional item, making literally thousands of decisions every day. I came upon one strange little card which I just couldn't decide whether to keep, so rather than break my rhythm, I simply stuck it in my pocket.

THE ANAL SPHINCTER
A Most Important Human Muscle

They say that man has succeeded where the animals fail because of the clever use of his hands, yet when compared to the hands, the sphincter ani is far superior. If you place into your cupped hands a mixture of fluid, solid, and gas, and then through an opening at the bottom try to let only the gas escape, you will fail. Yet the sphincter ani can do it! The sphincter apparently can differentiate between solid, fluid, and gas. It apparently can tell whether its owner is alone or with someone; whether standing up or sitting down; whether its owner has his pants off or on. No other muscle in the body is such a protector of the dignity of man, yet so ready to come to his relief. A muscle like this is worth protecting!

—Walter Bonemeir, M.D.

The sixties were over. Negroes became blacks. Girls became women. Hippies became freaks. Richard Alpert became Baba Ram Dass. Hugh Romney became Wavy Gravy, and his wife, Bonnie Jean, became Jahanarah. Keith Lampe became Ponderosa Pine, and his girlfriend became Olive Tree. My sister, Marge, temporarily became Thaïs. Indians became Native Americans. Cassius Clay became Muhammad Ali. LeRoi Jones became Amiri Baraka. And *Oracle* editor Allen Cohen became Siddhartha, but he moved to a commune where everybody called him Sid. They thought his name was Sid Arthur.

In the summer of 1970 I attended a weekend workshop at the Esalen Institute in Big Sur, conducted by Dr. John Lilly. It was about exploring mysticism with the scientific method. We weren't allowed to use words like "imagined" or "fantasized" or "projected." Whatever we experienced had to be accepted as reality.

Lilly read aloud from the manuscript of a book that he had decided not to have published, about his research with sensory deprivation tanks. During the workshop, I "experienced" communicating with Lenny Bruce in the grave. He told me to tell Lilly that he had a responsibility to have his book published.

I passed the message on, but Lilly replied, with total consistency, "That's Lenny's problem." Eventually the book was published, though.

John Lilly had worked with dolphins so long that he had begun to resemble one. He could practically speak dolphin language. His license plate was DOLFIN. He had done research on interspecies communication, and I told him of my acid encounter with that dolphin in Florida when the Yippies were conceived—the dolphin who had said, "If God is evolution, then how do you know He's finished?"

"No," Lilly corrected me. "How do you know *you're* finished?"

So it was up to me to evolve, not the God I didn't believe existed.

Jeanne was now living with somebody else, and had given birth to a son. Holly turned seven in January 1971. I promised her that we would stay in touch by phone and letters, and that I would be coming back to New York a few times every year to see her, and that she would spend summer vacations with me. But it was a painful parting. On our farewell afternoon, I took Holly ice-skating. She brought a little pillow along, which she stuffed inside her leggings in order to cushion her behind whenever she fell down.

I was finally ready to leave New York. I sat in my vibrating chair, listening to music, eating ice cream, and looking forward to a second chance in San Francisco. I had really fucked up my life, but this time I was determined to get things right.

Suddenly a gigantic fist burst through the clouds, and I heard a voice boom out: "Oh, yeah? *Pow! Pow! Pow!*"

CHAPTER 9

ONE FLEW INTO THE CUCKOO'S NEST

I MOVED TO SAN FRANCISCO IN FEBRUARY 1971. STEWART BRAND PICKED me up at the airport. On the plane I had been thinking about my trip to Cuba. At an educational community, some young students removed the string that was set up by a landscaping crew to mark off a cement foundation, and next morning, the school director lectured them. "Even a little thing like that," he explained, "does harm to the revolution." The children of Cuba were being programmed for cooperation rather than competition.

Now I asked Brand, "Do you think competition begins with the spermatozoa racing for the ovum?"

"I think the sperm don't race," he replied, "they *dance around* the ovum." He could be even more of a minimalist than Bob Dylan. I told Brand about the time I went to hear Ram Dass speak, and in the audience a heckler shouted out his capsule critique, "Words!" I told Brand I later learned that the heckler had once fucked a goat. Brand scoffed: "Deeds!"

Ken Kesey had already been in Palo Alto for a week. When I arrived, he was sitting in the backyard at a table with an electric typewriter. His parrot, Rumiako, was perched on a tree limb right above, and whenever he squawked, Kesey would type a sentence as though the parrot were dictating to him. Kesey looked up at me. "Hey, Krassner, I've just been sitting here, thinking about the anal sphincter."

I reached into my pocket, withdrew that bit of printed wisdom about the anal sphincter which I had transported three thousand miles, and handed it to Kesey. "My card," I announced. This was such an appropriate coincidence for a new beginning, it bordered on magic.

Hassler—that was Ron Bevirt's Merry Prankster name—served as our managing editor, chauffeur, photographer, and general buffer zone. A ritual developed. Each morning, Kesey and Hassler would come by the Psychodrama Commune where I was staying. We would have crunchy granola and ginseng tea for breakfast. Then, sharing a joint in an open-topped convertible, we would drive up winding roads sandwiched by forest, ending up at a large garage which was filled with production equipment.

Kesey and I would discuss ideas, pacing back and forth like a pair of caged foxes. Gourmet meals were cooked on a pot-bellied stove. Sometimes a local rock band came by and rehearsed with real amplification, drowning out the noise of our typewriters. Kesey had been reading a book of African Yoruba stories. The moral of one parable was "he who shits in the road will meet flies on his return." With that as a theme, we assigned R. Crumb to draw his version of the Last Supper for our cover of *The Last Supplement.*

At one point, Hassler told me that Kesey needed a short review of an esoteric cartoon book. I checked it out and suggested, "It made me say 'Far out' for the first time." Hassler's reaction: "You Zen Bastard." Until then, I had identified myself in *The Realist* as "Editor and Ringleader." Now I decided to change it to "Editor and Zen Bastard."

One day, two black women from Jehovah's Witnesses stopped by the garage, and within ten minutes Kesey convinced them that in Revelations where there's talk of locusts, it was really prophesizing helicopters. Actually, Kesey was a practicing Christian who also threw the *I Ching* every day as a religious ritual. When his daughter, Shannon, was invited out on her first car date, he insisted that she throw the *I Ching* in order to decide whether or not to accept.

Once he forgot to bring his family *I Ching* to the garage, and he seemed kind of edgy, like a woman who has neglected to take her birth-control pill, so I suggested that he pick three numbers, then I turned to that page in the unabridged dictionary, circled my index finger in the air, and it came down pointing at the word *bounce*. So that was our reading, and we bounced back to work.

One morning in the Psychodrama kitchen, I couldn't help but notice that Kesey was pouring some white powder—from a box he found on a pantry shelf—into his crotch. "I've used cornstarch on my balls for years," he explained. It seemed like an organic commercial in the making, so the next morning, Hassler brought his camera. Our public service ad would eventually appear on the inside back cover of the *Supplement*, with Kesey giving this pitch:

> Y'know how it is when you're swarthy anyway and maybe nervous
> like on a long freeway drive or say you're in court where you can't

unzip to air things out, and your clammy old nuts stick to your legs. Well, a little handful of plain old cornstarch in the morning will keep things dry and sliding the whole hot day long. Works better than talcum and you don't smell like a nursery. Also good for underarms, pulling on neoprene wet suits and soothing babies' bottoms. And it's biodegradable.

After a couple of months, we finished the *Supplement* and had a party. Somebody brought a tank of nitrous oxide to help celebrate. Kesey suggested that in cave-dwelling times, *all* the air they breathed was like this. "There are stick figures hovering above," he said, "and they're laughing at us."

"And," I added, "the trick is to beat them to the punch."

Kesey lived on a farm in Oregon, and also had a house in La Honda, across the street from a hill where a pair of speakers were embedded and could be turned on from the stereo system in his living room. One evening, after smoking DMT, we were sitting on the large front lawn, watching the sunset, when a car stopped on the road.

A couple inside were arguing fiercely. Kesey, with his wrestler stride, returned to the house and put on a record of Frank Sinatra singing "Strangers in the Night." The couple was stunned by such loud—and appropriate—music emanating from the hill. We could see them smiling as they shared that mystery, then drove away.

Kesey and I hung around La Honda for a while. We were smoking hashish in a tunnel inside a cliff which had been burrowed during World War II so that military spotters with binoculars could look toward the ocean's horizon for oncoming enemy ships. All we spotted was a meek little mouse right there in the tunnel. We blew smoke at the mouse until it could no longer tolerate our behavior. The mouse stood on its hind paws and roared at us, "*Squeeeeeek!*" This display of mouse assertiveness startled us and we almost fell off the cliff. The headline would've read, *Dope Crazed Pranksters in Suicide Pact.*

Before I interviewed Kesey at my new home in San Francisco—each of us using an electric typewriter on my dining-room table, passing paper with questions and answers back and forth—he used the remainder of my hash to boil a pot of tea for our creative fuel.

"Do you see the legalization of grass," I typed, "as any sort of panacea?"

"The legalization of grass," he typed, "would do absolutely nothing for our standard of living, or our military supremacy, or even our problem of high school dropouts. It could do nothing for this country except mellow it, and that's not a panacea, that's downright subversive."

"Since you're against abortion," I typed, "doesn't that put you in the position of saying that a girl or a woman must bear an unwanted child as punishment for ignorance or carelessness?"

"In as I feel abortions to be probably the worst worm in the revolutionary philosophy," he typed, "a worm bound in time to suck the righteousness and the life from the work we are engaged in, I want to take this slowly and carefully."

He proceeded to type quite a long, poetic justification, concluding:

"Punishment of unwed mothers? Bullshit! Care of neither the old nor the young can be considered to be punishment for the able, not even the care of the un-dead old or the un-born young. These beings—regardless not only of race, creed, and color, but as well of size, situation, or ability—must be treated as equals and their rights to life not only recognized but *defended*! Can they defend themselves?

"You are you from conception, and that never changes no matter what physical changes your body takes. And the virile sport in the Mustang driving to work with his muscular forearm tanned and ready for a day's labor has *not one microgram more* right to his inalienable rights of life, liberty, and the pursuit of happiness than has the three month's fetus riding in a sack of water or the vegetable rotting for twenty years in a gurney bed.

"Who's to know the value or extent of another's trip? How can we assume that the world through the windshield of that Mustang is any more rich or holy or even sane than the world before those pale blue eyes? How can abortion be anything but fascism again—back as a fad in a new intellectual garb with a new and more helpless victim?

"I swear to you, Paul, that abortions are a terrible karmic bummer, and to support them—except in cases where it is a bona fide toss-up between the child and the mother's life—is to harbor a worm of discrepancy."

Krassner: "Well, that's really eloquent and misty-poo, but suppose Faye [his wife] were raped and became pregnant in the process?"

Kesey: "Nothing is changed. You don't plow under the corn because the seed was planted with a neighbor's shovel."

Krassner: "I assume that it would be her decision, though?"

Kesey: "Almost certainly. But I don't really feel right about speaking for her. Why don't you phone and ask?"

I then—uncomfortably—called Faye Kesey in Oregon and reviewed that dialogue.

She asked, "Now what's the question—if I were raped, would I get an abortion?"

"That about sums it up."

"No, I wouldn't."

Before Kesey returned to Oregon, we went to a benefit for the United Farm Workers, and I saw Joan Baez there. When I gave her Dylan's message, I suddenly realized that I really *had* left New York.

A couple of years later, Kesey said to me, "If you're going to write about my position on abortion, I've changed, you know. It has to do with the war on drugs. The war is not on drugs, the war is on consciousness. Nobody has any right to come in and mess with your inside. They don't have any right to tell me what to do inside my head, any more than they have any right to tell women what to do inside their bodies. What's inside of us is *ours*, and we've got to fight for it."

★ ★ ★

I moved into a house on a cliff above the beach in Watsonville—between Santa Cruz and Monterey—with Hassler and his wife, Poopsie. She had a pair of pet porcupines that I hoped would stay off my waterbed. This was paradise for a city boy. I had to convince myself that the roar of the ocean was not the rumble of the subway. I could play music as loud as I wanted—there was a two-acre field between the house and a dirt road that led to the mailboxes, and there was a wooded area between the house and the edge of the cliff.

I had read that Disraeli used to embrace an oak tree for an hour so he could absorb its energy and be able to stay up all night. I tried that with a willow tree, not for an hour but just for five minutes, because I only wanted to stay up for a few hours.

I bought a used car, a Volkswagen convertible, for $500, although I still didn't know how to drive. Every weekend I would take a bus to San Francisco, where I had a room in the basement of a yellow-painted mansion that housed Prankster attorney Brian Rohan's law firm. Whenever anybody in the building flushed a toilet, I could hear it rushing through the pipes in my room. The caretaker lived in a little carriage house several yards from my room. He was a jazz drummer. I anticipated making love to the sound of his practicing. It would be fun to experience the buildup to an orgasm with the accompaniment of a drum roll.

My radio job bracketed the weekend, with one show early Saturday morning and another late Sunday night. My first show was on Easter weekend, and I opened with Lord Buckley's rendition of "The Nazz." I tried to get the name Rumpleforeskin listed in the phone book, but they refused. However, they did offer to list me as Foreskin Rumple.

I would eat meat only in the city on weekends. One evening, I was having dinner at a hamburger place before my show, and I sat at the counter watching a young ethnic chef with a white fluffy hat, as he placed one round piece of chopped dead meat after another onto the open fire to cook for rare, medium, and well-done strangers. I was intrigued by his serene expression, and talked about it on the air that night, inviting listeners to tell how *they* managed to survive boring, menial, repetitive jobs. The answers covered a spectrum of escapes that ranged from becoming a machine oneself to disengaging by astral projection.

Another time, I asked listeners to call in and tell about their moment of awakening. My favorite was from a woman who had been shopping at the supermarket. She took a jar of mayonnaise off the shelf—something which she had done dozens of times—but this time she noticed that it said *To open jar, remove lid*, and as if she had been struck by lightning, she suddenly realized how she had been programmed by the culture to become a consumer robot. Life was never the same for her after that.

Once, I suggested that listeners all get stoned or chant or do whatever got them high, and that they also have a jar of honey but not eat any until I gave the signal. First I played some Ravi Shankar sitar music. Then, while countless tongues were simultaneously savoring the taste of honey, I played a tape of a seventy-six-year-old beekeeper reading his epic poem about the nature of honey before playing some soulful numbers on his fiddle.

Another time, I orchestrated an electronic orgy. I requested that listeners wait to make love or masturbate until midnight. Then they could all get into it, knowing that they were sharing the pleasures of the flesh with a spirit of community that was like an invisible spider's web spun across the city. I provided the background music, from Janis Joplin singing "Down on Me" to Gene Autry singing "Back in the Saddle Again."

Although I occasionally had a celebrity guest on my show—Kesey, Jack Nicholson, Lily Tomlin, Country Joe McDonald—it functioned mostly as a sort of radio switchboard. I was able to connect exploited hippie craftspeople with a union organizer. When a woman called whose house had been set on fire by a neighborhood kid whose father was a cop, at the suggestion of other listeners, she ended up taking the kid out to dinner. And when actor Garry Goodrow called to find out if I knew a pickpocket who could serve as a technical adviser for his role in *Steelyard Blues*, I asked for anybody who was a pickpocket to please call, and one did.

Once I got a call from a man who was so hostile that I suggested he breathe deeply before we started talking. For ten solid minutes I allowed his heavy breathing to be broadcast, with music in the background, so that listeners who had never gotten an obscene phone call could finally get one over their radio.

There was never any pressure on me from anybody at the station, but when the head of ABC's FM division came out from the East Coast, he cornered me in the record library and advised me not to get too involved with talking about "the evils of capitalism."

"I've never even *mentioned* anything about the evils of capitalism."

"Well, just try and be subtle about it."

He instructed me to play music immediately after the news instead of commenting on the news. From then on I always played The Who's "Won't Get Fooled Again" right after the news, and *then* I would comment on it. One time I played "Garbage Dump" from an album by Charles Manson back to back with "The Ballad of Lieutenant Calley" of My Lai–massacre infamy. Another night I picked out records entirely on the basis of their album covers, and listeners thought it was a great mix. I always opened the show with Van Morrison's "Into the Mystic" and ended with his "Madame George." When the Fillmore Auditorium closed, KSFX broadcast it live, with disc jockeys on the scene, while I anchored the event from the studio.

One night Dick Gregory announced on my show that, until the war in Vietnam was over, he was going to stop eating solid foods. I in turn announced that, until the war was over, I was going to eat all of Dick Gregory's meals. Actually, my only *real* discipline was being silent one day a week. When Holly came out to stay with me that summer, she decided to join me on my silent day. We communicated with handwritten notes. Holly wrote, *Does laughter count?* Since we were making up the rules as we went along, I answered, *Yes, but no tickling.* Naturally she tried to make me laugh, but I held it in—and got a rush.

All the energy that normally gets dissipated into the air with laughter seemed to surge through my body instead. I decided to stop laughing altogether, just to see what would happen. The more I didn't laugh, the more I found funny. And, paying closer attention to others, I refined my appreciation of laughter as another whole language that could often be more revealing than words. Sometimes I would get a twinge of guilt if I nearly slipped and laughed, and I remembered what I had always known, that children must be *taught* to be serious. When I mentioned my laugh-fast to Dick Gregory, still on his food-fast, it didn't sound so far-fetched to him.

"That's two things people do out of insecurity," he said. "Eating and laughing."

"Well, what would happen to us if everyone in our audiences realized that?"

"Brother, we'd go out of business."

I almost laughed when he said that, but I had already decided to continue *not* laughing in order to see what finally *would* make me laugh out loud again.

After doing the Rumpleforeskin show for seven months, I got fired by the new station manager. His memo to the staff: "I have become deeply concerned about the inconsistency of being a formatted progressive rock station with an island of free form. The final clincher for me was the realization that we might in the future have to ask Paul to fit his program in more to our overall format—a restriction which I feel would be totally unfair to Paul and an aesthetic disaster. Please tell callers that Paul will be on KSAN Sunday night 6–9 PM for a one-shot and may get a regular series there."

At KSAN, I talked about the Attica prison riot, the evolution of Ram Dass, the ads in *Rolling Stone,* and chimpanzee behavior. Five minutes before I was due to sign off, in walked physician Gene Schoenfeld. Under the byline "Dr. Hip," he wrote a column syndicated to the underground papers. Now, his "Dr. Hip" advice program would follow my audition at KSAN. He was accompanied by his guest, Margo St. James. I couldn't help but notice that she was trying to unzip my fly, which was held up by a safety pin, and I realized that she intended to give me head while I was on the air.

"Be careful," I said, "the zipper's broken." She unpinned and unzipped me, then began to perform fellatio. "Would you please say something so that feminists who are listening will understand the context?" She looked up and said, "I'm doing this of my own volition." I maintained my composure, and continued talking. The radio audience had no way of knowing for sure what was actually happening.

I finally said goodbye to my listeners—"It's been a pleasure being with you"—then gave the proper station identification. "This is KSAN in San Francisco," I announced, "the station that blows your mind." Not only didn't I get a job, but I was temporarily barred from the station.

★   ★   ★

The first issue of *The Realist* that I prepared on the West Coast included a short piece by Tom Miller about "the first fatality of the waterbed fad sweeping nouveau-riche longhairs. He was watching a late-night talk show on his tiny Sony television, which had frayed electrical connecting wires. The set fell into a puddle—the result of his cat clawing at the waterbed—and he was electrocuted. The electrically charged water seeped up and surrounded his body before he could reach safety." Miller had invented this story, but it was picked up by the *San Francisco Examiner* and KCBS News. As a result, a California state commission passed a resolution calling for proper industry standards in the manufacture of waterbeds. How gratifying. It was a case of preventive journalism.

Still, what I *really* wanted to do was publish something that would top "The Parts Left Out of the Kennedy Book."

I had observed a disturbing element being imposed upon the counterculture—various groups all trying to rip off the search for consciousness—and I felt challenged to write a satirical piece about this phenomenon. Scientology was one of the scariest of these organizations, if only because its recruiters were such aggressive zombies. The stares of Scientology practitioners seemed to be tactical, their smiles unfelt. The goal of Scientology was to become a Clear—that is, a *complete* zombie—moving up to higher and higher levels by means of auditing sessions with an E-Meter, essentially a lie detector.

In confronting their guilt and fears through the medium of a machine, they had become machine-like themselves and they responded like automatons. Carrying their behavior to its logical conclusion, they could become programmed assassins. I chose Sirhan Sirhan as a credible allegory, since he was already known to have an interest in mysticism and self-improvement, from the Rosicrucians to Theosophy. In a list of upcoming features, I included "The Rise of Sirhan Sirhan in the Scientology Hierarchy."

Then I began to do my research. I was, after all, an investigative satirist.

Scientology founder L. Ron Hubbard's book *Dianetics* became a bestseller with the aid of an employee at *The New York Times* who leaked the names of those bookstores around the country which provide the basis for the *Times'* bestseller list. Hubbard's thesis was that traumatic shock occurs not only during early childhood, but also during the prenatal stage. In *Neurotica* magazine, G. Legman took off on that concept with his own cult, called Epizootics, "demonstrating the basic cause of all neurosis in father's tight-fitting jockstrap."

Not to be outdone by parody, Hubbard in 1952 turned *Dianetics* into Scientology, which traced trauma back to previous lives, not necessarily incarnations that were spent on this planet. In fact, Scientologists were forbidden to see the movie *2001* in order to avoid "heavy and unnecessary restimulation." By what? When Hal the Computer says "unclear"?

In 1955, Hubbard incorporated Scientology as a religion. This would enable its ministers to gain entry into hospitals and prisons, not to mention getting tax exemption. He issued the Professional Auditors Bulletin, a handbook for luring prospects into the Scientology fold. One example was the "illness research" method, taking out a newspaper ad, such as: "Polio victims—a charitable organization investigating polio desires to examine several victims of the after-effects of this illness. Phone so-and-so."

Hubbard explained, "The interesting hooker in this ad is that anyone suffering from a lasting illness is suffering from it so as to attract attention and bring about an examination of it. These people will go on being examined endlessly." Another example, under the subhead "Exploiting," was the "casualty contact" method, "requiring little capital and being highly ambulatory." All it needed was "good filing and a good personal appearance." Hubbard elaborated:

> Every day in the daily papers, one discovers people who have been victimized one way or the other by life. One takes every daily paper he can get his hands on and cuts from it every story whereby he might have a preclear. As speedily as possible, he makes a personal call on the bereaved or injured person. He should represent himself to the person or the person's family as a minister whose compassion was compelled by the newspaper story concerning the person. The goal is to move the customer from group processing to individual attention at a fee.

In 1962, Hubbard wrote to John F. Kennedy, claiming that his letter was as important as the one Albert Einstein had sent to Franklin D. Roosevelt about the atomic bomb. He insisted that "Scientology is very easy for the government to put into effect," and that "Scientology could decide the space race or the next war in the hands of America."

He offered to "train astronauts" for a fee of $25 an hour. "Don't think me a crackpot," he requested. Kennedy didn't respond, but the White House issued a memo to the Secret Service titled "Final Disposition," identifying Hubbard as a potential serious threat to the president's life.

The E-Meter had been presented as a panacea that could cure such "psychosomatic" problems as arthritis, cancer, polio, ulcers, the common cold, and atomic radiation burns. In October 1962, the FDA was investigating Scientology, so Hubbard wrote that the E-Meter is "a valid religious instrument, used in Confessionals, and is in no way diagnostic and does not treat."

Nevertheless, in January 1963, Attorney General Robert Kennedy ordered the FDA to raid Scientology headquarters. More than three tons of equipment, papers, and books were seized, including a hundred E-Meters. Scientology claimed that this violated their freedom of religion, and Hubbard wrote to President Kennedy again. He wanted to meet with him so that they could "come to some amicable answer on religious matters."

Then he wrote to Robert Kennedy, "even though you are of a different faith," asking for protection of the Scientology religion. Like his brother, Bobby didn't respond. Well, there it was—my satirical angle—Hubbard's motivation for programming Sirhan to kill Robert Kennedy would be revenge. Hmmmmm. Had I accidentally stumbled into a real conspiracy when I thought I was merely making one up?

In Scientology, Kennedy could have been declared an Enemy, subject to Fair Game, a penalty described in a Hubbard Policy Letter whereby an Enemy "may be deprived of property or injured by any means by any Scientologist. May be tricked, sue, or lied to or destroyed." In October 1968, four months after Bobby Kennedy was killed, Fair Game was "repealed," due to adverse publicity. "The practice of declaring people Fair Game will cease," Hubbard stated in a Policy Letter. "Fair Game may not appear on any Ethics Order. It causes bad public relations."

When Sirhan found himself awaiting trial, he was given several psychological tests. In one of these, he couldn't provide a simple yes or no response to only two specific statements: "At one or more times in my life, I felt that someone was making me do things by hypnotizing me." And, "Someone has been trying to influence my mind." During the trial psychiatrist Bernard Diamond used post-hypnotic suggestion to program Sirhan into climbing the bars of his cell. There were two different accounts of that experiment. In *Psychology Today* magazine, Dr. Diamond wrote:

> He went over toward the guards and climbed the bars like a monkey. I asked him why. He answered in that cool way he affected, "I am getting exercise." Then I played the tape to prove to him that he had been under hypnosis to do just that. But he denied it and complained that I was bugging him.

However, in the book *RFK Must Die* (a title borrowed from the phrase Sirhan had scribbled over and over and over in a notebook), author Robert Kaiser, who was present at that post-hypnotic experiment, wrote:

> Sirhan had no idea what he was doing up on the top of the bars. When he finally discovered that climbing was not his own idea, but Dr. Diamond's, he was struck with the plausibility of the idea that perhaps he had been programmed by someone else, in like manner, to kill Kennedy.

When Scientology was kicked out of Australia, the official inquiry concluded:

> It is only in name that there is any difference between authoritative hypnosis and most of the techniques of Scientology. Many Scientology techniques are in fact hypnosis techniques, and Hubbard has not changed their nature by changing their names.

Even Hubbard admitted the need for a "canceller," which was a contract with a patient that whatever the auditor said would not become literally interpreted by the patient or used in any way. So, immediately before patients were permitted to open their eyes at the end of a session, they were supposed to be told:

> In the future, when I utter the word Cancelled, everything which I have said to you while you are in a therapy session will be cancelled and will have no force with you. Any suggestion I have made to you will be without force when I say the word Cancelled. Do you understand?

When the word was used, it was not further amplified. Just that single word, *Cancelled*. Hubbard warned, "The canceller is vital. It prevents accidental positive suggestion. The patient may be suggestible or even in a permanent light hypnotic trance." In William Burroughs' book, *The Job*, he stated that "Hubbard has refused to publish his advanced discoveries. There is every indication that the discoveries of Scientology are being used by the CIA and other official agencies."

Ironically, Scientology obtained secret CIA documents through the Freedom of Information Act, proposing mind control experiments where hypnotized subjects would have an uncontrollable impulse to "commit a nuisance" on Groundhog Day on the steps of City Hall, in order to find out whether an unwilling subject could be quickly hypnotized, then made to undergo amnesia by "durable and useful post-hypnotic suggestion." The CIA also collaborated with the U.S. Army's Special Operations Division in bacteriological and chemical "open air tests" in the streets and subway tunnels of New York City.

My ultimate fictional connection between Sirhan and Scientology was inadvertently suggested by Burroughs in *Evergreen* magazine:

> Take a black militant and put him on the E-Meter. Tell him to mock up a nigger-killing Southern sheriff chuckling over the notches in his gun. The needle falls off the dial. He mocks up the sheriff again. The needle falls off the dial. Again, again, again, for two hours if need be. No matter how long it takes, the time will come when he mocks up the sheriff and there is no read on the E-Meter. He is looking at this creature calmly with slow heartbeat and normal blood pressure and seeing it for what it is.
>
> He has as-ised Big Jim Clark. As-ising does not mean acceptance, submission, or resignation. On the contrary, when he can look at Big Jim with no reaction, he is infinitely better equipped

to deal with the external manifestation, as a calm man fights better than an angry one. If you can't bring yourself to see the target you can't hit it. When the needle reads off, you are off target.

I had developed a source inside Scientology. I also had a friend who'd been on the crew of Hubbard's Sea Organization, a paramilitary fleet of ships. Crew members wore uniforms and had to sign an unusual contract:

> I do hereby agree to enter into employment with the Sea Organization and, being of sound mind, do fully realize and agree to abide by its purpose, which is to get Ethics in on this Planet and the Universe and, fully and without reservation, subscribe to the discipline, mores and conditions of this group and pledge to abide by them. Therefore, I contract myself to the Sea Organization for the next billion years.

Give or take a few centuries, of course. I began to work on "The Rise of Sirhan Sirhan in the Scientology Hierarchy." But then, in the course of my research, a strange thing happened. I learned of the *actual* involvement of Charles Manson with Scientology. In fact, there had been an E-Meter at the Spahn Ranch where his "family" stayed. Suddenly I no longer had a reason to use Sirhan as my protagonist. Reality will transcend allegory every time.

Manson had been abandoned by his mother and lived in various institutions since he was eight years old. He learned early how to survive in captivity. When he was fourteen, he got arrested for stealing bread and was jailed. He was supposed to go to reform school, but instead went to Boys Town, ran away, got arrested again, and began his lifelong career as a prison inmate. He was introduced to Scientology by fellow prisoners, and Charlie's ability to psych people out was intensified so that he could zero in on their weaknesses and fears immediately.

When he was released from prison in 1967, he went to the Scientology Center in San Francisco. The individual who accompanied him there told me, "Charlie said to them, 'I'm Clear—what do I do now?'" But they expected him to sweep the floor—shit, he had done *that* in jail. However, in Los Angeles, he went to the Scientology *Celebrity* Center. Now this was more like it—here he could mingle with the elite. I was able to obtain a copy of the original log entry: "7/31/68, new name, Charlie Manson, Devt. No address. In for processing = Ethics = Type III." The receptionist—who, by Type III, meant "psychotic"—sent him to the Ethics office but he never showed up.

At the Spahn Ranch, Manson combined his version of Scientology auditing with post-hypnotic techniques he had learned in prison, with geographical isolation and subliminal motivation, with sing-along sessions and encounter games, with LSD and mescaline, with transactional analysis and brainwashing rituals, with verbal probing and sexual longevity that he had practiced upon himself for all those years in the privacy of his cell.

Ultimately, in August 1969, he sent his well-programmed family off to slay actress Sharon Tate, some friends, and her unborn baby. Tate's husband, film director Roman Polanski, was in London at the time.

And, yes, Charles Manson *was* Rosemary's baby. A few months later, when the family members were captured and charged with the homicides, Manson was portrayed by the media as a hippie cult leader, and the counterculture became a dangerous enemy. Hitchhikers were shunned. Communes were raided. In the public's mind, flower children had grown poisonous thorns. But Manson was never really a hippie.

He had grown up behind bars. His *real* family included con artists, pimps, drug dealers, thieves, muggers, rapists, and murderers. He had known only power relationships in an army of control junkies. Indeed, Charlie Manson was America's Frankenstein monster, a logical product of the prison system—racist, paranoid, and violent—even if hippie astrologers thought that his fate had been predetermined because he was a triple Scorpio.

After having lived behind bars for most of his life, Manson began to explore and exploit the countercultural value system, from Haight-Ashbury to Strawberry Fields. Driving his family around in a school bus painted black, Manson stopped at the Hog Farm, whose school bus was painted in rainbow colors. While traveling, the Hog Farmers had found themselves at a fork in the road. Up above them, two sky-writing planes were playing tic-tac-toe, and the Hog Farmers decided to go one way if the X's won and the other way if the O's won.

Now they were back on their land, all in a circle, chanting "om," which somehow caused the visiting Manson to start choking and gagging, so *his* family began counter-chanting "evil." It was an archetypal confrontation. Charlie even tried to exchange one of his girls for Hugh Romney's wife, Bonnie Jean, but the black bus finally left, mission unaccomplished.

Manson had convinced himself and his family that the Beatles' songs—"Helter Skelter" and "Blackbird"—were actually harkening a race war, which he wanted to hasten by leaving clues to make it appear that black militants had done the killing. Stolen credit cards were deliberately thrown away in a black neighborhood. *Healter Skelter* (*sic*) was scrawled with a victim's blood on the refrigerator, and the word *war* was scratched onto a victim's stomach.

Roman Polanski put a $10,000 contract out on Manson's life.

After Tim Leary had escaped from Eldridge Cleaver's clutches, he was arrested by American agents and taken back to the States, then put in solitary confinement at Folsom Prison, in a cell right next to Manson's. The two "hole-mates" couldn't see each other, but they could talk. Manson didn't understand why Leary had given people acid without trying to control them.

"They took you off the streets," Charlie explained, "so that I could continue with your work."

During Manson's trial, Richard Nixon sprang his own leak in an encounter with the press corps, revealing the thrust of his speech to a gathering of law enforcement officials, where he had called Manson "guilty, directly or indirectly, of eight murders without reason." The next morning, a huge headline on the front page of the *Los Angeles Times* shouted: "Manson Guilty, Nixon Declares."

In court, Charlie held up a copy for the jury to see. When I saw that on the news, I said "right on!" for the first time. Behind my rhetoric was the false expectation that a mistrial would be declared because of Nixon's blunder. But the jury was polled, and in effect they said, "Oh, no, it won't affect *my* attitude toward the defendant—after all, Nixon is merely President of the United States."

Ed Sanders was covering the Manson trial for the *Los Angeles Free Press* and working on a book about the case, titled *The Family*. I wrote to him for permission to print any material that might be omitted from his book because the publisher considered it in bad taste or too controversial. Otherwise, I told him, I would have to make up those missing sections myself. Sanders put a notice in the middle of one of his reports: "Oh, yes, before we ooze onward, I am not, nor shall I be, the author of any future article in *The Realist* entitled 'The Parts I Left Out of the Manson Story, by Ed Sanders.'"

"A joke," he assured me—but, understandably, a safeguard.

I had known Sanders for ten years. He was always on the crest of non-violent political protest and outrageous cultural expression. In 1961 he got arrested with others for trying to swim aboard the Polaris submarine. The next year he published a parody catalog listing actual relics, such as Allen Ginsberg's cold-cream jar containing one pubic hair. He sent the catalog to universities and sold the items at outlandish prices. But now his courage and determination had taken a different path, and I flew to New York to pore through his Manson files. Sanders was a data addict, and his research notes were written in the form of quatrains. He had become an investigative poet.

When I returned to San Francisco, a young man with a child on his shoulders came to my house and rang the bell. I opened the door, and he served me with a subpoena. Scientology was accusing me of libel and conspiracy—simply for having *announced the nine-word title* of an upcoming article—"The Rise of Sirhan Sirhan in the Scientology Hierarchy"—which, ironically, I no longer planned to publish.

They were suing me for three-quarters of a million dollars. I published their complaint in *The Realist*, which allowed Scientology to reveal more about itself than anything I could have imagined about Sirhan. My attorney, James Wolpman, filed a petition to remove the suit to a federal court because of the constitutional question it raised concerning freedom of the press.

Scientology eventually offered to settle out of court for $5,000, but I refused. Then they said they would drop the suit if I would publish an article in *The Realist* by Chick Corea, a jazz musician and Scientologist (who required those working for him to be Scientologists), but that wasn't quite the way I made my editorial decisions, and I refused again. Scientology finally dropped their lawsuit altogether. However, their records show that they had other plans for me. Under the heading "Operation Dynamite"— their jargon for a frame-up—a memo read:

> Got CSW from SFO [San Francisco Office] to *not* do this on Krassner. I disagree and will pass my comments on to DG I US as to why this should be done. SFO has the idea that Krassner is totally handled and will not attack us again. My feelings are that in PT, he has not got enough financial backing to get out *The Realist* or other publications and when that occurs, will attack again, maybe more covertly but attack, nonetheless.

★ ★ ★

Coincidentally, as I was diving into my Manson research, I received a letter from Charlie himself. He had seen a copy of *The Last Supplement* in prison. During the trial, I had published a piece of apocrypha in *The Realist* about his stay at Boys Town—"Charles Manson was My Bunkmate" by Richard Meltzer. A defense attorney read it to Manson and he got pissed off. He complained, "You know how long I stayed in Boys Town? *Two days!*"

Now, in response to his letter, I mentioned that the article had been intended only as a satire of media exploitation. He replied: "Yes, brother, the world is a satire and I did see all sides of your story, 'Charlie's Bunkmate.' But I think in Now with no cover. Most people take into their minds bad thoughts and call it joking. Some lie and call it funny. I don't lie."

In pursuit of information, I visited Warren Hinckle. He was my editor at *Ramparts*, and after that folded, at *Scanlan's*, which also folded, but he had been planning to publish an article on the Manson case in *Scanlan's*, and now he brought me to former FBI agent William Turner, who had checked out Doris Day. The only connection she could possibly have with the Manson case was that her son, record producer Terry Melcher, had met Charlie and was interested in his music, and that Melcher was a former tenant of the Beverly Hills mansion where the massacre took place. *Aha!* I realized that could be the focal point of my satire—a torrid affair between Doris Day and Charlie Manson—a perfect metaphor for the coming together of the image and underbelly of Hollywood. Just for the hell of it, I wrote to Manson and asked if he ever had sex with Doris Day.

His reply: "Yes, and I also fucked Rin-Tin-Tin and the Virgin Mary."

I didn't know in what satirical direction I was heading, so I just continued to absorb whatever details I could find out about the Manson case. A prison psychiatrist at San Quentin told me of an incident he had observed during Manson's trial. A black inmate said to Manson, "Look, I don't wanna know about your theories on race, I don't wanna hear anything about religion, I just wanna know one thing—how'd you get them girls to obey you like that?" Manson replied, "I got a knack."

Hinckle also brought me to the renowned private investigator Hal Lipset, who informed me that not only did the Los Angeles Police Department seize pornographic films and videotapes that they found in Sharon Tate's loft, but also that certain members of the LAPD were *selling* them. Lipset had talked with one police source who told him exactly which porn flicks were available—a total of seven hours' worth for a quarter-million dollars. Lipset began reciting a litany of porn videos.

The most notorious was Greg Bautzer, an attorney for Howard Hughes, with Jane Wyman, the former wife of then-Governor Ronald Reagan. There was Sharon Tate with Dean Martin. There was Sharon with Steve McQueen. There was Sharon with two black bisexual men.

Lipset recalled, "The cops weren't too happy about *that* one."

But when he told me there was a videotape of Cass Elliot from the Mamas and the Papas in an orgy with Yul Brynner, Peter Sellers, and Warren Beatty—coincidentally, Brynner and Sellers, together with John Phillips of the Mamas and the Papas, had offered a $25,000 reward for the capture of the killers—suddenly there was a personal element intruding upon my investigation. In the summer of 1968, Tim Leary and I had been guests on the Les Crane show in Los Angeles; of course I publicized the upcoming Yippie counter-convention. After the taping, we went to a big party at Tommy Smothers's house, where I met Cass Elliot. We liked each other immediately.

The next day she called to invite me to dinner at her home that evening. Instead, we decided to meet Leary at a restaurant in Laguna Beach. David Crosby drove us there in a station wagon, while Cass and I cuddled and kissed on a foam-rubber mat. On the way we stopped at the Mystic Arts combination head shop and health-food store, with a magnificent meditation room. Two years later it would burn to the ground, on the same day that all the other head shops in the area were also destroyed by fire.

Although Cass and I slept together that night, we didn't have sex. In bed she kept talking about Billy Doyle, who was arriving from Jamaica the next morning. She seemed to be afraid of him. During breakfast the three of us sat around talking about the music scene, drug use, and the politics of protest. Doyle liked to act tough and mysterious.

"We know all about you," he told me. "You better watch your step."

Now I came across Billy Doyle's name in *The Family*. He was the drug connection for two of the victims, Voytek Frykowski and his girlfriend, coffee heiress Abigail Folger. Ed Sanders wrote:

> Sometime during [the first week in August] a dope dealer from Toronto named Billy Doyle was whipped and video-buggered at [the Tate residence]. In the days before his death, [another victim, Jay] Sebring had complained to a receptionist at his hair shop that someone had burned him for $2,000 worth of cocaine and he wanted vengeance. Billy Doyle was involved in a large-scale dope-import operation involving private planes from Jamaica.

And Dennis Hopper was quoted in the *Los Angeles Free Press:*

> They had fallen into sadism and masochism and bestiality—and they recorded it all on videotape too. The L.A. police told me this. I know that three days before they were killed, twenty-five people were invited to that house to a mass whipping of a dealer from Sunset Strip who'd given them bad dope.

Naturally, Billy Doyle felt it was rude of Sebring and Frykowski to tie him to a chair, whip him, and then fuck him in the ass while a video camera taped the proceedings before a live audience. But police investigators eliminated him as a suspect in the murders. However, on Friday evening, just a few hours before the massacre took place, Joel Rostau—the boyfriend of Sebring's receptionist and an intermediary in a cocaine ring

—visited Sebring and Frykowski at the Tate house, to deliver mescaline and coke.

During the Manson trial, several associates of Sebring were murdered, including Rostau, whose body was found in the trunk of a car in New York. Ed Sanders, who had already engaged in years of agonizing research into the Manson case, remarked that, personally, he had no desire for permanent meditation next to a spare tire.

So it appeared that the Manson family had actually served as some sort of hit squad for a drug ring. What a great satirical premise.

* * *

When President Kennedy was killed, Mae Brussell was a twice-divorced suburban homemaker with five children. Her seven-year-old daughter saw Lee Harvey Oswald on TV—he had a black eye and was saying, "I didn't do it, I haven't killed anybody, I don't know what this is all about." She decided to send him her teddy bear. It was all wrapped up and ready to mail when she saw Oswald murdered by Jack Ruby on TV. Mae had to wonder, "What kind of world are we bringing our children into?"

One bit of research led to another, and she started a weekly radio program, "Dialogue Assassination," originating on her local rock station, KLRB in Carmel, California, and syndicated to a half-dozen other stations. What had begun as a hobby turned into a lifetime pilgrimage. She purchased the Warren Commission report for $86, studying and cross-referencing the entire twenty-six volumes, without the aid of a computer. It took her eight years and 27,000 typewritten pages. She was overwhelmed by the difference between the evidence and the commission's conclusion that there had been only a single assassin. In fact, she concluded:

"Lee Harvey Oswald was set up to take the fall. But the Warren Commission ignored physical evidence from the scene of the crime—bullets, weapons, clothing, wounds—and based its judgment that Oswald was just a disturbed loner on the testimony of some thirty Russian emigres in the Dallas-Forth Worth area. Most of them, according to the testimony, were affiliated with anti-Communist organizations that had collaborated with the Nazis during the war."

Then she began to study the history of six hundred Nazis brought to this country after World War II under Project Paperclip. They were infiltrated into hospitals, universities, and the aerospace industry, further developing their techniques in propaganda, mind control, and behavior modification. She observed how the patterns of murder in the United States were identical to those in Nazi Germany. The parallels between the rise of Adolf Hitler and the rise of Richard Nixon were frightening to Mae. Hitler came into power as the result of more than four hundred political assassinations. So, rather than just investigating the death of John Kennedy, she collected articles about the murders of people *involved* in his assassination.

And, instead of limiting her research to the killing of Robert Kennedy, Malcolm X, Martin Luther King, and the attempted assassination of George Wallace, she began paying attention to the untimely, suspicious deaths of judges, attorneys, labor leaders, professors, civil rights activists, reporters, authors, Black Panthers, Chicanos, Native Americans—and Mary Jo Kopechne. Mae believed that Chappaquiddick was yet another CIA-orchestrated dirty deed; the National Safety Council had never found a single case of anybody escaping from a submerged car the way Senator Ted Kennedy supposedly had.

One afternoon in February 1972, Mae read in *The Realist* about the lawsuit in response to my announcement of "The Rise of Sirhan Sirhan in the Scientology Hierarchy." She immediately phoned to assure me that Scientologists had nothing to do with the assassination of Robert Kennedy. "Oh, I knew that," I told her, "but the article was just gonna be a satire, and they took it seriously. I'm working on something else now instead. Let me ask, do you know anything about the Manson case?"

"Of course," she said. "The so-called Manson murders were actually orchestrated by military intelligence in order to destroy the counterculture movement. It's no different from the Special Forces in Vietnam, disguised as Vietcong, killing and slaughtering to make the Vietcong look bad."

"Oh, *really*? Could I come see you?"

Hassler drove me to Mae Brussell's home. She was about fifty, plump and energetic, wearing a long peasant dress patch-worked with philosophical tidbits, knitting sweaters for her children while she breathlessly described the architecture of an invisible government. Her walls were lined with forty file cabinets containing 1,600 subject categories.

Every day, Mae would digest ten newspapers from around the country, supplementing that diet with items sent to her by a network of researchers and young conspiracy students known as Brussell Sprouts—plus magazines, underground papers, unpublished manuscripts, court affidavits, documents from the National Archives, FBI and CIA material obtained through the Freedom of Information Act, and hundreds of books on espionage and assassination. Each Sunday she would sort out the previous week's clippings into various categories as though she were conducting a symphony of horror.

"About 80 percent of all CIA intelligence information comes from printed news," she said, "so I am doing what they are doing, without being paid, and without selectively writing my own history, but using *all* the material."

"So how come *you're* still alive?" I asked.

"Well, I'm not," she chuckled. "I'm a robot."

But it was obviously a question that she had considered. If she knew so much, why *hadn't* they killed her?

"The CIA works on a basis of need-to-know," she explained. "Because if you know too much, you may not do what you're supposed to do. You must have a given order to do something, but if you know that the end result is that somebody's going to be blown up twelve miles away—and all you're supposed to do is deliver an envelope—you may think about it. One agent called me—he had killed ten people for the CIA. When members of the CIA cut his jugular vein, he had to sew it up, and he vowed vengeance against them because he had killed ten people, and when he was ordered to kill a member of Congress, he wanted to stop. Various agents listen to my program. It's a safety valve for them, on how far things are going."

"Are you saying that the intelligence community has allowed you to function precisely because you know more than any of *them*?"

"Exactly," she said, laughing at her own truth.

I stayed overnight, devouring material from her massive files. For Mae, although the ultimate mystery would remain forever inconceivable, assassination research had become her spiritual quest for truth. Conspiracy became her Zen grid for perceiving political reality, drawing her deeper and deeper into a separate reality that Carlos Castaneda never dreamed of. (The mysterious author of the New Age bestseller, *A Separate Reality*, was, of course, one of the three tramps arrested at the grassy knoll.)

I had originally intended to write a satirical article on the Manson case, but now I had stumbled upon an American version of the Reichstag fire. The next morning, my head was still swirling in the afterglow of a fresh conversion. On the bus, I pondered a theological question Mae had posed:

"How many coincidences does it take to make a plot?"

* * *

Voytek Frykowski's father had financed Roman Polanski's first film. He and Abigail Folger, were staying at the Polanski residence. She was paying the rent and supplying him with the money for their daily drug supplies. In July 1969, Billy Doyle promised Frykowski a new synthetic drug, MDA, made in Canada. I had tried MDA a few times—it felt like a combination of mescaline and amphetamine, acting as an extraordinary energizer and, if you were with the right person, a powerful aphrodisiac. The plan was for Frykowski to become the American distributor of MDA. He was hoping to sell a screenplay, but it's always nice to have something to fall back on.

In 1971, I flew to Kansas City to participate in a symposium at the University of Missouri with Ken Kesey and Ed Sanders. We ate in the cafeteria. Sanders ordered a full vegetarian meal and then couldn't eat any of it. I had never seen him so shaken. Ed was such a devout pacifist that he wouldn't even eat chicken soup because a chicken was killed to make it, and yet he had borrowed a pistol for a single night when staking out a possible cult animal sacrifice potentially connected with Manson. Now he was planning another book about the Manson case, titled *The Motive*.

"What *was* the motive?" I asked.

Ed seemed nervous. "Ask Peter Folger," he muttered through tight lips.

Folger was the coffee tycoon whose daughter, Abigail, had been one of the victims. She supported Tom Bradley as the first black candidate for mayor of Los Angeles, despite the objection of her father, who had a reputation as a fierce racist. While Ed Sanders was researching his Manson book, he received a Mafia kiss from a lawyer for Peter Folger. When Sanders advised me to "ask Peter Folger," I assumed he was referring to the fact that Folger had conducted his own investigation.

But then, in my paranoid fantasies, I began to believe that he meant Folger was *responsible* for the massacre; that he had actually *arranged* to have his own daughter brutally slain because she had violated family tradition by supporting a black mayor and living with a man who was going to distribute MDA, a drug that could provide tremendous competition for coffee. What once might have been a satirical premise had now become a serious possibility in the warped regions of my mind.

I even checked into the history of Folger's Coffee. A deal had been made with the FTC about their merger with Procter & Gamble. It was so suspicious that *Advertising Age* ran a front-page editorial. I watched Folger's Coffee commercials carefully. One took place in a supermarket, showing two white housewives standing in an aisle discussing the virtues of coffee when, almost subliminally, a black woman elbowed her way between them. In another commercial, the locale was a political convention hall, again with two whites and a black almost subliminally elbowing between them. Commercials were produced frame by precise frame, and I became convinced that Peter Folger was deliberately trying to program TV viewers with racism in his coffee commercials.

It was as though I were psychically playing the part of both characters in Roman Polanski's first film, *The Fat and the Lean*, where a wealthy landowner shoots an arrow into the air, and then his servant runs across the lawn carrying a target so that his master is assured of scoring a bull's-eye every time.

★ ★ ★

Within a week after the killings, there was a dawn raid on the Spahn Ranch, with a grand-theft-auto search warrant. The Manson group had been stealing Volkswagens and turning them into dune buggies. Manson and four family members—Linda Kasabian, Susan Atkins, Patricia Krenwinkel, and Leslie van Houten—were arrested, then released in three days. But, while they were in confinement, Atkins told her cellmate about the murders, and when the cellmate was released, she informed the Los Angeles police.

By this time, Manson and the others had moved to another ranch in Death Valley, where they were arrested again. Mae Brussell put me in contact with Preston Guillory, a former deputy sheriff at the Malibu Sheriff's Department, which aided the Los Angeles Sheriff's Department in the original raid of the Spahn Ranch. Guillory had participated in that raid, and I interviewed him at an apartment in San Francisco. He stated:

> We had been briefed for a few weeks prior to the actual raiding of Spahn Ranch. We had a sheaf of memos on Manson, that they had automatic weapons at the ranch, that citizens had complained about hearing machine-guns fired at night, that firemen from the local fire station had been accosted by armed members of Manson's band and told to get out of the area, all sorts of complaints like this.
>
> We had been advised to put anything relating to Manson on a memo submitted to the station, because they were supposedly gathering information for the raid we were going to make. Deputies at the station of course started asking, "Why aren't we going to make the raid sooner?" I mean, Manson's a parole violator, machine-guns have been heard, we know there's narcotics, and we know there's booze. He's living at the Spahn Ranch with a bunch of minor girls in complete violation of his parole.
>
> Deputies at the station quite frankly became very annoyed that no action was being taken about Manson. My contention is this— the reason Manson was left on the street was because our department thought that he was going to attack the Black Panthers. We were getting intelligence briefings that Manson was anti-black and he had supposedly killed a Black Panther, the body of which could not be found, and the department thought that he was going to launch an attack on the Black Panthers.
>
> Manson was a very ready tool, apparently, because he did have some racial hatred and he wanted to vent it. But they hadn't anticipated him attacking someone other than the Panthers, which

he did. Manson changed his score. Changed the program at the last moment and attacked the Tates and then went over to the LaBiancas and killed them. And here was the Sheriff's Department suddenly wondering, "Jesus Christ, what are we gonna do about this? We can't cover this up. Well, maybe we can."

I bet those memos are no longer in existence. The memos about what Manson was doing. Citizens' complaints. All those things I'm sure have disappeared by now. It shows the police were conscious of the fact that he had these weapons in violation of his parole. You've got at least involvement here on the part of Manson's parole officer, on the part of the Sheriff's Department, probably the sheriff himself, and whoever gave him his orders. Manson should have been [imprisoned] long before the killings, because he was on parole, period. He was living at the Spahn Ranch with an outlaw motorcycle gang. I feel that, to say the least, the sheriff of Los Angeles County is an accessory to murder.

The raid was a week after the Sharon Tate thing, and the intelligence information was coming in for about three weeks prior to the raid. They just didn't want any arrests made. It was obvious they wanted the intelligence information we were gathering for some other reason. Three days after they were arrested, seventy-two hours later, they were all released—lack of evidence—after this mammoth raid. This raid involved two helicopters, 102 deputies, and about twenty-five radio cars, and all the charges were dropped against everyone.

It appeared to me that the raid was more or less staged as an afterthought. It was like a scenario that we were going through. There was some kind of a grand plan that we were participating in, but I never had the feeling the raid was necessary or that it required so many personnel. Now, if you were a police official and you were planning a raid on the Spahn Ranch, utilizing 102 deputies and helicopters and all that, one would think that with all the information coming out a month prior to the raid, wouldn't you have them under fairly close surveillance? If you did have them under fairly close surveillance, wouldn't you see them leave the Spahn Ranch to go over and kill seven people and then come back?

So the hypothesis I put forward is, either we didn't have them under surveillance for grand-theft-auto because it was a big farce, or else they were under surveillance by somebody much higher than the Sheriff's Department, and they did go through this scenario of killing at the Tate house and then come back, and then we went through the motions to do our raid. Either they were under surveillance at the time, which means somebody must have seen them go to the Tate house and commit the killings, or else they weren't under surveillance.

You have to remember that Charlie was on federal parole all this time from '67 to '69. Do you realize all the shit he was getting away with while he was on parole? Now here's the kicker. Before the Tate killings, he had been arrested at Malibu twice for statutory rape. Never got [imprisoned for parole violation]. During the Tate killings and the Spahn Ranch raid, Manson's parole officer was on vacation, so he had no knowledge of Manson being incarcerated, so naturally Manson was released, but why wasn't a parole hold put on him?

It's like Manson had God on his side when all these things are going down, or else somebody was watching every move he made, somebody was controlling from behind the scenes. Somebody saw that no parole hold was placed. Manson liked to ball young girls, so he just did his thing and he was released and they didn't put any hold on him. But somebody very high up was controlling everything that was going on and was seeing to it that we didn't bust Manson.

Prior to the Spahn Ranch raid, there was a memo—it was verbal, I would have loved to Xerox some things but there wasn't anything to Xerox—that we weren't to arrest Manson or any of his followers prior to the raid. It was intimated to us that we were going to make a raid on the Spahn Ranch, but the captain came out briefly and said, "No action is to be taken on anybody at the Spahn Ranch. I want memos submitted directly to me with a cover sheet so nobody else can read them." So deputies were submitting memos on information about the Spahn Ranch that other deputies weren't even allowed to see. We were to submit intelligence information but not to make any arrests. Manson was in a free fire zone, so to speak. He was living a divine existence. We couldn't touch him.

And so it was that the presence of racism had morphed the Sheriff's Department into collaborators in a mass murder. But who was the higher-up that gave them the order to leave Manson alone? I was certainly prepared to believe that's what occurred. I had been gathering piece after piece of a mind-boggling jigsaw puzzle, trying to make them all fit snugly into one big cohesive picture, but without having any model to pattern it after.

Manson was on Death Row—this was before capital punishment was repealed (later reinstated, but not retroactively) in California—so I was unable to meet with him. Reporters had to settle for an interview with *any* prisoner awaiting the gas chamber, and it wasn't very likely that Charlie would be selected at random for me. In the course of our correspondence, there was a letter from him consisting of a few pages of gibberish about Christ and the Devil, but at one point, right in the middle, he wrote in tiny letters, *Call Squeaky*, with her phone number. I called, and we arranged to meet at her apartment in Los Angeles. On an impulse, I brought several tabs of LSD with me on the plane.

Squeaky Fromme resembled a typical redheaded, freckle-faced waitress who sneaks a few tokes of pot in the lavatory, a regular girl-next-door except perhaps for the unusually challenging nature of her personality plus the scar of an X that she had gouged and burned into her forehead as a visual reminder of her commitment to Charlie.

That same symbol also covered the third eyes of her roommates, Sandra Good and Brenda McCann. "We've crossed ourselves out of this entire system," I was told. They all had short hairstyles growing in now, after having shaved their heads completely. They continued to sit on the sidewalk near the Hall of Justice every day, like a coven of faithful nuns being witness to Manson's martyrdom.

Sandy Good had seen me perform at The Committee in San Francisco some years previously. Now she told me that when she first met Charlie and people asked her what he was like, she had compared him to Lenny Bruce and me. It was the weirdest compliment I ever got, but I began to understand Manson's peculiar charisma.

With his sardonic rap, mixed with psychedelic drugs and real-life theater games such as "creepy-crawling" and stealing, he had deprogrammed his family from the values of mainstream society, but *re*programmed them with his own philosophy, a cosmic version of the racism perpetuated by the prison system that had served as *his* family.

Manson stepped on Sandy's eyeglasses, threw away her birth-control pills, and inculcated her with racist sensibility. Although she had once been a civil rights activist, she was now asking me to tell John Lennon that he should get rid of Yoko Ono and stay with "his own kind." Later, she added, "If Yoko really loved the Japanese people, she would not want to mix their blood."

The four of us ingested those little white tablets containing three hundred micrograms of acid, then took a walk to the office of Laurence

Merrick, who had been associated with schlock biker exploitation movies as the prerequisite to directing a sensationalist documentary, *Manson*.

Squeaky's basic vulnerability emerged as she kept pacing around and telling Merrick that she was afraid of him. He didn't know we were tripping, but he must have sensed the vibes. I engaged him in conversation. We discussed the fascistic implications of a movie, *The French Connection*, and he remarked, "You're pretty articulate—"

"For a bum," I completed his sentence, and he laughed.

Next we went to the home of some friends of the family, smoked a few joints of soothing grass, and listened to music. They sang along with the lyrics of "A Horse with No Name": *In the desert you can't remember your name, 'cause there ain't no one for to give you no pain.*

I was basking in the afterglow of the Moody Blues' "Om" song when Sandy began to speak of the "gray people"—regular citizens going about their daily business—whom she had been observing from her vantage point on the corner near the Hall of Justice.

"We were just sitting there," she said, "and they were walking along, kind of avoiding us. It's like watching a live movie in front of you. Sometimes I just wanted to kill the gray people, because that was the only way they would be able to experience the total Now."

That was an expression Charlie had borrowed from Scientology. Later, Sandy explained that she didn't mean it literally about killing the gray people—that she had been speaking from another dimension. She told me that prosecutor Vincent Bugliosi once snarled at her as she kept vigil outside the courthouse: "We're gonna get you because you sucked Charlie Manson's dick." The girls just sat there on the sidewalk and laughed, because they knew that oral-genital relations did not constitute a capital offense.

When we returned to their apartment, Sandy asked if I wanted to take a hot bath. I felt ambivalent. I knew that one of the attorneys in the case had participated in a ménage à trois with Squeaky and Sandy, but I had also been told by a reporter, "It certainly levels the high to worry about getting stabbed while fucking the Manson ladies in the bunkhouse at the Spahn Ranch—I've found that the only satisfactory position is sitting up, back to the wall, facing the door."

Visions of the famous shower scene in *Psycho* flashed through my mind, but despite the shrill self-righteousness that infected their true-believer syndrome, they had charmed me with their honesty, humor, and distorted sense of compassion. They sensed my hesitation, and Squeaky confronted me: "You're afraid of me, aren't you?" she asked.

"Not really. Should I be?"

Sandy tried to reassure me: "She's *beautiful*, Paul. Just look into her eyes. Isn't she beautiful?"

Squeaky and I stared silently at each other for a while—I recalled that Manson had written, "I never picked up anyone who had not already been discarded by society"—and my eyes began to tear. There were tears in Squeaky's eyes too. She asked me to try on Charlie's vest. It felt like a perverted honor to participate in this ceremony. The corduroy vest was a solid inch thick with embroidery—snakes and dragons and devilish designs including human hair that had been woven into the multicolored patterns.

Sandy took her bath, but instead of my getting into the tub *with* her— assuming she had invited me—I sat fully dressed on the toilet, and we talked. I was thinking, *You have pert nipples*, but instead I said, "What's that scar on your back?" It was from a lung operation.

Brenda asked for another tab of acid, to send Manson in prison. She ground it into powder which she then glued to the paper with vegetable dye and the notation, *words fly fast*, explaining that Charlie would know what it meant. She stayed up late that night, writing letters to several prisoners with the dedication of a polygamous war wife.

Squeaky visited me a few times in San Francisco. On the way to lunch one day, she lit a cigarette, and I told her about the series of advertisements by which women were originally conditioned into smoking: a woman standing next to a man who was smoking; then a woman saying to the man, "Blow some my way"; and finally a woman smoking her *own* cigarette. Squeaky simply smiled, said "okay," and dropped her cigarette on the sidewalk, crushing it out with her shoe.

Another time, when I attempted to point out a certain fallacy in her logic, she responded, "Well, what do you expect from me? I'm crazy!" Once, she told me she had been beaten up by members of the Mel Lyman family from Boston because she wouldn't switch her allegiance to them, even though they'd had plans to break Manson out of jail while his trial was taking place, by means of a helicopter. She said they were "well organized."

Squeaky mailed me her drawing in red ink of a woman's face with a pair of hands coming out of her mouth. Written in script was the song lyric: "Makes me wanna holler, throw up both my hands . . ."

*　*　*

"Charles Manson was a patsy," Mae Brussell told me—"identical with Lee Harvey Oswald, Sirhan Sirhan, and James Earl Ray. The Manson thing was a hidden war against the youth culture. People sharing their housing, their food, their cars, recycling their old clothes. Make your own candles and turn off the electricity. It was an economic revolution, affecting every-thing from the cosmetic industry to the churches."

She believed that Tex Watson, the Manson family member who led the others on the night of the murders, had played a bigger part in planning the massacre than generally believed. Charlie had instructed the girls to do whatever Tex told them. When Manson was charged, Watson was also charged, but federal authorities held Watson in a Texas prison with no explanation—not even his own lawyers were allowed to see him—while Vincent Bugliosi prosecuted the Manson trial in California.

In order to find Manson guilty, the jury had to be convinced that Charlie's girls were zombies who followed his orders without question. However, in order to find *Watson* guilty, another jury had to be convinced that he was *not a zombie at all* and knew exactly what he was doing.

Mae gave me the heaviest lead in my Manson research. She told me that an agent for Naval Intelligence, Nathaniel Dight (not his real name), had been meeting with Tex Watson. Naval Intelligence—of course! L. Ron Hubbard was in Naval Intelligence. During World War II, imprisoned Mafia boss Lucky Luciano was pardoned at the urgent request of Naval Intelligence. The Committee to Investigate Assassinations stated that Lee Harvey Oswald had worked in Naval Intelligence. Even the infamous Zodiac Killer used obsolete Naval Intelligence ciphers in his notes.

Nathaniel Dight was taking courses at Naval Postgraduate School, and Mae claimed that only intelligence officers could do that. Mae said Dight had posed as a hippie artist, orchestrating the scenario of violence and witchcraft in meetings with Tex Watson, who then fulfilled the prophecy of this agent provocateur with all that shooting and stabbing.

Dight had done the artwork for a magazine which predicted that the counterculture would turn to violence and witchcraft. It was published by a corporation, which, Mae said, "was a conduit of CIA funds for medical research in mind control, intelligence money for electrode implants, and for LSD experiments, according to documents I got from the Pentagon."

Mae introduced me to Louise, a neighbor of Dight's, who told me she had recognized Tex Watson's photo in the newspaper as the one who had visited him. She told me about Dight's alleged strange behavior: "I would occasionally find a noose in my backyard, and it was always hanging from a tree or shrub. The nooses were made of a nylon type rope or cord, and were of varied weights. The nooses gradually crept closer to my house. The closer they were placed the smaller they became."

Although my interview with former deputy sheriff Preston Guillory had prepared me to accept Mae's theory on Dight, Guillory didn't recog-nize the name. Manson wouldn't answer any of my questions about him.

"Brother," he wrote, "names to me are like past dreams and my thought doesn't live in time. Much moves that I can never put on paper or express in words." Instead he discussed the jailhouse code against snitching.

I wrote back that there was *good* snitching and *bad* snitching—giving, as an example of the former, Daniel Ellsberg—but Charlie wasn't persuaded. I had also been corresponding with another prisoner at San Quentin, convicted mass killer John Linley Frazier, who wrote, "Me and Charlie are still trying to figure out how long our leashes are and who's been pissin' on 'em." Nor was I able to find anyone in the Manson family who could provide confirmation about Nathaniel Dight. Squeaky, Sandy, and Brenda had never heard of him.

Then came a break. My friend and Watsonville neighbor Jackie Christeve, who had started the first women's studies program in the country at San Diego State College, introduced me to Karlene Faith. They were both graduate students in the History of Consciousness Department at the Santa Cruz campus of the University of California.

Karlene invited me to participate in her activist thesis. She was writing a paper based on her project of bringing outside educators into the California Institute for Women at Frontera. I would conduct a workshop in creative journalism. Our visit to the prison was extended to include the Special Security Unit, which housed a trio of convicted killers—Manson family members Susan Atkins, Patricia Krenwinkel, and Leslie van Houten.

When we met them, Patricia and Leslie were needle-pointing a colorful dragon on muslin the size of a bedsheet. They had named the dragon Mao. "In case the Chinese take over," Patricia Krenwinkel explained, "we want to be ready." Jackie had brought an old film about dating that was more campy than instructional. She asked if they were interested in seeing it. "Yes," replied Leslie van Houten. "Anything with touching."

She said it with such tenderness, and yet they had used knives to butcher people to death—the ultimate *perversion* of touching. Later, we talked about the murders. "It was their karma," Susan Atkins reasoned. "In another life, our karma could have been reversed." That was the key to this puzzle. The Manson family had simply taken other people's karma into their own hands.

I asked if anyone there had ever met Nathaniel Dight. Susan replied, "Oh, yeah, Tex took me to sleep with him. And he gave us dope." Keeping my adrenaline rush anchored, I explained who he actually was. The others teased her. "Ha, ha, you slept with a CIA guy."

They asked me who really ran the country. I was carrying around in my pocket a pyramid-shaped seashell I had picked up on the beach. Using that as a model, I outlined the power structure of secret societies, culminating with an unholy coalition at the top—organized crime, military intelligence, and corporate greed. The three women passed the seashell around, caressing it with their fingers as if trying to capture the sensuality for future reference. I should've left it with them.

The next time I saw Squeaky, I told her about the meeting and gave her the seashell. She held it in her palm and rubbed it against her cheek.

"Wow," she said, "I can *feel* their energy."

* * *

Ed Sanders wrote in *The Family*, in reference to the Process cult, to which Charles Manson had ties:

> It is possible that the Process had a baleful influence on Sirhan Sirhan, since Sirhan is known, in the spring of '68, to have frequented clubs in Hollywood in the same turf as the Process was proselytizing. Sirhan was very involved in occult pursuits. He had talked several times subsequent to Robert Kennedy's death about an occult group from London which he knew about and which he really wanted to go to London to see.

The Process was an offshoot of Scientology. Could this be a case of satirical prophecy? I was tempted to return to my original premise involving Sirhan, but it was too late. I had already become obsessed with the Manson case.

In the summer of '68, while the Yippies were planning a Festival of Life at the Chicago convention, some zealots from the Process visited me in New York. They were hyper-anxious to meet Tim Leary and pestered me for his phone number. They were also busy recruiting new members. When a teenager known as Gloria Yippie became a Process initiate, she had to wear all black clothing with a silver cross around her neck, and she was required to be celibate. She explained to me that this temporary restraint on her libido was "just testing my obedience."

The Process first came to the United States in 1967. Members were called "mind benders" and proclaimed their "dedication to the elimination of the gray forces." They became the Process Church of the Final Judgment, a New Orleans–based religious corporation. They claimed to be in direct contact with both Jesus and Lucifer, and had wanted to be called the Church of the Process of Unification of Christ and Satan, but local officials presumably objected to their taking the name of Satan in vain.

The Process struck me as a group of occult provocateurs, using radical Christianity as a front. They were adamantly interested in Yippie politics.

They boasted to me of various rallies which their *vibrations alone* had transformed into riots. They implied that there was some kind of connection between the assassination of Bobby Kennedy and their mere presence on the scene. On the evening that Kennedy was killed at the Ambassador Hotel, he had been to a dinner party with Roman Polanski and Sharon Tate.

Bernard Fensterwald, head of the Committee to Investigate Assassinations, told me that Sirhan Sirhan had some involvement with the Process. Peter Chang, the district attorney of Santa Cruz, showed me a letter from a Los Angeles police official to the chief of police in San Jose, warning him that the Process had infiltrated biker gangs and hippie communes.

In 1972, Paulette Cooper, author of *The Scandal of Scientology*, put me in touch with Lee Cole, a former Scientologist who was now working with the Process Church. I contacted him and flew to Chicago. Cole met me at the airport with a couple of huge men whose demeanor was somewhat frightening.

They drove me to a motel, where I checked in, paying cash in advance. Cole arranged for a meeting with Sherman Skolnick, a local conspiracy researcher. He was in a wheelchair. Two men, one with a metal hook in place of his hand, carried him up the back stairs to my motel room. Lee Cole kept peeking out the window for suspicious-looking cars. It was becoming more surrealistic every minute.

Early the next morning, the phone rang. It was Sherman Skolnick. "Paul, I'm sorry to wake you, but you're in extreme danger." My heart started pounding, and I put my socks on. "That fellow from last night, Lee Cole, he's CIA." I got dressed faster than I had ever gotten dressed in my life, packed my stuff, and ran down the back steps of the motel without even checking out.

There was a cab outside. I got in and said, "NBC, please," because I knew somebody who worked there. The driver said, "Where's that?" If this were a movie, he wouldn't have spoken, he would've just started driving away, and then I'd say, "Hey, wait a minute, this isn't the way to NBC," so actually I was *relieved* that he didn't know where it was.

"Never mind," I said. "Do you know where the Playboy Building is?" And the driver knew. I'm sure he heard my sigh of relief. I was hoping to see Arthur Kretchmer, a friend who was the editor of *Playboy*, but this was Saturday and the offices were closed. I called him at home, and he said he'd be right there. While I was waiting, I called Ed Sanders in New York.

"I'm scared," I told him.

"Aw," he said, "they're just punks."

Somehow, that felt reassuring. After all, what exactly *was* I so afraid of? I met with Kretchmer, then decided to go ahead with my original plan, and he drove me to another motel. There, I called up Lee Cole. Of course he denied being with the CIA. We made an appointment to visit the Process headquarters. "And this time," I said—with Clint Eastwood bravado—"you can leave those *goons* of yours at home."

The Process men were dressed all in black, with silver crosses hanging from their necks. They called each other "brother" and they had German shepherds that appeared menacing. They tried to convince me that Scientology, not the Process, was responsible for creating Charles Manson. But what else could I have expected? Lee Cole's role was to provide information on Scientology to the Process.

To prove that he wasn't with the CIA, he told *me* stuff about Scientology. He described their plan to kidnap former boxing champion Joe Louis from a mental hospital, so that Scientology could get the credit for curing him. Back in San Francisco, I asked journalist Roland Jacopetti to check that out, and he discovered that Scientology actually *did* have such a plan, although it had been aborted.

Not that belonging to the CIA and Scientology were mutually exclusive, but I called Sherman Skolnick, and he apologized for scaring me. "You know us conspiracy researchers," he chuckled, "we're paranoid." Actually, conspiracy research had become his religious pursuit. He once called me up with a new piece of evidence and proclaimed: "I've discovered the holy of holies."

* * *

No wonder Mae Brussell was so excited. The attempted burglary of Democratic headquarters at the Watergate Hotel in Washington, D.C. in June 1972 had suddenly brought her eight-and-a-half years of dedicated conspiracy research to an astounding climax. She recognized names, methodology, patterns of cover-up. She could trace linear connections leading inevitably from the assassination of JFK to the Watergate break-in, and all the killings in between.

There was, for example, the murder of Ruben Salazar, a *Los Angeles Times* reporter, at the first Chicano-sponsored antiwar protest. Salazar had been working on an exposé of law enforcement, which would reveal secret alliances among the CIA, the army, the FBI, California's attorney general, and local police authorities.

L.A. District Attorney Robert Meyer received a phone call from L. Patrick Gray—who had recently become acting head of the FBI after J. Edgar Hoover's death—telling him to stop the investigation.

Meyer did quit, saying it was like the "kiss of death" to work with these people. Mae called Meyer, asking if he would help with her research. She wanted to find out why the Justice Department in Washington was stopping a D.A. in Los Angeles from investigating the killing of a reporter. A month later, Meyer was found dead in a parking lot in Pasadena.

And now L. Patrick Gray was involved in an even bigger cover-up. A year before the Watergate break-in, E. Howard Hunt, who had worked for the CIA for twenty-one years, proposed a "bag job"—a surreptitious entry—into the office of Dr. Lewis Fielding, a Beverly Hills psychiatrist who had refused to cooperate with FBI agents investigating one of his patients, Daniel Ellsberg, leaker of the Pentagon Papers. It was the function of the White House "plumbers" to *plug* such leaks.

The burglars, led by G. Gordon Liddy, scattered pills around the office to make it look like a junkie had been responsible. The police assured Dr. Fielding that the break-in was made in search of drugs, even though he found Ellsberg's records removed from their folder. An innocent black man, Elmer Davis, was arrested, convicted, and sent to prison, while Liddy remained silent. Mae Brussell corresponded with Davis, and after he finished serving Liddy's time behind bars, he ended up living with Mae. It was a romance made in Conspiracy Heaven.

Hunt also masterminded the Watergate break-in. Three weeks later— while Richard Nixon was pressing for the postponement of an investigation until after the election, and the mainstream press was still referring to the incident as a "caper" and a "third-rate burglary"—Mae Brussell completed a lengthy article for *The Realist*, documenting the conspiracy and listing the players, from the burglars all the way up to FBI Director Gray, Attorney General John Mitchell, and President Nixon.

"The significance of the Watergate affair," she wrote, "is that every element essential for a political coup d'état in the United States was assembled at the time of their arrest."

Mae proceeded to delineate the details of a plot so insidious and yet so logical that the typesetter wrote *bravo!* at the end of her manuscript. However, instead of my usual credit arrangement, the printer insisted on $5,000 cash in advance before this issue could go to press. I didn't have the money, and I had no idea how I would get it, but as I left the printing plant, I was filled with an inexplicable sense of confidence. When I got home, the phone rang. It was Yoko Ono.

I had known her in the '60s as an avant-garde conceptual artist. She had one project which took place on a wooden platform in The Paradox, a macrobiotic restaurant a few blocks from my loft. People would climb inside these huge black burlap bags, singly or with a partner, and then do whatever they wanted, providing a floor show for patrons while they ate their brown rice and sprout salad. I had helped support theatrical groups —the San Francisco Mime Troupe and the Free Southern Theater—but Yoko's project was so *absurd* that I gave her some money too.

As a token of appreciation, she presented me with a personally revised alarm clock. On the face of the clock, there was a blue sky with white clouds, but there were no hands. I wound that clock every day, leaving the alarm knob up, blindly changing the time it would go off so that I would have no way of telling when it would, but trying always to be psychically prepared.

It was just a Zen Bastard's way of learning to pay attention to the moment. I planned to do this for a whole year, but I decided to stop several months into it, on the day that I was in the middle of performing cunnilingus on a temporary soul mate on my vibrating chair when the alarm clock went off and we both screamed out loud in unison. I took that as an omen.

Yoko had since married John Lennon. Now they had arrived in San Francisco and invited me to lunch. At the time, the Nixon administration was trying to deport Lennon, ostensibly for an old marijuana bust, but actually because they were afraid he was planning to perform for protesters at the Republican convention that summer.

I brought the galleys of Mae Brussell's article, which provided a context for John and Yoko's current harassment. I mentioned my printer's ultimatum, and they immediately took me to a local branch of the Bank of Tokyo and withdrew $5,000 in cash. I had never intended for the money I once gave to Yoko in New York to serve as bread cast upon the water, but now it had come back all nice and soggy, *so precisely* when I needed it that my personal boundaries of Coincidence were stretched to infinity.

I could rationalize my ass off—after all, Yoko and Lennon had been driven across the country by their assistant, Peter, and they just *happened* to arrive in San Francisco at that particular moment—but the timing was so exquisite that Coincidence and Mysticism became the same process for me. John Lilly even told me about the Earth Coincidence Control Office—extraterrestrial guardians who protected him by manipulating human events so that he could carry out their higher purpose. At first I thought he intended this as a clever metaphor. Then I realized he meant it literally. And if they were doing it for *him*, maybe they were doing it for *me*.

Actually, that melding of Coincidence and Mysticism had begun in 1971 when I wrote a comic strip, drawn by Richard Guindon. It was about political witchcraft, a takeoff on *Rosemary's Baby*, directed by Polanski. A key scene in that film showed Rosemary moving around the letters from a Scrabble game so that instead of spelling out the name of her neighbor the letters spelled out the name of a warlock in a book she had been reading about witchcraft. And now, scrambling the letters of the vice president's name—SPIRO AGNEW—it became GROW A PENIS. Coincidence had been my religion, but this was *so* appropriate that it challenged my theology.

After all, when Senator Charles Goodell came out against the war in Vietnam, it was Agnew who called him "the Christine Jorgensen of the Republican Party"—thereby equating military might with the mere presence of a penis. Around that time, Mike Wallace interviewed me for *60 Minutes*. He asked me what the difference was between the underground press and the mainstream media, and I told him about the GROW A PENIS anagram.

"The difference," I said "is that I could print that in *The Realist*, but it'll be edited out of this program." My prediction was accurate.

Yoko Ono and John Lennon spent a weekend at my house in Watsonville. They loved being so close to the ocean. In the afternoon I asked them to smoke their cigarettes outside, but in the evening we smoked a combination of marijuana and opium, sitting on pillows in front of the fireplace, sipping tea, and munching cookies. We talked about Mae Brussell's theory that the deaths of musicians like Jimi Hendrix, Janis Joplin, Otis Redding, and Jim Morrison had actually been political assassinations because they were role models on the crest of the youth rebellion.

"No, no," Lennon argued, "they were already headed in a self-destructive direction."

A few months later, he would remind me of that conversation and add, "Listen, if anything happens to Yoko and me, it was *not* an accident." For now, though, we were simply stoned in Watsonville, discussing conspiracy, safe at my oasis in a desert of paranoia. At one point, I referred to Mae Brussell as a saint.

"She's *not* a saint," Lennon said. "*You're* not a saint. *I'm* not a saint. *Yoko's* not a saint. *Nobody's* a saint."

We discussed the Charles Manson case. Lennon was bemused by the way Manson had associated himself with Beatles music.

"Look," he said, "would you kindly inform him that it was *Paul McCartney* who wrote 'Helter Skelter,' not me."

Yoko said, "No, please *don't* tell him. We don't want to have *any* communication with Manson."

"It's all right," Lennon said, "he doesn't have to know the message came from *us*."

"It's getting chilly," Yoko said to me. "Would you put another cookie in the fireplace?"

Lennon was absentmindedly holding on to the joint. I asked him, "Do the British use that expression, 'to *bogart* a joint,' or is that only an American term—you know, derived from the image of a cigarette dangling from Humphrey Bogart's lip?"

"In England," he replied, "if you remind somebody else to pass a joint, you lose your own turn."

★ ★ ★

Mae Brussell believed that her article could literally prevent the reelection of President Nixon. We held a press conference—I had never done that for any issue before—but there was a lot of skepticism. It had been five years since I published "The Parts Left Out of the Kennedy Book," and I began to feel like the little boy who cried "wolf!" Only now there really *was* a wolf at the door, and I started running around like a graduate fresh out of Zealot School, getting copies of *The Realist* to the media and individual journalists.

Then, one sunny afternoon in Watsonville, I decided to take an acid trip to celebrate the publication. Hassler and Poopsie had moved, so I lived alone now. I ingested three tablets—a total of nine hundred micrograms of LSD—and went for a leisurely walk along the dirt road. On the way back, Jackie Christeve invited me to meet a man she described as her spiritual teacher.

He had a ruddy complexion and Satanic eyebrows. He was talking about having communicated with beings from outer space. Jackie gave him the new issue of *The Realist*. He began turning the pages with one hand and gliding his other hand a couple of inches above, back and forth, page by page, as though he were *sensing* the contents.

He said, "I feel a very strong sense of mission from everyone who has contributed to this."

"That's true," I said, flashing back to a conversation Norman Mailer and I once had about the tools of our craft. He used a pencil, and I used a typewriter. His rationale was that what you wrote *with* affects your style. A pencil is soft, he insisted, whereas a typewriter is clickety-clack. But, I argued, I wrote inside my head first, where it was not merely soft but *mushy*. So now, could Jackie's spiritual teacher be putting me on? Was he really just some kind of speed-reading con artist?

Although I could understand the concept of one's vibrational level being transmitted to paper through a pencil, I had presented the printer with typed manuscripts which were reset on another machine, photographed onto paper, run through presses, trimmed, and stapled. Yet here was this strange guy responding to the magazine in such an unusual way that I had to sit back and watch where my suspension of disbelief would lead.

"One of these writers," he continued, "has a higher consciousness than all the others. Not this material on fascism"—he must have seen the word standing out—"but, where was it, *this* is the highest consciousness of all." His hand glided over a column titled "Unintentional Satire." It was reprinted from *Horoscope* magazine—a poignant letter from a fifty-year-old reader who wanted to know what his chances were, astrology-wise, of getting a sex-change operation—he said, "I think I could face everything if I could do it as a little old lady instead of a broken old man"—together with the complicated text of a speculative chart the editors had set for him.

"Who's this author?" said the con artist. "I'm not familiar with the name. Is it an Oriental?"

He pointed to the byline at the top of the column: "by Wotsiur Syne."

"That's just a pun I made up. There's no such person."

Jackie left the room, and her spiritual teacher took on an air of confidentiality. "We've selected Jackie astrologically, you know."

Suddenly I felt extremely vulnerable.

"Who's we?" I said. "I don't understand what your purpose is."

"It's time for God to regain *control* of these bodies that have been entrusted to us."

His answer scared me. Once, when I had my radio show, I found a bubblegum football card, and I began to read it on the air, without mentioning the player's name, so that listeners could guess. It stated that he'd never had an injury in his entire professional career. "Well, we can fix that," I said, writing a note, "Season of the Witch," and I held it up for my producer to see and find the Donovan record.

"Let's all concentrate," I continued. "No, never mind, because then if anything happens to him, they'll blame us. You know, the word would finally reach him, and it might affect his performance on the field." As the song was being cued on the turntable by the engineer, I added, "The trouble with magic is, it works if you believe in it." So now, even though Jackie's spiritual teacher may not have been *trying* to psych me out, I was doing a pretty good job of it myself.

I fled from Jackie's house and ran along the dirt road back to my house. I had left the radio on and now Mae Brussell was talking about the assassination of Bobby Kennedy. But I had overdosed on conspiracy. I ran in one door and out the other, then down into the woods behind the beach. I found a cove at the bottom of a hilly area, sat under a tree, and then I let out a long, loud, *uncontrollable wail*—it must have been a ten on the

Primal Scream scale—releasing all the fear that had been building up in my psyche, from Scientology to Richard Nixon, from Naval Intelligence to Extraterrestrial Intelligence. Then I just sat there and watched the ground moving around in beautiful mosaic patterns.

At dusk, I moved to a dilapidated easy chair on the edge of the cliff. Through the fog I could see the silhouettes of some kind of space creatures. They were marking latitudinal and longitudinal lines on the ocean floor, as though it were a classroom globe. That evening I called Kesey. He said, "It has to do with a struggle for the will." And I called Mae. She said, "These people have their own reality. The occult is their safety valve for not having to deal with the problems on earth."

In fact, I was perceiving what had happened in mythical terms—the attempt to divert human compassion into otherworldliness. With that as my premise, I began to apply the logic of paranoia, and so now *Jackie* became part of the plot. Her last name was *Christeve*. Of course! Wasn't Christianity utilized for the prevention of rebels? Didn't Eastern religion rationalize the suffering of others as rotten karma? How long had that spiritual teacher been re-channeling Jackie's energy?

I recalled how I first met her when I was running on the beach and she was riding a bike slowly along the shore. *Aha!* She must've found out from the federal data bank that I had once been the winner of the Slow Bicycle Race. What a shrewd way to entrap me. I was seeing everything through a conspiratorial filter.

The next morning, when I went outside, there was a man on the road observing me with binoculars. Then there was another man, in a red sweater, running behind a tree. I counted seven men altogether. There was a helicopter circling overhead. I hurried to the cliff and down the rickety wooden steps onto the beach. There was a sheriff's car parked on top of the cliff, and a couple of deputies were watching me. They had my whole house staked out.

I walked along the beach, trying to appear nonchalant, back around into that cove in the woods. I sat under the same tree where I had howled like a helpless infant the day before. Now there was another *Mission Impossible* type standing in the woods, about fifty feet behind and above me, watching through binoculars.

Finally, choosing my words carefully, I turned around and called up, "What are you waiting for?"

He hesitated, then called back, "You seen any girls around here?"

"No."

"I heard they take nude sunbaths."

"Well, I haven't noticed any."

After a brief silence, he called to me, "What are *you* waiting for?"

"I just like to watch the way people act."

He grabbed his crotch and said, "You want *this*?"

"No, thanks."

I stayed there a few more minutes, just so he wouldn't think he scared me away. Then I got up and called out, "Well, good luck." I headed toward the beach, and he signaled to another plainclothes officer. All this was really happening. It was not my imagination. The LSD I took the previous day was very powerful, but it had worn off. These men were not any kind of hallucination. I was having a bad trip, but it was reality. I went back to my house, put all my dope in a jar, and buried it. I packed a few things and walked along the beach for about a mile.

It seemed like people were staring at me—every hippie surfer was an undercover cop—but somehow I managed to get away. I hitched a ride, making sure we weren't being followed. The driver gladly let me off at a phone booth. I called Frank Bardacke, an old friend from the Free Speech Movement who lived in the area. I knew I could trust him completely. He drove me to a bus station, and I went to San Francisco to hide out in my little room. The jazz drummer in the carriage house told me that a helicopter had been circling overhead there too.

Since I was a regular guest on Edward Bear's weekly TV show, I just went on that night and freaked out in public, spreading paranoia like apple butter. Although I was suffering from a severe case of information overload, I could still pass for sane in public. I even managed to keep a dental appointment without revealing the utter turmoil in my mind. I was desperately trying to maintain my balance between coincidence and conspiracy. But then two men showed up at my basement room.

They knocked on the door, and I asked for their ID. "Open up or we'll *break* the fucking door down." I decided to let them in. They were *huge*. They insisted on seeing *my* identification, but I didn't have any. They hassled, threatened, intimidated—scared the living shit out of me—but they wouldn't tell me who they were or what they were looking for. They didn't seem to want anything except my ID. The best I could do was show them mail addressed to me.

When they left, I was shaking. I decided to go back to Watsonville. On the bus, my thumb began to feel numb. It was obviously a direct result of the cavity in one of my molars having been filled. When the bus stopped in San Jose, I got off and called William Robbins. He was my dentist.

"Bill," I said, "I know who you work for, and I have two demands. I want everybody out of solitary confinement. And I want a cease-fire all over the world."

He hesitated a second. "Hold on, Paul, let me get your chart." He was stalling for time. When he came back to the phone, he asked, "Now, do you want my reaction?"

"No, that won't be necessary. I've gotta go. Goodbye."

I hung up the phone and got back on the bus. The man sitting in front of me, obviously an operative for the CIA, adjusted the ring on his finger in order to let his partner outside know that I was on the bus again. I had to let the man in front of me *know* that I was onto his game. So I took out my ballpoint pen. Clicking the top over and over like a telegraph key, I kept repeating, "Paul Krassner calling Abbie Hoffman"—just loud enough for the man sitting in front of me to hear—"Paul Krassner calling Abbie Hoffman." The CIA operative fidgeted nervously. He knew I was onto him now.

My mind had finally snapped. Allen Ginsberg's poem *Howl* began, "I saw the best minds of my generation destroyed by madness, starving hysterical naked," and I had always identified with the "best minds" part but never with the "madness" part. Eventually I told Abbie how I had tried to convince a CIA operative sitting in front of me on the bus that I was calling Abbie Hoffman by using my ballpoint pen as a telegraph key.

"Oh, yeah," Abbie said. "I got your call, only it was collect, so I couldn't accept it."

*   *   *

Lee Quarnstrom invited me to stay at his home and cool down. He was an original Merry Prankster who was now a reporter for the *Watsonville Register-Pajaronian*, bringing his acid consciousness to Santa Cruz County Board of Supervisors meetings. On the afternoon that he came to pick me up, there was a man on the dirt road using a surveyor's scope. As we drove toward him, it appeared that he was surveying *us*. Was Lee *delivering* me to him?

"Lee, I've trusted you up till now."

"I was afraid of that," he replied. To himself he thought, *Well, it was bound to come to this. Either Paul has trusted me up till now and still trusts me, or, more likely, he's trusted me up till now and suddenly thinks I'm part of the plot. Either way, he's really wacko.* Late that night, while Lee and his wife, Guadalupe, were asleep, I stayed up talking with another former Prankster, Julius Karpen, who had once been Lee's editor in Chicago. As we spoke, we were rolling billiard balls back and forth across the pool table in the living room, pushing and catching them with our hands rather than hitting them with a cue stick and waking anybody up.

Finally, I asked, "How long is it gonna go on?"

"How long is *what* gonna go on?"

"You know, this battle between good and evil, when is it gonna *end?*"

"Maybe never," Julius said.

Suddenly I felt a wave of relief. So it *wasn't* all my responsibility. Such a heavy burden had been lifted from my soul.

The turning point in my insanity came inadvertently one day at a gas station. While Lee was out of the car, I noticed two guys standing there, staring at me. Just as I was convincing myself that now *they* were out to get me, I flashed back to the West Side Highway in New York. Sheila Campion was driving her motor scooter, with me sitting behind her, my arms circling her waist. She was wearing a miniskirt. Truck drivers were making animal sounds and whistling.

"They *recognize* me," I joked to Sheila.

And now, the moment I realized that these two guys in the gas station were staring, not at me in the back seat, but at Guadalupe in the front seat, my perspective began to return.

I was fine by the time Holly, then eight years old, came to stay with me that summer. A group of us went to the Santa Cruz County Fair. As we were walking down the midway, a startlingly obese woman beckoned to us. She was an evangelist, and asked if Holly wanted to hear a story. Holly said okay, and they went into her tent. Several minutes later, Holly came out, carrying a balloon. "What was that all about?" I asked.

"Oh, she was telling a story about God. I don't even know if I believe in God."

"Neither do I. Well, at least you got a balloon out of it."

"And she gave me this too." Holly showed me a miniature police whistle. Then she started blowing the whistle and calling out, "Jesus! Here, Jesus!"

And I laughed . . . for the first time in a year. It had been *one whole year* since I started that experiment. I had gone an entire year without laughing. But now it began, just a chortle at first, but the dam had been broken, and that chortle turned into a side-splitting, knee-slapping, rolling-on-the-ground attack of laughter that alternated with spasmodic sobbing. Later I could analyze how Holly's spontaneous irreverence toward authority had finally broken through my thick shell, but for now I just surrendered to having one of those darned spiritual orgasms right there in public.

Losing my sense of humor had been the direction of my insanity. By taking myself as seriously as my cause, I had violated the Eleventh Commandment. I had an investment in my craziness, and I needed to perpetuate it. Only in retrospect would I find that, in response to my megalomaniacal demands, what my dentist had said—"Hold on, Paul, let me get your chart"—was unintentionally, screamingly funny.

By publishing Mae Brussell's work, I had been on a mission from the God I didn't believe in. I had bought into a *celestial* conspiracy. I had gone over the edge, from a universe that didn't know I existed, to one that did. From false humility to false pride.

But if existence was *not* absurd, then it was *planned*, and that was even *more* absurd. By adopting John Lilly's notion of the Earth Coincidence Control Office, I began to lose my own perspective. A couple of decades later, Lilly would dismiss his own concept. "Tooth problems," he explained. "I was trying to get in touch with my teeth."

★ ★ ★

It turned out that those inexplicable things which had helped frighten me into a state of acute paranoia could be explained logically. The space creatures who were dividing up the ocean floor were actually people in wet suits, clam-digging with long rods in the mud. The Sheriff's Department was never after me—they had been looking for a rapist in the area. The two men who intimidated me in my San Francisco basement room were from the Federal Bureau of Alcohol, Tobacco, and Firearms—they were Treasury agents, and they thought I was Brian Rohan.

In 1975, Squeaky Fromme tried to shoot President Gerald Ford. She was wearing a Red Riding Hood outfit, and I sent her a note in prison, teasing her about fading into the crowd. I wrote a piece for *Rolling Stone* titled "My Trip with Squeaky," including a paragraph about Nathaniel Dight being in Naval Intelligence, posing as a hippie artist, and meeting with Tex Watson. Dight sued for libel, and my sources had to give depositions.

Mae Brussell testified that I was "totally irresponsible" for publishing what she had told me.

Mae was an extraordinary researcher. While her father, Edgar Magnin, senior rabbi at the Wilshire Boulevard Temple, was entertaining Richard Nixon at his Beverly Hills home, Mae was busy revealing Nixon's rise to power as an incredible conspiracy. In the summer of 1972, she told me that the ultimate purpose of all the assassinations was to get Ronald Reagan into the White House.

But sometimes her heavy investment in conspiracy affected the objectivity of her perception. She was convinced that behind the death of John Belushi there was a conspiracy involving Robert De Niro and Robin Williams, who had both snorted cocaine with Belushi the night he died. I argued with Mae about this. After her death in 1988, I learned that, actually, the LAPD had been preparing a drug sting operation in which they planned to ensnare De Niro, Williams, and Belushi.

In any case, Dight's neighbor Louise was now in a state hospital. According to a psychiatric evaluation:

> Her feet are encased in the most unusual pair of slippers constructed of layers of garbage, including coffee grounds, bread crumbs, tea bags and lettuce and socks stiff with age and then plastic bags. The patient denies that this garb is out of the ordinary. In fact, she indicates that she was planning to use this foot gear as a pattern for a pair of slippers. She has related to the staff that she has been entered by the spirit of [Watergate burglar] James McCord and that she must die in order to free herself from this hex.

I realized that she wouldn't make a very good impression on the jury if she took the witness stand.

Susan Atkins was deposed at the California Institute for Women:

Q. Charles Manson, on occasion, he asked you or ordered you to sleep with men, whoever they might be, just men in general?

A. Many times.

Q. And Tex Watson did the same?

A. No, he never ordered me to sleep with anybody.

Q. So, on the occasion when you went to visit this friend of Tex Watson's with Tex, it was not at Tex Watson's request that you slept with this fellow?

A. No. There was a mutual attraction.

Q. So that was Charles Manson's function, and no one else had that prerogative?

A. Yes, I guess you could put it on that basis. I was kind of used, not kind of, I was used as a ploy to get guys to stay at the ranch. [She is shown a photo of Dight, whom she doesn't recognize.] Can I say something? I don't find him attractive at all to me, and I have this thing with men about overbites. I don't like men with overbites.

Dight was suing *Rolling Stone* for $450 million because he was never in Naval Intelligence. He claimed that my article caused him to lose interest in sex and his artwork. I considered pleading temporary insanity, but I realized that would be a cop-out. It was a moot point; the case was settled out of court for $100,000, and *Rolling Stone* published my letter of apology.

Meanwhile, Charles Manson has become a cultural symbol. In surfer jargon, "a manson" means a crazy, reckless surfer. For comedians, Manson has become a generic joke reference. I asked him how he felt about that. He wrote back: "I don't know what a generic is, Joke. I think I know what that means. That means you talk bad about Reagan or Bush. I've always ran poker games and whores and crime. I'm a crook. You make the reality in court and press. I just ride and play the cards that were pushed on me to play. Mass killer, it's a job, what can I say."

During Manson's lifelong career as a prison inmate, organized crime figures became his role models. He tossed horseshoes with Frank Costello, hung around with Frankie Carbo, and learned how to play the guitar from Alvin "Creepy" Karpis. On the night after the massacre of Sharon Tate and the others, Manson accompanied his family to kill supermarket mogul Leno LaBianca and his wife. Ostensibly, they were selected at random, but a police report showed that LaBianca was a heavy gambler. He owed $30,000 to Frankie Carbo's organization. I asked Manson about a little black book he was supposed to get from LaBianca.

He wrote back: "The black book was what CIA and a mob of market players had, Hollywood Park [race track] and numbers rackets to move in the Governor's office legally."

I had always felt that there was some connection between Charlie's executioners and their victims before the murders took place. I finally tracked down a reporter who told me that when she was hanging around with L.A. police, they showed her a porn video of Susan Atkins and Voytek Frykowski, even though, according to the myth, they had never met until the night of the massacre.

But apparently the reporter mentioned the wrong victim, because when I asked Charlie directly—"Did Susan sleep with Frykowski?"—he replied: "You are ill advised and misled. Sebring done Susan's hair and I think he sucked one or two of her dicks. I'm not sure who she was walking out from her stars and cages, that girl *loves* dick, you know what I mean, hon. Yul Brynner, Peter Sellers . . ."

I checked the photos of Jay Sebring. He did *not* have an overbite.

* * *

As I began to unwind from my psychotic episode, I could survey the damage I'd done. I had broken up with a girlfriend because I somehow convinced myself that the FBI had sent her to spy on me. She asked if we could at least have a dialogue, but that only made me more suspicious.

When I found a new girlfriend, I actually asked if there was a microphone in her cat's flea collar. Although I totally believed in the possibility at that instant, she of course thought I was just being my usual funny self. Twenty years later, I would read in an article by Harrison Salisbury in

Penthouse that "the CIA wired a cat to eavesdrop on conversations. Micro sensing devices were installed in its body, and its tail was wired as an aerial. But it was hit by a car before it got into action."

The most serious transgression of rationality concerned my history with Lyle Stuart. He had broken off our friendship in 1964. When his wife, Mary Louise, died in 1969, I was devastated. I didn't know what to do. So I just wrote a short note to Lyle: "I know the depth of your loss. I also know that you will smile again." It had been well intentioned, but I was trivializing his grief. I was also circumventing my own pain. I had never quite recovered from the shock of their rejection. I kept trying in vain to recoup the relationship.

Lyle gave me good advice. He said, "Friendship cannot be negotiated."

He had once published a collection of my interviews. When another publisher was readying an anthology of my pieces from *The Realist*, Lyle told them he had the rights to my next book and would sue. I had a letter from him *somewhere*, releasing me from that clause in our contract. I was desperate for money, but the new publisher was holding up my advance.

Lyle thought he was being funny, but I thought he was being sadistic. I fantasized about having him killed. Then I figured that wouldn't be ethical—I would have to do it myself. But the more I fantasized about it, the more I realized how self-centered I had become. To murder Lyle for being cruel to *me* would negate everything else in *his* life. I was shocked that I could have even *considered* taking anyone else's life, especially somebody who had done so much for me.

But now, years later, in the heat of my twisted psyche, I had lost the ability to trust, and somehow, as if to justify my severed relationship with Lyle, I managed to filter *him* into my occult conspiracy network. Because he had once published material on alternative ways of treating cancer in *The Independent*, yet Mary Louise had died of cancer, I reached the utterly insane conclusion that Lyle had made a deal with the Devil, sacrificing his own wife so that he could become a successful book publisher. I had to let him *know* that I knew, and yet some core of reality kept me from saying it outright, so instead I sent a message, a simple and shameful message: "The butler did it."

I had always considered myself to be a kind person. If I inadvertently gave somebody the wrong directions, it would bother me long after they had reached their correct destination.

Once, at a KSFX party where the guests were about evenly divided between blacks and whites, we were all making the cliché racial-stereo-type jokes—about tap dancing and eating watermelon and having giant penises—and everybody was laughing hysterically. Then, in the hallway, one black man said, "Hey, Paul."

"I don't remember your name," I pretended. "You all look alike." I expected him to laugh, but he reacted as if I had punched him in the solar plexus with all my might. "Yeah," he replied, bitterly, "we all *do* look alike." Suddenly I realized that he had just arrived at the party and wasn't in on the gag. I've never stopped feeling awful about that encounter.

I wasn't used to hurting people. And so, when I finally came to my senses about Lyle Stuart and the loss of Mary Louise, I was absolutely *horrified* that I had actually written, "The butler did it." How could I have committed such a cruel act? Especially toward someone who had, in effect, saved my life? How could I have deliberately tried to hurt the man who had been my first intimate friend?

I tried to trace back the roots of that intimacy. When I originally met Lyle in 1953, he had published an article in *The Independent* about how the Anti-Defamation League was secretly subsidizing anti-Semitic publications and then using them to scare contributions out of wealthy Jews. Lyle kept teasing me about being a spy for the ADL, but as our bonds deepened, we began to share our private thoughts.

Now, after my sanity had returned, I was able to pinpoint a specific conversation that had marked for me the moment of true intimacy between us. We had been talking about Lyle's relationship with Mary Louise. I admired the level of communication they maintained, but he said there were certain things that he couldn't discuss with her. The example he gave was how horrendous it would be for him if she were to die. Now, as I recalled that conversation, I was totally shocked by the loss of empathy that had allowed me to sink to such an ironic depth of cruelty.

* * *

Baba Ram Dass had dropped the Baba. He was now just plain Ram Dass. His father called him Rum Dum. His brother called him Rammed Ass. One afternoon Ram Dass was visiting me in Watsonville, and I taped our conversation.

"In 1963," I said, "I predicted as a joke that Tiny Tim would get married on the Johnny Carson show, and in 1969 it happened. You and I talked about that, and you called it 'astral humor,' but I never knew exactly what you meant by that phrase."

"Well, it's like each plane of reality is in a sense a manifestation of a plane prior to it, and you can almost see it like layers, although to think of it in space is a fallacy because it's all the same space, but you could think of it that way. And so there are beings on upper planes who *are* instruments of the law. I *talk* about miracles a lot, but I don't live in the world of miracles, because they're not miracles to *me*. I'm just dealing with the *humor* of the miracle concept from within the plane where it seems like a miracle, which is merely because of our very narrow concept of how the universe works."

Ram Dass knew of my involvement with conspiracy theory.

"I'm just involved in a much greater conspiracy," he continued. "You can't *grasp* the size of the conspiracy I understand. But there's no *conspirator*—it's the wrong word. That's why I say it's just natural law. It is all perfect."

"Would you agree with the concept—what William Blake said, that humans were created 'for joy and woe'—the implication of which is that there will always be suffering?"

"I think that suffering is part of man's condition, and that's what the incarnation is about, and that's what the human plane is."

And I asked Ram Dass, "If you and I were to exchange philosophies—if I believed in reincarnation and you didn't—how do you think our behavior would change?"

He paused for a moment. "Well," he said, "if you believed in reincarnation, you would never ask a question like that."

And then his low chuckle of amusement and surprise blossomed into an uproarious belly laugh of delight and triumph as he savored the implications of his own Zen answer.

I would find myself playing that segment of the tape with his bell-shaped spasm of laughter over and over again, like a favorite piece of music.

I had wanted to explore the Charles Manson case, but ultimately I had to face the reality of my *own* peculiar darkness. Originally, I had wanted to expose the dangers of Scientology, but instead I *joined* a cult of conspiracy. I had been skulking around like the Ancient Mariner, waving my grungy albatross in front of people's faces. I thought that what I had published was so important that I *wanted* to be persecuted, in order to validate the work. In the process, I had become *attached* to conspiracy.

"My whole identity got tied up in plots," I said to Ken Kesey.

"Always stay in your own movie," he advised.

"Yeah, but I'll tell you something—the FBI was right."

"About what?"

"I *am* a raving, unconfined nut."

CHAPTER 10

SHOWING PINK

In May 1974, Flo Kennedy presented the Feminist Party Media Workshop Award: "To Paul Krassner, publisher of *The Realist*. The longevity of which is a tribute to survival in a militaristic, genocidal, corrupt, police-state society. And with special recognition of his wit, humor, and irreverence." It was an unintentional kiss of death—the May issue of *The Realist* turned out to be my final issue. I had never *planned* to stop publishing. I simply ran out of money and taboos. Circulation had dropped off. Readers wanted me to be funny, while I had become obsessed with conspiracy.

"Sometimes you have to earn the right to be funny," I wrote.

In sixteen years of publishing, *The Realist* received two awards. One was from *Playboy*, for satire; the other was this one from the Feminist party, and I was particularly appreciative because I had always felt so strongly about equal rights. In 1959, I wrote, "From a completely idealistic viewpoint, the newspaper want ads should not have separate Male and Female classifications, with exceptions such as in the case of a wet-nurse." In 1964, that double-standard practice became illegal. It was an early tremor of the women's movement.

In November 1977, I attended the first National Women's Conference in Houston. There were more than four thousand delegates. Eldridge Cleaver was at the conference as an observer, but angry women surrounded him and chanted, "Out, rapist, out! Out, rapist, out!" Male TV reporters wearing makeup were busy interviewing female delegates who weren't wearing makeup. Placards shouted slogans: ADAM WAS A ROUGH DRAFT! I OWN MY BODY BUT I SHARE! LESBIANS FOR WAGES FOR HOUSEWORK!"

A counter-rally was held by anti-ERA leader Phyllis Schlafly, who had warned that the Women's Conference would be "promoting witchcraft." Her organization bought a half-page ad in two Houston papers, showing a little girl asking, "Mommy, when I grow up can I be a lesbian?" Ironically, Schlafly stayed at the same hotel as a lesbian motorcycle club, "Dykes on Bikes."

Over a thousand women stood in the rain to welcome a flaming torch that had been carried by a series of female runners for almost two months from Seneca Falls, New York, birthplace of the suffrage movement in 1848. Billie Jean King accepted the torch "as a symbol of what women can accomplish, not only in the world of sports, but in business, in government, and in the home." Bella Abzug thundered, "All of us run here for equality, and we will never run for cover." On the convention floor, there was a demand for the adoption of "Roberta's Rules."

While the conference was in progress, the nemesis of feminism, Larry Flynt, publisher of *Hustler* magazine, was flying in his private plane with Ruth Carter Stapleton, the evangelist sister of President Jimmy Carter. It was an alliance too outrageous for fiction. *Hustler* was, after all, the raunchiest men's magazine on the market. In the evolution of popular pornography, magazines had started out showing breasts but not nipples, buttocks but not anuses—and never, *never* a vagina. Nor did pubic hair used to be all over the place. Even nudist magazines had once rendered men and women into department-store manikins without genitalia playing volleyball.

The great pubic-hair breakthrough occurred first in *Penthouse*, and then *Playboy*. In a *Playboy* photo feature, "The Girls of Russia," one of the models was gazing at her naked body in a dressing-room mirror, and although her crotch had been air-brushed out of existence, her reflection revealed a triangular patch of dark curly hair that would serve to open Pandora's box wider and wider until *Hustler* eventually began "showing pink." Flynt's own wife, Althea, had shown pink in the pages of *Hustler*. Once issue even featured a Scratch 'n' Sniff centerspread. When you scratched the spread-eagled model in her designated area, a scent of lilac bath oil emanated from her vulva.

But now Larry Flynt was having a religious vision on his Lear Commander jet—which, when it belonged to Elvis Presley, had been painted red, white, and blue. Flynt purchased the plane for $1.1 million and had it painted pink. Up in the air with Ruth Carter Stapleton, he saw Jesus Christ together with a man calling himself Paul, who was laughing heartily. Flynt felt a warm, powerful sensation. There was a medicinal taste in his mouth. His entire body was tingling. He fell to his knees and clasped his hands in prayer to Jesus.

It was in this context that Larry Flynt was converted to born-again Christianity by the president's sister. It just seemed too bizarre to be true. Certainly there was suspicion at the White House as to Flynt's motivation, but there were also those who thought that Reverend Stapleton wanted Flynt to turn *her* fantasy of a Dallas religious center into a reality. But Flynt was putting out a tangible product every month, by which the sincerity of his conversion might be judged, so the intriguing question was: If he continued to publish *Hustler*, how could it possibly be changed?

At the time, I was writing a column which was syndicated to various alternative weeklies. Specifically I was working on my "Predictions for 1978," and I led off with this one: "Since Larry Flynt has been converted to born-again Christianity by Ruth Carter Stapleton, the new *Hustler* magazine will feature a special Scratch 'n' Sniff Virgin Mary."

* * *

Larry Flynt wanted me to write a profile of Lenny Bruce. He considered Lenny to be a satirical prophet. He'd recently read *How to Talk Dirty and Influence People*—which Lenny had ended with, "My friend Paul Krassner once asked me what I've been influenced by in my work," followed by a montage of cultural influences. Before I could begin writing the article, I was invited to *Hustler's* 1977 Christmas party in Columbus, Ohio. They would put me up at a hotel, there would be a prepaid round-trip ticket, and I would be picked up at the airport.

But I didn't know what to wear. I owned one pair of jeans, torn at the knees and backside. I had simply worn them out. This was before people paid extra to have fashion designers cut holes in their new jeans *before* they wore them. I could've worn my tattered jeans, but I didn't want to flaunt my poverty. Instead, I borrowed $15 from my friend Scoop Nisker, KSAN news commentator, and bought a new pair. I didn't know that there would be an official dress code at the *Hustler* Christmas party— "Men: Jackets or Shirt and tie. Women: Dresses or Pants Suits. *No Jeans.*" Otherwise I might have worn my tattered jeans just to be ornery.

The party was being held in some kind of union hall. There were meatballs which you had to impale on a toothpick and then dip in tomato sauce, but there were no napkins, so everybody was standing in a bent-over position to avoid dripping tomato sauce onto their good clothes while they ate their meatballs. That was a moot problem for me, since I was on the fourth day of a juice fast. Then I met Larry Flynt for the first time. "Whattaya doin'?" he asked.

"Stand-up comedy, now and then. I have a question for you, about your conversion. Do you believe that Christianity is the one and only true spiritual path?"

He answered, "I believe that Jesus was not a more important teacher than Buddha, and that neither Jesus nor Buddha is more important than any individual."

Dick Gregory was at the party, and Flynt asked each of us to perform, but first he would take the microphone himself. And so it came to pass that Larry Flynt, looking like a slick gambler, wearing a maroon jacket with velvet lapels, would stand and deliver unto his assembled employees, in a Kentucky hillbilly twang and rhythm, what I christened "The Sermon on the Mount of Venus":

> When *Hustler* moves to the West Coast we're gonna take Ohio magazine offices, and we're gonna be turning this into a daycare center which will be paid for by the company, so any of you females that have children, I don't think that you should leave them with babysitters, I think you should bring them into the daycare center, and we'll have professional people there to take care of 'em. I think you should spend lunch hours with your children, and I think you should spend your morning breaks and your afternoon breaks with your children because they need you. They need the kind of love and affection and cuddling and attention that they don't necessarily get from a babysitter . . .
>
> The first publisher's statement that I do under my borned-again theory, I intend to dress up as a baby with a diaper on and put a pacifier in my mouth and get in a crib and let a photographer take my picture, and then I'm gonna write about what happens when you become born-again. You see, everybody thinks that you get a little flaky. [*subdued laughter*] You know [*more laughter*]—everybody. Also you know [*laughter increases*]—will you people *please* shut the fuck up so I can *talk*—and that's the last time. I'm gonna put everybody out of here that don't keep their *mouth* shut till I finish . . .
>
> I'm happy to be able to announce tonight that Ruth Carter Stapleton is gonna allow Flynt Distributing Company to distribute her new magazine, *The Christian Woman*. We're also gonna be taking on *National Screw*. We're gonna be distributing a health magazine that Dick Gregory is gonna be publishing. Now, with *Hustler*, I am getting ready to write my last publisher's statement, and the new publisher of *Hustler* is gonna be a fellow by the name of Paul Krassner. And I'm starting Paul off at $90,000 a year. If he does a good job, I'll give him a raise. Now, he's gonna have all kinds of

excuses why he can't take the job, but he's not gonna have too much of a choice . . .

This was the first that *I* had heard of it. Suddenly I felt dizzy. Maybe it was from my four-day fast. Could I have hallucinated what I thought I had just heard? Very subtly I flapped my arms like wings, but I remained standing instead of flying, so I knew that this was really happening. I was in a daze while Flynt talked. Then came my turn. It had been twenty-five years since I performed at the *Mad* Christmas party, but my déjà vu was overshadowed by a slight state of shock. I managed to speak on automatic pilot:

Now there's a few things I have to think over, because when I first heard about Larry's conversion, I imagined the Martians coming to see *Hustler* magazine, and when you come from Mars you have very little conditioning to overcome so you look at stuff with like a child's eye, and you open up this magazine and, "Aha! Earth women trying to turn themselves inside out—and succeeding." So I've looked at *Hustler*'s pink, and I thought, well, maybe they use rouge, that's it. And they must use Crazy Glue to keep that outer labia stuck to the thighs there.

One of the photographers got some Crazy Glue stuck in his fingers when he was arranging a model and couldn't get his thumb and forefinger apart. So Larry fired him because he couldn't operate the camera with maximum efficiency. But then he got born-again, and as an act of Christian charity he hired this guy back again. Not as a photographer, but as a roach clip. He just goes around from desk to desk.

I'm looking forward to a Scratch 'n' Sniff Mary Magdalene. The Father, the Son, and the Holy Ghost go to a gay sauna bath. New tricks you can do with your rosary beads. Anyway, it's gonna be interesting to see how the change comes about in the magazine. I'm pretty jaded, but my mind got blown when I heard about Larry's conversion, because I figured either it's a scam or it's sincere, but either way it's real, because he said you are what you *think* you are and I've always said you are what you *pretend* to be. But it becomes the same thing anyway.

I mean I know one guy who got out of the army by saying "quack, quack" every time somebody talked to him. An officer would come up and say, "Attention!" And the guy'd go, "Quack, quack." And he would keep doing that until they finally had to get rid of him because they know anybody with that much determination ain't gonna stay and fight their war for them, or would probably shoot a sergeant on the wrong side. But once that guy got out of the Army, he was *still* saying "quack, quack" to people. See, it stays with you. So it doesn't matter if he was faking it or if it was real, because the "quack, quack" was real when he didn't *have* to do it.

So, there are two factors in my decision. One—about cigarettes—I was pleased to see that anti-cigarette ad on the back cover of *Hustler.* I'm more offended by seeing ads for cigarettes in magazines than pictures of vaginas, because one kills and the other gives life—and I think that's an important difference.

And the other thing, in Larry's conversion, he didn't put Jesus above Buddha and he didn't put Buddha or Jesus above any individual. So, as long as religion is going in the direction of liberation rather than control, then it's a healthy thing. So I guess I'll accept—since you made the offer publicly, I'll accept publicly [*loud applause*]. And I'd like to give a new slogan to the magazine: "Out of the toilet, onto the crucifix!" Now, in my fresh capacity as publisher of *Hustler,* I proclaim my first rule: At next year's Christmas party, everyone will be *required* to wear jeans.

People started coming up to me and shaking my hand and saying, "Congratulations." I was seeing this whole scene through a dreamlike haze. I had the sensation of having been thrust onto a movie screen, except that I could feel the flesh of their hands. Before, I had been wondering how *Hustler* would change, and now it turned out that I was the answer to my own question. What had irony wrought? For Larry Flynt to bring *me* in as redeeming social value was an offer too absurd to refuse.

He asked me if I had gotten anything to eat yet.

"No, thanks, I've been fasting for a few days."

"Oh really?" He seemed intrigued. "Why you been fasting?"

"Well, because I wanted to be real clearheaded when I got here. I was curious to see if you were a con artist or not. And you are. And you're good."

He hesitated for just a split second. Then he smiled and said softly, "I'm the best."

* * *

On Thanksgiving Day, Dick Gregory had been arrested in front of the White House for protesting the lack of human rights in South Africa. Larry Flynt had a premonition that there would be an assassination attempt on Gregory. Flynt contacted him a couple of weeks later, and they became friends. Gregory was now staying at Flynt's mansion in Columbus, helping him change to a vegetarian diet. Flynt had already taken off forty pounds. On the day before the Christmas party, Gregory was in the middle of giving himself an enema when Flynt walked in.

According to Gregory, "Larry said, 'Let me tell you about this fantastic guy I've got comin' out, and I don't know what I'm gonna do yet but I just wanna talk with him.' And I said, 'Well, who is it?' He said, 'Paul Krassner.' And I just fell out, and said, 'Are you serious? He's one of the hippest minds in the whole world.' Then he came back and said, 'How long you been knowin' him?' and I told him, 'All through the sixties,' you know. And I said it was a fantastic idea."

Of course, not everybody felt that way. A corporate executive at the party grabbed me by the collar and said, threateningly, "You're exploiting a very sick man." I didn't know how long I would last as publisher of *Hustler*, so when editor Bruce David showed me around the next morning, I began exercising my power immediately. The cover of the April 1978 issue—the one that would *not* feature a woman—was scheduled to have a teddy bear wearing a negligee. I changed it to an Easter bunny nailed to a crucifix, with a basket of painted eggs toppled over in the foreground, and assigned a staffer to write a piece on "The Commercialization of Easter."

I also went through Larry Flynt's publisher's statement and removed every masculine reference to God. That afternoon, Larry brought me into his office. I didn't know what to expect, but he said that he really liked my cover idea, and he agreed with me that God is genderless. "You know," he said, "I've always been of a philosophical bent." Then he gestured toward the wall. "You see these walls? I could make them come tumbling down by sheer will power."

"Oh, boy, this is gonna be some job."

"But I don't wanna misuse my power."

"Oh, shit, why doesn't anybody ever wanna misuse their power for me? C'mon, Larry, please, just once . . ."

Flying back to San Francisco, I decided—perhaps foolishly—not to ask him for a contract. If indeed I was exploiting a very sick man, at least I wanted him to be able to fire me as frivolously as he had hired me. Flynt told the *Los Angeles Times*, "I wanted someone Christ-like. I always felt Lenny Bruce was Christ-like. And Paul was closer to Lenny than Christ. Maybe I can provide Lenny with the last laugh."

On December 23, while I was spending the Christmas holidays with the Kesey family in Oregon, Larry Flynt's brother Jimmy and others were making arrangements to have Flynt locked up and declared insane. They were concerned about his behavior ever since his conversion—Flynt had been flying back and forth across the country, making speeches and deals, buying newspapers and real estate, attending religious revivals and subsidizing religious groups—and they convinced a probate judge to order his arrest and detention for a sanity hearing, not such an easy task since Flynt traveled with bodyguards.

Although the judge personally informed the sheriff, and plans for this legal kidnapping were put into effect, the order was withdrawn without explanation on Christmas Eve. Flynt called me in Oregon and invited me to the Bahamas for New Year's. Kesey's daughter, Shannon, was giving him a haircut, stretching out each individual coil and then clipping off the end of it while Kesey gave me his farewell blessing: "Christ's plan has a place for pink. All you have to do is lace it with love . . ."

★   ★   ★

Suddenly I found myself parasailing over Nassau Beach, harnessed to a long rope with a parachute attached to a motorboat. I was sailing high up enough that when I urinated into the air, my entire bladder was emptied before the stream of piss hit the ocean.

My "Predictions for 1978" had been published, and I gave a copy to Flynt in his hotel suite. "A Scratch 'n' Sniff Virgin Mary," he mused. "Hey, that's a great idea. We'll have a portrait of the Virgin Mary, and when you scratch the spot, it'll smell like tomato juice." Then he wanted to know who would be a good person to write an article for *Hustler* that would expose the pope as gay. I suggested Gore Vidal, who had already stated in an interview that Cardinal Spellman was gay. So much for our first editorial conference.

Dick Gregory was in the kitchen, diligently preparing a health drink for Larry—this must have been the birth of his Bahamian Diet powder—and he was also feeding unfiltered conspiracy theories to his eager student.

Althea Flynt was there too. She was a combination of *Evita* and *The Beverly Hillbillies*. When she was eight, her father murdered her mother, her grandfather, her mother's best friend, and then he killed himself. Althea was the perfect wife for Larry. When they met, she was a seventeen-year-old go-go dancer making $90 a week, jaded with street smarts. After they were married, she continued to bring home other women for him to fuck. And now she was making $500,000 a year.

Althea had been hostile to me at the Christmas party, but we became friends in the Bahamas, and she confided to me how upset she was that so many professional Christians were all lining up for money when Larry became so generous after his born-again experience. "God may have walked into his life," she said, "but twenty million dollars a year walked out."

Larry had never seen *The Realist*, but on New Year's Eve he offered to start publishing it again—with a staff. I accepted, as long as he agreed that I would have complete control of the contents. At midnight, we all went out on the dock and stood in a misty drizzle as Dick Gregory uttered truly eloquent prayers for each of us. When he finished, Althea whined, like Lucy in the *Peanuts* strip, "My hair's getting all wet." It was her way of saying "amen."

On New Year's Day, we were sitting in the sand, just relaxing. Larry had bought a paperback novel by Gore Vidal in the hotel store, but first he was reading the Sunday *New York Times* and worrying about the implications of juries with only six members. A moment later he was rubbing suntan lotion on my back.

"I'll bet Hugh Hefner never did this for you," he said.

* * *

In 1967, at the War Is Over demonstration in Los Angeles, police had forced thousands of protesters back into a grassy area where now stood Century City, an architectural phoenix rising out of the ashes of the peace movement. From my thirty-eighth-floor office in one of the twin towers, I could stare out a large plastic window which couldn't be opened, at the view of a restricted country club below. I found a tiny apartment in Beverly Hills for only $235 a month, and walked to work every day. I was the Lone Pedestrian.

Since Mother's Day falls in May, the idea was to have a nude pregnant woman on the cover of the May 1978 issue—another *Hustler* first—and, on the inside, an article, "Motherhood—Celebration of Life!" We found a pregnant model, and the photos combined beauty and dignity. There was a slight problem, though—you could see one of her nipples. An unwritten agreement existed among the publishers of men's magazines that human female nipples shall not be clearly visible on a cover, or else wholesalers were likely to refuse to distribute the magazine to retail outlets.

"But this is *insane*," I protested. "I mean, when that woman gives birth, there'll be no protuberances to nurse her baby with."

Yet I was learning by osmosis to accept certain arbitrary rules as the net in this pornographic tennis game. An erect penis must not be shown. Working hours are from 9 AM to 5:30. Semen must not be shown. Spring water must not be used to make coffee. Penetration must not be shown. If a call is interrupted by Larry Flynt's secretary, you must hang up immediately. Oral-genital contact must not be shown. This world of pornography was another separate reality that Carlos Castaneda never dreamed of. (Castaneda was, of course, one of the actors who got a blow job in *Deep Throat*.)

An Italian magazine, *Playman,* had published full frontal nude photos of Jacqueline Kennedy taken on a Greek island by the grace of a tele-photo lens. Lyle Stuart brought the issue from Italy and gave it to Al Goldstein, who reprinted the photos in his raunchy tabloid, *Screw*. Then Larry Flynt published a five-page spread in *Hustler*. But now he wanted to put the naked Jackie on the cover with a banner headline: *Did Onassis Kill Kennedy? Was Jackie Worth It?* On the inside, readers whose curiosity had been aroused would find "The Gemstone Papers," a conspiratorial amalgam of facts and apocrypha.

"But," I argued, "if you can't even put nipples on a cover, how are the distributors gonna let you get away with pubic hair?"

"If it's Jackie Kennedy's pubic hair," Larry replied confidently, "they'll display it."

The first born-again issue of *Hustler* would feature a heterosexual couple making love in various positions on a chair especially designed for that purpose. They were professional models who had never met before, but they both got so turned on that what had started out as simulated intercourse soon became quite real. The violation of the no-erection rule had been canceled out by the violation of the no-penetration rule. For here was the most paradoxical rule of all—penetration is allowed *if* it is so fully to the hilt that you cannot *see* the erection.

As for the cover with a nude pregnant model, that dilemma was resolved—instead of a photo, there would be an artist's version of a cut-away diagram of a fetus in the womb. The nipples of this unreal mother-to-be had high visibility, but that was no problem, because there were different standards for photography and art. However, another issue of *Hustler* was scheduled to include a portfolio of nineteenth-century miniature erotic paintings from India. Somebody noticed there was penetration that was clearly visible. Unlike the unknown couple, here was *visible* penetration, so these classics were altered at the printer, thereby reversing the usual double standard for photography and art.

★   ★   ★

As a symbolic act, I had my first lunch meeting with Dennis Banks of the American Indian Movement. They were planning a four-month march, from Sacramento to Washington, D.C., to protest anti-Indian legislation. When we finished eating, I reached for the check, saying, "This is my first editorial lunch." But Banks grabbed the check before I could.

"No," he said, "this is my first bribe."

Next, Wavy Gravy came to town, and he wanted to interview Tiny Tim for *Hustler*. I went to the hotel with Wavy. Even though I was now making $90,000 a year, I ate leftover food right off the room service trays that guests had placed outside their doors. Those old habits die hard. When I was a kid, my mother used to stand by the garbage can, warning me—"I'm gonna throw it away"—before she scraped the food off the plates. I took it on as my lifetime personal responsibility not to waste food.

Also, I was still too cheap to actually *buy* a box of facial tissues, so instead I always carried a few squares of toilet paper neatly folded in my pocket. It was only after the Kleenex people, who had a plant in El Salvador, dropped their sponsorship of *Lou Grant*—because the star of the series, Ed Asner, had demonstrated against the U.S.-financed death squads of El Salvador—that my frugality became a political protest. Almost three decades later, I was on a panel about "Fake News and Public Decency in the Age of Terror," and Ed Asner was in the audience, so I told that story. Later, as we were shaking hands, he said, "Listen, forget about the toilet paper—you have *my permission* to use Kleenex." Though I still don't.

Anyway, while Tiny Tim was rambling on about show business and Jesus, he confessed to spreading a lady's bottom with chunky peanut butter. It seemed appropriately kinky for *Hustler*, until Bruce David walked into my office, visibly agitated that I had even *suggested* such an interview. "I'm profoundly disturbed," he said, wrapping a long strip of Scotch tape from the dispenser on my desk around his hand and proceeding to remove the lint from his blue serge suit.

"The readers of *Hustler* are not interested in Tiny Tim," Bruce continued. Since he knew the magazine so intimately, I deferred to his judgment quite often. However, we did have one strong editorial disagreement. I had wanted to assign freelance reporter Laura Daltry to write an article, "Does Pornography Incite Men to Commit Rape?"—based on interviews she would conduct with convicted rapists serving time at San Quentin Prison. "But," Bruce asked, "suppose what she finds out makes *Hustler* look bad?"

"If it's a good piece," I said, "we'll publish it no matter what."

Bruce explained, "It isn't that I want to be dishonest and hide the information, but this would be stacking the deck against us, because I don't think the rapists themselves are in a position to know whether they've been influenced or not. I don't think they're necessarily smart enough or clearheaded enough."

Another editor added, "Laura Daltry has a feminist bent, so she'll be predisposed to find the connection." And, somewhere along the chain of command, my proposal got sabotaged. The article was never assigned.

Other articles I proposed were assigned, and published, ranging from Marilyn Katz on abortion rights to Eric Norden on the murder of Malcolm X, and I appointed science-fiction writer Theodore Sturgeon as *Hustler*'s book reviewer. I felt privileged to be reaching this otherwise neglected blue-collar audience with informative anti-establishment material, even if other pages of the magazine would undoubtedly become stuck together by several hundred thousand dried-up sperm cells that had mistakenly assumed they were heading toward the Fallopian tubes.

Moreover, I would have *The Realist* again as an outlet for my *own* peculiar vision. I began to gather together a small staff, people I'd worked with before—Art Kunkin, former publisher of the *Los Angeles Free Press*, as managing editor; Lee Quarnstrom as articles editor; and Jeanne as researcher and cartoon editor—she would move to Los Angeles with our daughter, Holly, and Holly's younger brother, Bill.

On the phone with Ken Kesey, I asked, "Does hiring one's ex-wife count as nepotism?"

"Well," he said, "nepotism is better than nopetism at all."

I repeated this to Larry Flynt. He laughed and said, "Look, the next time you perform somewhere, maybe you could use that line and mention that I said it."

"Oh, sure—in fact, why don't I call Kesey right now and tell *him* that you said it?"

In another building a few blocks away, *The Realist* shared offices with Flynt's conspiracy researchers, Mark Lane and Donald Freed. Lane discovered that when Lee Harvey Oswald was in the service, he contracted a venereal disease "in the line of duty," according to an official military document—proof positive that he was no ordinary Marine, but one who had gone to bed with a female Japanese spy in yet another brilliant career move.

Flynt had recently purchased the *Los Angeles Free Press*. When its editor, Jay Levin, founder of the *L.A. Weekly*, ran a story on Flynt in the *Free Press* with the wrong middle initial, Flynt insisted on a front-page correction. The "assassination squad"—as they were referred to by *Realist* staffers—published a special issue of the *Free Press* headlined, "JFK Murder Solved: Killing Coordinated by CIA." On the back cover, Flynt offered a million dollars to help bring the slain president's killers to justice. There were an awful lot of calls, but nobody collected the reward.

Flynt also offered a million dollars to various female celebrities, many nominated by readers, to pose nude and show pink for *Hustler*—Cher, Julie Nixon Eisenhower, Caroline Kennedy, Sally Struthers, Barbara Walters,

Lynda Carter (*Wonder Woman*), Lindsay Wagner (*The Bionic Woman*), Angie Dickinson (*Police Woman*), Barbara Eden (*I Dream of Jeannie*), Farrah Fawcett, Jaclyn Smith, and Kate Jackson (*Charlie's Angels*), and singers Olivia Newton-John and Linda Ronstadt—but none of them ever took him up on it.

He also tried unsuccessfully to give a million dollars in cash to President Jimmy Carter to re-establish the Commission on Obscenity and Pornography in order to find out if obscenity and pornography are really harmful. Meanwhile, shortly after my appointment as publisher of *Hustler*, Ruth Carter Stapleton suggested to Larry Flynt that he "get rid of" me. He refused. However, he did have an idea for a *Hustler* cover:

> I wanna have an illustrator draw a photograph of Jimmy Carter's face after he's just been told that Ruth, his sister, is in the centerfold of *Hustler*. His hair will be jumpin' out like an Afro and his teeth'll be poppin' out and he's gonna be all reared back holdin' a copy of *Hustler*. We're only gonna have one headline on that cover— "Ruth Carter Stapleton Shows Pink for *Hustler*! What Will Jimmy Think?" We're gonna shrink-wrap every single copy so nobody'll know what's in it, and Ruth is gonna issue a press release about a week before the magazine goes on sale.
>
> She's gonna go on vacation, and the press release is gonna say, "The reason why I decided to pose for *Hustler* is because I felt that if a middle-aged woman like myself decided to pose for a publication like *Hustler* it would help people in the world to become at ease with their sexuality." Now when you open it up to the center-fold, we're only gonna have one picture of Ruth in there, and it's gonna be a full-length centerfold shot of her wearing a very pretty pink dress, holding a pink Bible, wearing pink shoes, with a pink background, pink nail polish, pink stockings, pink lipstick, but she will be fully dressed.

Bruce David objected to the dishonesty of playing such a trick on those readers who would buy the magazine expecting to see Ruth Carter Stapleton totally naked, spreading her legs apart, with her pious pussy kept wide open by spirit gum, her love-tunnel glistening with glycerin and a staple in her belly button. Nevertheless, a realistic painting of her eventually appeared in *Hustler*, with Jimmy Carter's picture on the cover and a headline, "The President's Sister Shows Pink!" She didn't issue a press release, but *Hustler*'s publicity department did.

Althea Flynt was wistfully predicting that Walter Cronkite would announce, as the final item on the *CBS Evening News*, "The president's sister, evangelist Ruth Carter Stapleton, shows pink in the new issue of *Hustler* magazine—and that's the way it is."

* * *

Larry Flynt had been traveling around a lot, but he happened to be back in L.A. at the same time that Ram Dass was visiting, so I had the unique pleasure of introducing them. Larry, Althea, Ram Dass, and I went to a health-food restaurant, where we discovered that we shared something in common: We were all practicing celibacy—Larry at the suggestion of Dick Gregory, Althea by extension, Ram Dass for spiritual purposes, and me just for the sheer perversity of it.

Over lunch, Larry told me that I should "take more power." He said he was actually *bored* with pornography, but felt so strongly about his right to publish it that he had gone to Atlanta to defy a ban and sell *Hustler* personally. He got arrested for that, but first he had to stand trial for obscenity in Lawrenceville, Georgia.

The next week, he called me from Lawrenceville. "Now I know why you introduced me to Ram Dass," he said. "Is his name one word or two?" I told him it was two words, and he continued: "Ram Dass really helped me to get rid of my hang-up about labeling myself as a 'celibate.' I can just say that I'm not having sex."

"And you don't have to worry about the label 'fasting' either. You can just say that you're not eating food."

"Oh, listen, Paul—you know those ads for guns we have in *Hustler*—well, you know, I'm against violence, but I'm also against censorship, so just move 'em to the back of the magazine, okay?"

A few days later, while walking on the sidewalk in Lawrenceville during a lunch break in the obscenity trial, an American flag pin on his lapel, Larry Flynt was shot twice in the abdomen. The .44-caliber magnum bullets came from across the street, one lodging near Larry's spine. His local attorney was also wounded.

According to the doctors, if Larry hadn't taken an enema the day he was shot, he would not have lived, because the contents of his intestines would've caused a fatal infection. He'd had only grapefruit juice for lunch. His spleen and several feet of his intestine were removed. The *Hustler* staff was in a state of collective shock.

A group of employees donated blood for Larry. I flew to Atlanta on the Thursday before Easter and went directly to Emory University Hospital. Althea brought me to Larry's room. It was extremely unsettling to see such a powerful personality lying there so helpless, being kept alive by medical technology, with one tube feeding him and another tube breathing for him. He appeared bug-eyed with painkiller. Althea lifted the sheet and showed me his gaping wounds, a truly awesome sight.

"Oh, God, Althea—he's showing pink."

"I'm arranging for a photographer to come in here," she said. "We're gonna publish Larry's wounds in *Hustler*. I want people to see what they did to him."

I sat down in a chair by Larry's bed. I didn't know what to say. We simply clasped hands for a while. Finally I broke the silence. "Larry, tomorrow is Good Friday," I said. "So, uh, you don't have to go to work."

I glanced toward Althea to reassure myself that I hadn't indulged in irreverence that was too inappropriate, but she said, "Oh, Paul, *look*"—gesturing toward Larry—"he wants to show you something." Above the oxygen mask, Larry was blinking his eyes over and over again in rapid succession. "He's *laughing*," Althea said. It was a moment of unspeakable intimacy for the three of us.

As I was leaving the hospital, I heard Althea's voice from the other end of the corridor: "Oh, Paul!" I thought she was about to say something like, "Thank you for coming to see me in my hour of need." Instead, she called out, "Remember—go hard-core!"

Back home that night, I got into a bathtub full of burning hot water as if to experience Larry's pain, but it couldn't possibly feel the same. Besides, I was doing it out of choice and could stop voluntarily, whereas Larry would be confined to a wheelchair for the rest of his life, paralyzed from the waist down. I almost fainted when I got out of the tub.

The next day I was scheduled to have my photo taken for the upcoming born-again issue. I had been wearing the same old windbreaker to work every single day, but on this particular morning I decided to vary my wardrobe by wearing an old cowboy hat. The photographer asked me if I would take off my clothes and pose nude. I agreed, but I got caught up in *Hustler*'s editorial schizophrenia.

In the "Advise and Consent" column at the front of the magazine, you could read about how penis size doesn't matter, but in the ads at the back of the magazine, you could send away for penis enlargers. So, when I went into this little bathroom at the photo studio to remove my clothes, I fondled my penis just enough to make it a *little* larger without becoming erect.

Then I posed for the camera—completely naked except for my cowboy hat—shrugging my bare shoulders and smiling helplessly. This was the first time any publisher of a men's magazine had ever presented his own full frontal nudity. Moreover, the photo accompanied an interview wherein I admitted what no other publisher of a men's magazine had ever publicly admitted before:

Q. Have you ever jerked off to copies of *Hustler* or *Playboy* or *Penthouse?*

A. All of them. Sometimes I would pile them up, put *Playboy* on top, then *Penthouse* and then *Hustler,* so that the flowers would open wider as I went from one magazine to the next. I see showing pink as a reminder of vulnerability.

Q. And have you noticed that if you squint your eyes in a certain way the photographs become somewhat three-dimensional?

A. Well, I would have noticed it, but jerking off has made me blind. What I do notice is that every time I jerk off it's a mixed blessing, because I enjoy it and yet I know something's missing . . .

In my publisher's statement for the born-again issue of *Hustler,* I wrote:

The shooting of Larry Flynt has been referred to as "senseless violence." It kind of makes you wonder exactly what *sensible* violence is. The difference seems to be that senseless violence isn't permitted by law. Sensible violence allows landlords to ignore peeling paint that, when tasted by curious infants, can result in death by lead poisoning. Sensible violence enables the liquor lobby to persuade legislators not to pass a bill that would require funds to be allocated for the rehabilitation of motorists arrested for drunken driving.

Sensible violence is getting the highest possible percentage of the population hooked on coffee, and then—because caffeine is naturally bitter—there is mass sugar addiction to boot. Sensible violence is displayed in that TV commercial in which a famous actress tries to make parents feel guilty for not feeding their kids Twinkies, manufactured by ITT, the same folks who sabotaged the legally elected Allende government in Chile. Sensible violence is the production and distribution of cigarettes, justified by a printed warning that has become as meaningless as playing "The Star-Spangled Banner" before a ball game.

The advertising department thought I was trying to sabotage their efforts to obtain cigarette ads. They sent an advance copy of what I wrote to Althea at the hospital, asking her to veto it. Instead, she called it "the best publisher's statement we've ever had."

Meanwhile, heavy security procedures were put into force at the *Hustler* offices. I wanted to hire Frank Wills, the security guard who originally discovered the Watergate break-in when he noticed a piece of tape keeping a door unlocked even though the janitorial staff had already departed. But his current whereabouts were unknown.

Besides, while I was in Atlanta, Chick Canzoneri, a former bodyguard for Frank Sinatra, had been hired as our chief of security. Now he was concerned that I might be in danger because the *Los Angeles Times* mentioned in an article about me that I walked to and from work.

"Don't worry." I assured him. "Every morning, before I leave for the office, I check to see if there's a bomb in my boots."

★ ★ ★

Althea Flynt asked me, "What's the cover of the first issue of *The Realist* gonna be?"

"Well, this year will be the fiftieth anniversary of Mickey Mouse, so I'll have a quote from *Life* magazine, about how the three most powerful graphic images of the twentieth century are the Coca-Cola bottle, the Nazi swastika, and Mickey Mouse. And the cover illustration will show Mickey Mouse drinking from a Coke bottle and wearing a swastika armband."

"Have you talked to the lawyers yet?"

"Uh, no . . ."

Meanwhile, the cover of the April 1978 issue of *Hustler* featuring a crucified Easter bunny had resulted in the largest premature return of magazines by wholesalers in several months. And you couldn't even see the bunny's nipples. Maybe it was the blood and the crown of thorns that turned people off, who knew? It was too early to know the return status of the May issue with the cover featuring the cutaway illustration of a pregnant woman.

The cover of the June issue was scheduled to feature Larry Flynt's vow—"We will no longer hang women up like pieces of meat!"—and, as the quasi-logical extension of that quote, it would be accompanied by photo-artist Alfred Gescheidt's portrait of a woman as a piece of meat. Inside, there would be more of his work—a six-page menu of nude women, spread with appropriate condiments, mustard or tomato sauce—as if they were *actual* pieces of meat, superimposed on various dishes, a frankfurter or a plate of spaghetti and meatballs. An imitation government stamp on the cover would label this as the LAST ALL-MEAT ISSUE. A memo from one editor summed up the carnivorous machinations:

> The meatball shot will face the hamburger shot and that would give us two open pussy shots. The turkey shot was re-shot with open pussy, but Paul got the misimpression that we only needed

50% pink and so he okay'd staying with the original turkey shot. However, we convinced him that the entire object of re-shooting the meat spread was to get more pink, and so we persuaded Paul that the pink turkey shot should be chosen.

I approved the turkey spread, not because it contributed to the correct pink quota, but rather because an editor persuaded me that this was a better shot because the model's face was turned away from the camera.

"But ordinarily," I pointed out, "you've always wanted the model's eyes looking directly *at* you."

"Yeah, but when I eat a *turkey*, I don't wanna see the face looking at me."

However, the same photo-art selections by Gescheidt appeared in another men's magazine, and *Hustler*'s art department had to concoct a quick substitute. Bruce David brought in the new cover for my approval—a trick photo of a woman's body being stuffed into a meat grinder upside down, so that only her legs were still showing.

"What's this supposed to mean?" I asked. "Now that we aren't hanging women up like pieces of meat anymore, we're taking the next step and putting them into a meat grinder?"

But Bruce assured me that there was no time for anything else, and the production department backed him up. The cover immediately provoked protests in New York, San Francisco, and Los Angeles. I was accused of advocating attacks on women. I publicly apologized to those who felt hurt by the meat-grinder image, explaining that it was *Hustler*'s hurried attempt at self-parody.

Nevertheless, that cover was destined to become an unofficial symbol of male oppression at feminist rallies. In fact, when I attended a feminist conference with an old friend, Janet Bode—whose book on rape, *Fighting Back*, had just been published—she asked me to walk in separately from her and we would meet later.

★　★　★

A by-product of the attempt on Larry's life was a terrible cash flow problem at the Flynt empire. Creditors wanted to be paid immediately, while those who owed the company money held back their payments. Both the *Los Angeles Free Press* and *The Realist* were dropped from the publishing schedule. I didn't even have a chance to get out the first issue, and now I had to fire my entire staff. Althea had taken over the running of *Hustler*. As the staff began to get severely trimmed, the insecurity of those who remained increased. Morale got lower and tempers flared. Triggered by Bruce David yelling at a secretary, I finally sent this memo to all *Hustler* personnel:

> I would like to apologize for my lack of leadership in a particular area. Every time I've observed, but not spoken up about, the kind of sadistic disrespect which certain individuals have been increasingly displaying toward others, I have become a silent partner to that behavior. By allowing myself to become a figurehead, I lost sight of the fact that the reason people have taken so much shit is because they fear for their jobs. So, as of today, no one is to be fired without my approval. I cannot let my office turn into an isolation booth. It is not undermining authority if I refuse to permit blatant contempt to stifle a creative environment. This is not the Marine Corps. The misuse of power is a form of violence, and I will no longer tolerate it at *Hustler*. We will not treat employees like pieces of meat anymore.

"What is this," Bruce snarled, "Fuck-Your-Buddy Week?" The tension continued to escalate between us as several key staff members threatened mutiny if he stayed. Power-crazed and short-sighted, I ended up firing Bruce and sending a telegram to Althea. She flew both of us to Atlanta.

"You're the publisher," she told me, "and I won't interfere with your decision, but I'm hoping for a miracle."

Bruce couldn't conceive of working with me again, and I was prepared to quit rather than be maneuvered into having him back, but Althea proved to be a skillful mediator, and I ended up rehiring him. I was glad I did. He was a skillful editor under unusually heavy pressure, and I was a self-righteous fool.

In the hospital, I visited with Larry, who in his delirium was convinced that he had been walking around the room. He also told me that Hugh Hefner and *Penthouse* publisher Bob Guccione were directly responsible for his being shot. Straining to be rational, he asked if Gore Vidal had written that article yet, about the pope being gay, and I said that we were still trying to locate him. Larry also wanted to know about "the Jesus shoot," a photo spread he had previously described with this revisionist theory:

> Everyone knows who Mary Magdalene was, the prostitute that Jesus used to run around with. She was the one that was caught in the act of prostitution, and she was tried, and she was *stoned* to death. But if you get caught in the act of prostitution, that means you had to *fuck* somebody, right? So we're gonna show that picture,

and then we're gonna show her getting stoned, and we're gonna show Jesus walkin' up, saying, "Let *those* who have not lain with her cast the first stone."

Yes, I said that right. It's not, "Let those without sin cast the first stone." Because Jesus knows they'd *all* been fuckin' her, and that's why they stopped stonin' her, because, you see, he knew everything. And not only that, he was also troubled about why she was being stoned to death and the *man* wasn't being stoned, because if he hadn't *a-paid* her, she wouldn't've *fucked* him, and why should she be punished and him be let off the hook? Looks to me like somebody had something against the woman.

Althea had transformed the Coca-Cola Suite at Emory University Hospital into her office, where she was now studying the slides of that "Jesus and the Adulteress" feature. Dick Gregory was there, and he said, "This scares *me*." He was concerned about reaction in the Bible Belt, notwithstanding the fact that *Hustler*'s research department had already made certain that the text followed the Bible. And now Althea was checking for any sexism that might have slipped past the male editors' limited consciousness. The spread was already in page forms, but not yet collated into the magazine, and there was still a gnawing dilemma about whether or not to publish it.

The marketing people in Columbus were aghast at the possibility that wholesalers would refuse to distribute an issue of the magazine with such a blatantly blasphemous feature. Althea and I voted to publish. Dick Gregory and Bruce David voted not to publish. "I'm against it," Bruce said, "because we're already sucking wind with the lines of credit, and this is an issue that just simply will not be distributed."

Faced with this crucial decision, Althea made her choice on the basis of pure whimsicality. She noticed a pair of pigeons on the window ledge. One of them was waddling toward the other. "All right," she said, "if that dove walks over and pecks the *other* dove, then we *will* publish this." The pigeon continued strutting along the window ledge, but it stopped short and didn't peck the other pigeon, so publication of "Jesus and the Adulteress" was postponed indefinitely.

★ ★ ★

Larry Flynt had been transferred to a hospital in Columbus, and Althea traveled back and forth between there and Los Angeles. On one of her visits, I mentioned that I had been interviewed for *High Times* and that one of their questions was, "Have you slept with Althea Flynt?"

She said, "What did you tell them?"

"I just answered, 'No, but even if we had, I wouldn't *tell* you.'"

That was the truth, but Althea was visibly upset.

"Why'd they ask *that*?" she asked

"Well," I replied, "you know, just sensationalism."

The next day Althea called me into her office. Whenever she did that, I would always take my pen and pad with me. She might have an idea for an article—on the quality of food in public schools, for example—but this time we both sat down and she got immediately to the point.

"Paul—I have to fire you."

I wrote down *fired* on my pad.

Then I asked, "Does Larry know about this?"

"No, not yet. But the readers wanna see a picture on the publisher's page of somebody who looks like he *works* for a living."

"Althea, I *do* work for a living. I work for *you*."

Of course, I knew what she meant. In the photo on the publisher's page, I was wearing green shades and a cowboy hat over my long hair. But still?

"No, I didn't mean it that way," she said. "Look, *Hustler* is really Larry's baby, and people wanna see *his* picture back on the publisher's page. We've been getting a lot of calls from readers and wholesalers complaining that they don't feel the magazine is really *Hustler* without Larry, and now that he's recuperating, he should be publisher again. It's nothing personal—I like you better than Ruth Carter Stapleton or Dick Gregory or anybody else Larry introduced me to. But whenever I walk past the office he built for himself here—he never even got a chance to use it . . ."

She started to sob. I didn't know quite how to react. She said, "My mascara's running." I handed her a tissue from my pocket. It is proper etiquette to comfort one's employer when one has just been fired. Althea started wiping her face. "This tissue is falling apart," she complained.

"It's not a Kleenex," I explained. "It's toilet tissue." She looked stunned. "But," I quickly added, "it's two-ply."

She laughed. "You really are crazy."

"Althea, listen, I don't have any money. I didn't save a penny. I've spent it all paying back debts. I'll need to get a severance check."

"How much do you want?"

"Well, I think ten percent of my salary would be fair. That would be $9,000."

"I was thinking of $5,000."

"All right, let's compromise—$7,000."

"Okay, that's fine," she said. "Seven is God's lucky number."

We embraced, and Althea whispered, "I love you, Paul."

I went back to my office and locked the door. I felt an overwhelming sense of relief. I phoned family and friends to tell them the news before they learned it in the media. When I called Ken Kesey, he said, "Well, why don't you come to Egypt with us? The Grateful Dead are gonna play the Pyramids." What perfect timing! I put my radio on and started dancing around the office. I belonged to this vast army of secret dancers who only dance when they're alone. There I was, dancing and singing, "Oh, thank you for firing me, Althea, thank you, thank you, thank you."

My main editorial regret was that I hadn't been able to publish that "Jesus and the Adulteress" photo spread. The nearly life-size poster which was supposed to be included as a pull-out centerfold would instead remain on my wall at home as a memento of those six months at *Hustler*. There was Jesus, a generic barbershop-calendar Jesus, looking reverently toward the sky as he covered up the prone Adulteress. Her head was bleeding from the stones that had been cast upon her. And she was showing pink. Sweet, shocking, vulnerable pink. This poster was a startling visual image, unintentionally satirizing the ostensible change from the old *Hustler* to the new *Hustler*.

But I was through there now. That evening, I walked home totally elated. Although *Hustler* had been accused of exploiting women, actually it was guilty of exploiting some men's addiction to pornography. I had been catering to an unseen audience who all had one particular quality in common—the security of never being rejected by a centerfold—but now I finally had my own life back. If you play a role long enough, there comes a point where the role begins to play *you*. So now I felt as though *I* had been born-again.

To celebrate this transition, I snorted the balance of my cocaine stash (when in Hollywood . . .)—and then I cut off all my hair with a little pair of toenail scissors.

★ ★ ★

Bob Weir looked up at the Great Pyramid and cried out, *"What is it?"* Actually, it was the place for locals to go on a cheap date. The Pyramids were surrounded by moats of discarded bottlecaps. The Grateful Dead were scheduled to play on three successive nights at an open-air theater in front of the Pyramids, with the Sphinx looking on.

A bootleg tape of Dean Martin and Jerry Lewis doing filthy schtick was being used for a preliminary sound check. Later, an American general complained to stage manager Steve Parish that the decadence of a rock and roll band performing here was a sacrilege to five thousand years of history. Parish said, "I lost two brothers in 'Nam, and I don't wanna hear this crap." The general retreated in the face of those imaginary brothers.

But there *were* a couple of *real* injured veterans. Drummer Bill Kreutzmann had fallen off a horse and broken his arm. He would still be playing with the band, using one drumstick. Or, as an Arabian fortune cookie might point out, *In the land of the limbless, a one-armed drummer is king.* Basketball star and faithful Deadhead Bill Walton's buttocks had been used as a pincushion by the Portland Trailblazers so that he could continue to perform on court even though the bones of his foot were being shattered with pain he couldn't feel. Having been injected with painkilling drugs to hide the greed rather than heal the injury, he now had to walk around with crutches and one foot in a cast under his extra-long galabia. Maybe Kreutzmann and Walton could team up and enter the half-upside-down sack-race event.

An air of incredible excitement permeated the first night. Never had the Dead been so inspired. Backstage, Jerry Garcia was passing along final instructions to the band: "Remember, play in tune." The music began with Egyptian oudist Hamza el-Din, backed up by a group tapping out ancient rhythms on their fourteen-inch-diameter tars, soon joined by Mickey Hart, a butterfly with drumsticks, then Garcia ambled on with a gentle guitar riff, then the rest of the band, and as the Dead meshed with the percussion ensemble, basking in total respect of each other, Bob Weir suddenly segued into Buddy Holly's "Not Fade Away."

"Did you see that?" Kesey said. "The Sphinx's *jaw* just dropped!"

Every morning my roommate, George Walker, climbed to the top of the pyramid. He was in training. It would be his honor to plant a Grateful Dead skull-and-lightning-bolt flag on top of the Great Pyramid. This was *our* Iwo Jima.

In preparation for the final concert, I was sitting in the tub-like sarcophagus at the center of gravity in the Great Pyramid, after ingesting LSD that a Prankster had smuggled into Egypt in a plastic Visine bottle. I had heard that the sound of the universe was D-flat, so that's what I chanted. It was only as I breathed in deeply before each extended *om* that I was forced to ponder the mystery of those who urinate there.

I had a strong feeling that I was involved in a *lesson*. It was as though the secret of the Dead would finally be revealed to me, if only I paid proper attention. There was a full eclipse of the moon, and Egyptian kids were running through the streets shaking tin cans filled with rocks in order to bring it back.

"It's okay," I assured them. "The Grateful Dead will bring back the moon."

And, sure enough, a rousing rendition of "Ramble on Rose" would accomplish that feat. The moon returned just as the marijuana cookie that Bill Graham gave me started blending in with the other drugs. Graham used to wear two wristwatches, one for each coast. Now he wore one wristwatch with two faces.

(Before the original edition of this book was published, the young lawyer at Simon & Schuster who vetted the manuscript asked if I had gotten Graham's permission. Otherwise, he could sue for libel. She thought I was referring to *Billy* Graham, the evangelist, who presumably was not a doper. When I explained who *Bill* Graham was, she said I had to precede his name with "rock impresario." I did so, but I told her, "On the day that Billy Graham gives me a marijuana cookie at a Grateful Dead concert in front of the Great Pyramid, the revolution will have begun.")

There was a slight problem with an amplifier, but the sound engineer said that it was "getting there."

"Getting there ain't good enough," Garcia responded. "It's gotta fuckin' *be* there."

This was a totally outrageous event. The line between incongruity and appropriateness had disappeared along with the moon. The music was so powerful that the only way to go was ecstasy. That night, when the Dead played "Fire on the Mountain," I danced my ass off with all the others on that outdoor stage as if I had no choice.

"You know," Bill Graham confessed, "this is the first time I ever danced in public."

"Me too," I said. That was the lesson.

The next day a dozen of us had a farewell party on a felucca—an ancient, roundish boat, a kind of covered wagon that floats along the river. Jerry Garcia was carrying his attaché case, just in case he suddenly got any new song ideas. There were three guides who came with our rented felucca: an old man whose skin was like corrugated leather, a younger man who was his assistant, and a kid whose job was to light the *hubbly-bubbly*—a giant water pipe which used hot coals to keep the hashish burning.

We were all completely zonked out of our minds in the middle of the Nile. The Egyptians kept us dizzy on hash and we in turn gave them acid. The old man mumbled something—our translator explained, "He says he's seeing strange things"—and gave *me* the handle of the rudder to steer, which I managed to do in my stoned stupor. The felucca was a vehicle of our cultural exchange.

While I was still unwinding from my experience at *Hustler*, I had been simultaneously adapting to Egyptian consciousness, where a woman had to be clothed from head to foot with a chador so that only her eyes were showing. The mere sight of her flesh was officially barred because it could create anxiety and excitement in a man.

A woman was not permitted to worship with men because her presence would serve as a distraction from Allah. Nikki Scully of our group decided to walk around the streets of Cairo wearing a chador. She said that the nonverbal message she kept getting from her eye contact with the Egyptian women was: *We are one! We are one! We are one!* Of course, she might well have been projecting her own feminist attitude.

Coincidentally, Ruth Carter Stapleton was visiting Egypt. She had been conducting prayer meetings and inner healing sessions. When *Washington Post* reporter Rudy Maxa told her I was in Cairo, she asked him to invite me to meet with her. "After all," she said, "mine is supposed to be a ministry of reconciliation, isn't it?"

But when Maxa wrote in the *Post* that "only the inability to determine Krassner's whereabouts saved him from a dose of inner healing at the base of the Pyramids that afternoon," he had no idea that I'd been tripping on LSD and chanting *inside* the Pyramid that same afternoon.

On the return flight from Egypt, we ate whatever dope was left, and had an extremely pleasant trip. I joined the Mile High Club, making out with Mobilia Growlight in the airplane bathroom.

"This," said Mobilia, "is *really* flying United." She didn't know that it was an old Bob Hope joke.

Back in the States, I wrote to Ruth Carter Stapleton, expressing my surprise that she wanted to meet me inasmuch as she had previously asked Larry Flynt to fire me. She phoned in response to my letter.

"I want to apologize," she said. "I had been advised that you were not the correct individual to change the image of *Hustler*, but I shouldn't have judged you before I met you. I don't usually judge people before I meet them."

"Well, if you were a *true* Christian," I teased, "you wouldn't judge me even *after* we met."

She laughed graciously. Then we talked about the blatant contrast between *Hustler* and Egypt.

"I went from one extreme to the other," I told her. "It was like getting out of a hot sauna and jumping into the freezing snow."

"How do you mean that?"

"Well, I had gone from showing pink to wearing chador."

* * *

Larry Flynt had started out as the son of a simple sharecropper. A facsimile of the shack he lived in would be constructed in the basement of his mansion in Ohio. He lost his virginity to a chicken at the age of fourteen. When he married Althea, he arranged for a chicken to be a guest at their wedding.

In 1984 a grand jury indicted Joseph Paul Franklin for shooting Flynt and his attorney. Investigators said the possible motive was his anger over sexually explicit photos of interracial couples in *Hustler*. There has never been a trial, because he is already serving two life terms at a maximum security prison, for racist killings.

Flynt published a parody of a Dewar profile ad, claiming that Reverend Jerry Falwell, head of the Moral Majority, had lost his virginity with his mother in an outhouse. Falwell sued, and a court awarded him $200,000, not for libel but for malice. The case ended up before the Supreme Court, while Flynt was sitting in a wheelchair, wearing an American flag diaper, and calling members of the court "eight assholes and a cunt."

Nevertheless, the Court voted unanimously in favor of Flynt, overturning the lower court's decision. Otherwise, it would have established an awful precedent that could apply to Garry Trudeau's *Doonesbury* strip. If Falwell's feelings had been hurt, that was simply the risk of democracy.

When Flynt became a born-again Christian and was praying to Jesus, he recalls, "I promised to give up my wife for Him. I promised to see myself castrated, to look down and see myself with no sexual organs and look up and say, 'Yes, God, it's okay, if that's Your will, that's fine.' I spoke in tongues. There were animals eating at my neck, like baboons and monkeys, gnawing at me. He told me my calling—to bring peace to earth."

Larry Flynt's prayers were answered. Althea became heavily addicted to narcotics, and in 1987 she drowned in a bathtub. Flynt had a penile implant and married a mail-order bride. He now attributes his conversion to "a chemical imbalance" in his brain.

Postscript:

I still like pubic hair, but Internet porn sites now present several choices—completely shaved, vertical landing strips that look like exclamation points, heart-shaped, the Charlie Chaplin with just a little patch above the clitoris, and a tiny triangle that serves as an arrow *pointing* to the clit—yet, for a full bush, one would have to search the Web for "hairy" sites that are considered as "specialty," "kinky," or "fetish." The bald-pussy trend has gone mainstream, though Joy Behar observed that "no pubic hair creates a wind tunnel."

CHAPTER 11

HOLLY TOMOLLY

HOLLY'S FIRST WORD WAS "MORE." HER SECOND WORD WAS "TITTY." AFTER my marriage with Jeanne broke up, I continued to be haunted by the memory of her nursing Holly with one breast while I suckled the other. It was one of the sweetest feelings of my life, and my heart would flash upon that memory every time I witnessed Holly's childhood innocence fading away.

The first time it happened, we were having lunch in Greenwich Village, at a sidewalk café across the street from the Women's House of Detention. From behind the barred windows of an upper floor, inmates were shouting curses at their fate and tourists alike.

Holly asked, "Daddy, were there *supposed* to be jails?"

It happened again at a peace rally. "Isn't war stupid?" she asked. I was carrying Holly and a placard with a large illustration of *The Realist*'s worried-looking birdlike icon, Sir Realist. She observed a group of young people with tambourines, singing "Hare Krishna" over and over. "It sounds like they're saying my name," she said, and then we started singing, "Holly Krassner, Holly Krassner . . ."

* * *

Valerie Solanas served as an angry harbinger of the feminist revolution. She wore a man's outfit and her hair was stuffed under a Bob Dylan cap. When she walked into Andy Warhol's office to persuade him to make a film of a rather raunchy play she'd written, he accused her of being a cop. "And here's my badge," Valerie replied, unzipping her fly to expose her vulva. Previously she had telephoned him, and he invited her up to his famous loft because he thought her title, *Up from the Slime*, was so wonderful.

Originally, she had sent her manuscript to *The Realist*. I rejected it, but we met at the Chelsea Hotel and had lunch. Valerie hated men. She told me of her "organization"—SCUM—the Society for Cutting Up Men, and her plan to herd all the men in the world and keep them caged up for the purpose of stud farming. Now she had written *The SCUM Manifesto*, a document of heavy-handed proselytization. Sympathizing with the anguish of a pamphleteer, I lent her $50, not expecting her to pay it back. That was on Friday, May 31, 1968.

On Monday, June 3, I went to Jeanne's apartment to pick up Holly for lunch. She was now four years old. First we stopped at Woolworth's on 14th Street. Holly had seen a propeller beanie advertised on *Romper Room*, and I promised to buy her one. There was only one beanie left, but one of its two propellers was broken off.

I told Holly, "We can wait and get one that's *not* broken another time, or we can get the broken one now if you don't mind."

"I mind," she said, meaning she *didn't* mind.

We headed east—Holly wearing her new broken beanie and carrying the other propeller in her hand—turned left on Union Square, and happened upon Valerie Solanas on 16th Street, just a block away from Andy Warhol's place. She seemed less tomboyish than usual. Her Dylan cap was gone; her hair had been cut and styled in a feminine fashion. She seemed calm, friendly, in good spirits. We talked a little while about nothing special, then said goodbye, and I took Holly to Brownie's, a vegetarian restaurant. Valerie headed west. Five minutes later, Holly and I were seated at a table, and Valerie walked in.

"Do you mind if I join you?" she asked.

"Well, yeah, I do mind, actually, but only because I don't get a chance to see my daughter that much."

"Okay, I understand," she said, and left.

Holly was confused by the use of the word *mind*.

"That lady wanted to join us," she observed.

"I know, but I wanna be alone with you."

Holly smiled. "And I wanna be alone with you."

This was at 11:30 in the morning. Three hours later, Valerie went looking for Andy Warhol, but he wasn't there. Two hours after that, she found him and shot him. For all I knew, she had bought the gun with the money I'd lent her. It turned out she borrowed it from Motherfucker Ben Morea.

If I had known when she wanted to join us that Valerie's intention was to shoot Warhol, who knows, I might have been able to talk her out of it. Was she actually asking me for help in the restaurant? Or did she simply want company? That would've been a switch; she usually charged lonely men on the street $6 for an hour of conversation.

Could my quasi-rejection of Valerie have been the final straw? Maybe Andy Warhol was just a victim of her displaced hostility. Still, he had been the source of her persecution fantasies. She convinced herself that he was responsible for her literary difficulties.

Then again, she could've shot *me*—*and Holly*—right there in the restaurant. "Whattaya mean, I can't join you for lunch?" *Bang! Bang!* That easy. That absurd. That horrific.

In a 1996 interview with actor Taylor Mead, Warhol cohort Paul Morrissey said, "In the spring of 1968, Solanas approached underground newspaper publisher Paul Krassner for money, saying, 'I want to shoot [Olympia Press publisher] Maurice Girodias.' He gave her $50, enough for a .32 automatic pistol."

* * *

One day Holly unintentionally inflicted a severe emotional wound on me. She simply said—referring to the guy Jeanne was living with—"I have two daddies now." A terrible sense of loss went searing through my psyche. Moreover, if I was visiting at *her* apartment, Jeanne would ask me to leave before Holly's other "father" got home.

After I moved to California, whenever Holly and I talked on the phone we would always end with a big "wowee" hug. She would write to me about how she went to Central Park and climbed on the rocks like a monkey, and how she got dressed as a witch on Halloween. She signed all her letters, *Holly Tomolly.*

The first summer that she came to stay with me, when she was seven, one afternoon she said, "Daddy, let's kiss the way they do in the movies and on TV."

"Well, what do you mean?" I asked, trying to hide my discomfort.

"Like this," she answered, putting her arms around me, her little lips directly on mine, moving her head around just like they did in the movies and on TV. Then we both giggled, and that was all there was to it, but somehow I felt grateful that nobody had walked in on us. "Listen," I fantasized, "this was *her* idea. *She* was the aggressive one . . ."

When she was eight, a man exposed himself to Holly. The police asked her to describe him. She said that he was cross-eyed. The cops wanted to know if she remembered anything else about him.

"It was big and hairy," she said.

By the time she was nine, Holly was a true anarchist. She wouldn't even accept the rules of *games*. She challenged Stewart Brand to play a game of checkers with each of their checkers half red and half black. She also insisted on playing tic-tac-toe blindfolded. But her supreme moment came when she wanted to play hide-and-go-seek while riding in a taxicab.

She would also ask me great questions, like, "Is laziness a form of hypochondria?"

When Holly was ten, on one of my visits to New York I took her and Jeanne out for dinner.

"Mommy told me all about sex," Holly announced in the restaurant.

"Oh, really? What did you learn?"

"Oh, she told me about orgasms and blow jobs."

I blushed. They laughed.

*   *   *

In 1975, when Holly was eleven, she decided to come stay with me in San Francisco for a whole year. This was a courageous move for her—new city, new school, new friends. Her best new friend was Pia Hinckle—whose father, Warren, was now editing *City* magazine, published by Francis Ford Coppola. It was the film director's brief foray into print journalism. The girls used the *City* color photocopying machine to reproduce dollar bills.

Holly and Pia enjoyed playing tricks. Once they rolled a marijuana joint for me, filled with herbal tea. Actually, I had a healthy stash of pot in my desk drawer, but mice kept getting inside and eating right through the baggie in order to get their cannabis fix. I would find mouse turds in the drawer each day. We had no mousetrap, but Holly had an idea.

"Doesn't the mouse get the munchies after eating the marijuana?"

So we left on the floor a large paper bag containing a piece of cheese and a lollipop. Sure enough, in the evening we would hear the mouse rustling inside the paper bag, and I'd capture it by closing the top before it could get out. Then we would bring the bag with the stoned mouse out to an empty lot across the street and let it go free, only to be caught sooner or later by a stray cat who in turn would get zonked out from having eaten a stoned mouse. Although we had literally invented a better mousetrap—a nonviolent one—the world wasn't exactly beating a path to our door.

I had been performing occasionally, and naturally that experience turned into a bit onstage. I would weave an imaginary story about how I had found myself getting especially stoned on this stash but couldn't figure out what made it so powerful, so I sent a sample to Pharm-Chem, a sort of People's FDA, and they said that a preliminary test showed there was an additive in my marijuana.

They could ascertain only that it was organic, but further testing indicated that it was mouse turds, so I began to entice the mice by leaving marijuana out and capturing them with the old lollipop-in-the-bag ploy. I would collect their turds till I had enough to roll a dynamite joint. I had discovered a new and cheap way of getting high—smoking mouse turds.

I decided to present a comedic equivalent to Tony Orlando and Dawn. What stand-up comic had ever featured backup singers before? I held an informal rehearsal with Holly and Pia for the debut of Paul Krassner and Dusk. They choreographed their own dance steps to perform behind me, singing the appropriate *doo-ah doo-ahs*, while I proceeded to tell the tale of my discovery of a new way to get high at no expense except for a lollipop and rolling papers, culminating with a spectacular musical chant by Dusk—"Mouse turds! Mouse turds! Mouse turds!"—as they rhythmically flailed their arms in the air.

At another show, a local *Rolling Stone* "No Talent Contest," I decided to play my musical saw for the first time publicly. As I was putting resin on the bow, I confessed to the audience, "This is slightly humiliating for a child prodigy violinist, but . . ." And then I surrendered to an impulse, just as I had done at Carnegie Hall. Instead of playing "Indian Love Call" as I had practiced, I simply sawed my bow in half.

Holly berated me for wasting money like that, and I promised never to do it again.

* * *

Our apartment was halfway up a long, steep hill, and in the back was what Holly called "our magic garden." States Street was just off the intersection of Castro and Market—the heart of the gay ghetto—and there was a Chinese laundry at the foot of the hill called the Gay Launderette which, even though it had changed owners several times, always kept that name for goodwill.

There was a clothing store named Does Your Mother Know? And a bulletin board announcing an "Anal Awareness and Relaxation Workshop." And jokes that gays told about themselves, like, "Why do the Castro clones all have mustaches?" The answer: "To hide the stretch marks."

Warren Hinckle introduced me to Harvey Milk at his camera shop, and I watched him develop into the gay equivalent of Martin Luther King. Had he lived, he might have been elected the first openly gay mayor.

Holly took classes in computer math and trampoline, chemistry and gymnastics, played clarinet in the orchestra, took pantomime lessons, and on Saturdays she fed the animals at the Junior Museum across the street from our home. Once an iguana bit her on the hand, and I worried that Jeanne would think I wasn't taking proper care of her.

Holly and I enjoyed walking around and exploring the charms of San Francisco. She would read aloud the signs in store windows: "Yes, we're open." "Sorry, we're closed." But she would cover her eyes to avoid memorizing the phone number on the side of a delivery truck—something I had done as a kid myself, although she was imitating her mother.

Another time we crossed a street, and she made the same philosophical observation that sages across the ages have made. "No matter where I go, I'm always there." If I would spit in the gutter, she would not only imitate me, she would spit backward over her shoulder. We would walk along harmonizing the Grateful Dead song "Ripple"—not the lyrics, just "wa, wa, wa, wa . . ."

Holly was thinking about getting a kitten, but she didn't want to have it spayed. "If you had Mommy spayed," she explained, "I wouldn't even be here today." When I was Holly's age, I still didn't even know where babies came from. But she had learned about the basic facts of human reproduction when she was three, and now here we were, discussing the implications of abortion.

Holly was a very physical girl. She loved to have her back scratched, and we would always hold hands when we walked. Of course, men in the gay ghetto felt free to be equally affectionate.

She asked, "How come it feels strange to see two men holding hands?"

"I guess because they don't do it in *your* neighborhood."

"That's true," she said.

I added, "When I first moved to San Francisco, it seemed strange to me, and then I just got used to it."

And she said, "I guess I will too."

Eventually, Holly and Pia planned to visit a Glory Hole. These were establishments where a man would stick his dick through a hole in the wall, and an unseen man on the other side would suck him off. The girls thought of disguising themselves as boys, with rolled-up socks in their crotches.

* * *

On my wall there was *San Francisco Chronicle* reporter Paul Avery's photo of a Vietnamese child and his mother, both severely burned by napalm, just staring out at you with a look of disbelief and horror.

Holly said, "Daddy, can I ask, how come you keep that picture there?"

"Well, because whenever I have a problem, I try to explain it to that little kid and he gives me perspective."

"What's perspective?"

"It means, by comparing my problem with his, I just can't feel sorry for myself."

Holly observed my eccentricities, which, in my hermit-like lifestyle, I had come to take for granted. For example, I didn't have any liquid dish soap. She found it very odd that I would wash dishes using only hot water and my fingernails. She also noticed that I didn't have a vacuum cleaner. She wasn't completely satisfied with my explanation that I would just wait for enough dust to gather so that I could sort of wrap it around my hand and roll it away like tumbleweed. And yet I would request that she throw her banana peel into the kitchen garbage can instead of my office wastebasket.

Naturally, there were certain eccentricities that even Holly wasn't aware of. Occasionally I would pick up the phone and say "I love you" to the dial tone. And often I would be a model of efficiency by simultaneously using one hand to brush my teeth and other hand to urinate. But I would always put the toilet seat back down out of respect for Holly. It was a simple exercise in consciousness.

I had my limits, though. Holly was a skateboard enthusiast to the point of evangelism. She loved skateboarding down the hill, and even though she showed me how she could stop before she came to the corner, I couldn't stop myself from worrying. She urged me to try her skateboard.

"No, thanks. I'm too old to start scraping my knees."

"Oh, come on, Daddy, if you wanna have fun, you gotta get bruised."

For fun, Holly and Pia skipped down the street, arm in arm, singing, "We're off to see the Wizard, the wonderful Wizard of Oz . . . ." For fun, they got dressed up as prostitutes on Halloween and went from door to door, saying, "Trick or treat?" For fun, they pretended that Holly was having her period by leaving ketchup-stained tissues floating in our toilet.

One afternoon they were going to see the film *Carrie*—in which Sissy Spacek is confused by her first menstrual flow. Holly had read the book and was curious to see how it got translated to the screen.

As she was leaving to meet Pia, I said, "Hey, Holly, wouldn't it be funny if you had your first period right in the middle of the movie?"

"Very funny, Dad." And she went on downstairs. Then she came back up the stairs, smiling. "You're right, it *would* be funny."

One day I decided to make a chef's salad for dinner. At the Safeway supermarket I bought lettuce, tomatoes, cheese, and dressing, but, perhaps because I was becoming a vegetarian, I somehow felt justified in shoplifting the ham—a slight perversion of situational ethics. But I stuck the package into my back pocket carelessly enough for a security guard to notice. He followed me out of the store and brought me back in. He took me upstairs where I could watch *other* shoplifters through a one-way mirror.

The manager ordered me, "Open your sweater." I was wearing a bulky wool sweater, which looked suspicious under the circumstances, but when I opened it, there were no other stolen goods. I didn't fit the usual profile. He held out the package of ham and asked, "Do you have the money to pay for this?" I nodded my head yes.

"Okay," he said, "I'm gonna let you go this time, but listen, you ever steal anything here again, we'll bust you."

The security guard led me downstairs and said, "You can wait on that line—it's for nine items or less." We both smiled. It was a moment of intimacy. Herb Caen heard about this incident at a party for *City* magazine and mentioned it in his *Chronicle* column.

I had been assigned to write an article about Ken Kesey for *City* magazine, but even after it was published, they still didn't pay me. I was concerned about the dwindling supply of food money for Holly and me. She noticed my habit of constantly counting the money in my pocket. I even had to sell my collection of original *Mad* comics to pay the rent one month.

So, while Holly was languishing in my waterbed wearing her curlers, I put on my boots, took a dime to call a lawyer, and walked diagonally across town to the *City* office in North Beach, psyching myself up all the way there. I was planning to take the receptionist's typewriter and throw it through their front window if they didn't pay me the money they owed me within half an hour.

Although I knew where Francis Coppola ate lunch, and could have gone to that restaurant and embarrassed him—"Oh, Godfather, please help me"—this wasn't really his fault. It would be more proper to confront directly those staffers who had ignored my letters and phone calls. My threat was taken seriously, and I received my check in twenty minutes—but more out of public relations than justice. They knew that if they had me arrested, it would get into Herb Caen's column. Coppola accused me of "betraying" him, but Warren Hinckle told me that I had done the right thing.

* * *

Our favorite neighborhood restaurant (founded by Dennis Peron, later coauthor of the medical marijuana referendum, Prop. 215) was named Island, after Aldous Huxley's utopian novel. Holly would sit there quietly reading *Lolita*, Vladimir Nabokov's novel about a pedophile, and if I felt at all embarrassed, well, that was *my* problem.

We often went to the movies together. Her favorite was *Paper Moon*, with Ryan O'Neal and his daughter, Tatum, playing a father-and-daughter con-artist team. Holly would end up seeing that movie nine times. She relished the scene where they're sitting in a restaurant, and Tatum tells her father very loudly, "I want my $200! I want my $200!" So it didn't come as a *total* surprise when Holly and I were sitting in a restaurant and she started shouting, "I want my $200! I want my $200!"

Holly resembled Tatum O'Neal. Her friend Diane—daughter of conspiracy researcher Mae Brussell—resembled Linda Blair, who played the young girl possessed by Satan in *The Exorcist*. So there they were, Holly and Diane, sitting poolside in Carmel and pretending to be a pair of young actresses, graciously signing their autographs—*Tatum O'Neal* and *Linda Blair*. Diane was chewing bubble gum, wearing platform shoes, and talking about Neil Diamond.

"He's good, sure," she said, "after they've knocked off thirty *other* singers."

While Holly was at school, I covered the Patty Hearst trial for the *Berkeley Barb*. She had been kidnapped by the Symbionese Liberation Army, led by Cinque (Donald DeFreeze). Patty was kept in a closet, then she joined the SLA, changed her name to Tania, adopted radical rhetoric, and robbed a bank with them.

Now, the philosophical question which had plagued the history of human consciousness—*Is there is, or is there ain't, free will?*—was finally gong to be decided by a jury. While they were deliberating, I took Holly to the empty courtroom, and she sat in Patty's chair. Mae Brussell called, worrying that *our* daughters might be kidnapped. I passed her warning on to Holly and offered to accompany her to school.

"Oh, Daddy," she said, "that's not necessary. Mae's just paranoid."

Holly then bought a gift for me—a plastic clothespin-like paper holder labeled *Threats*.

On one hand, there was Mae Brussell, busily documenting the rise of fascism in America. On the other hand, there was Holly, standing on Pia Hinckle's front porch, yelling, "Hitler! Hitler!" That was the name of Pia's cat, so named because of a square black patch under its nose, just like the mustache on Adolf Hitler's face.

I asked Holly, "Do you know who Hitler *was*?"

"Didn't he lead the Jews out of Germany?"

"Well, not exactly . . ."

* * *

I had become involved with Bread and Roses, an organization founded by folksinger Mimi Farina to provide free entertainment at institutions ranging from juvenile centers to retirement homes. I was scheduled to perform at a drug rehabilitation center in Marin County, and Holly came with me.

I had been developing a routine about the Deaf Mute Liberation Front, which began as a takeoff on the fact that, until Henry Kissinger's image as a harmless philanderer had been established, President Nixon's chief of staff, H. R. Haldeman, would not allow the audio of Kissinger's statements to be broadcast—and the electronic media complied—but it was my contention that lip-reading viewers, who could tell that Kissinger had a German accent, were warning their friends: *Henry Kissinger is a Nazi.*

So now I became a fake ventriloquist, and Holly sat on my lap, playing a hearing-impaired dummy who simultaneously translated into sign language whatever I was supposedly making her say.

"Well, Holly, how are you today?"

"Just fine, thank you. Would you like to hear a riddle?"

"Okay, sure. How does it go?"

"All right—why is Anita Bryant like a Polish lesbian?"

"I give up. Why is Anita Bryant like a Polish lesbian?"

"Because she fucks men"—and now Holly switched from her facsimile of official sign language to that universal gesture, making a circle with the thumb and index finger of one hand while pushing the index finger of her other hand in and out of that circle. We may not have been politically correct, but we were a team.

Holly and I spent Thanksgiving with the Hinckles, and Christmas with the Keseys at their farm in Oregon. The whole Kesey family lived in a huge, sectioned-out barn, with a metal fireplace that hung from the living-room ceiling. Outside, there were cows and peacocks and a dog who dropped stones on your foot because he wanted you to throw a stone so he could fetch it. There was a swarm of bees to provide honey, and there was a beautiful colt, which we tried to catch, but the mother horse kept running along and blocking us like a football player.

Chuck Kesey, Ken's brother, ran a creamery, and he bought over a large supply of homemade ice cream with liquor in it. I ate so much—the coldness and the sweetness covered up the taste of the alcohol—that, without even knowing it, for the first time in my life I got drunk—on ice cream—throwing up and passing out.

"I'm not used to taking legal drugs," I explained.

* * *

In April 1976, on the same day that the pope announced he was not gay, I received a registered letter from the FBI informing me that I was on a "hit list" of the Emiliano Zapata Unit of the New World Liberation Front, but that "no action will be taken, since all of those who could carry it out are in custody." I was more logically a target of the government than the NWLF—unless, of course, they happened to be the same.

Was the right wing of the FBI warning me about the left wing of the FBI? A communique from the NWLF charged that "the pigs led and organized" the Zapata Unit. Jacques Rogiers, aboveground courier for the underground NWLF, told me that the reason I was on the hit list was because I had written that Patty Hearst's kidnapper, Cinque, was a police informer.

"But that's *true*," I said. "It's a matter of record. Doesn't that make any difference?"

Not to him it didn't. "If the NWLF asked me to kill you," he admitted, "I would."

"Jacques," I replied, "I think this puts a slight damper on our relationship."

That's when Holly and I moved to a new apartment on States Street, without telling Jacques. I kept the FBI letter in that plastic *Threats* holder that Holly had given me. She was in Oregon, spending her Easter vacation at the farm with the Kesey family.

At that drug rehabilitation center where we performed our ventriloquist act, I had met a musician, Doreen, who later told me that she was so inspired by our visit that she gave up dope. Now that she was released, she contacted me, we began to date, and she turned me on to snorting heroin. I got high on the irony but sick from the smack, neglecting to feed Holly's goldfish in the process. They died, their bloated bodies floating in the tank, and I had to flush them down the toilet. Perhaps because I knew them as individuals with names, Jaws and Lily (after Lily Tomlin), I never even considered replacing them with substitute goldfish.

When Kesey flew back with Holly, I met them at the airport.

"Listen," I told her, "I have some bad news and some good news. Which do you want to hear first?"

She cringed. "Which is worse?"

"Well, the good news is that I was on a list of people to be killed, but the FBI captured the group who were planning to do it. And the bad news is that I got very sick and neglected to feed Jaws and Lily, and they died. Holly, I'm really sorry."

She started hitting me mock hard with her little purse, a poignant mixture of frustration and affection.

When a drug rehabilitation counselor came to give a guest lecture at her school, he informed the students that they couldn't fool their parents about smoking marijuana, because it was obvious from their dilated pupils, slurry speech, and short-term memory loss. Holly couldn't resist asking, "What about if somebody's *parents* have those symptoms?" The counselor had to admit that this was sometimes a problem.

The students were warned that if they took a quaalude and smoked a joint three days later, they would still feel the effects of the quaalude. Some students took this as a homework assignment. "Day one . . ."

One student wanted to know if Silver Rectangles was good LSD. The counselor was aware of Orange Sunshine and Green Triangle, but he had never heard anything about Silver Rectangles. They were actually tiny electronically treated strips of foil that were intended to set off a metal detector if a library book was being stolen. I extended that premise onstage, recounting how the kid ate a Silver Rectangle, and the security guard made him take off his jacket when he set off the metal detector, then his sweater, then his pants, until he was completely naked, but he still set off the metal detector, so it was sent back to the factory for repairs.

The drug counselor's visit had one other side effect. Holly asked me if I had ever tried heroin, and I finally gave her the details of what happened with Jaws and Lily.

She said, petulantly, "That drug rehab guy *told* us that people would kill for heroin, but he didn't say that it would be my *goldfish!*"

★   ★   ★

In the film *Save the Tiger*, Jack Lemmon plays a middle-aged man who has a brief affair with an assertive teenage hippie. At one point they match role models—one pair of names after another—from their own particular cultural and countercultural backgrounds. Lemmon would name baseball star Cookie Lavagetto and the hippie girl would counter with Baba Ram Dass. But in real life, when I told Holly that Ram Dass was coming to visit us, she had never heard of him. The game was different. Now Ram Dass was *my* Cookie Lavagetto.

Holly had adapted easily to my assortment of friends, listening intently whether it was Super-Joel reminiscing about the Yippies or Margo St. James talking about organizing prostitutes or Ram Dass discussing masturbation as a form of spiritual meditation. Holly thought that for a guru he was a pretty regular guy.

Her year with me was coming to an end.

"When I go back to live with Mommy," she said, "I'm gonna call you more often."

"Oh, yeah?" I teased. "How come?"

"Because I *know* you now."

"Well, who'd you think I was before?

"Fred Astaire."

Intuitively she had understood the symbolism of Fred Astaire as a romantic figure in tuxedo and top hat, dancing across tabletops and ceilings, as opposed to me, this funky Daddy who didn't have a vacuum cleaner, who sawed his violin bow in half, who got caught shoplifting, and who accidentally killed her goldfish.

When Holly left, I started leaving the toilet seat up again.

In the summer of 1977, I got a magazine assignment to cover the trial of Roman Polanski. Holly was now thirteen—the same age as the girl Polanski was accused of seducing (I didn't know yet that it was actually rape)—and Holly had decided to come to Santa Monica with me, sit in the front row of the courtroom, and just stare at Polanski. She also planned to write an article about the trial from *her* point of view. However, Polanski pleaded guilty to a lesser charge, then fled the country on the day he was supposed to be sentenced.

I told Holly, "I'm gonna write about the trial anyway."

"How can you do that?"

"I'll just make it up as if it actually occurred. Roman Polanski's defense will be that the statutory rape laws are unconstitutional because they discriminate against kids."

"How would you feel if the kid was *me*?"

"Well, I'm a liberal father, but . . . you're right. I'm not gonna write the article."

*　*　*

When she was fourteen, Holly went to Mexico to learn Spanish at a school where no English was spoken. The next year, in the summer of 1979, she served as my translator on a three-week expedition to Ecuador, focusing on shamans and healers. She was the only adolescent among a dozen adults, so the experience would have elements of an archetypal rite of passage for her.

After we left Quito, our bus stopped at a marker signifying the exact dividing line between the Northern and Southern hemispheres. I couldn't resist the territorial urge to urinate on both sides of the equator with one bladder splatter merely by adjusting my aim. Later on in our journey there would be a billboard proclaiming a NASA tracking station, and I would urinate on that too. Still another of my Great Moments in Urinating series would occur in an old-fashioned bullfight stadium. It was empty, but as I walked to the center of the arena, I could hear a roar—the wild cheering of an invisible crowd of spectators, anticipating my moment of urinary truth.

There in Ecuador, I had an affair with one of the women on the trek. Holly was observing us very carefully. On July 23, she wrote in her journal:

> Today's my half birthday! I'm exactly 15-½ years old! Oh, yeah, I haven't written anything about the only romance on the trip. Daddy and Dinah! They are sharing a room & Daddy says that if him & Mommy had treated each other as good as he & Dinah are treating each other they'd still be together. I know that's bullshit but it's a sweet thing to say and it's nice to know things are working so well for them.
>
> Daddy seems like a kid again, holding hands in the taxi & when they're eating, little kisses on the cheek, and he's so happy. Dinah is 29, really pretty & intelligent. Daddy says she reminds him of Mommy. She lives with her boyfriend. They really make each other laugh. I'm so happy for Daddy! For my "birthday" they gave me a rhinoceros beetles shell that they found . . .

Because Dinah and I both knew—and agreed in advance—that we would go our separate ways when the expedition ended, our affair had that much more intensity.

For the final week, our group lived deep in the jungle. Our home had belonged to a shaman who died a few months previously. The structure sat on stilts and had a sturdy thatched roof, but no side walls. A raised deck was the kitchen area. There was no toilet, except for a cluster of bushes, and the Cayapa River was for washing and—if you boiled the water for fifteen minutes—drinking.

Every day, three generations of the shaman's family arrived early in the morning. These indigenous Cayapa Indians would sit serenely, as though posing for an official portrait. The women were bare-breasted. One was playing with the penis of her small child. Adults were required to live together for six months before they were permitted to marry. At their wedding ceremony, a couple would be given ten lashes each as a sample of the 150 lashes either would receive for marital infidelity.

We were like a bunch of Martians who had suddenly dropped in on their primitive culture. We were *their* live TV show. They were fascinated by one of us practicing Tai Chi. They listened to another singing "there's a riot going on in cell block number nine." They watched a psychiatrist taking notes on their curiosity. They had become the observers, and we had become their subjects.

As a Zen Bastard exercise, I once trained myself to laugh when I stubbed a toe. It had become second nature. I had been searching for an example of how humor could transcend language, and when I stubbed my toe and laughed out loud automatically, our hosts shared the universality of such an incongruous reaction to pain.

* * *

Shamanism goes back fifty thousand years. The *curandero* (healer) communicates with those unseen evil spirits responsible for illness. But it's also a family business. Built into the overhead costs of our trip was the transfer of enough *sucres* to insure the privilege of participating in their healing ceremonies.

The Christian influence was evident in the name of one shaman—Jesusito. He wore a long silk shirt with short sleeves. In front of him was a shrine of hand-carved wooden figures—a soldier, a *Mama Grande* (female figure) with white beads, a policeman, a bishop, Otahulpa (the last Inca king)—bronze eagle-head staffs, polished stones, a prehistoric clay cast of an ox head, money, and a pair of holy objects: a gray, clamshell-like item that opened up to reveal a head of the Virgin Mary that could be lifted out in case you wanted to make Jello in the mold; and the most sacred of all, a sealed-beam headlight from an old Buick which was transformed into a kind of crystal ball. There were forty thousand Cayapa Indians, but none had ever seen a car.

Our journey would climax with a group ingestion of ayahuasca, a hallucinogenic vine similar to yagé, used by shamans throughout the Amazon basin to have visions and communicate with jungle spirits during their healing ceremonies. Holly had hoped to participate. Wanting to be a responsible parent, I gave her some literature to read, including an article by Andrew Weil, author of *The Natural Mind.*

"Vomiting is the first stage of the effect of yagé," he wrote. "It is not fun, and I say that as someone who likes to vomit in certain circumstances."

He suggested fasting after breakfast, but our group ate lunch anyway, rationalizing that as long as we were all going to vomit that night, we might as well put something into our stomachs now to throw up later.

Ayahuasca means "soul vine." It is innocent-looking enough, an inch or two thick, curving into and beyond a complete circle. Who can imagine how its psychedelic use was originally discovered? First it is chopped vertically, then horizontally, and then boiled. In *Wizard of the Upper Amazon,* Bruce Lamb wrote:

> Drinking a carelessly prepared extract would only cause violent vomiting, acute intestinal cramps and diarrhea, [an old Peruvian healer] said, and he went on to tell me that *ayahuasca* must be handled with care and reverence, simmered slowly in a special earthenware pot over a low fire under constant, proper attention.

However, ours was being boiled in an aluminum pot by a young Canelos Indian couple in the midst of a lovers' quarrel. But we couldn't very well tell them that they were preparing it the wrong way. A leaf, datura (similar to belladonna), was added to the potion, an unappetizing, rusty colored, muddy liquid which tastes so putrid that a bottle of rum must be held in your other hand for an instant chaser.

Inevitably, the sounds of our violent retching would echo through the jungle. One by one we would go outside and vomit as though we were wet towels being wrung out by invisible demons. When Holly's insides declared that it was her turn to throw up, I accompanied her outside. It was a mini-volcanic retching that temporarily took over her body. I thought, *I hope I'm doing the right thing.*

When Holly finished, I began. The power of peristalsis possessed me so thoroughly that I vomited and farted simultaneously. Holly's tears turned to laughter at my involuntary duet, which in turn made me laugh. There I was in the middle of the jungle with my daughter—vomiting, farting, and laughing.

"I think this is known as quality time," I managed to say.

As we were walking back to the shack with our arms around each other and feeling weak, Holly said, "It's nice to be near someone you love when you're in misery."

Under the influence of ayahuasca, the local people traditionally have visions of jaguars and anacondas (water snakes). But instead our group saw elephants and mice, spider webs of memory, and a woman wearing an 1890's gown and a large hat, eating a loaf of French bread. The corrugated metal ceiling was moving like ocean waves for me. During the healing ceremony, two shamans kept sucking the poisons out of a patient's head, and then, although the shamans didn't actually vomit, they did make these awful *sounds* of regurgitation to get rid of those poisons.

All through the night, we were forced to divert our psychic energy away from exquisite visionary flights simply in order not to throw up again. The shamans were laughing at us whenever anyone succumbed to vomiting. A flash of paranoia convinced me for a moment that there was some kind of sorcerer's trick being played on us.

Before we left, one of the shamans asked our medical doctor for Lomotil, to be used for diarrhea, and the cultural exchange was completed. Our return hike through the rainforest was accompanied by a tremendous rainstorm. While getting thoroughly soaked, Holly and I harmonized "Singin' in the Rain" over and over and over as loud as we could.

* * *

After I had moved back to San Francisco from my *Hustler* stint, Holly remained in Los Angeles with Jeanne, so our visits to each other were much more frequent than when they were living in New York. They both came to a show I did in L.A., and just before I went onstage to perform, Jeanne said, "Paul, I have to tell you something. Holly's not yours." It was Jeanne's way of saying, "Break a leg."

Holly was attending Fairfax High School and working at a Baskin-Robbins ice cream parlor just off Sunset Boulevard. She had come to know her hooker customers by their favorite flavors, and pointed them out to me as we walked along. "That's Rocky Road. That's Pralines 'n' Cream. That's Strawberry Shortcake." Holly was taking on an almost scary sophistication. In a book report for her English composition class, she wrote:

> The most important and interesting news that I found from reading *The Victims* were the statistics. They show that nine out of ten rape victims are emotionally unable to have sexual relations with men for at least one year after the assault. The time between the assault and when the women may want to participate in sexual activities is known as the *Seul* period, meaning 'alone' in French. The length of time of the *Seul* period may vary, the time depending on the intensity of the attack and the previous mental stability of the victim.

But, not only was there no such book as *The Victims*, Holly had also invented the *Seul* period. I was really quite proud of her.

One evening, when she was sixteen, Holly called me. "Hold on a second," she said, then held her telephone to the speaker of her stereo. And I heard Carly Simon singing, "Daddy, I'm no virgin, and I've already waited too long . . ." Then Holly hung up quickly.

I began to laugh and cry simultaneously. I was laughing at the creative way she had chosen to tell me this news—my generation had avoided communicating with parents about sex altogether—and I was crying because I never got any when *I* was sixteen. The sexual revolution had still been just a horny dream back then. Now I was delighted to see its legacy in action, but I also felt a certain vestigial resentment. "Why, these young kids today, they just don't appreciate the joy of *yearning*." I had to be careful not to let the memory of my own blue balls turn into sour grapes.

When Holly visited me that Thanksgiving, I teased her, "Did you bring your diaphragm?"

"Oh, Daddy, even if I fall in love with someone, it doesn't mean we have to go to bed right away."

She had found her own place on the spectrum between abstinence and promiscuity. Still, she got in trouble for having a hickey on her neck during a gymnastics competition. When Holly graduated high school, she was designated "Class Flirt" in the yearbook, exactly the same title Jeanne had earned when *she* graduated high school. It gave one a sense of continuity.

★ ★ ★

Scoop Nisker managed to maintain his balance between current events and the infinite void. He was now the news director of KSAN, and his slogan was "If you don't like the news, go out and make some of your own." He was also a practicing Buddhist, and his slogan was, "Stay high, but keep your priorities straight." Together, we've led humor workshops at Esalen and other New Age resorts.

In 1981 Scoop persuaded me to attend a ten-day meditation retreat where I would have to do without any of my usual media distractions. I was afraid at first, and decided to go only in order to *confront* my fear. But then Holly called. She was now seventeen. She wanted to go to college in San Francisco and live with me again. So—keeping my priorities straight—I immediately canceled out of the Buddhist retreat. That whole experience would only have been polluted by my irresponsibility in not being home to help Holly with her re-entry.

I liked the way she challenged me. Once I was smoking a joint very early in the day, and she said, "Dad, how come you have to escape reality the first thing in the morning?" When I was a kid, my parents would refer to "a colored guy" and I would tell them that "Negro" was correct. Now, when I would refer to somebody as "Oriental," Holly would tell *me* that "Asian" was correct.

She didn't like small talk. "Oh, Dad, that's trivial bullshit," she would say. The vestigial old-fashioned parent in me wanted to chastise her, "Hey, you can't talk to me that way, I'm your *father*." But the contemporary New Age parent in me knew that Holly had made an accurate observation. What I had said *was* trivial bullshit. I took a deep breath.

"I'll tell you something, Holly. I'm glad you feel free enough to tell me that what I'm saying is trivial bullshit, but I hope *you're* glad that *I'm* free enough to *recognize* my own trivial bullshit when it's pointed out."

Nobody I knew had ever said "trivial bullshit" to *their* parents. Certainly I never said it to mine, even though they specialized in trivial bullshit. I had learned to pretend that my parents were a Buddhist monk and nun whose sole purpose on earth was to test my patience with trivia. So, when they showed me how many electric outlets were in the kitchen, I eagerly *examined* them. "Oh, look, here's a three-pronger!" That way there was no friction between us. They felt good, I felt good, and what a commendable goal that was.

When my mother opened up the bread of a sandwich—*while* I was eating it—and put more food inside, I could only smile with gratitude for this whole new form of generosity to contemplate. And when my father gave me his old parka—literally *showing* me how to put the hood on—I didn't remind him that I was no longer five years old or accuse him of freezing in his parental role. I just said, "Let me practice that a few times."

Conversely, Holly gave me a pair of red cotton long johns for Christmas, and she *didn't* show me how to put them on. I wore them for the first time when I was performing on a cold night in Sebastopol, and at one point in my monologue, I decided to show them to the audience. But when I turned my back and pulled my jeans down, the long johns stuck to the jeans, and I found myself accidentally displaying my bare buttocks, in a spotlight, to a large group of assembled strangers.

This was a very dreamlike moment, but I couldn't very well flap my arms like wings as a reality check—not without resembling a human bellows. I was merely a victim of static cling. I had heard that phrase in fabric-softener commercials, but I had never actually *experienced* it.

Recovering my composure, I told the audience, "You see, actually, I came here to join the Moonies, and this is my initiation." After that, I began to moon audiences deliberately, but only once in each city, because I didn't want it to become a comedy gimmick. When I mooned the audience at the Roxie Theater in San Francisco, Holly reminded her friends in a loud stage whisper, "That's my Dad."

* * *

"Fashion is fascism," Abbie Hoffman once declared.

The political side of me had accepted that slogan as a truism. But Holly was interested in fashion—she had a definite flair for it—and her sense of justice was the antithesis of fascism.

She might glance at *Vogue* magazine, but individuality was the key to her wardrobe. She had bleached her blonde hair platinum, and when the roots grew in, she maintained a two-tone hairstyle. Later on, she dyed her hair pitch black and kept it in a style that completely covered one of her eyes. She wore a leather jacket with chains hanging from it, and plenty of makeup, including a multicolored lightning streak on one cheek. She wanted to get a kitten, which she planned to name Bonzo and dye pink.

Once I was visited by a stereotypical longhaired friend. He was sitting on the floor in the lotus position when Holly came home. They looked at each other. "Punk," he said. "Hippie," she responded.

Although Holly was going out to clubs and dancing away the nights, we still managed to play a haphazard version of the domestic game. We had taken to piling up the paper bags from shopping on the kitchen table—neither of us would bother to flatten them out and put them away—but one time Ken Kesey came over and just crumpled all the bags up into one big bag which he tossed out the back window into our magic garden.

Kesey teased Holly and said she looked like a neo–Hell's Angel, but she got *truly* hassled from all sides. On one occasion a woman wouldn't let her in the subway door, calling Holly a "punk bitch!" Another time we were walking along and a *real* punk with green and purple hair called out to us from her window. "Hey, will ya tell that girl stripes are out!" I had come to understand how easily rhetoric could take the place of reason.

Abbie was wrong. Fashion is *not* fascism. Dress codes are.

★ ★ ★

One afternoon, Holly and I were waiting at a bus stop, on our way to a movie, and there was a luscious teenage girl also waiting for the bus.

"Ooh, yummy," I whispered.

"Daddy, she's *my* age!"

Her words echoed around in my cranial cavity. Lust for teenagers permeates the culture. Over the years, I had slept with four seventeen-year-olds, but now I found myself caught between a line of dialogue in *Stripes*, where Bill Murray mentions getting "wildly fucked by teenage girls," and a line of dialogue in *Tempest*, where John Cassavetes says, "If you touch my daughter, I'll kill you."

When Holly got involved with a new boyfriend, they cooked spaghetti in our kitchen, and they threw a few strands up at the ceiling, where they stuck, thereby passing the gourmet chef test. She spent a lot of time at his place, and my moment of truth arrived, not in a bullfight ring, but in the form of a question from Holly. She wanted to know if her boyfriend could spend the night at our house. I pretended to be nonchalant. I prided myself on being a permissive parent. Holly and I had agreed that I wouldn't tell her what to do unless it involved health, safety, or the rights of others. And now she was calling my bluff.

"Okay, sure," I said, "but tell him that he can't smoke cigarettes in the house."

At least I felt justified in exerting *some* parental authority. When I was Holly's age, I used to lie in bed wondering if my parents did *it*. Now I lie in bed knowing that my daughter *was* doing it. She was no longer my little girl saying, "Daddy, would you scratch my back?" She was no longer that innocent youngster standing on a porch and calling out for a cat, "Hitler! Hitler!"

Since then, she had read *The Diary of Anne Frank* and seen *Holocaust* on TV. Now she was going to audition for a New Wave band called The

Vktms. One of their song lyrics went, "Hey, you know I ain't no martyr, but I ain't no Nazi." She also wanted to change her stage name to Holly Hard-On, but she had the flu that week, so her audition and name-change became moot. Ah, yes, but she would've been following in my footsteps. Introducing Rumpleforeskin and his daughter Holly Hard-On.

How proud could a father get?

And, whenever I found myself looking lustfully at a teenager, I would automatically hear Holly's voice saying, "Daddy, she's *my* age!"

* * *

I continued to perform occasionally. When I was booked in Minneapolis, I spent the afternoon hanging around the indoor mall, soaking up atmosphere, and gathering last-minute material. The men's room in the mall had a long one-way mirror in front of the urinals, so that while I stood there peeing, I could watch people walking casually by. It was surrealistic to be shaking out those last few drops of urine while a woman who couldn't see me appeared to be looking right at me as she applied her lipstick.

When I returned to my motel, there was a message that Holly had phoned. I called her back. She was about to be taken to the hospital by a neighbor. She had been bitten by a spider and her arm was painfully swollen. I called again later, right before my show, and she was crying because a doctor had told her that if the infection reached the bone her arm could be paralyzed. Somehow I went onstage and did a surprisingly good show, perhaps because I had to concentrate so hard in order to keep my emotions on hold.

The next morning, in my motel room, I got a call from Jeanne. "I've raised that girl for seventeen years, and now *you're* killing her." I could see my jaw drop in the mirror. I was absolutely speechless. "Paul"—I heard Jeanne's voice say—"you're not laughing." She had zeroed in on the core of my vulnerability, but the relief that she was only joking was worth the tension of that brief moment when I thought she was serious.

There was a line I sometimes used onstage: "Pope John Paul has issued a *pronunciamento* that, under extreme circumstances, a one-night stand may be considered a form of monogamy." And that's exactly what happened when I performed in another city—instant intimacy. Now, a few months after one such encounter with a young woman named Bernadette, I got a call from her. She was planning to visit San Francisco and wanted to stay with me. She confessed to having fantasies of being spanked by me.

When I was a kid, my father bought a cat-o'-nine-tails—a stick with nine little leather whips—which he used to punish my brother, my sister, and me. I was lucky enough to understand on some gut level that he was a victim of his own conditioning. When he finally realized that he couldn't break us, he broke the cat-o'-nine-tails and threw it away.

After Holly was born, I began researching child abuse for *The Realist*, and learned that those parents who abused their offspring had consistently been abused by *their* parents, so that the practice was passed on from one generation to another, as if it were in the genes rather than imitative behavior. But I never had the slightest doubt that I would break that pattern.

When I was a guest on *The Mike Douglas Show*, I mentioned that I didn't spank my daughter, and the matronly audience started *booing* me. During a commercial break, another guest, Minnie Pearl of *Grand Ole Opry* fame, said to me, "I'm a'scared of nonconformity." I was surprised.

"Are you kidding?" I said. "You're wearing a bonnet with the price tag still hanging from it."

So now here was Bernadette on the phone saying, "I've been having fantasies of being spanked by you. Would you do it?"

"But," I protested, "I'm nonviolent."

"So am I," she said.

I asked, "Were you spanked as a child? I have this theory that when kids get spanked, but then the parent feels guilty and hugs them, the kids begin to associate pain with warmth."

"I wasn't spanked as a child," she said.

"Well, there goes that theory." Women were now asserting themselves and saying out loud what pleased them sexually. And men were expected to *do* those things which women were now free to tell them they wanted. "All right," I said, "when you visit, I promise I'll spank you. But when you say stop, I promise I'll stop."

"No, no—don't say that. It's the *vulnerability* that turns me on."

"Yeah, but it's *fake* vulnerability, because you trust me. I mean, you didn't call Melvin the Mauler."

She never did visit, but I fantasized about it. I imagined that in my room I would be spanking a twenty-seven-year-old woman, while in another room slept my seventeen-year-old daughter, who I had gotten booed by the audience on *The Mike Douglas Show* for *not* spanking.

* * *

Economic security had always been very important in my family. My father moonlighted as a short-order cook, and he used to put three piles of change from his tips on the floor, for my brother, my sister, and me. When my parents came back from a vacation in Las Vegas, my father gave each of us a silver dollar, with the admonition, "You are never to spend this. It's a reminder that you can always come to your mother and me if you ever need money." So now I passed on *my* silver dollar to Holly, with that same admonition, thereby carrying on my father's tradition.

The year 1982 became a turning point for both Holly and me. She was celebrating her eighteenth birthday, and I was mourning my fiftieth. On January 23, I presented her with one of those novelty newspaper front pages bearing the headline "Holly Krassner Becomes Legal!"

On April 9, she presented me with a foot massager, a gift certificate for ice cream, and several pads so I could write down all her telephone messages. I had been somewhat melancholy as I approached the half-century mark, brooding over projects that had remained long undone and regretting relationships that had never been properly nurtured. I was rationalizing my current spate of celibacy when Holly gave me some advice.

"Dad, have fun while you're young. Not having fun is what makes you older."

So I started going out again. One afternoon Holly came home with her new boyfriend, only to find me in bed with my new girlfriend, who felt slightly awkward.

"It's all right," Holly reassured her. "I'm a liberal daughter."

"I'm glad you guys are here," I said. "My cock is about to fall off."

"*I'm* glad we're here," Holly's boyfriend replied. "*My* cock is about to fall off."

We all laughed heartily, but I felt some kind of archetypal discomfort at this reference to his sexual prowess with my daughter, as though some unspoken primordial taboo had just been shattered. But I was the one who had triggered it.

* * *

Holly began to remind me more and more of her mother. The way she walked, the way she said certain words—like "*wonderful*"—the way she prepared food, biting the ends off string beans, then spitting them into the sink. She could even fit twenty-four checkers into her mouth.

One day I noticed that the wedding photo of Jeanne and me was missing from the wall behind Holly's bed. At first I thought it might be a symbolic gesture of adolescent independence, but she explained that a friend had brought over some cocaine, and they used the glass on the frame to chop it up with a razor blade. "But you can't write about that," she quickly added.

We had an agreement that Holly could approve anything I wrote about her, because, after all, you can't tell your own daughter, "Nyah, nyah, you forgot to say that was off the record."

"Too bad," I said. "It would show how you don't have any false senti-mentality, and that we communicate with such honesty."

"I just don't want people to think I'm a dope-head."

"What difference does it make what other people think? You know, there was a time when John Lennon and Yoko Ono were getting a lot of bad publicity, and they were really upset about it, so I gave them this little strip of paper from a Chinese fortune cookie that I'd been carrying around. It said, *If you are standing straight, it doesn't matter if your shadow is crooked.* But look, of course I'll respect our agreement."

However, Holly had a heavy date that evening, and she couldn't find her car keys. She was starting to panic.

"Dad," she said, "if you can find my car keys, you can tell the coke story, okay?"

I found her car keys, but I told her she didn't have to keep her part of the bargain. She insisted on keeping it, though.

Holly was nineteen when she decided to leave San Francisco and go to school in London. I finally removed the spaghetti from my kitchen ceiling. It had been sticking up there for two years. And Ken Kesey came over and removed from the wall my photo of the napalmed child and his mother. It had remained there for twelve years.

Before Holly left, I did another show at the Roxie Theater. She checked the sound system, made sure there was a stool and that I had a glass of orange juice. "Dad," she said, just as I was about to go onstage, "I have to tell you something. I'm not yours."

* * *

I was going through some sort of midlife crisis. I missed Holly, I missed publishing *The Realist*, I missed having a girlfriend. Then I met Rachel Hickerson. She was a writer who used the pseudonym Pheno Barbidol. We were both scheduled to be in New York at the same time, and arranged to spend a few days together.

When I returned to San Francisco, I called and asked her to marry me, and she said yes. Radio personality Alex Bennett agreed to perform the wedding ceremony on his morning radio show, and Herb Caen announced it in his column. This all sounded like great fun in the media, but in reality it was a terrible romantic illusion. We hardly knew each other. I kept asking myself, *What have I done?* I had apparently lost my sense of cause and effect. Rachel stayed at my apartment for six schizo-phrenic weeks, with me serving as both the cause of her pain and the source of her comfort.

I might just as well have abducted Rachel. She was a culmination of the way my relationships with women had become an extension of my relationship with pornography. Each new magazine—and each new woman—was like an investment, and of course I wanted a return on that investment. Then I would discard a woman as easily as a porn magazine.

I had lived alone for the eighteen years since my marriage ended, always holding back commitment from every new girlfriend as though intimacy would still be a betrayal of Jeanne. Now I was determined to break that pattern.

Right after Christmas 1983, I was booked as the opening act for Professor Irwin Corey, the elderly "world's foremost authority," in a four-day run at the Julia Morgan Theater in Berkeley. Backstage, Corey and I smoked a joint, and he told me how he used to read Nazi hate literature to get him in the mood to perform. Rachel came to the theater with me a couple of times, but not on closing night, when I met Orli Peter, a graduate student in psychology.

Although we only talked briefly, there was an electric spark between us. We were supposed to get together, but Rachel was still living at my apartment, and I kept postponing my first date with Orli. Finally, on the day before Rachel was gong to leave, Orli called (actually, it was her sister, pretending to be Orli), insisting we meet either that evening or the next. Naturally I chose the next evening. Rachel left at 4 PM the next day, and Orli arrived at eight o'clock. I was amazed at my own resilience.

Orli and I ended up living together. Our relationship was confrontational but fun. There was an age difference—I was fifty-two and she was twenty-eight—which was not really a problem, but she wanted to have children someday, and I was extremely ambivalent about starting a new family at this stage in my life. Jeanne gave me her blessing.

"Good luck," she said, "you'll just be an old fart with a young kid."

In 1985 I sent a letter to Holly in London, and this was her response:

Dear Dad,

I received your "father-to-daughter-turning-21" birthday letter. Thank you, it made me laugh & cry. Only moments before the mailman slipped the letter through the door I was telling my friend what wonderful parents I had & how much I missed them—what timing. I think it's wonderful that you & Orli have been together a whole year now, she must be an incredible lady. I love you very very much, not only because you are my father but because you are also a wonderful friend. What a surprise to find out you are actually considering raising a family.

I know that I've always wanted to be your only child—but that's pure daughter selfishness. I've always been my daddy's little girl, in all the years I didn't live with you, in the few years I did, & even now, turning 21, living so far away, I am & will always be your little girl. I guess I'm now at an age that I can take care of myself & I guess you are too. As you said—your kids could play with mine—what a funny idea. Just make sure that's what you really want before you do it. I suppose this is my daughter-to-father lecture. Regardless of the fact that I grew up with my parents separated & slightly crazy, I can't imagine anyone loving their father & mother more than I love mine, nor can I imagine having grown up differently.

So—if I'm about to have any more brothers or sisters I want them to have the same happiness & the same strength (without needing it so much) that I have had. They couldn't ask for a better father although I can hardly conceive the idea of you changing diapers & playing baseball in the park. I'm sure Orli would be a wonderful mother, although I haven't met her yet. I know what you're like so I can only guess what a woman living with you would be like. I also know that out of all the girlfriends you have had you couldn't have picked anyone better to be my mother.

I just don't want you to do anything rash. I do remember a wedding announcement a little over a year ago which has long since been forgotten. You must realize by now that us kids—well—we're a lifelong commitment. You're right, it is a hard but enjoyable process to know what you really want (sometimes). I have complete faith in you & I'm sure you'll make the right choice. Don't worry about my daughter selfishness, my support is with you whatever you do.

I think I had to write all this down because your letter was such a shock to me, not a bad shock, more of a surprise. No matter what happens I love you lots & it *will* be a real trip for both of us to see what I do with my life.

Holly's letter forced me to admit that I really didn't want to be a new daddy. *Us kids—well—we're a lifelong commitment.* I realized that I simply didn't want to make that commitment. Orli and I loved each other, but we had different goals in life. Despite the bond between us, we would have to go our separate ways.

That summer I worked at Winnarainbow, a camp for the performing arts run by Jahanarah and Wavy Gravy. I was the comedy counselor. At the end of the season, I made out with another counselor on the outdoor trampoline one night. The next morning, I noticed a stain on the trampoline from my semen. I found a piece of chalk and drew an outline around the stain. It was, after all, the corpse of Holly's sibling.

Holly had gone to visit a Greek Island and stayed there, working as a dishwasher and cleaning squid for a dollar an hour, eight hours a day, seven days a week. To take a bath she had to climb into her kitchen sink. But now she was back in London, and she was planning to return to America. She sent a photo taken in one of those booths with a curtain where you get four poses on a filmstrip. She had written a different word on four rectangular cards and, switching quickly, she held up one card with each pose, so that you could read this vertical message in front of her smiling faces:

DEAR
DAD
SEND
MONEY!

Her friends borrowed those cards, went into the photo booth, and sent that same message to *their* fathers.

* * *

I moved to Venice Beach, and Holly stayed in San Francisco. By 1991, she had become the manager of community and government relations at KQED, the PBS and NPR affiliates there. I was performing in town and staying at her apartment. Because it was raining hard and she traveled by motor scooter, I was tempted to call her at work and tell her that if the ground was too slippery to drive on, I'd be glad to pay for a cab.

But Holly was now twenty-seven (old enough to spank), and I realized that if I were in Venice and it was raining in San Francisco, I wouldn't phone her about the rain, so now, even if she were to die because her motor scooter slid in the rain, and I would have to live with that horror for the rest of my life, I still had to let go of my paternalism and trust her judgment. I decided not to call. When Holly came home, I told her how I had resolved my dilemma.

"Oh," she said, casually, "if it was raining too hard, I would've taken a bus home."

Over dinner, we were talking about the way you realize how dependent you are on appliances when the electricity goes off.

"Speaking of appliances," she said, "do you ever use that microwave oven Mom and I gave you last Christmas?"

"Yeah, once in a while, to heat up soup and things. You know what, though, I left the microwave door open and I found a few mouse turds on the tray inside."

"Oh, remember that time on States Street, when we invented that mousetrap—the paper bag with a lollipop and cheese in it?"

"Of course I do—and if I ever actually caught a mouse inside the microwave, I'd try to shut the door before it could escape."

"Dad, I can't believe you'd nuke a mouse!"

"No, I'd never do that. I would just unplug the microwave and carry it outside, and let the mouse go free."

"And then you'd race it to see who could get back to the house first."

"And the mouse would win."

CHAPTER 12

I WAS A COMEDIAN FOR THE FBI

THE TABOOS WERE RETURNING TO TV COMEDY IN THE EARLY EIGHTIES with a vengeance. When *Saturday Night Live* poked fun at religion, an organized write-in campaign resulted in seven out of thirty sponsors canceling. As a result, religion was no longer accepted as a valid target on that show. The writers were told specifically to "lay off" Jerry Falwell. They were also instructed to "de-emphasize" political humor, because the average age of their viewers had dropped to fifteen years and, said the producer to the staff, "Fifteen-year-olds are not interested in politics."

Although NBC would never censor Johnny Carson's references to sidekick Ed McMahon's alcoholic adventures, the head of broadcast standards admitted to me that "if you were going to make jokes about Ed McMahon getting stoned on an illegal substance, it would not be approved." In a society where arbitrary distinctions were drawn between legal and illegal drugs, children were being taught that it was wrong to put cyanide in Extra-Strength Tylenol but acceptable to spray paraquat on marijuana crops.

Cable TV now allows more freedom of expression than the networks, but not so in the summer of 1980, when Emmy-Award-winning producer Ann Elder hired me as head writer for a TV special, satirizing the presidential election campaign. This was the first time HBO would feature an independent production. The show, titled *A Funny Thing Happened on the Way to the White House*, would take place in a modern newsroom, with Steve Allen as anchor. There would be a bank of TV monitors serving as segues to various correspondents and the sketches they introduced. I was told that HBO wanted hard-hitting satire, but what they would finally broadcast was refried cotton candy.

This was the first time in American history that three major presidential candidates—Ronald Reagan, Jimmy Carter, and John Anderson—had all publicly declared themselves as born-again Christians. So the election was no longer a choice between the lesser of two evils; it had become a matter of choosing between the least of three sinners. But Ann Elder told me that my concept of a "More Born-Again Than Thou" competition was "not appropriate" for HBO.

Another idea that never saw the light of TV was concerned with the issue of unemployment. The premise was for incumbent Jimmy Carter to dream that he lost the election and had to stand on the unemployment line. He would have to deal with a clerk who'd observe that "life isn't fair"—Carter's own words when the Supreme Court upheld the Hyde Amendment, which forbade the use of federal funds to pay the cost of an abortion for a woman who could not afford one herself.

Although abortion involved a personal decision to be made by each individual, here again it became a major political issue in the presidential campaign. All the candidates had to take public positions. Our original presentation to HBO included my idea for a sketch, "The Big Sister Abortion Clinic," wherein a poor teenage girl who is pregnant and unmarried arranges for a fetal transplant to a wealthy woman who *can* afford an abortion. There was no objection from HBO, but Steve Allen sent this memo:

> You could run into problems with the abortion sketch. More than any other important issue of our time, this one has become a deadly grim business. I wrote the book that comedy is about tragedy, etc., but because of the fact that killing—justified or not—is involved here, the issue is far more touchy than any other. If you decide to do such a sketch anyway, I would not want to be involved with it.

And so the sketch was aborted. I respected Steve for sticking to his principles, but it was still frustrating. Every idea I came up with got knocked out somewhere along the chain of command. Ronald Reagan made a campaign promise that he would take a senility test if the proper authorities concluded that he had become senile—and indeed, as if to *prove* his senility, he promised that, if elected, he would end the inheritance tax for rich and poor alike—but my sketch about the "Senility Liberation Front" was eliminated from the show.

Only one sketch from the original presentation remained in the final script. It took place in a bar where Secret Service agents hung out. But ultimately, after the sketch was thoroughly filtered and homogenized and diluted, it retained only one line of dialogue from the original script—a Secret Service agent ordering his drink through a walkie-talkie: "Bartender, I'll have a Lee Harvey Wallbanger." And even that was a setup which became a punchline when the *real* punchline was eliminated—the bartender answering through his walkie-talkie: "Yes, sir, will that be one shot or two?"

During the two months that the show was in production, I shared a room at the Magic Motel with one of the writers, Rex Weiner, an old friend from New York. Every morning we would take a bus from Hollywood to Century City. The *Hustler* offices had been in one of the twin towers; the HBO offices were in the other. There were signs on the bus: WARNING— THERE ARE UNDERCOVER COPS RIDING THIS BUS.

The bus was pretty crowded, but I wanted one of those signs. I thought it would be a real coup to have one because obviously it would have been lifted from a bus, and there wasn't an undercover cop on that bus or he would've busted me for taking the sign that warned about him. So I stood up on my seat and started taking down the sign. The other passengers were watching me, but nobody said anything. Except Rex.

"*Stop, thief,*" he yelled. "*He's taking that sign!*"

I was blushing, but I took the sign and explained, "I'm just checking to see if there are any undercover cops on this bus."

Rex and I went to a wake for Doug Kenney, the producer of *Animal House*. It was held in a Japanese restaurant right above the Magic Motel, and there were trays of goodies to eat. We were severely tempted to start a food fight—"Doug would have wanted it that way"—but out of respect for other mourners, we resisted the temptation.

When HBO premiered *A Funny Thing Happened on the Way to the White House* on election eve, it was filled entirely with froth and fluff. I felt grateful that the closing credits rolled by swiftly. But the experience had been so stultifying that I decided to return to stand-up comedy, where there would be just me and a microphone and the audience, and no filters in between. In 1971 Groucho Marx had written to my publisher—"I predict that in time Paul Krassner will wind up as the only live Lenny Bruce"—and now I was ready to run with that satirical torch.

* * *

I was scheduled to perform at Budd Friedman's Improvisation in Hollywood in April 1981. Friedman asked me to try and get some advance publicity.

Near the end of March, I delivered a keynote address at the Youth International Party convention in New York. These were the latterday Yippies, originally launched as the anti-Yippie "Zippies" during the 1972

Republican convention in Miami. I asked the audience a rhetorical question, "How would *you* like to be a Secret Service agent guarding Ronald Reagan, *knowing* that his vice president, George Bush, is the former head of the CIA?" Once again, satire would be outdistanced by reality. On March 30, the president was shot by John Hinckley in order to make a favorable impression on actress Jodie Foster so he could take her bowling. Moreover, Hinckley came out for gun control, and Reagan came out against it.

On April 2, 1981, the *Los Angeles Herald-Examiner* quoted a dispatch from the New Solidarity International Press Service:

> A group of terrorists and drug traffickers linked to *Playboy* magazine met in New York City's Greenwich Village area and publicly discussed an assassination of President Ronald Reagan and Vice-President George Bush. The meeting convened by the Yippie organization, featured former *Playboy* editor [*sic*] Paul Krassner and numerous individuals associated with *High Times* magazine, *Hustler* magazine, and the *Chicago Sun-Times*.
>
> In a statement this afternoon, national Democratic Policy Committee advisory board chairman Lyndon H. LaRouche, Jr., urged that this information be made public at this time as a means of assisting government investigators pursuing the assassination attempt against President Reagan. *Playboy* magazine, as an international dossier released in the March 30, 1981, issue of *New Solidarity* indicates, is at the center of an international apparatus that has in the past been directly implicated in high-level political assassinations.

The *Herald-Examiner* published *Playboy's* response: "Absolute, unequivocal nonsense." And Budd Friedman said to me, "Paul that's not exactly what I meant by advance publicity."

In July, *New Solidarity* escalated the attack and published a whole dossier on me:

> In the early 1950s, Paul Krassner was recruited to the stable of pornographers and 'social satirists' created and directed by the British Intelligence's chief brainwashing facility, the Tavistock Institute, to deride and destroy laws and institutions of morality and human decency. Among Krassner's circle of Tavistock iconoclasts, peddling smut in the name of humor and 'creative expression,' were Lenny Bruce . . .

These people were taken seriously in certain quarters. Lyndon LaRouche received enough campaign contributions to qualify him for matching funds from the government. And the U.S. Labor Party's newsletter, *Investigating Leads*, was subscribed to by police departments across the country.

Indeed, when two thousand demonstrators protested the construction of the Seabrook nuclear power plant in New Hampshire, Larouche's private intelligence network briefed a state police lieutenant that the demonstration would be "nothing but a cover for terrorist activity"—the exact same phrase the governor would use to the media a few days before the rally.

But . . . *Tavistock* . . . *Tavistock* . . . I just couldn't seem to remember anything about ever having been brainwashed at the Tavistock Institute.

They must've programmed it out of my consciousness.

* * *

As a performer, I was a bundle of paradoxes. I was a hermit, yet I would go out to do shows and talk to a hundred people at once. I was a social critic, yet my spiritual path was trying not to judge others. Irreverence was my only sacred cow, yet I wouldn't allow victims to become the target of my humor. So, there was one particular routine that I stopped using in 1970. It called for a "rape-in" of legislators' wives in order to impregnate them so that they would then convince their husbands to decriminalize abortion.

But feminist friends objected. I resisted at first, because it was such a well-intentioned joke. But I reconsidered. Even in a joke, why should women be assaulted because men make the laws? Legislators' wives were the victims in that joke, but the legislators themselves, and their laws, should have been the target. For me to stop doing that bit of comedy wasn't censorship; it was conscious evolution. And the subject of sexism became a running theme of my work as I began to tour in the fall of 1981.

At the Village Gate in New York: "There's definite sexism in the movie *E.T.*—I mean, how do we know E.T. is male? Because the little boy says, 'I'm keeping *him*.' This is a blatant male chauvinist assumption. I've seen *E.T.* and there's no penis. And even if there were, it would be *human* chauvinism to assume it was a penis. How do we know it's not just a spare battery holder for E.T.'s finger with the red light?"

At Cross Currents in Chicago: "We've all heard the expression, 'Don't bogart that joint.' It comes from the old macho image of Humphrey Bogart with a cigarette dangling from his lower lip. I think there should be a feminist campaign of re-education, so that the next time somebody holds onto a joint rather than passing it, instead of saying, 'Don't bogart that joint,' you say, 'Don't *bacall* that joint.'"

At the Improvisation in Los Angeles: "They did a test on Canadian mice and discovered that when male mice smoked marijuana they grew female breasts. And the same phenomenon has been found with humans.

Men who smoke marijuana have actually been growing female breasts. That's the bad news. The good news is that it's cutting down on sexual harassment in the office. The men just fondle their *own* breasts."

While I was in New York, a nun was raped. When I got to Chicago, the rapist was also there. He had given himself up to the police. Onstage I explained the true reason why: "He heard that the Mafia, in a rush of Christian compassion, put a $25,000 contract out on his life. So now I'm asking the Mafia to use their clout to end the war in El Salvador since *four* nuns were raped and killed there." They must've heard my request. By the time I got to Los Angeles, the *Herald-Examiner* was reporting that the Mafia was "probably the largest source of arms for the rebels in El Salvador."

★　★　★

In the spring of 1982, there was a Radical Humor Festival at New York University. On the opening night panel, I described the abortion sketch excluded from that HBO show:

> This was around the time that the Hyde Amendment had been up-held by the Supreme Court. Which meant that poor women could not get an abortion paid for by Medicaid. So I was gonna write this sketch about the Big Sister Abortion Clinic. There's a teenage girl who is pregnant and unmarried, but she can't afford an abortion, and she's not ready to be a mother yet. So they introduce her to her Big Sister, who's a wealthy woman who *is* married, has a successful career, does social work, has three kids of her own, but has never had an abortion and feels unfulfilled as an emancipated woman because the real issue is choice, and she just wants to exercise her choice.
>
> So they arrange for a fetal transplant. This is where the fetus is transplanted from the womb of the poor teenage girl to the womb of the wealthy woman. Now this is a perfectly safe operation, it's legal, and best of all it's paid for by Medicaid. So now, that wealthy woman, the Big Sister, is not going to carry this pregnancy to term—she's not gonna be a surrogate mother—but as soon as the scar from the fetal transplant heals, then she'll get an abortion, be-cause she can afford it, while the teenage girl doesn't have to bear an unwanted baby, and neither of them is violating any laws.

A *Village Voice* critic wrote:

> In sniping at the Hyde Amendment, Krassner had taken potshots at middle-class women—they had become his victims, the real tar-

get of his piece. And we had all laughed. For me, that's one of the scariest aspects of comedy.

That weekend, the festival sponsored an evening of radical comedy. The next day, my performance was analyzed by an unofficial women's caucus. Robin Tyler ("I am not a lesbian comic—I am a comic who is a lesbian") served as the spokesperson for their conclusions. What had caused a stir was my reference to the use of turkey basters by single mothers-to-be who were attempting to impregnate themselves by artificial insemination.

Tyler explained to me, "You have to understand, some women still have a hang-up about penetration."

Well, I must have been suffering from Delayed Punchline Syndrome, because it wasn't until I was on the plane, contemplating the notion that freedom of absurdity transcends gender difference, that I finally did respond, in absentia: "Yeah, but *you* have to understand, some men still feel threatened by turkey basters."

I could hardly wait to share this concept with my next audience.

The San Francisco Socialist School had booked me to perform at the Women's Building on May Day evening. Three days before the show, the Women's Building contacted the Socialist School, asking that I not be allowed to perform because it had just come to their attention that I had once been associated with *Hustler* magazine. The female organizers at the Socialist School refused to call off the event and switched the location to Modern Times, a feminist bookstore.

Performing in the Bay Area always had an extra dimension for me, because the audiences there were beyond hip—and Berkeley was the absolute epicenter of political correctness. One night I was performing at Ashkanaz:

> You know, men wouldn't be so worried about having a premature ejaculation if they could only have *multiple* orgasms. Then it wouldn't be a *premature* ejaculation, it'd just be the *first* one. Women can have multiple orgasms—but they also have to menstruate—that's Emerson's Law of Compensation. If I could have multiple orgasms, I would be totally willing to have a regular menstrual cycle every month. I'd suffer through a heavy flow for a few days—get a little bitchy, maybe—but it'd be worth it. So, is there a Devil in the house? I'll sign a pact right now.

A young woman in the audience approached me after the show. She thought that it was inappropriate for me to talk about menstruation as a negative process. She felt it was a *sacred* process which kept her in touch with the cycles of Nature. I always welcomed this kind of dialogue. I even encouraged audiences to interrupt me while I was onstage. At one show, a woman called out, "I'm so tired of hearing this sexist bullshit."

"Which sexist bullshit?" I asked. "Could you be specific?"

"That sexist *bullshit*," she repeated. "Why don't you say *cow*shit?"

At another show, I happened to mention that "I have a pathological resistance to memorizing stuff." A woman stood up and identified herself as a member of NAPA, the Network Against Psychiatric Assault. She objected to my use of the word *pathological*. She said, "Friends of mine who committed no crime have been incarcerated in mental institutions against their will because some authority figure labeled them as 'pathological.'"

"I'm sorry," I said, " I didn't mean to offend you, and I know that what you say is true, but I was just making fun of *myself*, really, so let's not get paranoid—I know, I know, that's *another*." The woman from NAPA laughed along with the rest of the audience, and I knew I was doing my job right.

★   ★   ★

ABC Evening News anchor and *60 Minutes* correspondent Harry Reasoner wrote in his memoir, *Before the Colors Fade*:

> I've only been aware of two figures in the news during my career with whom I would not have shaken hands if called to deal with them professionally. I suppose that what Thomas Jefferson called a decent respect for the opinion of mankind requires me to identify those two. They were Senator Joseph McCarthy and a man named Paul Krassner or something like that who published a magazine called *The Realist* in the 1960s.
>
> I guess everyone knows who McCarthy was. Krassner and his *Realist* were part of a '60s fad—publications attacking the values of the establishment—which produced some very good papers and some very bad ones. Krassner not only attacked establishment values; he attacked decency in general, notably with an alleged "lost chapter" from William Manchester's book, *The Death of a President*.

I appreciated Reasoner's unintentional irony—having started my career as a political satirist by making fun of McCarthyism—but I resented being coupled with Senator McCarthy. Whereas he had senatorial immunity for his libels, I risked lawsuits for what I published.

What I really wanted to do, though, was crash a party where Harry Reasoner would be. "Excuse me, Mr. Reasoner, I just wanted to say how much I enjoy your work on *60 Minutes*." And then, as a photographer captured us shaking hands, I would say, "I'm really glad to meet you. My name is Paul Krassner or something like that."

I booked myself to perform at a theater in Hollywood for a series of Monday nights. One Sunday morning, I was scheduled to be a guest on Michael Benner's KLOS show. I still didn't know how to drive a car, and there were no buses or cabs in sight, so I was hitchhiking to the radio station. A police-car megaphone advised me to pull over to the side, and two cops got out. "Don't you know it's against the law to hitchhike?"

"No, I didn't know that."

One cop frisked me and the other wrote a citation for "hitch hiking w/ thumb out." Where it said, *Make of Car*, he wrote down "Ped" for pedestrian. Where it said *Approximate Speed*, he indicated that I was going three miles an hour in a thirty-five-mile-per-hour zone. Then he asked for my ID.

"I'm sorry," I told him, "I never carry any ID."

"Why not?"

"Well, I know who I am."

He wasn't amused—I could tell by his expression—and I realized that I had lost my empathy for a moment. Seeing it from the cop's point of view, I had come across as a wise guy. So now I wanted to do something to reconcile the tension between us. I took out of my pocket an ad from the *L.A. Weekly*. The headline said, "An Evening with Paul Krassner," and the photo was one of me mooning an audience. I had a slight doubt about handing the ad to him, but I did anyway.

"Here," I explained, "this isn't exactly my ID, but it's all I have."

Out of habit, the cop looked at the photo of my ass, then at my face, and he said, "Is this you?"

It was another one of those rare and precious moments.

The next night Scott Kelman came to my show. We had met twenty years previously, when I performed at Town Hall in New York. Now he was planning to start a new theater in downtown Los Angeles and wanted to produce me there—but my show would need a name. Thanks to Harry Reasoner, I decided to call it *Attacking Decency in General*. My show opened at the Wallenboyd Theater in 1984, and it ran for six months. I received awards from *Drama-Logue* and the *L.A. Weekly*.

Scott and I became friends in the process. He slept at his office and let me stay at his apartment in Venice Beach. I fell in love with the neighborhood and that's when I decided to move there, but for a while I also kept my place in San Francisco, shuttling back and forth.

"It's really decadent," I confessed to the audience. "I mean, there are people living in cardboard boxes just a block away from this theater, and I still have two apartments. I was feeling very guilty until the other day, when I was walking down the street and I saw a guy who had two card-board boxes."

★ ★ ★

David Letterman was winding up his interview with sex therapist Ruth Westheimer.

"Do you have a favorite question?" he asked.

"Funniest question lately was . . . a caller called and said, 'Dr. Ruth, I do use contraception. But one of the things we like to do, my lover and myself, she likes to toss onion rings on the erect penis.' And I thought"— But Letterman reached over to hit the sound-effects buzzer and said, "I'm sorry, time's up, Ruth, uh—" He was interrupted by applause from the audience. "Good heavens," Letterman said, "this is not a jack-in-the-box. We, uh, on that note we have to pause. Believe it or not. Good luck with your television show. Come back and see us. Dr. Ruth Westheimer, ladies and gentlemen."

And that was the end of it. Letterman never did find out what Dr. Ruth thought, but that bizarre onion-rings image would remain embedded in my consciousness. In 1984, in the introduction to an anthology, *Best of The Realist*, I included in a long paragraph about changing taboos:

> Did Nancy Reagan actually sit on Mr. T's lap while he was wearing a Santa Claus suit and kiss him on the cheek, or was this one of those doctored photos on the cover of the *National Enquirer*? Was I only dreaming when I saw Phil Donahue ask the long-awaited question, "What does the Old Testament have to say about vibrators?" Did I merely hallucinate Dr. Ruth Westheimer advising David Letterman that his girlfriend could vary their foreplay by tossing onion rings onto his waiting erection? Did I just imagine I heard a young boy call the Alex Bennett show and discuss the taste of chocolate pubic hair?

I didn't realize until too late that the sentence about Dr. Ruth and David Letterman was missing. I called up my editor to find out why.

"Paul," he said, "that's actionable."

"But it's *true*—how can it be libelous?"

"Well, I thought you made it up. I'm not familiar with Dr. Westheimer, and I don't stay up late enough to watch the Letterman show."

"Look, I don't blame you—if I hadn't seen it myself, *I* would've thought I made it up—but I wish you would've checked with me."

The depressing aspect of this incident was that fear of litigation had permeated the mindset of publishers and producers so deeply—as though

David Letterman might actually sue me if I *had* made it up—or, more likely, Dr. Ruth might sue. I sure would have enjoyed covering *that* trial.

I could envision her on the witness stand, telling a jury, "The defendant caused me great mental anguish and also severely harmed my professional reputation, because I would *never* recommend such a practice—playing ringtoss on an erect penis with onion rings—I mean everybody knows, fried foods are not *good* for you."

But it was this touch of censorship in the guise of editing that provided the specific impetus for me to start publishing *The Realist* again in 1985, after an eleven-year hiatus. "The taboos may have changed," I wrote, "but irreverence is still our only sacred cow." I felt like the old alcoholic doctor in those classic Western movies where the school-marm, having been impregnated by the sheriff, is about to give birth in a barn, and the doctor's hands are shaking, but he says, "I can still do it—get me hot water and blankets—and hurry!"

I had no staff, but an old friend, Lynn Kushel, would handle circulation. I thought that the subscription price of *The Realist* would be $24, but Robert Anton Wilson told me of William Burroughs's observation about how often the number twenty-three occurred in his life, and then Wilson began to notice that same coincidence in *his* life. Two of his children had been born on the twenty-third. My own daughter was born on the twenty-third. My Venice post office box number included twenty-three. So I took Wilson's suggestion as an omen—it was a leap of faith in the irrational—and the rate became $23. One subscriber referred to it as "the official Illuminati rate."

There seemed to be a renewed need for *The Realist* since the Reagan administration had begun conducting government by public relations. Although the taboos were different—bad taste, in fact, had become an *industry*—social commentary itself was now the biggest taboo of all.

I published the return/premiere issue of *The Realist*—this incarnation was in newsletter format—in the summer of 1985. It featured an interview with Jerry Garcia:

Q. Does the world seem to be getting weirder and weirder to you?

A. Yeah. The weirdest thing lately for me was that thing of the Ayatollah and the mine-sweeping children. In the war between Iran and Iraq, he used kids and had them line up like a human chain, holding hands, and walk across the minefields because it was cheaper than mine detectors.

Q. That's just unfathomable.

A. It's amazingly inhuman. And people complained about the Shah—a few fingernails and stuff—but this is kids walking across minefields. It's absolutely surreal. How could people go for that?

Q. But how do you remain optimistic? There's 48 wars going on now simultaneously—and yet the music is joyful—even "Please don't murder me" is a joyful song.

A. Well, when things are at that level, there's kind of a beauty to the simplicity of it. I wrote that song when the Zodiac Killer was out murdering in San Francisco. Every night I was coming home from the studio, and I'd stop at an intersection and look around, and if a car pulled up, it was like, this is it, I'm gonna die now. It became a game. Every night I was conscious of that thing, and the refrain got to be so real to me. "Please don't murder me, please don't murder me."

For a feature story in the second issue of the born-again *Realist*, I contacted Robert Anton Wilson. There was a one-inch news item about a convention in Italy of the Married Roman Catholic Priests Association, representing seventy thousand priests who had married in defiance of the Vatican. I gave the clipping to him.

"Bob, should you choose to accept this assignment, I'd like you to cover this event as though you had actually been there."

Wilson wrote his report, and even *I* almost believed that he had actually gone to the married priests convention. Next, there was a tiny news item about the first International Orgasm Conference, and I assigned him to cover that event, too, as though he had actually been there. *The Realist* was back in apocryphal business.

(The final issue was published in Spring 2001. Several years later, Austin artist Ethan Persoff began to post all the issues online, four at a time, on a website, The Realist Archive Project.)

* * *

Venice was paradise, especially for a nondriver like me. It was my desert island. I could walk to the post office, the grocery store, the laundromat, the bank, the pharmacy, or take a bus to the mainland (Santa Monica) if I wanted to see a movie. I had a sense of community in Venice—a little Philippine restaurant prepared a special drink for me, Ginger Treat, and the mail carrier talked about "the spirit of the sidewalk."

At a "Freedom to Read" event at Small World Books on the Venice boardwalk, I met Matt Groening, creator of *The Simpsons*. He told me, "I've been reading *The Realist* since 1966, when I was eleven years old, and

I must say that it warped me for life." Now *that* was gratifying.

I lived in a tiny two-room apartment on a walk street, Clubhouse Avenue, one block from the boardwalk. I could take long barefoot walks on the beach, and I could see the ocean from my kitchen window. The waves had different moods—calm, frisky, angry—but their momentum always gave me a sense of perspective. They were rolling onto the beach long before I was here, and they would continue rolling in long after I was gone.

Nancy Cain was one of my neighbors. She lived right across the sidewalk from me. When she was sixteen, Nancy listened over and over to Mort Sahl's first album until she memorized it, just as she did with the score of *My Fair Lady*. As an actress she worked in summer stock in Detroit, and as a singer she performed on a bill with Lily Tomlin and Madeline Kahn in New York. She left her show-business career to become active in Videofreex, pioneers in guerrilla TV, documenting the counterculture and antiwar movement. Then she programmed a pirate television station, Lanesville TV, in upstate New York.

She was a producer on the PBS series *The '90s*, and would eventually launch *CamNet*, the first camcorder network, with her partner, Judith Binder. *Rolling Stone* designated *CamNet* second only to HBO in their list of "the ten things in 1993 that didn't suck," heralding it as "a peoples CNN" and "the inevitable next step in the liberation of television from network owners and broadcasters." In 2011, Nancy's memoir, *Video Days: And What We Saw Through the Viewfinder*, was published.

Nancy and I shared a certain shyness, but she was the only one I ever saw who stopped and talked with a guy who shouted gibberish poetry on the boardwalk. After a while, they had a conversation in English. And, as Nancy and I became friends, we developed our *own* peculiar frames of reference. Once, just as she said, "I have no personal problems," my smoke alarm went off for no discernible reason, and that became a running gag between us. Whenever either one would utter a sentence that sounded like it was tempting fate, the other might say, "Oops, did I just hear the smoke alarm just go off?"

Nancy had been saving two capsules of the designer drug Ecstasy, not wanting to try it alone, and we took it together on the beach one afternoon, savoring the sensuality of the sand. Later, we were walking along the shore, and I had a severe case of dry-mouth. She dipped her finger in the ocean so that I could lick the salt water off. That moment of intimacy smoothed the transition for us to evolve from friends into lovers.

So, I was publishing *The Realist* again, I was performing regularly, and Nancy and I were growing closer and closer. I finally felt happy again about the way things were going in my life.

And then my smoke alarm went off.

A dozen police cars had been set on fire, which in turn set off their alarms, underscoring the angry shouts from five thousand understandably angry gays. This was in 1979. I had been covering the trial of Dan White for the *San Francisco Bay Guardian*. The ex-cop had confessed to killing Mayor George Moscone and Supervisor Harvey Milk.

Dale Metcalf, a former Merry Prankster who had become a lawyer, told me how he happened to be playing chess with a friend, Steven Scherr, one of White's attorneys. Metcalf had just read *Orthomolecular Nutrition* by Abram Hoffer. He questioned Scherr about White's diet and learned that, while under stress, White would consume candy bars and soft drinks. Metcalf recommended the book to Scherr, suggesting the author as an expert witness. After all, in his book, Hoffer revealed a personal vendetta against doughnuts, and White had once eaten five doughnuts in a row.

Hoffer didn't testify, but his influence permeated the courtroom. White's defense team presented that biochemical explanation of his behavior, blaming it on compulsive gobbling down of sugar-filled junk-food snacks. Psychiatrist Martin Blinder testified that, on the night before the murders, White "just sat there in front of the TV set, binging on Twinkies." Another psychiatrist stated, "If not for the aggravating fact of junk food, the homicides might not have taken place."

In my notebook, I scribbled "Twinkie defense," and wrote about it in my next report. On the 25th anniversary of that double execution, the *San Francisco Chronicle* reported that, "During the trial, no one but well-known satirist Paul Krassner—who may have coined the phrase 'Twinkie defense'—played up that angle." And so it came to pass that a pair of political assassinations was transmuted into voluntary manslaughter.

And I got caught in the post-verdict riot. The police were running amuck in an orgy of indiscriminate sadism, swinging their clubs wildly and screaming, "*Get the fuck outta here, you fuckin' faggots, you motherfuckin' cocksuckers!*" I was struck with a nightstick on the outside of my right knee and I fell to the ground. Another cop came charging at me and made a threatening gesture with his billy club. When I tried to protect my head, he jabbed me viciously on the exposed right side of my ribs. *Oh, God, the pain!* The dwarf in the clown costume had finally caught up with me, and his electric cattle prod was stuck between my ribs.

At the hospital, X-rays indicated that I had a fractured rib and pneumothorax, a punctured lung. The injuries affected my posture and my gait, and I gradually began to develop an increasingly unbalanced walk, so that my right foot would come down hard on the ground with each step. My whole body felt twisted, and my right heel was in constant pain.

I limped the gamut of therapists—from an orthodox orthopedic surgeon who gave me a shot of cortisone in my heel to ease the pain, to a specialist in neuromuscular massage who wondered if the cop had gone to medical school because he knew exactly where to hit me with his billy club, to a New Age healer who put one hand on my stomach, held the receptionist's hand with the other, and she asked her whether I should wear a brace. The answer was yes. I decided to get a second opinion—perhaps from another receptionist.

Meanwhile, my twisted limp became increasingly worse. In 1987 I went to a chiropractor, who referred me to a podiatrist, who referred me to a physiatrist, who wanted me to get an MRI—a CAT scan—in order to rule out the possibility of cervical stenosis. But the MRI ruled it *in*. The X-rays indicated that my spinal cord was being squeezed by spurring on the inside of several discs in my neck. The physiatrist told me that I needed surgery.

I panicked. I had always taken my good health for granted. I went into heavy denial, confident that I could completely cure my problem by walking barefoot on the beach every day for three weeks. "You're a walking time bomb," the podiatrist warned me. He said that if I were in a rear-end collision, or just out strolling and I tripped, my spinal cord could be severed, and I would be paralyzed from the chin down. I began to be conscious of every move I made. I was living, not one day at a time, not one hour at a time, not one minute at a time—I was living one *second* at a time.

The head of orthopedics at UCLA assured me that I really had no choice but to have the operation. I asked if I could have avoided this whole situation with a different diet or by exercising more. He shook his head no. "Wrong parents," he said, referring to hereditary arthritis. My condition had been severely exacerbated by the police beating, or vice-versa.

I was one of 37 million Americans who didn't have insurance—by November 2011, the number would reach 53 million—nor did I have any savings. Fortunately, I had an extended family and friends all over the country who came to my financial rescue. The operation was scheduled to take place at the Hospital for Joint Diseases in New York, where my brother and I had once played our violins on Christmas Day.

A walking time bomb! I was still in a state of shock, but since I perceived the world through a filter of absurdity, now I would have to apply that perception to my own situation. The breakthrough for me came when I learned that my neurosurgeon moonlighted as a clown at the circus.

"All right," I told myself, "I surrender, I surrender."

Paralyzed from the chin down! I tried to dial—I mean push—Nancy's phone number with my nose. I fantasized about using a voice-activated word processor to write a novel called *The Head*, in which the protagonist finally dies of suffocation while performing cunnilingus because he can't use his hands to separate the thighs of the woman who is sitting on his face.

I met my doctor the night before the operation. He sat on my bed wearing a trench coat, and he called me Mr. Krassner. I thought that if he was going to cut me open and file through five discs in my upper spinal column, he could certainly be informal enough to call me Paul. He was busy filling out a chart.

"What do you do for a living, Mr. Krassner?"

"I'm a writer and a comedian."

"How do you spell comedian?"

Rationally I knew that you don't have to be a good speller to be a fine surgeon, but his question made me uneasy. At least his *hands* weren't shaking while he wrote. Then he told me about how simple the operation was and he mentioned almost in passing that there was always the possibility I could end up staying in the hospital for the rest of my life. *Huh?* There was a time when physicians practiced positive thinking to help their patients, but now it was a requirement of malpractice prevention to provide the worst-case scenario in advance.

The next morning, under the influence of Valium and Demerol, I could see that my neurosurgeon had just come from the circus, because he was wearing a clown costume, with a big round red nose over his surgical mask. He couldn't get close to the operating table because his pointed shoes were so large, and when he had to cleanse my wound he asked the nurse to please pass the seltzer bottle . . .

"Wake up, Paul," the anesthesiologist, said, "Surgery's over. Wiggle your toes."

Nancy was waiting in the hall—there she stood, "my favorite biological quirk," as she had once described the meaning of her existence—and I was never so glad to see her smile.

That evening, at a benefit in Berkeley, Ken Kesey told the audience, "I spoke with Krassner today, and the operation was successful, but he says he's not taking any painkillers because he never does any legal drugs."

Then Kesey led the crowd in a chant: "Get well, Paul! Get well, Paul!"

And it worked. The following month I was performing again, wearing a neck brace at a theater in Seattle.

★ ★ ★

Bruce Springsteen and Vanna White were scheduled to costar in an epic Western musical to be filmed in Arizona, according to a front-page article in *The New Times*, which also carried an ad for hiring extras. More than a thousand calls came to the phone number listed, which turned out to be the governor's office. It was April Fool's Day, 1987.

A worldwide humor movement had been developing, and I was

attending the sixth International Humor Conference, at Arizona State University, where the causes and effects of laughter were being taken very seriously by 1,500 theoreticians from thirty-five countries. I was the only performer among all these pedagogues, who delighted in analyzing that which I did instinctively.

I had dinner with the Russian delegation at the Holiday Inn. They were all having barbecued pork ribs, so the waitress placed gigantic bibs around their necks. The bib on the editor of *Krokodil,* the satirical tabloid published by the Soviet government, read "Superman." The bib on their art director read "Miss America."

We were discussing censorship. They insisted they had none, although it came out in conversation that a particular cartoon idea—showing British Prime Minister Margaret Thatcher spread-eagled on a bed, with an American saying, "Where do you want these missiles?"—was not published because it was "too coarse." I said that I could publish anything I want in *The Realist,* but that I also wrote for *National Lampoon,* and they had turned down my account of snorting cocaine with the pope; the *Lampoon* editors loved it but were afraid of an organized letter-writing campaign to their advertisers.

"Would *Krokodil* be interested in publishing that piece?" I asked.

Superman and Miss America graciously declined my offer.

On the final day of the conference, the Russians took the stage. The subject was "Soviet and American Humor." With charming sarcasm, the *Krokodil* editor admitted that American humor was greater, holding up an envelope labeled "rattlesnake eggs." He and his colleagues were "quite frightened" by this novelty-store item, which had been presented by one of their hosts.

He expressed the hope that "explosions of bombs would be replaced with explosions of laughter, and stereotypes based on hatred would be converted to handshakes of friendship." When the session was almost over, a man in the audience called out to the Russian panelists, "Who among you is the KGB agent? Please identify the FBI agent traveling with you!" Suddenly feelings of discomfort and embarrassment filled the auditorium. I stood up and acknowledged that *I* was the FBI agent. The tension was broken by a burst of appreciative laughter, but I had blown my cover.

Then we took the show on the road. There was a special event at UCLA—"Soviet Humorists Meet American Humorists." As a panel member, I was asked to try and make the Russians laugh. I chose what I felt would be an appropriate demonstration of freedom of humor, pausing after each sentence so that the interpreter could translate:

"For a political satirist," I said, "there are ripe times. Of course, the arms-for-hostages scandal is different from the Watergate scandal. There we had the Nixon tapes, with eighteen and a half minutes missing. Now all we have is former CIA Director William Casey getting a brain operation. But what makes this suspicious is that they only removed the section from August 1985 to November 1986."

First the Americans in the audience laughed, and then the Russians on the stage laughed.

There was a slide show scheduled, and a spotlight was now on the wall, but no slides yet. I made a shadow face with my hand, and it spoke silently on the lit-up wall. Then the art director of *Krokodil* made a shadow face with *his* hand, and we engaged in a silent conversation. The audience applauded this positive omen, heralding the end of the Cold War.

(A couple of years later, after the Berlin wall had crumbled, Ron Kovic, the author of *Born on the Fourth of July*, was the guest of honor at a benefit for the Alliance for Survival, and I presented him with an original FUCK COMMUNISM! poster. "You didn't have to fuck Communism," I told him, "because Communism fucked itself.")

I covered that Humor Conference for the *Los Angeles Times*, titling my report "I Was a Comedian for the FBI." Actually, I had once recognized two FBI agents taking notes at my comedy performance, so I started talking about *them*, and they continued to take notes. The promotional headline on the cover of the *Times* Sunday Calendar section blared out: *Paul Krassner—"I Was a Communist for the FBI!"*

According to Herb Caen in the *San Francisco Chronicle*, "Fearing Krassner would sue, the *Times* recalled and destroyed some 300,000 copies at a cost of about $100,000. Krassner would have laughed, not sued." Or maybe I would've settled out of court for $50,000 and *really* laughed.

But what the *Times* had in common with the neurosurgeon who operated on me was that neither knew how to spell comedian.

I also covered the first annual Comedy Convention in Las Vegas. As comedy had become an industry, the product had become standardized. For three days, an assembly line of sixty-four stand-up comics did fifteen-minutes showcase performances.

There were so many references to ancient and current TV shows—from *Marcus Welby* to *Max Headroom*, from *Gilligan's Island* to *Love Connection*, from *The Brady Bunch* to *Cagney and Lacey*, from *Perry Mason* to *Hulk Hogan*, from *Soupy Sales* to *Oprah Winfrey*—it became yet another separate reality that Carlos Castaneda never dreamed of. (Castaneda was, of course, the neighborhood barber in *Leave It to Beaver*.)

★ ★ ★

During the Iran/Contra hearings, Peter Bergman (formerly of the Firesign Theater) and I teamed up to do a weekly commentary of KPFK. Since Oliver North and his fellow conspirators used code names—North was Steel Hammer—Peter became Commandante Baldie and I became Thunder Heart. Listeners had to identify themselves by *their* code names when they called—for example, Slush Fund.

Meanwhile, Scott Kelman, who had produced both Peter's show and mine, thought that "Peter, Paul, and Harry" would be a great title for an evening of political satire at the Museum of Contemporary Art. He asked curator Julie Lazar if she knew of an appropriate performer who happened to be named Harry. She suggested Harry Shearer. Scott called me to ask about Shearer. "He's brilliant," I said, "let's do it." And so they co-produced a completely sold-out series. If Shearer had been named after his *other* grandfather, "Peter, Paul, and Harry" might never have happened.

Each of us prepared to perform in our own particular way. Peter would stare at himself in the mirror and make strange sounds to exercise his vocal chords. Harry would sit in a separate room where his make-up woman had flown in from Iowa to transform him into Derek Smalls from *Spinal Tap*. And I would be off hiding behind some boxes, toking away on a joint of the marijuana that served as my creative fuel.

Scott was sure that I performed better when I wasn't high, and he was under the impression I was straight when he told me one night, "That was the best show you've ever done." I confessed that I had smoked a giant doobie before I went onstage. The irony was that Scott sold pot to help pay the rent, and that was exactly the stash that got me stoned.

A producer from *The Late Show* came on closing night and later invited me to be a guest. Joan Rivers had been fired and now the Fox network was continuing the show with a different host each week, Arsenio Hall becoming the most popular. At MOCA, I had related the story about taking LSD at the Chicago conspiracy trial, and the producer wanted me to tell it on *The Late Show*.

"I don't want to be frozen in the sixties," I said. "I'd rather talk about contemporary issues."

"Such as?"

"The Iran/Contra hearings."

"Don't you think that's outdated?"

"It's only been two weeks. You want me to talk about something that happened two *decades* ago."

And so I was given six minutes, live on network TV, to observe that

Gary Hart wouldn't have made a good president because he obviously didn't know how to conduct a covert operation or how to practice plausible deniability; to explain that the Harmonic Convergence was just a bunch of virgins getting together to play their harmonicas; and to describe the Iran/Contra hearings as a convention of wimps.

Imitating a senator, I said, "We don't mind if you wanna have a secret government, we just wanna be *told* about it—how else are we gonna pretend that we're the *real* government?"

A couple of weeks later, the new producer, Barry Sand, a refugee from the Letterman show, called. He had seen me on *The Late Show* and wanted to hire me as a writer on the program that would replace it, *The Wilton North Report*, hosted by a pair of drive-time radio disk jockeys who referred to a woman's breasts as "mcguffies." Eventually Sand asked me to do an on-camera commentary for one of the run-throughs.

I didn't own a suit, and I refused to wear one from the Fox wardrobe room, so instead they dressed me in a sweater, shirt, slacks, socks, and shoes. Only the underwear was mine. I was ready now for my commentary:

> I'm here to say that marijuana rots your brain. I speak from personal experience. Recently I was experimenting with pot, and suddenly I had this weird hallucination. I saw Mr. Potato Head surrendering his pipe to Surgeon General Koop. It all seemed so real. So I think it's a good thing we found out about Supreme Court nominee Judge Ginsberg smoking those joints. It explains how he could block the Environmental Protection Agency's effort to eliminate cancer-causing asbestos.
>
> His mind had been totally destroyed by marijuana. Why else would he derail the EPA's regulation on toxic chemical leaks from underground storage tanks? And it *must* have been burned-out brain cells that caused him to squelch a Public Health Service study of the impact of federal budget cuts on infant mortality. I'm telling you, marijuana caused a combination of plaque and smegma to grow between the lobes of his brain . . .

"I don't think we can get away with the pot stuff," Barry Sand said. "There's a law against that at NBC."

"Barry, we're not *at* NBC. I'm confused. You said you wanted me to do a hard-hitting, funny commentary."

"Don't be confused. You're right. If we can't do it on Fox, where *can* we do it?"

Later on, he asked me to do another commentary. This one would be on the air, and if that worked out, I could do one every night. My ship had finally come in, only it happened to be the *Titanic*. Fox executives met with the affiliate board, which recommended that *The Wilton North Report* be canceled. The show would be broadcast for one more week, and I would have my fifteen minutes of fame on the installment plan.

It was a modern American dream come true. *Click!* There's Johnny Carson: "Tammy Faye Bakker took her makeup off, and people thought it was Ernest Borgnine." *Click!* There's Ted Koppel interviewing Henry Kissinger. *Click!* There's *me*, talking about how the U.S. Information Agency had adopted a policy that would allow the government to label documentary films as propaganda when certifying them for distribution in other countries. Now I was applying that same policy to news inside the United States. I had the word *propaganda* flashing on and off the screen, superimposed on film clips of President Reagan signing a farm bill, and New York's Mayor Koch defending his homeless policy.

On the hundredth anniversary of the *National Geographic*, I recalled in my commentary how, as an adolescent, I used to look at that magazine for photos of topless native women: "It was permissible to show nakedness because these were women of color. Of course, this was before *Playboy*, *Penthouse*, and *Hustler*, but even these men's magazines have an unspoken agreement never to show nipples on the cover, no matter how gynecological they get on the inside pages."

The word *nipple* rubbed Barry the wrong way. I had to come up with a euphemism. Protuberance? No, too clinical. Centerpiece? No, sounds like a floral arrangement. Then I found one—"How about *complete* breasts?"—and Barry approved. So I said "never to show complete breasts on the cover." It was either that or "mcguffies."

At a farewell party for the staff in the Fox garage, the cleaning lady got an ovation. She was the one, after all, who took care of the mess every evening after we had finished constructing our electronic sandcastles.

* * *

Once again I returned to stand-up comedy. I continued to learn about the craft with every performance. My reviews had progressed over the years from a *Chicago Tribune* critic who wrote, "Paul Krassner's career as a comic may be as dead as a doornail," to a *Los Angeles Reader* critic who wrote, "Krassner delivers ninety minutes of the funniest, most intelligent social and political commentary in town." But, after I had performed at the Village Gate, I would read in an article about Barry Sand in *Spy* magazine:

> She [Gale Silverman, Barry's girlfriend] was known to leave rude and/or threatening messages on the answering machines of former

"Wilton North" staff members. One afternoon, while paging through *The Village Voice*, she spotted an ad for a nightclub comedy act by Paul Krassner, who had been a writer and performer on "Wilton North." Silverman felt Krassner had betrayed her and Sand by writing a frank article about "Wilton North" for the *Los Angeles Times*, and so, understandably, she picked up the phone and prepared to call in a bomb threat to the club.

"If Paul Krassner plays there," she said while dialing, "the place is going to blow up." When a horrified colleague grabbed the phone away from her just in time, she shrieked, "Fuck him! I'm going to get that cocksucker back! What he did to us was horrible!"

In July 1988, I was booked to perform at Lincoln Center. Also on the program would be poet Allen Ginsberg, New Age musician Phillip Glass, and performance artist Karen Finley, whose infamous reputation for shoving a sweet potato up her ass preceded her appearance.

Nancy and I had gotten married in City Hall on April Fool's Day, and this trip was our belated honeymoon. I forgot what traffic was like for a pedestrian—I had already received two citations for jaywalking in Venice—but now I remembered that in New York it was a crime *not* to jaywalk. Dodging between cars on Seventh Avenue, we made it safely across the street to the Carnegie Deli.

Henny Youngman was standing near the door. Nancy's sister, Linda, asked permission to take a photo of him. Then she criticized him for his appearance on the Larry King show, where he had argued with attorney Gloria Allred about the admission of women to the Friars Club. Now Youngman was pleading his case to Linda.

"Don't you think I have a right to privacy?"

"Yes, and when you feel that way, you should stay home."

That afternoon there was a sound check at Lincoln Center. I stood onstage with the microphone in my hand, doing Henny Youngman.

"Take my sexism—please."

Before the show that evening, I was chatting with Allen Ginsberg backstage. We had been fellow protesters over the years. The poem he would read had previously been done at a benefit for Vietnam veterans. As Country Joe McDonald said, "We were against the war, not the warriors." Ginsberg had come out of the closet long before gay rights became a public issue. With equal fervor he had been a spokesperson for hallucinogenic drugs and an uncompromising peace activist.

Instead of my usual rambling hour and a half, this night I would have only twenty-five minutes. It had to be really tight. The performance was sold out, and the critics would be there. I was extremely nervous. I was supposed to go on right after intermission. I sat in the bathroom of my dressing room and smoked a joint. Less than fifteen minutes to go. The tension had a certain stoned quality about it now. Finally the stage manager knocked on my door. It was time to confront myself. This is real. This is me. This is not a dream.

I had made a bizarre choice. Since I was both an atheist and an absurdist, I decided that the most absurd thing I could do would be to develop an intimate relationship with the deity I didn't believe in.

"Please, God," I prayed, "help me do a good show."

And I heard the thundering voice of God answer, *"Shut up, you superstitious fool!"*

Now another offstage voice was introducing me to the audience, and I walked out there, picking up the same microphone I held that afternoon. I had been psyching myself up for an entire week in preparation for the immediacy of this instant. Lenny Bruce had taught me by example about the magic of an opening line that intuitively articulates the consciousness of the audience.

"Well," I began, "Allen Ginsberg is very disappointed. He thought that Karen Finley was gonna shove a sweet potato up *his* ass."

The laughter of the audience was like an explosion of sweet music. We connected immediately. I felt a rush of security. I started talking about the Reagan administration: "For nearly eight years we've had an after-dinner speaker in the White House." This was intended as a simple throwaway transition line, but to my surprise the audience applauded. That image must have struck a raw nerve. Then I conducted an imaginary press conference:

> "Mr. President, members of the Secret Service have been caught doing dope."
> "Well, that just goes to show how far the problem extends."
> "Mr. President, the Pentagon is involved in a terrible bribery scandal."
> "Well, there are a few rotten apples in every barrel."
> "Mr. President, the U.S. Navy has shot down an Iranian plane and killed 190 innocent civilians."
> "Well, that was a wrongful accident."

To which I added, "There used to be a sign on the desk in the Oval Office that said THE BUCK STOPS HERE. Now it's been changed to a sign that says SHIT HAPPENS."

It was really working—and when it really works, it's like surfing on waves of laughter. Outside Lincoln Center, I was confronted by a real-life version of the character, Rupert Pukin, played by Robert De Niro in *King of Comedy*. This fellow kept telling me jokes, one after another. He said, "Here's my card," and he handed me a card that read *My Card*. "You wanna see my pride and joy?" This time the card had photos of two products, Pride (furniture wax) and Joy (dishwashing liquid).

"I've gotta leave now," I told him, "but if we ever meet again, let's see if we can relate to each other without telling a single joke."

He hesitated a split second, then took on the demeanor of Curly from the Three Stooges, exaggeratedly twirled his index finger in the air, and said, "Why, *soitanly!*"

And we both laughed. It was our first real contact.

★ ★ ★

America was hungry for spontaneity. Michael Dukakis lost his debate with George Bush because of the *non*-spontaneity of his answer to the first question posed by CNN's Bernard Shaw: "If your wife, Kitty, were raped and murdered, how would you feel about the death penalty?" The answer seemed extremely impersonal.

Two days before the final debate, I got a call from Dukakis headquarters in search of jokes, "self-deprecating one-liners," that Dukakis could use. At the time, he was being criticized for the pollution of Boston Harbor. "At some point during the debate," I suggested, "Dukakis could say, 'If what Mr. Bush says is true, I'll go swimming in Boston Harbor.'" But that was a trifle *too* self-deprecating. "Okay, then, how about, 'I'll *walk across* Boston Harbor?'" But that was too self-laudatory.

On the day of the debate, Dukakis headquarters phoned again. "Let me emphasize," the caller added, "we're desperate." This time I suggested that Dukakis say, "Mr. Bush keeps saying that I'm a card-carrying member of the ACLU, but I'm a dyslexic, and I thought he was accusing me of being a card-carrying member of UCLA." Not only was that too local a joke, but apparently they didn't want to take a chance on offending the dyslexic vote, not realizing that to a dyslexic a vote for Bush would *be* a vote for Dukakis.

The only one-liner that Dukakis actually used in the final debate was "a flexible freeze [a phrase Bush used]—that sounds like an economic Slurpie." It fit right in with a presidential campaign of easily recognizable pop-culture references: Dukakis calling Bush "the Joe Isuzu of politics"—he was TV car salesman—Arnold Schwarzenegger belittling Dukakis as Pee-Wee Herman, Bush referring one day to the popular sitcom

Thirtysomething and the next day referring to Vanna White from *Wheel of Fortune* as "Vanna," thereby perpetuating his delusions of intimacy.

* * *

In the summer of 1991, *Friends* producer Kevin Bright hired me as a writer on "The Ron Reagan Show," seemingly an ironic association in view of the kind of material I had done about his father in *The Realist* and onstage—plus, *High Times* had just published my fake interview with Nancy Reagan, in which she admitted that she'd had an affair, not only with Frank Sinatra but also with L.A. Police Chief Daryl Gates.

However, young Ron was a fellow cultural mutation, and he understood that I was treating his parents as political symbols. I had met Ron's sister, Patti Davis, ten years previously, when their father was still president. A San Francisco district attorney had taken a few folks out on his sailboat. I told her, "I really respected your decision to appear at that anti-nuke rally."

"I was doing that *before* my father was president," she said. "I *have* to do it. I'm serious about that. It's the *planet*." This was a logical extension of the time Graham Nash told Patti that she had a cute ass for a president's daughter, and she responded, "I had a cute ass *before* I was the president's daughter." Patti's Secret Service guards had been at the anti-nuke rally, but they didn't come sailing with us. "I wanted to take a stand," she said, "by having all female Secret Service guards, but there's very few of them."

Now, at lunch, a restaurant hostess shook hands with Ron Reagan and said, "I thought it was really cool for your sister to talk about masturbation in *Vanity Fair*."

My friend from *Wilton North*, Lane Sarasohn, was the other writer on this show, and he drove me to work every day. One morning, I noticed a bumper sticker that said SUBVERT THE DOMINANT PARADIGM, which I mentioned to Ron, and he adopted it as the show's unspoken credo.

We decided to defuse the fact that he was the son of the former president, in a promo which included a recent clip of Ron as host of *Evening at the Improv*, saying, "I am the love child of Frank Sinatra"—followed immediately by an old black-and-white film clip of Ronald Reagan saying, "Can you imagine what the Commies will do with this!"

But Fox head Barry Diller happened to be watching TV at home. He felt that the promo was exploitative and yanked it off the air.

I told Ron that he had been falsely outed by militant gays in New York. We knew that issue was bound to enter the dialogue on an upcoming program about gay rights, so he was prepared. "I was a ballet dancer," he said on the show, "and any straight ballet dancer gets a rather thick skin about this sort of thing. But it occurred to me that it's insulting to my wife of eleven years, because it says she's living a lie, and I don't like that."

Ron Reagan had a charming sense of irreverence. In the conference room, we were watching a clip from the movie *Rapture*, which was to be included on a show about religion.

"I met a guy," Mimi Rogers is telling her husband. "You should meet him. You could love him too."

"You fell for some rich homosexual," the husband says, laughing.

"He's the Lord Jesus Christ."

"And," Ron added, "he's hung like a stallion."

On another show, about television, one of the panelists, Chris Albrecht, the producer of *Roc*, a sitcom about a black garbage collector, described the character as "middle class."

I whispered to Lane, "Doesn't he mean working class?"

"From his point of view, anybody who has a job is middle class."

"That must mean that working class is anybody who's waiting on the unemployment line."

"The Ron Reagan Show" was not renewed, and a few weeks later, Lane and I found ourselves waiting on the unemployment line.

★   ★   ★

I turned down invitations to audition for roles in a couple of situation comedies. On *What a Dummy*, I could have auditioned for the part of a disc jockey stuck in the sixties who wears platform shoes and plays Peter, Paul and Mary records backward, but I didn't want to perpetuate that kind of stereotype.

And on the new Mary Tyler Moore show, I could have auditioned for the part of a man who kills a cable TV repairman because he can't get a clear picture on his TV set—he says, "All I wanted to do was watch *Tic-Tac-Dough* without ghosts"—but I didn't want to contribute one iota to the notion of casual violence as a solution to problems, especially with a laugh track to hide the propaganda.

I was spoiled. I had gotten used to speaking my own words. So it was back to stand-up comedy again. Instead of appearing at comedy clubs, my venues varied—from the Committee for the Scientific Investigation of Claims of the Paranormal, where subliminal learning tapes were debunked and psychics were denounced, to the New Age Renaissance Fair, where subliminal learning tapes were sold and psychics could read everything from your palm to chicken bones; from an art gallery to the Brentwood Bakery, where chairs were set up and audience members were each given a free pastry of their choice; from a conference sponsored by the Society for the Scientific Study of Sex, where I learned a new oxymoron, "codependency support group," to a fundraiser for openly gay Tom Ammiano's campaign for San Francisco supervisor, at a gay cabaret, where a few callers wanted to know if I was gay.

"Krassner isn't gay," the manager told them, "but he *is* queer."

Ammiano, later a California assemblyman, would introduce a bill not only to address the state's economic crisis, but also to begin a discussion about how best to regulate its largest cash crop, marijuana, which brings in $14 billion a year.

"The best scenario," he told me, "would make it a states' rights issue, but in the meantime California's out of the gate early. 'Oh, but federal law pre-empts it.' Well, I've got to be candid here. Since when has San Francisco given a fuck about that?"

"States' rights," I said. "It's not just for racists anymore."

*　*　*

Flapping my arms like wings to determine the difference between the news and dreaming had become the signature of my performances. At the Hundredth Monkey Project to Stop Nuclear Testing, I talked about insane priorities and what is *considered* sane:

> In the recent trial of Jeffrey Dahmer—you know, that serial killer who dismembered and cannibalized his victims—the final witness for the prosecution was a psychiatrist who testified that Dahmer was *sane* because he wore condoms when he had intercourse with those corpses. I did this [*flapping my arms*] for *that* one. But here's my public service announcement: "If Jeffrey Dahmer is sane enough to have safe sex, what about *you*?"

And, at another event, in Minneapolis, "Early Warnings: Media and the Environment," sponsored by the *Utne Reader*:

> I'm not sure why, at this stage of the game, with the state of the earth, why this conference is being called Early Warnings. I guess maybe that means that Rachel Carson and others, a couple of decades ago, were merely indulging in premature ejaculations. The New Age movement has really come a long way since there was originally a cult of seven hippies who derived their entire theology from Celestial Seasonings tea bag boxes. And then it expanded, they got into colonics, which is an enema with an ideology.
>
> And there's a whole industry now, there are companies that do nothing but produce New Age music, which is sort of like Muzak,

but without the melody. We're all environmental journalists who have that New Age sensibility now. People don't say, "This is off the record." They just say, "Look, I'm feeling very vulnerable." But I want to give you something very practical to take back—a way to tell the difference between the news and dreaming—because it's getting more and more difficult—you know, there's so much imagery.

So you flap your arms like wings, then if you see something in the news, like they're not gonna spray malathion on some field because there's a rat there that's an endangered species, you just go like this [*flapping my arms*], and if you fly, then you know you're dreaming. The first time I tried this was when I read that Bob Dylan had become a born-again Christian.

I thought, *Wait a minute, here's a guy who sang about don't follow leaders, and now he's chosen one.* I flapped my arms like this and I remained stationary, so I knew it was a true news item, that Dylan had actually become a born-again Christian. Of course, now he's going to back to his Hebraic roots. He's currently in a halfway house for secular humanism.

It was at this conference that I had an epiphany. I met a man who owns a ranch in Australia. He told me about an Aborigine child he knew who slept on a bed made of leaves and twigs, but he went to a school where they had two computers, run by a generator. This Aborigine child had already broken the code at MIT, and his next target would be the Pentagon.

CHAPTER 13

PRANKS FOR THE MEMORIES

ONE NIGHT IN 1968, STILL IN NEW YORK, STEVE POST ASKED ME TO GUEST-host his radio show. At the time, a mass student strike was going on at Columbia University, so Marshall Efron, Bridget Potter, and I pretended that we were Columbia students who had taken over WBAI.

We used code names—Rudi Dutschke, Emma Goldman, and Danny the Red. In nasal tones, I explained that we were all taking a course in alternative media, that our assignment was either to write a term paper or participate in an activity, and that we had decided to take over a radio station for credit.

"The airwaves belong to the people," we chanted.

We had planned to carry on this hoax for fifteen minutes, but it lasted four hours. KNBC in San Francisco and several other stations put us on the air, live. Local listeners called the police, but when they arrived we told them it was a put-on. Then, after they left, I went on the air again, snickering as I described the way we had fooled the cops. And they came again.

* * *

When I moved to California, I took along my Donald Duck with eight arms (Shiva Duck, also known as Donald Sutra), and there it stood on the mantel over the fireplace at my home in Watsonville. But on this particular day, there was something vaguely different about it.

Then I realized what it was—he had *ten* arms now.

The additional arms were actually two pairs of shoelaces. Ken Kesey had been around. He had bought a pair of shoelaces for himself, but they only came in packages of three.

★ ★ ★

While visiting New York, I was a guest of Yoko Ono and John Lennon for the celebration of Yoko's show, *This Is Not Here,* at the Everson Museum of Art in Syracuse. I found myself sitting on the floor in a large room where Ringo Starr led a large group of friends and associates singing "He's Got the Whole World in His Hands," with each individual singing the chorus. When it was my turn, I sang, "*She's* got the whole world in *her* hands . . ."

Later, I was about to enter an even larger room, which was quite crowded. As I walked through the doorway, Phil Spector stood up at the far side of the room, pointed at me, and shouted, "You killed Lenny Bruce!" I was stunned. Rather than ratchet up the sour vibe that Spector had created, I turned around and left. John and Yoko ran after me, apologizing profusely for Spector's insane outburst.

A couple of years later, at the A&M recording studio, he pointed a gun at Lennon, chasing him through the corridors.

★ ★ ★

In August 1974, *Variety* reported: "John F. Kennedy will be impersonated in a play, with Vaughn Meader in the lead. Meader hasn't played the Kennedy role since the assassination."

Two days later, Richard Nixon became the first president in American history to resign from office, and Lenny Bruce whistled from the grave, "*Whew!* David Frye is screwed *again!*"

Chic magazine assigned me to write "A Sneak Preview of Richard Nixon's Memoir." I had a poster of him on the wall for inspiration. There was this scene between Nixon and his chief of staff:

> I stood up, and walked around my desk to where Haldeman was sitting. I ran my hand back and forth over the top of his crew cut. I am not very physically demonstrative, but I had always wanted to do that. Still, for me, this was almost a spontaneous gesture.
>
> "*You* stuck by me, Bob," I said. I suddenly began weeping uncontrollably.
>
> "Sir—is there anything I can do?"
>
> Between sobs I blurted out, "Oh, sure"—and I certainly did not intend for this to be taken literally—"why don't you try sucking my cock, maybe *that'll* help."
>
> To my utter astonishment, Haldeman unzipped my fly and proceeded to do exactly what I had *facetiously* suggested, with what can only be described as extreme efficiency. He must have had some

practice during his old prep school days. But neither of us said a word—before, during, or after.

It occurred to me that this misunderstanding was comparable to the time that Jeb Magruder remarked how convenient it would be if we could get rid of Jack Anderson, and G. Gordon Liddy assumed this was a direct order and rushed out to accomplish the act. If Liddy had not blabbed his "assignment" to an aide in the corridor, Anderson might not be alive today.

As for my own motivation, here was an experience, not of homosexuality but of power. I realized that if I could order the Pentagon to bomb Cambodia, it was of no great consequence that I was now merely permitting my chief of staff to perform fellatio on me. In fact, I was fully cognizant of what an honor it must have been for him.

When the incident was over, I simply returned to my desk and, although the tension of vulnerability was still in the air, we resumed our discussion as if nothing had occurred.

"Now," I said in a normal tone of voice, "what's on the agenda?"

Was my sneak preview of Richard Nixon's memoir an example of what Ram Dass had labeled "astral humor"? Liz Smith wrote in her syndicated column that Haldeman had been in the Oval Office with Nixon, and that his trousers were down to his ankles.

Hoping to smoke out the truth, I retyped one page of the manuscript, adding a phrase (shown in italics) to this sentence in the former president's memoir: "When the incident was over, I simply returned to my desk and, although the tension of vulnerability was still in the air *and my trousers were still around my ankles,* we resumed our discussion as if nothing had occurred." Then I photocopied the manuscript and sent it to Liz Smith.

I assumed she would check with her source. Instead, she wrote in her column that she had been fooled by me, implying that her source had based the revelation on my article in *Chic*. Somehow my hoax on Liz Smith had backfired. I became a victim of my own satirical prophecy.

Then one day I sensed that there was something vaguely different in Stewart Brand's San Francisco apartment where I had a little room. I finally realized what it was—my Richard Nixon poster. His eyes, which were usually looking toward the right, were now looking toward the left.

It had that eerie effect of a platter with the face of Jesus, whose eyes follow you as you pass a novelty-shop window, except that Nixon's eyes were frozen in this new position. I examined the poster more closely and was able to discern that the original eyeballs had been whited out from the right side, and new eyeballs had been drawn in at the left-hand corners.

Then I checked to see whether the eyes in Holly's photo had also been changed, but no, she was still looking directly at me. Only Nixon's eyes had been altered. But it would've been out of character for Stewart to do that.

Ken Kesey had been around again.

★   ★   ★

G. Gordon Liddy and I had something in common. A few years after I answered "no" when the bailiff at the Chicago conspiracy trial asked, "Do you swear to tell the truth, the whole truth, and nothing but the truth," Liddy answered "no" to that same question at the Watergate conspiracy trial. And he wasn't even on acid at the time. On the other hand, Liddy once ate a rat and I've never even tasted one, so things do balance out.

Back in 1966, when Liddy led a midnight raid on Millbrook, it was a shrewd career move. Arresting Tim Leary was a giant step up Liddy's ladder, to the FBI, to the CIA, to the White House Plumbers—and, after serving time in prison, he started his own counterterrorist company, played a role on *Miami Vice*, held hands with Betty White on *Password*, starred in *Nowhere Man*—as a man who fakes his own death to throw cops off the trail so he can make a huge drug score—and finally Liddy got his own TV talk show. Another typical American success story.

The essential difference between Tim Leary and G. Gordon Liddy was that Leary wanted people to use LSD as a vehicle for turning themselves on to a higher consciousness, whereas Liddy wanted to put LSD on the steering wheel of columnist Jack Anderson's car, thereby making a political assassination look like an automobile accident. But who could have predicted that—sixteen years after the original arrest—Leary would end up traveling around *with* Liddy in a series of debates?

I decided to attend the debate in Berkeley in April 1982. Julius Karpen wouldn't go with me.

"Liddy is Hitler," he said. "Would you pay to see Hitler?"

Lee Quarnstrom answered, "*I'd* pay to see Hitler." Then he turned to me. "Wouldn't *you* pay to see Hitler?"

"Well, first I'd try to get a free backstage pass."

"Sure," said Lee, "and you could tell the security guard, 'It's okay, I'm with the *bund*.'"

Leary warned the audience that Liddy was a lawyer—"trained in the adversary process, not to seek truth. I was trained as a scientist—looking for truth, delighted to be proved wrong." He confessed that "Liddy is the Moriarty to my Sherlock Holmes—the adversary I always wanted—he is the Darth Vader to my Mr. Spock."

"As long as it's not *Doctor* Spock," said Liddy.

He argued that "the rights of the state transcend those of the individual." Not that he was without compassion. "I feel sorry," he admitted, "for anybody who uses drugs for aphrodisiacal purposes."

"Gordon doesn't know anything about drugs," countered Leary. "It's probably his only weakness." He looked directly at Liddy. "It's my duty to turn you on," he said, "and I'm gonna do it before these debates are over." Then he made a unique offer: "I'll eat a rat if you'll eat a hashish cookie."

Liddy turned down the offer—one can carry machismo only so far, and he had to draw the line somewhere—but he did provide appropriate grist for my stand-up comedy mill:

> According to Liddy's book, he actually ate a rat. He did it to overcome his fear of eating rats. Certainly a direct approach to the problem. None of that gestalt shit. Now, I'm not sure how he ate the rat, whether he just stuck it between a couple of slices of bread, or barbecued it first, or chopped the rat up and mixed it with vegetables in a stew.
>
> But there were rumors that when Leary and Liddy were on tour, the Psychedelic Liberation Front found out their itinerary and began feeding hash brownies to rats and releasing them, one by one, in Liddy's room at the various motels he stayed at, while he was debating, in the hope that nature would sooner or later take its course, and one night Liddy would feel in the mood for a midnight snack, *catch* the rat that was left in the room, eat it and, by extension, the hash brownie the rat had eaten, and then Liddy would think he got stoned from eating the rat. This would, of course, be right on the borderline in the ethics of dosing.

* * *

In 1974, at a party in San Francisco, Abbie Hoffman was talking with Sheriff Richard Hongisto. "Are you really the sheriff?" Abbie asked. Hongisto took out his gold badge—the design included a peace symbol—and Abbie feigned snatching it from him. "*I'm* the sheriff now!"

It was a poignantly ironic gesture to those of us who knew that this was really a farewell party for Abbie. He was about to go underground. He had made the mistake of introducing one individual who wanted to buy cocaine to another who wanted to sell it, and they were both cops. Now he was facing a sentence of fifteen years to life.

"I got caught behind enemy lines," he whispered to me, "without proper identification."

So Abbie went on the lam, changed his name to Barry Freed, and started another life. He felt "like a hunted animal" but, with the aid of plastic surgery, managed to become an environmental activist.

In January 1977, Jimmy Carter was scheduled to be inaugurated, and I was scheduled to perform at the Counter-Inaugural Ball. I went to Washington and met up with my old friends, Walli and Sam Leff. They were grinning as we strolled through the streets toward the swearing-in of Carter that afternoon, because they knew there was a surprise in store for me.

We encountered some guy leaning against a building. He had a beard, he was wearing shades, and there was a hood covering his head. I didn't know who it was, but then I recognized Abbie's laugh, and we embraced. Walli and Sam served as Abbie's main aboveground support system, and they had cunningly orchestrated this reunion.

"Somebody's staring at us," Abbie whispered to me. "I hope it's *you* they recognize."

He introduced me to his "running mate," Johanna Lawrenson, and we all continued walking.

"Do you think," I asked Abbie, "that Gerald Ford could've been re-elected if he hadn't pardoned Nixon?"

"Plea bargaining always has its risks," he replied.

Now we were standing in the midst of a huge crowd on the sidewalk, just a few yards away from Jimmy and Rosalynn Carter. Instead of riding in a limo, the new president and First Lady were walking hand in hand down the street just like ordinary folks.

"Hey, Jimmy!" Abbie yelled, aware that his voice was being safely drowned out by the cheering of the crowd. "Hey, Jimmy! Why don'tcha gimme a pardon as your first act in office!"

Who could have dreamed that, several years later, Abbie would be joining Carter's daughter, Amy, and two hundred other students protesting CIA recruitment at the University of Massachusetts? When Abbie finally met Jimmy Carter, he told him about that scene at the inauguration.

The former chief executive responded, "I *would've* pardoned you."

★　★　★

In San Francisco, shortly before Christmas 1979, my phone rang. A voice said, "You wanna buy me coffee?" It was Abbie, still on the lam.

"I'll meet you at City Lights Bookstore in half an hour," I said.

Johanna was with him. He called her Angel. They had become each other's psychic anchor.

"Our relationship is completely nonsexist," he explained. "She's my bodyguard, and I do the cooking."

They spent more time together than any couple I knew. But, Abbie confided, there was one problem: "She wants to have a kid."

"Oh, yeah? You gonna have one?"

"Don't you remember? I had a vasectomy."

"Oh, I forgot about that." In fact, a film—*Vas!*—had been made of his operation. "Well," I offered, "if you need a donor—after all, what are friends for?"

We wandered around North Beach. Abbie was not exactly keeping a low profile. He stood next to a Salvation Army Santa Claus on Broadway, borrowed his bell, and rang it vigorously, urging unsuspecting passersby to drop some cash into Santa's cauldron. We moved on. He did a Harpo Marx parody of a tourist responding to a barker in front of a strip joint. Then he proceeded to take the place of the barker.

"Come on in," he shouted. "Whatever you want, we got. You want ladies with stretch marks? We got 'em here!"

Abbie was frustrated about a film, *The Big Fix*, in which a character obviously based on him sells out and works for an advertising agency. In real life, as Barry Freed, Abbie was an organizer in the anti-nuclear-power movement. In fact, one day, in separate stories in the same issue of his local newspaper in upstate New York, there were photos of both Abbie and Barry. While Abbie was being written about as a fugitive, Barry was being honored as an environmentalist. Abbie confessed that he had come to prefer his new identity.

"Angel is in love with Clark Kent, not Superman," he said. "Abbie Hoffman becomes like a third person in bed with us."

"Then why are you thinking about emerging?"

"I don't like being chased."

In 1980, Abbie emerged from underground by way of an exclusive interview with Barbara Walters. She was taken to meet him by Bob Fass and Cathie Revland, whose code names were Mork and Mindy.

It wasn't too long before Abbie found himself onstage at the University of New Mexico, debating G. Gordon Liddy. The moment had come for Abbie to ask Liddy a question he had been pondering for months. Abbie braced himself.

"Liddy," he shouted, "I got just one question for you. Do you eat pussy?" The audience cheered. This was really off the wall. "Come on, Liddy, answer me! Do you eat pussy?" Liddy couldn't respond over the roar of the crowd, and Abbie bleated over and over, "*Do you eat pussy? Do you eat pussy?*"—like some kind of sexual street fighter chanting his mantra—"*Do you eat pussy? Do you eat pussy?*"

The audience went wild. Abbie was triumphant. Finally, Liddy was able to reply, "You have just demonstrated, more than I ever could possibly hope to, the enormous gap which separates me from you."

* * *

In the summer of 1982, there was a celebration of the twenty-fifth anniversary of Jack Kerouac's novel *On the Road*, at Naropa, a Buddhist college in Boulder, Colorado, where presumably they referred to his book as *On the Path*. I was invited to moderate a discussion titled "Political Fallout of the Beat Generation."

The panel would consist of William Burroughs, Allen Ginsberg, Abbie Hoffman, and Tim Leary. At a pre-panel brunch, Burroughs mentioned communicating with Jack Kerouac from beyond the grave.

"But how can you tell," I asked Burroughs, "whether the experience is a subjective projection or an objective reality?"

Burroughs replied, in his jaded nasal voice, "Subjective, objective—what's the difference?"

We were all asked to sign posters for the event. Abbie was writing his signature extra large and with great care. "The guy who shot John Lennon," he said, "complained that Lennon gave him a sloppy autograph, so I ain't takin' any chances."

Since Abbie and Leary had both debated Liddy, they were now comparing notes. Abbie told Tim about his fundamental question, did G. Gordon Liddy eat pussy?

"I can attest to the fact that he does," said Leary. "At least he made it a point at some of our debates to announce that he is definitely *not* monogamous."

I asked, "Does that mean there are Liddy groupies?"

"Oh, definitely," said Leary.

"I guess my father was right. There really *is* a law of supply and demand."

On the panel that evening, Allen Ginsberg was speaking:

> I think there was one slight shade of error in describing the Beat movement as primarily a protest movement, particularly Abbie. That was the thing that Kerouac was always complaining about; he felt the literary aspect or the spiritual aspect or the emotional aspect was not so much protest at all but a declaration of unconditioned mind beyond protest, beyond resentment, beyond loser, beyond *winner*—*way* beyond winner—beyond winner or loser, a declaration of unconditioned mind, a visionary declaration, a declaration of *unworldly love* that has *no hope* of the world and cannot change the world to its desire—that's William Carlos Williams—unworldly

love, which means the basic nature of human minds, which is totally open, totally one with the space around, one with life and death.

So naturally, having that much insight, there'll be obvious smart
remarks that might change society, as a side issue, but the basic theme
was beyond the rights and wrongs of political protest. I was always
interested in political protest in a way Timothy disapproved of, and
that Kerouac thought was new reasons for spitefulness—actually,
new reasons for malice—out of my old socialist, communist, gay,
funny intellectual eyeglass background, maybe, but the basic thing
that I understood and dug Jack for was unconditioned mind, negative
capability, totally open mind—beyond victory or defeat. Just awareness, and that was the humor, and that's what the saving grace is.
That's why there *will* be political after-effects, but it doesn't have to
win because having to win a revolution is like having to make a million dollars.

In my role as moderator, I asked, "Abbie, since you used to quote Che
Guevara saying, 'In a revolution, one wins or dies,' do you have a response
to that?"

HOFFMAN: All, right Ginzo. Poems have a lot of different meanings for different people. For me, your poem *Howl* was a call to
arms.

GINSBERG: A whole boatload of sentimental bullshit.

HOFFMAN: We saw in the sixties a great imbalance of power,
and the only way that you could correct that imbalance was
to organize people and to fight for power. Power is not a dirty
word. The concept of trying to win against social injustice is
not a dirty kind of concept. It all depends on how you define
the game, how you define winning and how you define losing—
that's the Zen trip that was learned by defining that you were
the prophets and we were the warriors.

I'm saying that you didn't fight, but you were the fighters.
And I'll tell you, if you don't think you were a political movement and you don't like winning, the fuckin' lawyer that defended *Howl* in some goddamn obscenity suit—you wanted *him*
to be a fuckin' winner, I guarantee you that. That *was* a political
debate.

When the applause subsided, I added: "And by the same token, Tim Leary
didn't want *his* lawyer to 'drop out.' But I must add in fairness that I once
said the same thing about Leary's doctor. I said, 'Well, you don't want

your doctor to drop out of medical school, do you?' And he answered, 'Well, you're talking about doctors, and I'm talking about healers.' So I do remember my lessons. Tim, while Abbie was talking, you muttered, 'That sounds like G. Gordon Liddy.' Would you care to expand on that?"

LEARY: Is this [microphone] on? At this moment, Liddy would say, "I always have trouble with bugs," right? Yeah, I was debating Liddy the other night, and he put on the blackboard the word *Power*. When it was my turn I put *The Evolution of Intelligence*. And in a very interesting way, Abbie, you and Gordon have much more faith in the political system's ability to change things, and I believe with William Burroughs that it's the culture that changes—you change the way men and women relate to each other, you change the way people's consciousness can be moved by themselves, you change their music and their dress, you change the way they relate to the land and to other forms of plants and animals, and you've got yourself a revolution—to use your word, a fuckin' revolution—that'll make the politicians and the power-mad people . . . it's gonna happen so fast they won't know it's gonna happen.

HOFFMAN: Well, I don't wanna argue, because there's so many good vibes, and standing in front of the Albanian flags up here, and everybody's so happy and high—shit, it's like *The Love Boat*—but I will say this about my debate with G. Gordon Liddy. For me it was a Voltairean experience, namely—once, a philosopher; twice, a pervert—and I'm never gonna do it again. And I whipped his ass. Easy. And I wanna say, Tim, if you don't regard the four years you spent in prison as a political act, you took one trip too many.

Because a lot of people during those times—just growing your hair long—I mean I look out and I see people with long hair, short hair, no hair, green hair, blue hair—you know, earrings in their ears—and that happened because other people had to stand up, whether it was against their families, their church, their school—cops would drag 'em into alleyways and shave their heads—it was a political act. So, to separate what is cultural from political when we are talking about American society in the fifties and sixties is an absolutely hopeless and ridiculous task.

But Leary *had* become politicized, as indicated by his revised slogan for the eighties.

"Turn on," he advised the audience, "tune in and, *please*, take over!"

* * *

A couple of months after the Chicago convention in 1968, antiwar organizers became a target of the House Committee on Un-American Activities. At the hearing, there was a plan for witnesses and their lawyers to protest the focus and manner of the proceedings by standing up at a predetermined signal. I stood up too, and a pair of marshals carried me out by the armpits while I continued to take notes: *carrying me out . . .*

Abbie Hoffman got arrested for wearing an American-flag shirt. When he appeared on *The Merv Griffin* show wearing another American-flag shirt, network officials blacked out his image, or blued it out if you were watching on color TV.

Ironically, Jerry Rubin wore a Vietcong flag as a cape and *didn't* get arrested. He had appeared before the same Un-American Activities Committee a couple of years previously, wearing an American Revolution soldier's costume. On another occasion he got dressed in black pajamas like a Vietcong. Later on, he wasn't sure whether to go to Washington dressed as Santa Claus or a clown. He went as Santa, but got his accompanying statement mixed up, and said, "These hearings are a circus anyway."

An FBI memo had stated:

> To enlarge upon this obvious personality conflict [between Abbie Hoffman and Jerry Rubin], our New York Office has prepared a leaflet in the jargon of the New Left which necessitates the use of obscenities to make the document authentic. The leaflet implies that Hoffman is using Rubin, Yippies, and the "Street People" for his own personal gain. This leaflet, mailed to a select few New Left activists and publishers of New Left publications, will unquestionably widen the personality gap between these two individuals and will tend to fragmentize the organization and hopefully lead to its complete disintegration.

But, in 1984, Jerry and Abbie were together again. Jerry had become involved in the world of finance. He once wrote that a necktie was a hangman's noose, but now he was wearing one. "Money is the long hair of the eighties," he announced. He even sent out a press release requesting that the media no longer refer to him as a former Yippie leader. I envisioned the headline: "Former Yippie Leader Asks Not to be Called Former Yippie Leader!"

Now, Jerry and Abbie were on tour with a debate titled "The Yippies versus the Yuppies." One evening they were doing two debates at the

Stone, a San Francisco nightclub. Alex Bennett moderated the first one, and I moderated the second. Jerry began:

> You may remember me from the sixties. I led thousands of youths into the streets, and presidents fighting wars quivered at the sound of my name. I was known and not wanted in many states. I was the cause of thousands of family arguments around the table between parent and child. Now I've taken off my beard and no one recognizes me anymore, so I carry my American Express card wherever I go [displaying it as in the TV commercial]. You too can have one. But first you've got to become a Yuppie. Now what is a Yuppie, anyway? The word stands for young urban professional, and was coined for the first time as the result of my networking events in New York which brought Yuppies together, exchanging business cards and advancing their careers.

Abbie, in turn, suggested that Jerry "merge with Jane Fonda, so they can have 'networkouts.' What could be better—strong, muscular bodies with shallow, underdeveloped minds?" He had come prepared with props and proceeded to make a Yuppie pie for Jerry.

Into a Cuisinart he poured the ingredients—spirulina, Brie, wine ("from Chile, made by stepping on the eyeballs of political prisoners"), some tofu ("soft, rubbery, sort of like the intestines of a Cabbage Patch doll"), natural vitamins, stock certificates ("stocks and bondage: Yuppie sex"), credit cards, business cards, the keys to a Porsche, a gold watch ("How does a Yuppie spell relief? R-o-l-e-x")—and then he processed it all down to a fine, unappetizing mess.

As moderator, I summed up:

> This debate perpetuates the myth that there is a separation between Yippie and Yuppie. We each have a combination of both spirits. The Yippie in us knows that there must be some kind of social revolution to counter the injustices that horrify us every day. The Yuppie in us knows that, too—but we want to watch it on our VCRs, maybe have some friends over for Sunday brunch. After all, what good is a social revolution if you can't watch it at your convenience? If Abbie Hoffman were to throw money in the stock exchange today, this time Jerry Rubin would invest it.

* * *

I never went to any of my high school or college reunions, but I couldn't resist attending the twentieth anniversary of the Summer of Love in San

Francisco. At noon on the summer solstice of 1987, young and middle-aged hippies—gray hair and potbellies not having erased a certain gleam in their eyes—were marching in an All Beings parade down Haight Street. Costumes ranged from a giant snail to Zippy the Pinhead.

One fellow still in civilian clothes explained, "I was supposed to be Tarzan, but I had to wash the dishes."

Local countercultural fixtures were all there: The Mime Troupe, Rosie Radiator and her fleet of tap dancers, the Automatic Human Jukebox, and a panhandler asking, "Can you spare $100?" The buses now had posters that suggested SHOP THE HAIGHT.

The charm of that entrepreneurial urge was not to be confused with the mission of the Haight-Ashbury Preservation Society, whose targets were symbolized by a walking Big Mac cheeseburger, a prisoner of Thrifty's in chain-store chains, mock pallbearers carrying a casket to mourn the wished-for death of Round Table Pizza, a sign warning DON'T MALL THE HAIGHT! and somebody in a Merlin the Magician outfit with a placard, YOU DON'T NEED MAGIC TO FIGHT THE FRANCHISING. A lone, sad-faced clown bore a banner with a white dove in a red heart.

In Golden Gate Park, an emcee asked the crowd a series of rhetorical questions to rev them up: "How many people were here in the sixties? . . . How many are here now? . . . How many don't know? . . . How many don't care?" A musician announced, "We were told not to have amplifiers, but we decided to break the law today." Hog Farmer Sharon Share-alike offered her roll of hard candy to novelist Herb Gold, which immediately aroused his fear of dosing. "These really are Life Savers," he asked, "right?"

The Summer of Love reunion continued at the I-Beam, a disco on Haight Street. Onstage, I compared the decades:

In the sixties, marijuana was $10 an ounce. In the eighties, it's $300. In the sixties, teenagers used to hide their pot smoking from their parents. In the eighties, parents have to hide it from their kids. In the sixties, the favorite chemical drug was LSD. In the eighties, it's Ecstasy. In the sixties, Ken Kesey wasn't allowed to donate blood because he had ingested acid. In the eighties, there are those who are afraid to get a blood transfusion because of AIDS. In the sixties, Lenny Bruce got arrested for saying "cocksucker" onstage. In the eighties, Meryl Streep got an Academy Award for saying it in *Sophie's Choice*. Now, almost the entire audience at a Grateful Dead concert is younger than the number of years the band has been together—but these kids have less deconditioning to go through than we did. They have less innocence to lose.

When a group of students and other protesters, including Abbie Hoffman and Amy Carter, won their case against CIA recruiting on campus by using a "necessity defense," attorney Leonard Weinglass told me that the turning point for the jury was the testimony of Ralph McGehee, who revealed how he had been recruited right off the football field by the CIA, only to become a star player in their assassination-squad program. Members of the jury would not have voted that way in the sixties because they weren't prepared to believe such testimony as they are in the eighties.

In the sixties, we knew that the CIA was smuggling heroin from Southeast Asia. And in the eighties we know that they're smuggling cocaine from Central America. The same planes that fly weapons for the Contras to airports in Panama, Honduras, and Costa Rica come back to Florida, Louisiana, and Arkansas with their cargoes filled to the brim with cocaine, even though the administration is carrying on its anti-drug campaign. The pilots only have to be careful to evade the radar screen. So while Nancy Reagan is saying, "Just say no," the CIA is saying, "Just fly low."

Meanwhile, the quality of co-option had not been strained. The slogan "Today is the first day of the rest of your life" was used in a TV commercial for Total breakfast cereal. Tampax promoted its tampon as "Something over thirty you can trust." Beatles songs were used to sell cars, or, if you preferred to walk, they also sold sneakers. *Time* magazine was being peddled by the Byrds' version of Pete Seeger's song, "Turn, Turn, Turn"— based on Ecclesiastes—there's a *time* for this and a *time* for that, get it?

The Youngbloods once sent a copy of their song "Get Together" to every member of Congress and the Senate, with a suggestion that it be established as the new national anthem, but who could ever have guessed that it was really destined to become a jingle in a jeans commercial? Or that a Jefferson Airplane song would be used in a bank commercial? Or that Timothy Leary would model a Gap shirt for a full-page ad in *Interview*, and Ram Dass would peddle a rejuvenating skin cream at a Saks Fifth Avenue counter? *People* magazine was selling the twentieth anniversary of the Summer of Love with a feature story set off by a double-paged cover with psychedelic artist Peter Max's signature on both pages.

In red spray paint, on a brick wall just off Haight Street, standing out among the graffiti like John Hancock's signature on the Declaration of Independence, this message summed it all up: LOVE IS REVENUE.

* * *

In the summer of 1988, I attended a conference in Chicago, celebrating the twentieth anniversary of the mass protest at the Democratic national convention. The conference was being held in the very same International Amphitheater where Hubert Humphrey had been nominated. As we were driving there, Dave Dellinger asked Carl Oglesby a rhetorical question: "And we were gonna *walk* all the way here?" Former Black Panther leader Bobby Seale was already at the amphitheater.

"Bobby," I said, "I've been saving this question for you for twenty years now. When you guys flew into Chicago for the convention in 1968, were you armed?"

"Oh, absolutely—we didn't know what to expect. So we had concealed weapons—this was before they searched people at the airport, you know."

Onstage, Yippie organizer Judy Clavir was speaking: "I work for a statewide agency that's concerned with alcoholism prevention and drug addiction prevention. The sixties was a time of 'just say yes to drugs, but just say no to war, just say no to exploitation, just say no to racism, just say no to sexism.' We were definitely very experimental with drugs, there's no question about it, and what we did not understand at the time was the nature of the disease of addiction."

Then it was my turn: "It's a little bit strange to think that if Dan Quayle were a year older, he might've been in Chicago twenty years ago—but with the National Guard. The difference is, then we would've put flowers in the barrel of his rifle—today we would be putting a condom over it."

I couldn't help but notice that Abbie Hoffman was sitting exactly where Mayor Richard Daley sat in 1968 when Senator Abraham Ribicoff was on the dais at the amphitheater saying, "With George McGovern [as president] we wouldn't have gestapo tactics on the streets of Chicago," and Mayor Daley shouted from his seat, "Fuck you, you Jew son of a bitch, you lousy motherfucker, go home!"

And the déjà vu became even more twisted. When I referred to the debate between Abbie and Jerry, I said, "It was a Yippie event in and of itself, but it was also a Yuppie event since they were grossing $5,000 a throw," then *Abbie* started shouting at *me*: "That's not true!"

Although he knew it *was* true, he remained adamant about not being perceived as performing politically for financial gain. He once got a $25,000 check for the movie rights to a book, and he endorsed it to the Black Panthers to bail out a prisoner who he knew in advance was going to flee the country. I asked why, and he said, "Jewish guilt." Abbie hated it when anybody would mistake him for Jerry and ask, "Do you still work on Wall Street?" But now his fury with me went much deeper than simple truth or falsity. Not only had I defied his wish, I had also gone back on my word. Later, we would have our confrontation.

"Why the fuck did you have to *do* that?" he demanded. "I don't want you deciding what's on or off the record."

"Abbie, you debated Jerry *publicly*."

"And you insulted me publicly. You promised the Leffs that you would drop that debate shit from your routine. Then within a month you not only did it again, you did it right in *front* of me."

"I'm sorry. I just keep blurring the line between friendship and cultural chronicler."

"Look, Paul, I'm a public figure trying to build a movement, and I live a very dangerous life. Obviously I'm used to being publicly attacked or ridiculed or worse, and even by a few people who are friends, but I hardly am friendly or honest with them today. Sure, life is as funny, absurd, and ironic as you portray it, but it's also extraordinarily fragile. You seem willing for the sake of a public joke or story to put in jeopardy the fragility of my life and friendship."

I apologized. That was the last time I saw Abbie, but we continued to correspond and talk on the phone. In one conversation, he poked fun at Robert McFarlane's "feeble attempt at suicide" during the Iran/Contra hearings by downing "just a few measly tranquilizers." Abbie killed himself in April 1989 by taking 150 phenobarbital capsules plus alcohol—exactly what his recommendation to McFarlane for a successful suicide would have been. Abbie was clinically manic-depressive. He chose to end his life because he couldn't stand the pain of living.

Both the Los Angeles City Council and the San Francisco Board of Supervisors voted unanimously to adjourn in Abbie's memory. A Hearst newspaper published an editorial in praise of his radicalism. In Central Park a marijuana smoke-in was held in his honor. At UCLA there was a write-in campaign of Pigasus for President.

A week after Abbie's death, the autopsy report was released, and his picture was on the front page of the *Los Angeles Herald-Examiner*, on the left side. On the right side was a photo of Lucille Ball, who was about to undergo serious surgery. That evening, I had dinner at a Hollywood restaurant with Steve Allen. CNN's entertainment reporter had made an appointment to meet Steve at the restaurant, and he interviewed him there, *twice*, once for if Lucille Ball survived the operation and once for if she didn't. Although I could understand the practicality of such foresight, somehow I was offended by it.

Sure enough, the next day, there was Steve Allen on CNN, standing outside the restaurant saying, "We all hope Lucy will pull through. There have been many success stories in the history of television, and yet the affection that millions of Americans hold for Lucille Ball is unique."

A week later, she died, and sure enough, there was Steve Allen on CNN again, standing outside the restaurant and saying, "Lucy will be greatly missed." Then George Burns came on and said, "I had a lot of fun with Lucy," and I couldn't tell whether he had taped that before or after she was dead. There's no business like show business.

*   *   *

A memorial for Abbie was held at the live-porn O'Farrell Theater in San Francisco. It took place upstairs in their office, although I considered this possibility: In the Ultra Room, two naked ladies are dancing and diddling each other. Now one puts a candle in her ass and the other is lighting it. Men are standing in little booths, watching through the glass, and jerking off. If a man puts a twenty-dollar bill through the slot in the glass, one of the women will attach herself to the glass like a Garfield-the-cat doll. Suddenly, a man who is about to come, feels someone tap him on the shoulder.

"Excuse me," I say, "is this the Abbie Hoffman memorial?"

"Uh, oh, yeah," he answers, "I think so—Abbie would've wanted it this way."

In Los Angeles, the memorial took place in a Unitarian church. I met Jackson Browne there. I told him that Abbie thought his song "Running on Empty" should've been used as background music for the movie of the same name, and Browne told me that his mother used to read *The Realist*. Backstage, Vietnam veteran Ron Kovic said, "I'm gonna get out of my wheelchair and say, 'Abbie gave me the courage to walk!'" Onstage, Whoopi Goldberg said, "Abbie gave me the courage to be different."

When it was my turn, I mentioned to the audience that in Abbie's honor, I had rolled a joint "on the cover of *People* magazine," which featured a picture of Abbie wearing his American-flag shirt. (The *Los Angeles Times* quoted me as saying that I had rolled a joint *with* the cover of *People* magazine.)

The most touching moment at this memorial occurred when Daniel Ellsberg unfurled a banner given to him by young people at an anti-nuclear protest, beautifully embroidered with this message: *Sweet dreams, Abbie. You helped start it. We'll help finish it.* The audience went wild with emotion as Ellsberg presented the banner to Johanna in the front row, and they embraced.

A few months later, another memorial was held in New York at the Palladium, a glitzy theater which usually presented rock concerts. As I ended my few minutes onstage, I pretended that I was being channeled by Abbie. I took on his Boston accent, his rabble-rousing growl, and—referring to the recent massacre in Tiananmen Square—I raised my fist in the air.

"Free the Chinese one billion!"

As I left the stage, there was the next speaker, a Chinese student. "Thank you very much," he said, shaking my hand.

"Wow," I said, "that was fast."

Allen Ginsberg was backstage and gave me a tip on poetic emphasis.

"Free the Chinese one *billion!*" he suggested.

Daniel Ellsberg was also there, waiting to speak. I noticed he had something tucked under his arm. I asked him what he had there, and he showed me. It was the same banner that he had unfurled at the memorial in Los Angeles.

"How'd you get *that* back?" I asked.

"Johanna gave it to me," he replied, "so that I could present it to her again today."

And I finally understood. Re-staging the unfurling of the banner dedicated to Abbie Hoffman was just a variation on the CNN reporter interviewing celebrities twice about Lucille Ball. And hadn't *I* mostly repeated at the New York memorial, almost word for word, what I said at the Los Angeles memorial? I could no longer feel self-righteous about CNN's premature sentimentality. There *was* a business like show business after all, and it was the radical memorial business.

When I mentioned this incident to Steve Allen, he responded, "American reality has become part show biz through and through, whether you're talking about politics, religion, the military, or whatever. The Jewish scriptures report God frequently doing tricks and schticks to get people's attention."

★ ★ ★

Twenty-two years after Tom Wolfe wrote *The Electric Kool-Aid Acid Test*, mythologizing the cross-country trip of Ken Kesey and his Merry Band of Pranksters, they were once again driving the psychedelic bus, *Further*, from the farm in Oregon to the Smithsonian Institution in Washington, D.C. There would be various stops along the way. Tim Leary asked me to be sure to call him when the bus arrived in Los Angeles before heading east. Kesey told me that in Philadelphia, a troop of Girl Scouts with a hip scout leader was scheduled to board the bus.

"We're calling it Cookies and Kool-Aid," he said.

This was not the first time such a trip was planned. In 1974, a group of second-generation Pranksters were repainting the designs and symbols and inner-vision comic strip characters on *Further*, because there had been an inquiry from the Smithsonian. Kesey figured that if the outside of the rusting bus could be brightened anew, why, then, the inside would automatically work again and it could be driven all the way to Washington.

In 1984, the bus was still there on the farm. In fact, *People* magazine was planning to publish a special section on the sixties, and a photo of *Further* would be on the cover, with Wavy Gravy perched on the hood, Kesey and me sitting on each of the front headlights. Posing for the cover of *People*, I couldn't resist holding onto my crotch with one hand. However, they made Michael Jackson the main story instead, and put *his* carefully chosen picture on the cover with his gloved hand grabbing *his* crotch. That photo of us on top of the bus was a full page on the inside, identifying me as "father of the underground press." I immediately demanded a paternity test.

On a Saturday morning in November 1990, I flew to San Francisco so I could join the pilgrimage. I was on assignment from the *Examiner*. It had always been impossible for me to cover Kesey's trip without getting personally involved, but this time I also found myself torn between reporting the truth—that this was *not* the original bus—or snitching on a friend. I had a slight conflict of interest.

Was my responsibility to reveal what I knew or to be loyal to Prankster tradition? The original bus, a 1939 International Harvester, was still resting in peace at Kesey's farm, a shell of its former shell, metal rusting and paint fading, a psychedelic relic of countercultural history. But the bus I boarded now was a 1947 International Harvester. The Grateful Dead had donated $5,000 for a sound system, which was blaring out Ray Charles's "Hit the Road, Jack" as we left San Francisco.

This version of *Further* had been deemed the Most Historical Float in an Oregon Fourth of July parade. It was painted by fifteen individuals starting in April. The result was a magnificent visual feast. A sun god with refraction discs so the eyes followed you. A totem pole and a tiger. Adam and Buddha. Pogo and Silver Surfer. A lizard following Dorothy and her companions down the yellow-brick road—referred to as the Lizard of Oz. A banner on the side of the bus warning NEVER TRUST A PRANKSTER.

A helium tank on the back platform, so Kesey could blow up balloons and give them to kids. One parent offered him a quarter. "I'm an important author," he explained with mock pride, "you can't give me a *quarter*." So now the parent wasn't sure whether the balloon was free or she should give Kesey seventy-five cents.

Pedestrians flashed the V sign and the *Star Trek* signal as the bus continued on its way. Drivers waved and honked their horns. A police car was behind us, and the cop inside it used his megaphone to call out, "Good luck on your journey." Our hood ornament was a beautiful sculpture of a court jester holding a butterfly net, named Newt the Nutcatcher, with a profile resembling Neal Cassady, legendary driver of the original *Further*.

On the inside, a picture of Cassady watched over the current driver, Kesey's nephew, Kit, who refused to wear a taxicab cap. Kesey's son, Zane, was also on the crew, so the trip had a strong sense of continuity. Altogether there were twelve males plus one female, a twenty-three-year-old Deadhead who got on the bus in Berkeley instead of going to a Halloween party dressed as Pippy Longstocking.

Lee Quarnstrom had quit his job as a reporter to join the original Pranksters, and he was covering this event for the *San Jose Mercury-News*. Since we were now in San Jose, the bus circled around the parking lot of the *Mercury-News*. Kesey quickly found a CD of sixties songs and played "Mr. Lee" by the Bobbettes over the sound system. Lee was sitting on the top deck of the bus as the editorial staff stood outside the building, cheering for him while the lyrics rang out: "One, two, three, look at Mr. Lee . . ."

Ed McClanahan had been a classmate of Kesey's in the Stanford writing class where it all started. He gave up a chance to go on the original journey, regretted it for twenty-six years, and was now covering this trip for *Esquire*. "If the bus goes past the *Esquire* building," he asked Kesey, "are you gonna play the theme from *Mr. Ed*?"

Later, I happened to overhear Quarnstrom whisper to fellow ex-Prankster Zonker, "Shhh, Paul doesn't know." There was some sort of hoax in the air. I was tempted to corner him and say, "Lee, I've trusted you till now," but instead I decided to maintain conscious innocence and just allow events to unfold.

Quarnstrom and Kesey had something awful in common. They had each lost a son. Eric Quarnstrom had been shot in a meaningless street encounter. Jed Kesey was killed in an accident when the van carrying his wrestling team skidded off a cliff. I had just come offstage at the Wallenboyd Theater when my producer, Scott Kelman, said he had to tell me something. I assumed it was about my performance—Scott always gave me complete freedom *and* helpful feedback—but now he was telling me about Jed's death. Scott had held back from telling me before the show.

I was shocked. Jed and I had a special relationship. I flew to Oregon. Faye was stalwart, but Ken was shaking with emotion as we embraced. "You were his favorite," he sobbed. Kesey had always been against seat belts—"They sanction bad driving," he claimed—but after this tragedy he would campaign for legislation that would *require* vehicles to have seat belts, the kind that could've saved Jed's life. But now he had only unspeakable grief.

"I feel like every cell in my body is exploding," he said.

During the reunion bus trip, Quarnstrom and Kesey talked with each other about their mutual tragedy for the first time, in the kitchen at Wavy Gravy's house.

"I think about Eric every day," said Quarnstrom.

Kesey said he thought about Jed every day, adding, "And it's appropriate that we should."

When his son died, Kesey confided in me, "I'm so sad about losing Jed, it made me realize that when I die, it's gonna make a lot of people sad." It turned out to be a true observation. When Kesey died on November 10, 2001, a lot of people were indeed saddened. Some were sad because they had been affected by the books he wrote. As for *Cuckoo's Nest*, he told me, "I wasn't trying to write a novel, I was trying to go all the way."

Others were sad because they identified with and were inspired by the mission of *Further* and its inhabitants, the equivalent of wanting to run away with the circus. Still others were charmed by his charismatic zest for life. Family and friends loved him simply for who he was.

And then there was his little granddaughter.

"Now," she asked plaintively, "who will teach us how to hypnotize the chickens?"

*   *   *

Meanwhile, a color photo of the bus had appeared in *Time* magazine, and an employee at the Smithsonian immediately recognized it as *not* being the original *Further*. Their spokesperson issued a statement: "The current bus is not even close to the original. Even if it were, the Smithsonian is not interested in a replica." Kesey was aghast. He mused out loud:

> I don't think of this bus as a replica. The Smithsonian—they want to clone the other one from the carburetor, which is about all that's left of it—the way they wanted to do in that Woody Allen movie, *Sleeper*, when they only had the nose for that. And they wanted to put on new metal, new chassis, new motor, and hire some artists to paint, you know, they're going to restore it, and I thought, *In what form?*
>
> Are they going to go back to when it was bright red and we all drove it into Berkeley on Vietnam Day with swastikas and Stars of David and American flags all over, with guns stickin' out of the top? Or when we went to New York with Pop Art stuff on it? It's had dozens of different permutations. If they really want to restore it, they'll take it back to yellow.

But the thing about the Smithsonian is that I've never spoken to them. They've been dealing with some rich people up in Portland—they wanted me to give them the bus—they're going to fix it up and donate it to the Smithsonian. My metaphor for this is that they've also been negotiating for Tom Selleck's dick but they haven't mentioned it to Tom.

We reporters had a discussion about journalistic ethics, specifically how we planned to handle any possible use of drugs on the bus. What with stomach paunches, gray hair, and bifocals, the drug of choice this time around could well be Metamucil. Kesey would permit neither cigarettes nor diet soda on the bus. In response to a decade of "just say no" propaganda, he advised, "Just say thanks."

He was disinvited from a *Nightline* panel on drugs because he was pro-marijuana. He made a distinction between pot, mushrooms, LSD, psilocybin—"the organic, kinder, gentler, hippie drugs"—and cocaine, crack, meth—"drugs that make you greedy and produce criminals." He called drugs "my church" and confessed that he had taken psychoactives "with lots more reverence and respect than I ever walked into church with."

On Sunday morning in San Jose I ate a marijuana cookie. It was coming on powerfully just as the bus arrived at the Rosicrucian Egyptian Museum. Appropriately, the painting on the back door of our bus was a splendid eye-in-the-Pyramid. Kesey's video crew had been filming the reporters reading their articles aloud, and he wanted me to read mine from inside a tomb in the museum, the king's sarcophagus.

"But I haven't written anything yet," I protested.

"You have twenty minutes," Kesey said.

However, the marijuana cookie had an extraordinarily pleasant physical effect, and I was feeling very nonlinear. Instead of writing anything, I just stared at the mummies. There were framed X-rays in their cases to prove that actual human beings were buried with their arms crossed inside all that adhesive tape. Now the Pranksters were ready to bring me into the tomb, but I felt totally unprepared. My mouth was extremely dry, so I ingested another "drug," a vial of Chinese herbal tonic labeled *Deer's Tail Extract.*

Maybe they planned to seal me inside the king's sarcophagus! Could *that* be the secret they weren't telling me before? But with a leap of faith I lowered myself into the hole in one corner of the tomb. Only my face was now visible. Ordinarily I would get in trouble for this, but we were also being filmed by CBS, and the manager of the museum only wanted to know when it would be shown on TV. Kesey gave me the signal to start.

"Well, as Yogi Berra once said, this feels like déjà vu all over again. The last time I was in a sarcophagus was 1978, when we accompanied the Grateful Dead to Egypt, where they played the Pyramids, and won. But that time we walked there from the hotel. This time the bus brought us here, this bus that the Smithsonian doesn't want because it's not the original. You know, it's not really Fonzie's leather jacket at the Smithsonian—that was actually worn by Penny Marshall.

"And it's not really Archie Bunker's easy chair there, either—they just found it on some other set and said it was Archie's. But this bus has been turning on whoever sees it, like a traveling oasis, transcending age, transcending gender, transcending race, transcending class. The Smithsonian doesn't *deserve* this bus. A man from the Peace Center here in San Jose told me, 'This bus was painted by the spirit of time.' If God wanted the bus to be in a museum, God wouldn't have given it an engine."

When I finished babbling, Kesey directed me to disappear back into the tomb. But first I couldn't resist saying, "And now I'd like to share with you the secret of eternal life." Suddenly I began writhing around in agony and grabbed my throat—*Aarrgghhh! Yaarrgghhh! Braagghhh!*— then fell back into the sarcophagus, as my choking sounds continued until they finally faded out. I vowed to myself, "I surrender to the Unknown." Then I emerged from the tomb, and Kesey's fellow Prankster, Ken Babbs, announced, "As we say in Mummy Land, 'That's a wrap.'"

I called Holly to tell her that we were at the Rosicrucian Museum and that I had just been in the king's sarcophagus.

"The king's esophagus?" she said. "What were you doing in his throat?"

On Monday, we headed north for Stockton, where Kesey was scheduled to speak at the University of the Pacific. And the machinations of the prank began. I was the only one who didn't know what the plan was. But while Kesey was inside speaking, Zane was drawing a chalk outline on the street around the perimeter of the bus. Inside, Kesey was finishing up his question-and-answer segment.

"Okay," he finally said, "that's enough. Now we will sing our national anthem."

And he led the audience in the Grateful Dead song, "What a Long Strange Trip It's Been."

Outside, the crew made sure my bag was off the bus. They were staging a fake mutiny. Inside, Kesey left the stage.

He said to Zonker, "Why don't you run out there and tell us the bus is missing?"

Zonker replied, "Because I didn't know it *was.*"

Lee rushed in and reported, "Kesey, they done left us!"

Kesey shouted, "The bus is gone! The bus is gone!"

Where the bus had been, there was now only that chalk outline and a message in white tape spelling out: NOTHING LASTS! The bus was on its way back to Oregon. Kesey and a couple of others would stay at a hotel in Stockton and take the train back. They had planned from the very start that the bus would not be driven to the Smithsonian.

"I always knew we wouldn't carry this prank too far," Kesey said, adding in mock shock, "*That's* not the real Elvis!"

I called Tim Leary to inform him that the bus was *not* coming to Los Angeles after all. Leary had been in Europe, returning with an East German flag which he wanted to donate to the Smithsonian, but he didn't say whether it was the original flag or just a replica.

Zonker offered to drive me to San Jose, where I could catch a plane back home the next morning. Before I went to get my bag from Kesey's room, I told Zonker, "I hope I don't come out of the hotel only to find a chalk outline of the car." Kesey asked me to call Herb Caen at the *Chronicle* and tell him that *Further* had disappeared. I suddenly realized that I was experiencing the Stockton hostage syndrome. A hoax was played and, although I had been a victim of that hoax myself, I was now expected to help perpetuate it.

"Tell him there's been a mutiny," Kesey instructed me, "and that you're an irate Prankster who's been left behind."

"What, and ruin my credibility?"

★ ★ ★

An obituary in the *Los Angeles Times* began: "Bernie Boston, the photojournalist who captured the iconic image of a young Vietnam War protester placing a flower in the barrel of a rifle held by a member of the Army's Military Police Battalion, died . . . The photo known as Flower Power became Boston's signature image and earned him acclaim in the world of photojournalism. Taken during an antiwar march on the Pentagon on Oct. 22, 1967, the photo was a finalist for the Pulitzer Prize."

The protester, not identified, was Joel Tornabene. Earlier in this book, I described him as "an unheralded Yippie organizer known as Super-Joel. His grandfather was Mafia boss Sam Giancana." In 2006, Joel's sister, Fran, informed me, "Our grandfathers were a Sicilian doctor and a Norwegian Irish carpenter. I can't imagine how anyone would actually believe that Giancana relationship."

I contacted her immediately, apologizing "for passing on false information." I added, "Although I included that story in my autobiography, recently I've had the rights reverted back to me, and I plan to have it republished in an updated edition, so I will certainly include a postscript revealing that hoax." She replied:

> I think that Joel must have had quite a good time with the "Giancana connection hoax." I was first made aware of this story after his death in Mexico in 1993. His attorney, Dennis Roberts, came to Chicago to meet with my mother and our family. He seemed to be quite surprised to see a simple middle-class family home in Franklin Park, rather than a River Forest Mafia compound. I wasn't aware of the extent of this story until Prairie Prince, who I know Joel was close to for years, asked me a few years ago which side of the family was Giancana. Since then, I've seen your tale regarding his being moved to the unindicted co-conspirator list due to the "grandfather connection."

"I'm embarrassed to admit that I believed it," I confessed, "simply because Joel was extremely convincing when he told me—so I'm a professional prankster who got pranked himself—but I really had no way of double-checking his personalized put-on."

And I'm not the only one who's been fooled like that. Another sister, Felicia, located an interview in which Tom Waits was asked who Joel is. Waits replied:

> He's in the concrete biz. Mob guy. He was the grandson of Sam Giancana from Chicago. He did some yard work for me, and I hung out with him most of the time. He died in Mexico about five years ago. He was a good friend of [producer/composer] Hal Wilner, and he was a good guy. He had an errant—I don't know how to put this—he used to go around, and when he saw something he liked in somebody's yard, he would go back that night with a shovel, dig it up, and plant it in your yard.
>
> We used to get a kick out of that. So I stopped saying, "I really like that rosebush, I really like that banana tree, I really like that palm." Because I knew what it meant. He came over once with twelve chickens as a gift. My wife said, "Joel, don't even turn the car off. Turn that car around and take those chickens back where you found them." He was a good friend, one of the wildest guys I've ever known.

Waits has written a song—"How's It Gonna End," on his album *Real Gone*—that includes this lyric: "Joel Tornabene lies broken on the wheel..."

And Joel's ten-year-old nephew used him as a topic for a history project. He centered it on the 1968 convention in Chicago—titled "Someone Who Took a Stand."

* * *

The process of writing an autobiography becomes part of the autobiography. The healing of my relationship with Lyle Stuart became intertwined with the writing of my manuscript. He had been justifiably bitter toward me, but as I came to understand what I had done during my psychotic episode, and was able to share it with him, forgiveness followed.

After twenty years of estrangement, it made me happy that he became my severest critic again, and his encouragement immensely enhanced my confidence in writing this book. I don't know how my *whole life itself* would have turned out if I had never met Lyle in the first place.

My friend Robin Clauson has *An Astrological Mandala* which features trance readings for all 365 phases of the Zodiac. Mine is: "A Revolutionary Magazine Asking for Action . . . Whether the revolutionary action is violent or peaceful, bitterly resentful or loving, the one desire is *to reach beyond established forms.*"

Robin believes I was *fated* to publish *The Realist,* but that's much too mystical a concept for me. I can only observe how the combinations of chance and choice in my life have ultimately merged into some kind of random destiny. Coincidence is still my religion. I believe that life on earth was the result of inconceivable coincidence rather than conscious design, and that my own individual conception was the result of inconceivable coincidence. It was much easier believing that my parents had purchased me in a hospital.

When my father died, my mother wrote in that day's box on the kitchen calendar: "No more Mike." Although my father had never approved of my work, preferring to avoid controversy, my mother told me, a year after he died, that he had really admired what I did, and would've liked to have done it himself. The last time we spoke, I told him how his talking about the law of supply and demand had influenced me so strongly as a kid, and he said, "Aw, I don't believe in that anymore." I asked, "Why not?" And he said, "The manipulation of the human mind."

Just as the counterculture of the sixties evolved and exploded out of the blandness and repression of the Eisenhower-Nixon years, so has the counterculture of the twenty-first century been evolving and exploding out of the blandness and repression of the Bush-Cheney years and beyond, in a myriad of forms.

While we've gone from the Zapruder film to the Rodney King video to YouTube, from entertainment to evidence, things have been happening so fast that even the rate of acceleration has been accelerating, and irreverence has been increasing along with everything else. Although it took more than a decade after the assassinations of John and Robert Kennedy for there to be a band called the Dead Kennedys, it took only a few months after the attempted assassination of Ronald Reagan for there to be a group called Jodie Foster's Army. Other bands have been named Sharon Tate's Baby, Jim Jones and the Suicides, and Lennonburger.

Whenever I've performed on the anniversary of John Lennon's death, I've worn a T-shirt he once gave me. It has a lithograph of John playing the piano and singing. Above the illustration is the word *IMAGINE*. In Chicago, a woman in the back of the audience asked, "Why are you wearing that T-shirt?" I explained what John Lennon had meant to the culture and to me.

She called out, "Why are you telling us all that?"

"Because you asked me why I was wearing this T-shirt," and I proceeded to describe the T-shirt.

"Oh," she exclaimed. "I thought it said *I. Magnin.*"

Lennon would've liked that.

* * *

Like other editors, I was willing to tolerate Hunter Thompson's irresponsibility in the process of presenting his talent. In 1997, at a memorial for Allen Ginsberg that I emceed, Thompson—true to his reputation—was supposed to make an appearance, but he didn't show up. Johnny Depp, who played him in the movie version of *Fear and Loathing in Las Vegas*, did.

I told the audience that I was disappointed because I was hoping to present Depp, Thompson, and Bill Murray (who played him in *Where the Buffalo Roam*) all standing together, and then I would say, "Will the real Hunter Thompson please fall down?"

In 2005, I learned of Thompson's suicide when Associated Press Culture Correspondent John Rogers phoned to ask what my reaction was. He would write, "'I'm stunned,' said Krassner, who was nearly speechless for several minutes after hearing the news. 'It's hard to believe I'm referring to him in the past tense.'" This was on a Sunday evening in the middle of a three-day Presidents' Day holiday weekend. I don't know who else or how many others Rogers had called before or after me, but apparently I was the only one who happened to be accessible at the time.

As a result, after the AP report was dispatched, I was deluged with interview requests from print, radio, and TV outlets. Each time, I found myself uttering some new observation, if only to keep myself from getting jaded. During one call, I said, "Hunter was larger than life, sort of like a Macy's Thanksgiving Day Parade float." On the next call, I added, "Except that it was filled with nitrous oxide."

Among the interviews was NPR's *All Things Considered*. After it was broadcast, I learned that I was considered "big enough now" to merit the preparation of an advance obituary for NPR. I don't take it personally. This is a purely pragmatic practice in the media world. I'll be right up there with Charlie Manson, who is certainly a high achiever in his own field of endeavor. My personal definition of success is simply trying to do the appropriate thing every moment. As Ken Kesey once told me, "I think of my energy and my image as two separate entities. My energy is what I do. My image is what other people think I do."

My friend, radio journalist Jon Kalish, was given the assignment to put me "in the can." He allowed me the rare opportunity of fact-checking my own obituary. I asked him if it would be possible to include my website. Actually, I was slightly disappointed that my electronic obit doesn't mention my role as an underground abortion referral service, because that was such a turning point in my life. I had crossed a line, from observer to participant, from satirist to activist.

After Kalish finished interviewing Steve Allen for my NPR obit on October 30, 2000, Steve was driving to his son's home, and a car backing out of a driveway struck his car. Everything seemed okay, but later, while taking a nap at his son's home, Steve had a massive heart attack and was pronounced dead. An autopsy indicated that the heart attack had been triggered by the traffic accident. Ah, if only Kalish had asked Steve one more question—or one less question—then Steve would still be alive today.

★   ★   ★

I've noticed that the network news shows are all targeted at middle-aged and elderly viewers. They are all sponsored by prescription drugs promising to cure erectile dysfunction. A Viagra commercial—with background music by Queen singing "We are the Champions"—features men dancing in the streets, ecstatic at the prospect of asking their doctors if a free sample is right for them. Personally, I don't have any problem getting a hard-on, but I've begun to worry that it's *really* rigor mortis setting in on the installment plan.

My friends have grown older, and the musicians we listened to in the sixties have grown older along with us. I imagine myself emceeing the Geezerstock Festival, standing on an outdoor stage, looking out at a vast audience of gray-haired hippies with paunches and granny glasses, as I speak in a slow, shaky voice:

"Are you having fun? . . . I can't hear you! . . . No, I mean *I really can't hear you!* . . . I have an announcement. The Port-o-Potties that are painted green should be used only by those who have to pee at least once an hour. The Port-o-Potties that are painted red should be used only by those who have to pee less than once an hour. . . . It's now my pleasure to introduce the Rolling Stones. They've been very busy gathering moss. Here comes Mick Jagger with the aid of a walker. And Keith Richards is being carried out on a gurney . . . Oh, wait, I've just been handed another announcement: Warning—do not take the brown antacid . . ."

When I was seventy, I wrote a piece for the AARP magazine, *Modern Maturity*. My subscription copy arrived—it was the issue in which my article was supposed to be featured—but it wasn't in there. I checked with my editor, who asked how old I was. I told her that I didn't understand what difference that would make. She explained that there were three editions: one for readers fifty and over, one for readers sixty and over, and one for readers seventy and over. I was too old to read my own article.

There was a time when I was considered too young to read certain things, and now I'm considered too old to read certain things. Obviously, something must have happened to me in between. Like, say, most of my life?

Once a short-lived magazine, *Cheetah*, published a fake obituary of me. An AP reporter called, and I explained that it was a hoax.

"Are you sure?" he asked.

"Of course," I replied. "I'd tell you if I was dead."

On WBAI, Bob Fass was taking phone calls, and listeners were discussing whether that obit was legit. Someone called and said, "You know, I didn't even know that Paul Krassner was alive until I heard that he was dead." And, at that precise moment, my sense of false humility was restored.

* * *

If the universe is infinite, then the paths to connect with it are also infinite. There was, for example, a woman who won a clam-shucking contest, and her husband said, with genuine pride, "I think she was *born* to shuck clams." To him, she was the personification of Lennon's working class hero.

In 1976, I attended "The American Hero: Myths and Media," a symposium held in Sun Valley, Idaho. I delivered a keynote address, "The Heroism of Failure":

> Remember the guy whose car crashed into Gerald Ford's car when he was campaigning in Connecticut? Well, he was asked to stand up in the audience of Howard Cosell's variety show. The audience hesitated just a beat before they applauded, realizing that it was *all*

right to clap because this guy *had not succeeded* in killing President Ford. If he had, he never would have been invited even to *sit* in the audience.

However, Squeaky Fromme and Sara Jane Moore both failed in *their* attempts to kill Ford, yet neither of *them* was invited to stand up in the audience of the Howard Cosell show. Is this still another example of male chauvinism in the presentation of heroes as role models? Not quite. Although it's true that Squeaky and Sara Jane were unsuccessful assassins, it's the intent that counts. An audience will applaud for the perpetrator of an unsuccessful accident, but not if you shoot somebody on purpose, even if you miss.

At that Heroes conference, I met Lindsay Wagner, star of *The Bionic Woman*. She was unaware that the CIA served as technical adviser to her series, but she spoke poignantly of the positive influence that her TV alter-ego had on young amputees she visited in hospitals.

I also met Tom Laughlin, of *Billy Jack* movie fame. A couple of years later, he and his wife, Delores Taylor, invited me to a dinner party. They were Thomas Jefferson enthusiasts. In their home, there was Thomas Jefferson's furniture, Thomas Jefferson's silverware, Thomas Jefferson's recipes—we started with peanut soup—and even Thomas Jefferson's violin. I mentioned playing the violin as a child, and Laughlin invited me to play this one. I hadn't held a violin for twenty-five years, not since I had used it as a prop when I started doing stand-up comedy, and four decades had passed since that concert in Carnegie Hall. It felt like a previous incarnation. But now Billy Jack himself was handing me Thomas Jefferson's violin. How could I resist?

"I'd like to dedicate this to Thomas Jefferson's slaves," I said.

And then I played the only thing I felt competent enough to perform— "Twinkle, Twinkle, Little Star." While I was playing, I stood and, as unobtrusively as possible, balancing on my left foot, I scratched my left leg with my right foot. It was a private joke between me and the god of Absurdity.

CHAPTER 14

BLOOPERS AND OUTTAKES:
THE PARTS LEFT OUT OF THIS BOOK

THE "EARLY YEARS" SECTION OF THE WIKIPEDIA ENTRY FOR ME BEGAN: "Krassner was a child violin prodigy (and was the youngest person ever to play Carnegie Hall, in 1939 at age six). He is Jewish . . ."

I felt that was inaccurate, and I contacted the Wiki-people, requesting a correction. I gave as a required source the autobiography you now hold in your hands—specifically, the Lenny Bruce chapter, with this quote of mine:

"I don't consider myself Jewish. I equate religion with organized superstition. And anyone who thinks of Judaism as a race rather than a religion is accepting the Nazi tenets."

And so now the entry for me reads: "His parents were Jewish . . ." To that was added: ". . . but Krassner is firmly secular, considering Judaism 'organized superstition.'"

This time I was, in effect, misquoted. I contacted the Wiki-people again, giving the same required source.

And so now that sentence ends: ". . . considering religion 'organized superstition.'"

* * *

What if I didn't happen to cross paths with an old Yippie friend, Jim Fouratt, near the post office in Venice Beach shortly after *Confessions* was originally published in 1993? He told me that Danny Goldberg—producer of music albums, anti-nuclear activist, and head of the Southern California branch of the ACLU—really enjoyed reading it. I wrote to Danny, and he suggested I do a stand-up comedy CD. He ended up overseeing six such albums, two at Mercury Records and four at Artemis Records.

One of them—*Irony Lives!*—was recorded in February 2002 in Los Angeles. Dan Castellaneta, who does the voice of Homer on *The Simpsons*, graciously agreed to introduce my performance, which he did from an offstage microphone in order to maintain the image of that blustery animated–cartoon character. However, the attorneys at Fox TV wanted to hear the whole album before granting permission to include the introduction, and they asked for seven copies of the tape.

Finally, in June, I was informed by an attorney for Artemis that, "unfortunately, Fox declined our request, and in doing so failed to go into any detail as to what their reasons were." It may have been because the album included such tracks as "Terrorist Attacks," "In the Guise of Security," and "My Cannabis Cup Runneth Over."

Naturally, I leaked the banned introduction to my own website, which then crashed because there were so many hits. Ironically, more people heard the intro there than would have heard it on *Irony Lives!* Well, Fox may own Homer's voice—when it's done by Dan Castellaneta, that is—but they do *not* own the following transcript of his introduction. Whoever thought that Homer Simpson would be considered intellectual property? *D'oh!* And now I'd like to introduce Homer introducing me:

> Hello. I'm Homer Simpson. There have been many great counter-culture heroes I have admired over the years. Steve McQueen, Dr. Demento, Dr. Denis Leary, and Wavy Gravy. Mmmmm, gravy. But even some counterculture heroes go too far and step over that line between dissent and in-dissent-cy. I'm speaking of Paul Krassner.
>
> The first problem I have with Paul Krassner is that the only good song he wrote for Jefferson Airplane was "Crown of Creation." And even then his name is spelled K-a-n-t-n-e-r even though it is pronounced Krassner.
>
> I also have a problem with the fact that he is an atheist. If there is no God, then who has placed a pox on me and mocks me every day? Of whom do I live in fear and mortal terror? Buddha? I think not. He's way over in China where thankfully he can't get at me.
>
> I have a problem with his constant use of words such as "penis," "Larry Flynt," "premature," "ejaculation," "CIA," and on several occasions he has been known to use the words "Bush" and "Bush Jr." in mixed company. Did I mention "penis"? Yeah, here it is—"penis" (*Laughs*). (*To self*) "Penis."
>
> Let's see, where was I? I mentioned, "penis," "gravy," "Buddha," "God," "Jefferson Airplane" . . . No. That's it . . . Will everyone please put their hands together for that raving, unconfined nut

. . . here's hoping he opens with "Crown of Creation" . . . Paul Krassner!

*   *   *

At the first annual Portland (Oregon) Book Festival, "Wordstock," in 2005, I was invited to open for Norman Mailer and then introduce him. I said:

> The thing I most admire about Mailer is a combination of his courage as a writer and how much he respects the craft. He writes in longhand with a number two pencil, he once told me, because it puts him in more direct contact with the paper that he's writing on, and I felt so guilty because I was still using an electric typewriter at the time. You remember typewriters, don't you? But I have a niece who saw a manual typewriter, and she said, "What's that for?" I explained, and she said, "Well, where do you plug it in?" "You don't have to plug it in, you just push the keys." And she said, "That's awesome."
>
> Anyway, one aspect of Norman Mailer's craft is that he chooses his words very carefully. Or, as he would say, "One chooses one's words very carefully." The thing that I recall, the words that he chose most carefully, of all the books he's written, was something that he said when I asked him how he felt about circumcision. He thought for a moment, then he chose his words carefully and, with a twinkle in his eye—one of his main characteristics—he said, Well, I believe that if Jews didn't have circumcision, they would punch their babies in the nose and break them."

When Mailer came onstage, walking with the aid of two canes because of a severe arthritic condition, he received a standing ovation. He eased himself onto a high chair behind the podium. He said:

> Gee, Paul, I didn't know how to start tonight, but maybe you got me going. Now, if I ever made that remark, that the reason Jews get circumcised is to keep them from breaking their babies' noses, all I can say is that I must have been down in the lower depths of a very bad marijuana trip. But I think, even at my worst, I couldn't really have said that. Paul is a master of hyperbole. He loves hyperbole, as for example when Lyndon Johnson attacked the wound in JFK's head.
>
> At any rate, if I did say it, I would forgive myself now for having said it, because circumcision happens to be something that every Jewish male thinks about every day of his life. It makes us obsessive

for a very simple reason. We don't know if it's an asset or a liability. And I'm not speaking of it lightly. I'm speaking of psychic castration that may make us smarter or it may not. We worry about things like that. So I will say categorically, that if I ever made that remark, I was out of my head, and to the best of my marijuana memory, I never made it. I want to thank you, Paul, for making that up and giving me a beginning tonight, and for warming up this audience . . .

Ah, yes—dueling memories.

* * *

When Hunter Thompson's first book, *Hell's Angels,* was published in January 1967, I assigned a behind-the-scenes article for *The Realist* about his promotional tour. He was broke, so I paid him $200 in advance, and I offered to send him some LSD if it would help.

He replied, "You can send me some acid to help me level out. And I'll send you a dozen just-born marijuana weeds. You can plant them in Central Park."

On a visit to New York in February, Hunter arranged for me to meet him and his copy editor, Margaret Harrell—an attractive redhead, smart and witty—for dinner.

Apparently I forgot her name, so it's possible that I called the publisher and asked for the name of the copy editor. In March, I sent her this letter:

> Dear Barbara,
>
> If you ever decide to try LSD, this is just to offer my services as guide. Incidentally—no, not incidentally—you are one of the most delicious females I've ever seen, and since there was already a mild establishment of intellectual rapport, I feel compelled to state my—to de-ulteriorize—my motivation. I would like to make funny, passionate, friendly, cosmic, absurd love with you. Ho hum. I think I'll attach a questionnaire with this. It is not a form letter, by the way.
>
> Paul
>
> Barbara—check one:
>
> [   ] I like your honesty. Please call me at [phone number].
> [   ] I believe in equal rights. I'll call you at [two numbers].
> [   ] Your honesty is appealing but I have a spontaneity hang-up.

[ ] But didn't you know I'm a virgin, and intend to remain one?

[ ] I'm not a hymen-fetishist, but you're just not my type.

[ ] You're my type, but I'm just not socially available.

[ ] I'm a lesbian; do you have a cute sister?

[ ] You men are all alike, you're only after one thing, bla bla bla.

[ ] I'm sorry, I can't go out with a man who doesn't drink.

[ ] You'll have to get a new trench coat first.

[ ] Ha ha, I'm not even going to send this back to you.

[ ] I'm an independent spirit and I'm afraid you'll be possessive.

[ ] I don't *have* to give you *any* reason, see.

[ ] Barbara Willson is somebody *else;* you and I never even met.

[ ] You writers will do anything to get your book published.

After a weekend rendezvous in Los Angeles with Hunter, Margaret arrived at work at noon on Monday. Now flash ahead to 2011. In her memoir, *Keep This Quiet: My Relationship with Hunter S. Thompson, Milton Klonsky, and Jan Mensaert,* she wrote:

> In my absence that morning Swedish copy editor Barbara Willson had received a letter from Paul Krassner. He had written it to her, *thinking that was me* . . . Unknown to him, this one was half right: "Barbara Willson is somebody *else;* you and I never even met." Barbara turned the letter over immediately—downstairs to the Random House obscenity files. I wasn't told.
>
> Sometime later Paul phoned me at work. He said he'd asked Hunter's permission to invite me out. Hunter said yes. I winced. So Paul wrote the letter. Then told Hunter he'd invited Barbara Willson on a date. Hunter said fine, but who's Barbara Willson? Krassner was phoning to tell me to retrieve the letter, I'd get a kick out of it.
>
> I retrieved it. Obviously, I would not say yes and wondered why Hunter would, but it was part of his contradictory character. Would he really not mind? Would he say he didn't mind as a test? Then I passed [that test]. So much blood shot to my head that I did not reason out the possibility that Hunter too had no idea what Paul was talking about.

I know *I* don't have any idea what I was talking about. It's all a mystery to me. Did I actually call Hunter and ask for his permission to date his copy editor, not knowing yet that she was his paramour? All I know is, he never wrote that article, but he *did* return the $200.

* * *

On the morning of April 1st, 1995, I flew to San Francisco. It remains my one of my favorite cities, and I jumped at any excuse to return there. My excuse for this visit: I was scheduled to emcee a benefit for Jack Kerouac's daughter, Jan, who had been on dialysis treatment for the last few years.

On that sunny afternoon, I was standing around stoned in Washington Square Park, wearing my *Mad* magazine jacket that Holly had given me the previous Christmas. The smiling face of Alfred E. Neuman—stating his renowned philosophy, "What—me worry?"—graced the back of my jacket. That's exactly how I felt that day, like a harmless innocent.

I was waiting for the arrival of the annual Saint Stupid Day Parade, led this year by Grand Marshal Ken Kesey and his sidekick Ken Babbs in an open-topped convertible. The event was sponsored by the First Church of the Last Laugh. Their sound equipment was surrounded by yellow plastic tape warning, *Police Line—Do Not Cross*. Somebody in a clown costume handed me a three-foot section of that tape and, April fool that I am, I graciously accepted.

The celebration featured music, comedy and a traditional free brunch, along with such favorite rituals as the Sock Exchange and the Leap of Faith. Kesey, also in town to speak at the benefit, was in fine form. He delivered an optimistic pep talk to the audience sitting contentedly on the grass.

"It ain't over," he concluded, "until the fat lady gets high!"

Then he led a "gong bong," where everybody stands up, forms a circle, holds hands and, as a single unit, takes a dozen long, deep breaths, letting out the final exhalation with upraised arms and a group wail of exultation. During this moment of spiritual hyperventilation, a young woman fell to the ground and broke her nose. She was a casualty of peace.

That night, at the benefit for Jan Kerouac—held only because she happened to be the daughter of a ground-breaking literary celebrity, even though he had abandoned her mother when she was pregnant with Jan—I said to my friend Julius, who drove me there, "It's not enough any more just to be a sperm donor."

Jan had met her father only twice. The first time she was nine. The second time, six years later, he sat there, drinking a fifth of whiskey and watching *The Beverly Hillbillies*. Jan would eventually die of kidney failure at the age of forty-four, never having fulfilled her fantasy of becoming drinking buddies with her father, who died when she was a teenager.

Now, backstage, someone I knew handed me a baggie of what I assumed to be marijuana. I thanked him and put it in my pocket. Ah, yes, one of the perks of the benefit biz.

Later, as the final members of the audience were straggling out of the theater, I was sitting with Julius in his car in the parking area at Fort Mason Center. He was busy rolling a joint in a cigar box on the dashboard with the map light on. There was a police car circling around in the distance, but we foolishly ignored it. Suddenly, a moment later, there was a fist knocking heavily on the passenger-side window, and a flashlight shining in my eyes. Shit! Fuck! Caught!

We were ordered outside and, with our arms outstretched against the side of the car, with the face of Alfred E. Neuman smiling at the cop and asking, "What—me worry?" And indeed, the cop was worried. He asked me if I had anything sharp in my pockets. "Because, he explained, "I'm gonna get very mad if I get stuck," obviously referring to a hypodermic needle.

"No," I said, "there's only a pen in this pocket"—gesturing toward the left with my head—"and keys in that one."

He found the coiled-up three feet of yellow plastic tape warning, *Police Line—Do Not Cross*, and said, "Where'd you get this?"

"At the Saint Stupid Day Parade."

"What's it for?"

"To keep people away."

But then he found the baggie. And, to my surprise, it contained psilocybin—magic mushrooms. He examined the contents. Then, with blatant sarcasm, he said, "So you like mushrooms, huh?" Under the circumstances, it was such a ridiculous question that I almost laughed, but I realized that, from his point of view, this was a serious offense.

The cop's question reeked with archetypal hostility, and it kept reverberating inside my head. So you like mushrooms, huh? It was not as though I had done anything which might harm another human being. This was simply an authority figure's need to control. But control what? My pleasure? Or was it deeper than that?

Julius was given a $50 citation for possession of marijuana, but I was arrested on the spot, handcuffed behind my back, and my Miranda rights were read to me. I stood there, heart pounding fast and mouth terminally dry, trying to keep my balance on the tightrope between reality and unreality. With the aid of a terrific attorney, Doron Weinberg, I got off with a $100 fine and nothing on my permanent record.

And I finally understood what that cop when he snarled, "*So you like mushrooms, huh?*" What was his actual message? Back through eons of ancestors—all the way back to what Terence McKenna called "the unstoned apes"—this cop was continuing a never-ending attempt to maintain the status quo. He had unintentionally revealed the true nature of the threat he perceived. What he *really* said to me was, "So you like the evolution of human consciousness, huh?"

"Well, yeah, now that you mention it, I do. I mean, when you put it like that—*So you like the evolution of human consciousness, huh?*—sure, I do. I like it a whole lot."

★ ★ ★

In 2005, I got a letter from *Vanity Fair* editor Graydon Carter, and then a call from Brett Morgen, director of *The Kid Stays in the Picture*. They were coproducing a documentary about the sixties antiwar movement. It would have no narrator and no talking heads, only archival footage and animated reenactments based on actual events and transcriptions of trial testimony. However, Allen Ginsberg floating a few feet above the floor in the lotus position while he chants can be construed as cartoonic license.

Morgen invited me to write four specific animated scenes:

1. Birth of the Yippies: The hurricane, the meeting, and the press conference.
2. Got Permit?: Trying to get permits from Chicago deputy mayor.
3. Acid Testimony: Ingesting a tab of LSD at lunch before testifying.
4. Women's Liberation: The feminist protest outside the Miss America Pageant.

Although Brett Morgen "loved, loved, loved" the scenes I wrote, the backers objected to the use of LSD, fearful of diverting attention from the main focus of the film. It was Brett's baby, but it was being diapered by the backers. I was disappointed, if only for the sake of countercultural history. Anyway, my suggestion—instead of referring to it as acid, Abbie could yell, "Hey, this is pretty powerful fuckin' aspirin"—was rejected.

Thus, the trippy hurricane segment of the "Birth of Yippies" scene, which was originally going to open the film, was omitted. My implied "threat" in the "Got Permit?" scene that the Yippies would pour LSD into the reservoir, plus the entire "Acid Testimony" scene, were also out. And, unfortunately, the "Women's Liberation" scene wasn't included because of time constraints.

Brett named the film *Chicago 10*, encompassing the eight defendants plus attorneys William Kunstler and Leonard Weinglass. I was concerned that people would think it was the ninth sequel to the musical *Chicago*.

During an interview with Videofreex during the trial, Abbie had said, "We don't wanna be martyrs. We wanna live to see the overthrow of the government. Be a great fuckin' movie." But Brett's goal now wasn't quite as ambitious as overthrowing the government. When he called to tell me that the documentary had been selected to open the 2007 Sundance Film Festival, he mused, "Wouldn't it be great if Abbie's legacy turns out to be that he helped to end the war in Iraq?"

Brett got a standing ovation at Sundance. There was another screening a couple of days later, not intended so much for festival-goers as for folks who lived in Salt Lake City. I ate a chocolate candy loaded with psilocybin to enhance the experience, unaware that Brett planned to bring me onstage to speak to the audience and then join him in a Q & A session.

Brett warned me, "This is the heartland." Still, I began with a joke I'd heard in town: "A Mormon decided to go hiking in the beautiful mountains of Utah, but first he stopped to buy some equipment at a Mom and Mom and Mom and Pop store."

One of the questions was "What advice would you offer to young people today?"

My mind was swirling like a multicolored whirlpool. I assigned my subconscious to come up with an appropriate answer, while I stalled for a moment, leaning on the lectern. "My advice to young people is," I said, "if you go to a restaurant and order a club sandwich, be sure to remove the toothpick before you take the first bite."

When my subconscious came through, I said, "Always remember that the political system acts as a buffer between the status quo and the force of evolution. Example: In order to get Republican votes for the children's healthcare bill, Democrats agreed to fund $28 million to their abstinence-only program."

Brett wanted *Chicago 10* to open during the election year, and he was pleased that it opened in theaters around the country in February 2008 and was on PBS two weeks before the election. In October 2007, *Chicago 10* opened the Austin Film Festival. Brett was unable to attend, so I went there as his proxy.

I decided to smoke a joint before I left my hotel for the screening that evening. However, I was in a nonsmoking room, and there was a notice on the desk: "Should you choose to smoke in a nonsmoking room, a $250 cleaning/deodorizing surcharge will be added to your room bill." So I toked it in the bathroom with the door closed, sitting on the tub and exhaling into the toilet. During the Q & A session, someone asked a question about the differences between the Vietnam War and Iraq. My response:

Both wars were both based on lies and fear-mongering. One of the differences is that there was a draft during the Vietnam War. That personalized it, sadly. People wore buttons that said NOT WITH MY BODY YOU DON'T. The Bush administration deliberately doesn't have a draft now because they know that whatever disconnect there is between the public and the horror that the government is conducting in their name, would dissolve. People have certainly protested (more than thirty million worldwide before the war began)—and been ignored—but with a draft in the U.S., citizens would take to the streets in multitudes to demonstrate against the war. When Latinos marched through Los Angeles over the immigration issue, there were a million of them. What we need to do now is hire Mexican workers as guest protesters, so they can do the job that Americans don't want to do . . .

★   ★   ★

During the 1968 Democratic convention in Chicago, I was among 15,000 protesters who had gathered in Grant Park for a rally when the police, triggered by the actions of one of their own provocateurs, attacked the demonstrators and sadistically beat as many as they could reach. It seemed impossible that we could ever work within the system. But in 2008, forty years later, there were 200,000 celebrants who had gathered in that same park, giddy with the excitement of Barack Obama's victory. They had worked within the system.

During the past four decades, there had been a linear progression from Jimi Hendrix playing "The Star-Spangled Banner" at Woodstock to Aretha Franklin singing "My Country, 'Tis of Thee" at Obama's inauguration. Was it possible that this event signified the early tremors of a nonviolent revolution? As the late singer/songwriter Harry Chapin once told me backstage at a benefit: "If you don't act like there's hope, there *is* no hope." And remember, placebos work. My hope was that I wouldn't become disappointed in President Obama. But I did.

Now I find myself comparing and contrasting the Yippies and the Occupy Wall Street protesters.

We had to perform stunts to get media coverage of our cause, so a group of us went to the New York Stock Exchange and threw $200 worth of singles onto the floor below. Now, an Occupy placard, WALL STREET IS WAR STREET, gave me a sense of continuity. Other anonymous Occupiers carried posters proclaiming: GOD FORBID WE HAVE SEX & SMOKE POT. THEY WANT US TO GRAB GUNS & GO TO WAR! I AM AN IMMIGRANT. I CAME HERE

TO TAKE YOUR JOB. BUT YOU DON'T HAVE ONE. $96,000 FOR A BA IN HISPANIC TRANSGENDER GAY & LESBIAN STUDIES AND I CAN'T FIND WORK! And, a woman in a wheelchair: STAND UP FOR YOUR RIGHTS!

By the sheer power of numbers without the necessity of stunts, the Occupiers have broadened public awareness about the economic injustice perpetuated by corporations without compassion conspiring with government corruption that has resulted in immeasurable suffering. The Yippies were a myth that became a reality. The Occupiers are a reality that became a myth. The spirit of nonviolent revolution is what connects them.

NPR waited until eleven days of Occupy Wall Street had passed before reporting its existence. The executive news editor explained that the Occupiers "did not involve large numbers of people" (actually, there were already several hundred), no "prominent people" showed up (thus ignoring Michael Moore and Susan Sarandon), the lack of "a great disruption" (the police pepper-spraying protesters trapped in a cage of orange netting finally met that need), "or an especially clear objective" (oh, right, just like all those flip-floppy pandering politicians whose clear objective is to get elected).

The Occupiers appear to be a leaderless community—most likely, you can't name a single one; not yet, anyway—whereas Abbie Hoffman, Jerry Rubin, and I served as spokespeople for the Yippies. We had media contacts and knew how to speak in sound bytes. If we gave good quotes, they gave free publicity for upcoming demonstrations. It was mutual manipulation.

The Yippies were inspired by a Buddhist monk in Vietnam who set himself on fire in order to call attention to the war. The photo of that incident traveled around the globe, and I wore a lapel button which featured that flaming image. Similarly, in 2010, a street vendor in Tunisia refused to pay a police bribe, then immolated himself, which inspired a revolution there, and next in Egypt, then spreading into Arab Spring, which ultimately inspired American Autumn in 2011.

Inspired by the Yippies attempt to levitate the Pentagon, Aron Kay wanted to get fellow Occupiers to levitate Wall Street, to no avail. Likewise, inspired by the Yippies nomination of an actual pig for president, Michael Dare tried unsuccessfully to persuade fellow protesters at Occupy Seattle to carry out his notion that "if corporations are people, let's run one for president." I offered myself as Secretary of Greed.

The evolution of technology has changed the way protests are organized and carried out. The Yippies had to use messy mimeograph machines to print out flyers that had to be stuffed into envelopes, addressed, stamped, and mailed. The Internet generally—and social media such as Facebook and Twitter—have enabled Occupiers to inexpensively reach countless people immediately.

When the Yippies were being tear-gassed, beaten sadistically and indiscriminately, we chanted, "The whole world is watching!" But now, when a bloodbath was expected to happen if the New York police forced the Occupiers out of the park—and then that didn't happen—Michael Moore asked a cop, "Why don't you think the eviction happened?" The reply: "Because the mayor's afraid of YouTube."

One month later, Mayor Bloomberg apparently lost that fear; by his order, the eviction happened at 1 AM The next afternoon, a protester, before being allowed back in, was overheard remarking, "The cops have occupied Zuccotti Park. We're just trying to figure out what their demands are."

What occurred in Chicago in 1968 was officially labeled "a police riot" by a government-sponsored investigation. Now, as the Occupy model has spread around the country, police brutality has increased, and it's not surprising that there have been accusations of provocateurs sabotaging the nonviolent principle, including an assistant editor at a conservative magazine who infiltrated a group of protesters in Washington, D.C., later claiming that his purpose was "to mock and undermine them in the pages of the *American Spectator*," and that he helped incite a riot at the National Air and Space Museum, getting pepper-sprayed in the process.

The Yippies were essentially countercultural, and, although the Occupiers are essentially mainstream, right-wing media pundits have been demonizing them like mad.

Bill O'Reilly called the Occupiers "drug-trafficking crackheads" and "violent America-hating anarchists." Sean Hannity said they "sound like skinhead Nazi psychos." Ann Coulter referred to them as mobs of "teenage runaways" and "tattooed, body–pierced, sunken-chested nineteen-year-olds getting in fights with the police for fun." Glenn Beck warned that they "will come for you and drag you into the streets and kill you." Andrew Breitbart declared that Occupy Wall Street is "a group of public masturbating violent freaks." Rush Limbaugh labeled them "dumbed down" and "propagandized" and asked a rhetorical question reeking with layers of irony: "Whatever happened to the '60s—*Question Authority*!" At this point, Limbaugh is sort of like a castrated canine that is still busy humping the living-room sofa by force of habit.

I'll conclude here with a little gift for the infamous 1 percent in the form of what could eventually become a riddle for reactionaries: "What do corporations and fetuses have in common?"

And the answer is: "They're both persons."

In December 2010, the Oakland branch of PEN, the international writers' organization, honored me with their Lifetime Achievement Award. Here are some excerpts from my acceptance speech:

> I really appreciate that introduction. That's the best intro I've gotten since, at the Just for Laughs Comedy Festival in Montreal, where there was a bunch of comedians who were gonna do about six minutes each, and so the emcee came into the Green Room and just asked each one how they wanted to be introduced. So I said, "Well, just say I'm a social satirist." About fifteen minutes later, it was my turn to come on, and there was the emcee, looking at the scratchy notes that he had written, and he said, "Our next comedian is Paul Krassner, a sociopath." It's on my resumé now.
>
> I appreciate the irony here—I've had a lifetime of being an iconoclast, and now this Lifetime Achievement Award is making me an icon. And so I have to search around for my oclast and see what happened to it. I appreciate this plaque—probably made in China [it was]. I told my dentist I was getting a plaque, and he said, "Well, I'll remove it." Anyway, you know, to get an award like this does not imply that I did it alone.
>
> There are so many to thank who have contributed and supported me all of these decades, and I just want to thank a few of them quickly in chronological order. But first and foremost, in terms of my spiritual quest, I would like to thank—*Satan!*—just kidding. It was a real competition getting this award. I beat out Justin Bieber, I beat out Levi Johnston, and Johnny Knoxville, not to mention Christine O'Donnell.
>
> I want to thank my parents, who really were very embarrassed by my work, if not ashamed, and yet they were supportive of me and they nurtured my irreverence. My brother George and my sister Marge, who were also very supportive. My former wife, Jeanne Johnson, who taught me that responsibility is fun. Our daughter, Holly, who once said to me, "Dad, don't be offended, but I don't want to be a writer when I grow up, because it seems like a very insecure profession." My current wife, Nancy Cain, who for twenty-two and two-third years has been my mate and my muse. Lyle Stuart, editor of *The Independent,* a forerunner of the alternative press, where I served my apprenticeship in journalism. And Lenny Bruce, my inadvertent mentor in satire . . .
>
> So, I just want to conclude with—I hardly remember anything from my entire higher education—the only thing I remember from

college was in an anthropology course, and it was a definition of happiness—"having as little separation as possible between your work and your play"—and I've been very fortunate, being able to do that, and to get an award for it is really the icing on the cake, because the process was the goal. And also I know that, in my lifetime I've met so many people who deserve a lifetime achievement award, except that they didn't do it publicly. I do want to say how happy this award makes me, and the only thing that makes me happier is that it's not posthumous. Thank you.

* * *

So many people who were important in different aspects of my life have died in addition to those already mourned in this book.

Family: My mother, Ida Krassner. And my first wife, Jeanne Johnson.

Friends: Lyle Stuart. Bill Gaines. Lou Swift. Scott Kelman. Bill Graham. Alan Watts. Paul Jacobs. Phil Ochs. Dave Dellinger. Anita Hoffman. Jerry Rubin. Stew Albert. Timothy Leary. John Lilly. Robert Anton Wilson. Norman Mailer. Kurt Vonnegut. Terry Southern. Gus Reichbach. Lotus Weinstock. Tony Russo. John Lennon. Jerry Garcia. Cass Elliot. Jean Shepherd. Tuli Kupferberg. John Francis Putnam. Marv Davidov. Bill Kunstler. Albert Ellis. Bob Abel. Peter McWilliams. Mae Brussell. Jack Herer. Peter Bergman. Ralph Gleason. Herb Caen. Janet Bode. Dick Schaap. Jerome Washington. Ken Kelley. Del Close. Owsley Stanley. Steve Ben Israel.

And one more for the road . . .

George Carlin died in June 2008. He was a generous friend. When I performed in Los Angeles, he sent a limousine to pick me up at the airport, and I stayed at his home. And such a sweet man. When I opened for him at the Warner-Grand Theater in San Pedro, we were hanging around in his dressing room, where he was nibbling from a vegetable plate. I watched as he continued to be genuinely gracious with every fan who stopped by. If they wanted his autograph, he would gladly sign his name. If they wanted to be photographed with him, he would assume the pose. If they wanted to have a little chat, he indulged them with congeniality.

I said, "You really show respect for everybody."

"Well," he responded, "that's just the way *I* would want to be treated."

As a performer, Carlin was uncompromising, knowing that his audience trusted him not to be afraid of offending them. In fact, he was excited by that possibility. The day before one of his live HBO specials, he called and told me to be sure to watch it, because he would devote the first ten minutes of his performance to the subject of abortion.

Carlin had long been vocal in support of the right to smoke and ingest various drugs, and he posed this rhetorical question: "Why are there no recreational drugs in suppository form?" I was pleased to inform him that teenage girls have been experimenting with tampons soaked in vodka, inserting them vaginally or rectally as a way of getting intoxicated without their parents detecting booze on their breath.

No matter what else Richard Nixon accomplished in his lifetime, his obituaries always mentioned him as the first American president to resign, and no matter what else George Carlin accomplished in *his* lifetime, his obits always connected him with the Supreme Court ruling on "The Seven Words You Can't Say on Television."

When asked in the Green Room at the Warner-Grand Theater by producer Dan Pasley why he didn't include the word "nigger" in that list, Carlin replied, "There's nothing funny about it—that really *is* a dirty word—but repressed words about sexual functions and bodily parts were truly funny. I had only been thinking about the 'dirty' words in terms of sex and bodily functions, and how uptight these religious freaks have made us. *That's* fun, that's some funny shit."

At a private memorial for family and friends, Carlin's daughter, Kelly, read from his burial instructions, written on May 1, 1990:

> Upon my death, I wish to be cremated. The disposition of my ashes (dispersal at sea, on land or in the air) shall be determined by my surviving family (wife and daughter) in accordance with their knowledge of my prejudices and philosophies regarding geography and spirituality. Under no circumstances are my ashes to be retained by anyone or buried in a particular location. The eventual dispersal can be delayed for any reasonable length of time required to reach a decision, but not to exceed one month following my death.
>
> I wish no public service of any kind. I wish no religious service of any kind. I prefer a private gathering at my home, attended by friends and family members who shall be determined by my surviving family (wife and daughter). It should be extremely informal, they should play rhythm and blues music, and they should laugh a lot. Vague references to spirituality (secular) will be permitted.

Kelly added, "There will be no mention of God allowed" and "no one will be allowed to say that 'George is now smiling down at us from Heaven above.'"

Carlin once told an audience of children how to be a class clown as a way of attracting attention. "I didn't start out with fake heart attacks in the aisle," he explained. Ah, if only that's what he was doing *this* time.

But a reporter did once ask him how he wanted to die.

"I'd like to explode spontaneously in someone's living room," he replied. "That, to me, is the way to go out."

And, through his CDs, DVDs, books, and online, George Carlin does indeed continue to explode spontaneously in living rooms across the country and around the world.

★ ★ ★

Orson Bean is my oldest living friend. He's a Christian libertarian conservative, and we've had an ongoing email dialogue about religion, but he's still a Christian and I'm still an atheist. Not a militant atheist, as I used to be, though. I changed when I realized that Martin Luther King was a Christian, but I was inspired by his actions, and George Lincoln Rockwell, head of the American Nazi Party, was an agnostic, but I abhorred what he stood for. It no longer mattered to me what anybody's religious belief was, only how they treated others. And Orson Bean is a true mensch.

I decided to email him: "If you can arrange for me to interview Andrew Breitbart"—his son-in-law—"I'll believe in God."

Orson must've forwarded my email to Breitbart, because *he* sent me an email saying, "Apparently there is a God," with his own phone number. I called, we spoke, and he agreed to do an interview. My only ground rule would be that neither of us would interrupt the other.

I contacted Steve Randall, my editor at *Playboy,* and I got the assignment. I immediately sent an email to Orson with the good news. The subject line was "Praise the fucking Lord."

My discussion with Breitbart—maybe his last interview—was published in the December 2011 issue of *Playboy.* Here's how it began.

> KRASSNER: I was surprised to learn that you consider my work to be one of your inspirations. But you also claim that the mainstream media had a double standard and didn't criticize me the way they do with you and the conservative movement that you represent. It's not true, though. I've been excoriated in papers from the *Los Angeles Times* to the *Chicago Tribune* to *The Washington Post.* My favorite headline was, "Give This Man a Saliva Test." And you've also praised Abbie Hoffman and the Yippies, and Ken Kesey and the Merry Pranksters, as heavy influences. They were both close friends of mine and remain as my touchstones, and yet you're at the other end of the social and political spectrum. So what I want to know is, how do they fit into the context of your own personal mission?
>
> BREITBART: Well, at the time that you were doing what you were doing and trailblazing and causing mischief and mirth and

affecting the type of political and social change that you were attempting to do, there's no doubt that you were being challenged by others at the time. What I'm talking about is the current order of the media in the twenty-first century and how history now looks upon the Merry Pranksters and the Abbie Hoffmans and the Ken Keseys and Hunter Thompson with great reverence, and it's as if they've been given their own wing of the journalism school. And so I don't want to simplify history.

I understand at the time that you went through hell, and the same could be said of Matt Drudge. From 1995 until about 2002, the same forces were trying to claim that Matt Drudge had no right to be doing what he was doing, which now everybody accepts as commonplace and accepted practice, and *The Huffington Post* was just purchased for $350 million by AOL for replicating what Matt Drudge does on the left-of-center bent. So the trailblazers, while they're trailblazing, can beget the arrows and slings hurled at them, and I'm not trying to diminish the peril that you went through. I'm stating that right now, when I'm reporting truths on Wednesday and causing mirth on Thursday, the press has a problem dealing with that. And I'm saying, no, you're not going to define me; I'm going to define what it is that I do, and you're going to have to deal with it. And I gained my inspiration from the knowledge that you guys went through the same process, and I'm using you guys as a model.

* * *

I'm in pretty good health, but over the decades, stemming from that old police beating, my gait has gradually gotten gimpier and gimpier. My hip became so out of kilter that my right foot turned inward when I walked, and my left foot was continuously tripping on my right foot. More and more often, I found myself falling all over the place. Dozens of times. Several fractured ribs.

Finally, when I fell at a book festival in Australia, I began accidentally knocking down *other* people like dominoes, and I realized that I would definitely need to start walking with a cane. Since then, at any airport, I have to put my cane on the conveyor belt, along with my carry-on bag and my shoes. And then the security person hands me a *different* cane—a wooden one, painted orange—to help me walk through the metal detector without falling.

One time in a restaurant, I tripped on *my own cane* and fell flat on my face—bruising myself badly, yet grateful that I hadn't broken any teeth. That's my nature—to perceive a blessing in disguise as soon as I stop bleeding. However, this time I was left with a dark, square-shaped scab between my nose and my lips. It looked like a Hitler mustache, and I became somewhat self-conscious about it.

I really *am* a walking time bomb. I cannot afford to fall again. I must be careful when I walk. I just have to be fully conscious of every single step. Left. Right. Left. Right. Left. Right. Any fall could injure me. It might even be fatal. So I've surrendered to a process of survival that's truly an ongoing lesson in mindfulness. I'm learning that when you're mindful in one aspect of your life, you'll strengthen mindfulness in other aspects.

I am, after all, a Zen Bastard, and I certainly have no desire to trip while hobbling along my peculiar path.

★ ★ ★

For several years, I've been writing a column for *AVN* (Adult Video News), a trade journal for the porn industry. In March 2011, I received an email from the editor:

"We are just on the verge of completely revamping the magazine, and it is my unhappy duty to tell you that we are going to have to discontinue your 'One Hand Jerking' column. With the focus of the magazine shifting to a more business/retail-oriented editorial content, we're going to have to use the space differently. I have been procrastinating making the cut because your column was one of the bright spots in my job, so I was really loath to let it go."

I wasn't too surprised. I think there's so much free porn on the Internet that it's become a substantial competitor of pay-for-porn. Exactly one week later, I got an email from the editor of *High Times*, for which I've been writing a column titled "Brain Damage Control" for a few decades.

"There's no easy way to put this," I was informed, "but [another writer] will be taking over your column slot in the magazine. I hate to be the one to tell you this. I have great admiration for you and your writing."

I continued to contribute occasional pieces on a freelance basis, but Holly was right. Writing *is* a very insecure profession. I was in a state of being-fired shock. Suddenly, Social Security had become my only source of income. I was depressed for one day, but then, fortunately, my perspective returned—I mean I wasn't buried alive under earthquake rubble in Japan, I wasn't shot dead in the streets of Syria—and I realized that I had to be proactive. So, what was the silver lining in this double-media-whammy cloud? I took my plight as an omen and decided to work full-time on my long awaited (by me) first novel.

It's about a contemporary Lenny Bruce–type satirist. Those scenes where my protagonist performs, I've developed onstage myself, although at times it felt like I was actually channeling Lenny, until the day that he said, "C'mon, Paul, you know you don't believe in that shit." Well, that ended *that* wishful-thinking delusion.

I told my friend Avery Corman—author of *Oh, God* and *Kramer vs. Kramer*—how I welcomed the challenge of writing a novel.

"But, you know," I added, "fiction is really hard to write. You have to make everything up."

And he said, "Hey, listen, you've been making stuff up all your life."

"Yeah, but that was journalism."

* * *

There were more than four hundred authors at the 2012 *Los Angeles Times* Festival of Books. The participants ranged from the late Rodney King (whose videotaped severe beating twenty years ago by sadistic police officers resulted in a riot that caused over fifty deaths and devastating destruction) to Judy Blume (her books for children and adults have sold more than eighty million copies) to T.C. Boyle (the author of more than twenty novels).

Rodney King was there, at the University of Southern California, to discuss his book, *The Riot Within: My Journey from Rebellion to Redemption.* He had made famous his rhetorical question—"Can we all get along?"— but he spent the $3.8 million he was awarded in a lawsuit, and now that he was broke again, the new question for him, and so many of us, might as well be changed to "can we all get a loan?"

There was a panel titled "E Cannabis Unum." This event served as one more step toward the decriminalizing of marijuana being accepted by the mass media and mainstream culture as the logical and humane thing to do. The panelists were Mark Haskell Smith, author of *Heart of Dankness: Underground Botanists, Outlaw Farmers, and the Race for the Cannabis Cup;* Heather Donahue, an actress who has written a memoir, *Growgirl: How My Life After* The Blair Witch Project *Went to Pot;* and me, the editor of a collection, *Pot Stories for the Soul,* which includes true tales by Ken Kesey, Hunter Thompson, Michelle Phillips, Wavy Gravy, and Jack Herer, among others, with an anti-intro by the prolific science-fantasy author Harlan Ellison.

That collection was published by High Times Books in 1999. It won the Firecracker Alternative Book Award and later became a Quality Paperback Book Club selection. Now a new, expanded and updated edition has been published by Soft Skull Press. The attorneys for the *Chicken Soup for the Soul* series had originally sent a "cease and desist" warning. Although scientists and theologians alike agree that, while the soul cannot be located, apparently it *can* be copyrighted.

So the sequel, *Acid Trips for the Soul,* was re-titled *Acid Trips for the Mind,* but the distributor insisted that it be changed to *Psychedelic Trips for the Mind.* The second sequel, *Magic Mushrooms for the Soul,* was re-titled *Magic Mushrooms for the Body,* but then I changed that to *Magic Mushrooms and Other Highs: From Toad Slime to Ecstasy.*

I sent a copy of *Magic Mushrooms and Other Highs* to my friend Todd McCormick, who wrote two articles for that book, but the warden rejected it "because on pages 259–261, it describes the process of squeezing toads to obtain illicit substances which could be detrimental to the security, good order and discipline of the institution."

This was pure theater of cruelty. Federal correctional facilities do not have a toad problem, and outside accomplices have not been catapulting loads of toads over barbed wire fences to provide the fuel for a prison riot.

The panel I was on was moderated by Dean Kuipers, an editor and writer at the *Times,* and the author of *Burning Rainbow Farm.* He called on me first. I told the audience that if they looked under their seats, they would find a little baggie. Several optimists actually looked. It was my Oprah moment.

"The priorities are insane," I said. "Tobacco is legal, and it kills 1,200 people every day, in this country alone. Whereas, marijuana is *not* legal, and the worst thing it can do is give you the blind munchies that lead you to raid your neighbor's refrigerator. My position is, as long as any government can arbitrarily decide which drugs are legal and which drugs are illegal, then anybody behind bars for a nonviolent drug conviction, they are political prisoners.

"I personally found out that pot enhances a nice dinner, it enhances going to a movie, it enhances making love—I even smoke a joint before I roll one, because it enhances the rolling experience. *High Times* once published a questionnaire, and one of the questions was, 'Is it possible to smoke too much pot?' And a reader responded, 'I don't understand the question.'

"I owe my longevity to never taking any *legal* drugs. Except, a few months ago I took an aspirin. But it was at a party. It was social toking. There was a lot of peer pressure."

A review of the panel in the *Times* stated:

"Smith held forth on his experiences tagging along with the folks trying to find the world's best weed (an honor that earns one an award called the 'Cannabis Cup') and Donahue described her life as part of a medical marijuana community in Northern California community that she refers to as 'Nugget Town.'

"But it was Krassner who, to borrow pot parlance, Bogarted the show. An old hand at working the cannabis crowd for laughs, he rolled quip after quip that had the crowd chucking throughout . . ."

I assume that was a typo, that the reporter meant "chuckling," not "chucking." As in upchucking. On the other hand, there were a few students who *did* vomit. But it wasn't my fault. I had seen them earlier, chasing toads around the campus, hoping to catch one and lick that slime at 4:20.

*　*　*

When I mentioned to Holly that on April 9, 2012, I would be eighty years old, she said, "Dad, that's crazy."

"I know," I said, "but you can't fight chronology."

To celebrate the occasion, we had a family reunion. My brother and his wife came from Maine, my sister came from Florida, and Holly and her husband Dan came from Napa with their adopted-at-birth three-month-old baby, Talia Jeanne Dawson. Holly and Dan had been present in the delivery room, and he cut the umbilical cord.

The highlight of my birthday was meeting my granddaughter for the first time. While I held Talia in my lap, Holly put the radio on for some music, and Talia started conducting. Holly turned the radio off and Talia stopped conducting. Holly turned the radio back on and Talia began conducting again.

I showed Holly *The Onion's* review of the 2011 MTV Video Music Awards:

"The first 'pre-show performance,' by someone called Cobra Starship: because I am very old, I experience a shiver of terror at the thought that they might be the latest iteration of the cryogenically frozen leftovers of Jefferson Airplane. They turn out to be a briskly paced anthology of everything I thought was cool when I was nine: shiny pants, sunglasses insouciantly thrown aside, fog machines, lots of G-rated writhing. I am not entirely sure that the disembodied head of Paul Krassner isn't directing all this from behind the wings . . ."

I remarked, "To become a joke reference can be even a bigger honor than my lifetime achievement award."

And Holly said, "A good joke lasts longer than a lifetime achievement award."

Printed in the United States
by Baker & Taylor Publisher Services